SIMON JOHN DE VRIES is Professor of Old Testament at Methodist Theological School in Ohio, Delaware, Ohio.

Time and History in the Old Testament

YESTERDAY, TODAY AND TOMORROW

Simon J. DeVries

William B. Eerdmans Publishing Company   Grand Rapids

Library of Congress Cataloging in Publication Data

De Vries, Simon John.
  Yesterday, today and tomorrow.

  Includes bibliographical references and indexes.
  1. Time (Theology)—Biblical teaching. 2. History
(Theology)—Biblical teaching. I. Title.
BS680.T54D48   231'.7   74-31322
ISBN 0-8028-3457-4

to BETTY
JUDY, PETER, and JENNIFER
GARRY

who shared, share, and will share
most of my yesterdays, todays, and tomorrows

hindering me little
helping me much

אשתך כגפן פריה בירכתי ביתך
בניך כשתלי זתים סביב לשלחנך

Ps. 128:3

Foreword

Secular thinkers have recently joined theologians and historians of comparative religions in their common interest in the meaning of time. They discern in this notion an urgency which has been heretofore the distinctive mark, on the whole, of sectarian religionists. As the second millennium of the Christian era draws to a close, one of our more gnawing preoccupations centers on the eventuality of the annihilation of life on the surface of the planet Earth.

Not unlike the Romanticists who would sigh over the passing of an enchanted hour, contemporary man echoes unconsciously the cry of Lamartine,

"O temps, suspends ton vol!"

The difference of mood, however, is stunning. Nineteenth-century poets were haunted by the loss of the present moment. Twentieth-century temper has to do with the fear of a catastrophic future. One mourned on account of the ephemerality of time and the other begs for "more time." Some political scientists and most ecologists are asking whether mankind will be able to learn how to behave properly before the biological margin of survival is irremediably thinned out. Eschatology has become a field of scientific research. The problem of time has displaced the problem of nature.[1]

This cultural development points to the quality of time as well as its quantity. *Kairos* is never to be ignored if one thinks of *chronos*. Thus, the biblical notion of time as "the opportune season" is by no means obsolete. In this "timely" volume, Professor De Vries shows that ancient Israel's notion of days and seasons is entirely relevant to the study of time in the contemporary age.

Although books of value have appeared on this subject in recent decades, this work is perhaps the first that examines rather exhaustively the Old Testament references to the categories of past, present, and future. Using a comprehensive methodology, the author rightly reacts against the onesidedness of approach that has characterized much of biblical scholarship in the modern period. Exegesis of a particular passage cannot be confined to philological investigation, indispensable as this may be. Literary

---

1. Cf. Clement Rousset, *L'anti-nature: éléments pour une philosophie tragique* (Paris, Presses Universitaires de France, 1973).

and historical criticism as well as redaction criticism may not be ignored for the sake of the newer methods of form-critical analysis and traditio-historical criticism. All these modes of inquiry have a contribution to offer to the explanation of a text, and they actually penetrate one another. The author disregards none of them, for he is not satisfied by any of them alone. Moreover, he seeks to go beyond a merely exegetical examination of isolated pericopes by looking at the sweep of the biblical tradition from a broad perspective. Nevertheless, he devotes a great deal of his attention to the critical interpretation of several Hebraic expressions which deal with the future, the adverbial references to the present, and especially the manifold uses of the words for "day," "today," and "the day of Yahweh."

Some of the semantic conclusions that arise from this work may eventually deserve to modify entries in biblical dictionaries, while the interpretation of several passages of the Old Testament literature may affect future commentaries. Professor De Vries's conclusions have a bearing, for example, on the composition of the book of Deuteronomy, the function of editorial prefaces or additions to the sermons of the great prophets, the ideology of the dynastic historians.

One of the valuable aspects of this undertaking resides in the care with which attempts have been made to determine the relationship of special words to the chronological events they describe and to the quality of time to which they point. The whole book stresses the theological nature of the literary genres in which the motif of time appears. Holy War, Covenant, Proclamation of Judgment, Announcement of Salvation, all of them are presented as springing out of the agency of the Deity. The interpretation of the past and the prediction of the future are formulated in such a way that the Hebraic apprehension of history always assumes a revelatory character.

Whether history is revelation or revelation is history is a well-known theological question for which there is no ready or undebatable answer. The theologians of the next generation will find here at least a critical presentation of the relevant data.

Especially pertinent in this respect are the author's remarks on the final redaction of the prophetic books. The editors of these books were epitomists who, in the light of new situations, and through the processes of selection and juxtaposition, expanded, qualified, and sometimes profoundly modified an individual prophet's proclamation of the future. Canonical hermeneutics receives its style from the Hebraic and later early Jewish use, with radical revisions, of ancient predictions in unprecedented contexts of cultural history. Canon is dynamic interpretation of the past for illuminating a bewildering present.

The prophets and the preachers of the covenant recited Israel's memory in almost every generation, but they adapted this memory as they preserved its form, for they were aware of the need to change the national character and to induce their contemporaries to take responsible decisions while time was still available to them. They restated the motif of "the Day of Yahweh" because they knew that the future of the covenant people was always a "now." Old Testament eschatology, thanks to this volume, is replaced in its parenetic milieu and the notion of event is viewed as inextricably bound to the proclamation of the word. As prophetism moved into apocalyptic, the time of God became equated with the end of history.

This book helps us to situate the biblical awareness of history as distinct from that of the ancient Near Eastern peoples, especially Egyptian, Hittite, and Mesopotamian. The quantitative aspect of chronology which confers upon history its sense of continuity was never ignored by the Hebrew prophets and poets. Even early Jewish historiographers, however, contributed to the theological understanding of time, for they apparently referred to royal annals and genealogies in order to shake a naive belief in institutional security. The stress on genealogies and chronological structures which characterizes much of Judaism at its birth during the Exile and the Persian times sprang from the pastoral intent of the descendants of the Jerusalem priests who had survived the Babylonian onslaught and attempted to confer meaning to a meaningless situation.

The historicization of agricultural feasts which had been inherited from the Middle Bronze Canaanites constitutes the most eloquent witness to the power of the Hebraic notion of time. In the ancient Near East in general and in the Fertile Crescent surrounding Israel in particular, feasts had been almost exclusively seasonal celebrations of nature myths. This book suggests that in almost every feast of the covenant people, the category of nature has been displaced by that of time. In her holy seasons, Israel celebrated not the deified forces of nature but the transcendence of her God over the forces of nature and his ultimate sovereignty over the nations. According to the author, however, these festivals represent not only the triumph of Hebraic faith over the fascination of Northwest Semitic syncretism but also a certain compromise. They tend to dilute the uniqueness of a historical event into the repetition of a ritual. Sacramental celebration risks reducing the timely into the timeless.

Some readers may wish to pursue this line of discussion further, since the ambiguous complexity of the Hebrew cultus and its precise relation to historical memory requires continuous attention from contemporary scholarship. Professor De Vries, at any rate, provides some of the evidence which will contribute to a reexamination of the old problems of myth and ritual, history and cultus, this-worldly against other-worldly eschatology, as well as the theological dynamics of sacramental acts through which worshipers participate in the *telos* of creation.

The stage is thus set for a new appraisal of the Jewish-Christian apocalyptic and of this peculiarly eschatological fever, yet anti-apocalyptic stance, of Jesus and of the first generation of Christians.

In the twentieth century as in the first, to borrow the words of Mr. Auden,

"... *the Kingdom of Heaven may come, not in the present*
And not in the future, but in the Fullness of Time."

The Bible reverses the romantic concept of time. Instead of moaning over the "happy days that are no more," it convinces the sons to assume the burden of the trust which the fathers have placed upon them. Rather than lamenting over the "first careless rapture" which may never be recaptured, the Bible endows the present with a quality of continuity through transformation and even revolution. Far from exuding impatience over the lateness of the future ("When will these things come to pass?") or indifference upon its shape ("Après moi, le Déluge!"), the Hebraic notion of time sharpens the claim of generations to be born.

Hebrew-Christian eschatology neither discards the old for the sake of the new nor despises the passing moment by neglecting it in the name of some utopian futurity. It respects the instant of now but never at the expense of a better tomorrow.

—SAMUEL TERRIEN
Professor of Hebrew and the Cognate Languages, Union Theological Seminary
Adjunct Professor of Religion, Columbia University

Preface

The theme to which this book addresses itself is without gainsaying one of the most important in the entire range of philosophical and theological topics. No one will charge that the biblical view of time and history is a piddling and inconsequential matter. Biblical revelation is an historical revelation, the product of an unfolding of transcendent truth in the lives and minds of persons living over many centuries of time, experiencing drastic changes in their physical and spiritual circumstances. Itself produced by history, the Bible wrestles with the puzzle of history and temporal event. All who aspire, therefore, to take adequate account of the biblical tradition within the thought of the church and synagogue, as also the influence of the Jewish and Christian heritage in western culture as a whole, will acknowledge that crucial issues are at stake.

The writer of the present volume makes no claim to have handled the chosen theme in all its aspects. Far from it: an awareness of one's own scholarly limitations and the limits of publishing possibilities have demanded that a single group of related phenomena be selected. But two things may be said. First, the phenomena selected—the use and function of certain formal expressions involving the Hebrew word for "day"—are among the very most central, and at the same time most neglected, data within the orbit of relevant investigation. Second, the phenomena chosen have been studied intensively and comprehensively, allowing our results to stand on an edifice of sound building blocks, each carefully put into place.

It is the writer's devout hope that this book will not be used solely by specialists in biblical exegesis and criticism. It is for them, assuredly—especially at the point of showing a better way to penetrate into the textual history of difficult passages that may contain words for elements of time. But this is a book that systematic and speculative theologians will, one hopes, want to study for possible application to broader investigations. Biblical scholars and systematicians desperately need each other. We protest against the all too common practice of exegetes who keep their work so esoteric that nonspecialists can receive scarcely an inkling of consequences for theology in general; we protest also against theologians who ignore current biblical research and write as if the Bible (or at least the Old Testament) has nothing to say to modern man.

Should a nonspecialist take this book in hand, we invite him first to read Chapter One in order to get our intended effort into perspective, then

11

to read Chapter Five in order to savor its consequences and implications. But we urge such a reader not to imagine that the results summarized in Chapter Five may be forthwith either appropriated or rejected. These results are distillations from lengthy and detailed textual study. As factual data have been sacred to the writer, so, we hope, they will be sacred to those who use our results or repudiate them. It is, to be sure, our hope that through the example of this book many theologians will be encouraged to submit themselves to the yoke of scientific textual study, while our fellow biblical scholars learn once again, if they have forgotten it, that exegesis is a *theological* discipline.

A few words are needed respecting certain technical aspects of this book. The original Hebrew of the Old Testament has been reproduced in two forms: transliterated and with the Hebrew consonants. This is neither arbitrary nor due to considerations of economy. The transliterated text is best used wherever linguistic matters stand in the foreground since it is the word, not the written form of the word, that is important. The consonantal Hebrew is rightfully employed when textual and literary-critical considerations predominate, since here the written form of the words does matter. It is also used for uninflected Hebrew roots. However, it has not been deemed necessary to reproduce the Hebrew vowel points inasmuch as these are readily available in the biblical text from which citation is being made.

The footnotes are intended not only for documentation but as a running commentary on our own text. While numerous works are cited in these notes, we make no pretense at having provided a full and exhaustive bibliography for the various passages entering into study. Solely literature that the writer sees to have an immediate bearing on his own analysis has been cited. Truth to tell, all too few commentaries make anything whatever of the temporal phenomena that have interested us.

This book has needed to have a length commensurate with the importance of the chosen theme and the demands of the required methodology. Nevertheless, as it now appears in print, it is appreciably shorter than in its original manuscript form. Some of the eliminated material has found its way into print elsewhere. As a supplement to our treatment here, we invite attention to the following articles by the present writer: "David's Victory over the Philistine as Saga and as Legend," *JBL* 92 (1973), 23-36; "The Development of the Deuteronomic Promulgation Formula," *Biblica*, 55 (1974), 301-16; "The Time Word *māḥār* as a Key to Tradition Development," forthcoming in *ZAW*, 87 (1975); "Temporal Designatives as Structural Elements in the Holy-War Tradition," *VT*, 25 (1975), 80-105; "Deuteronomy: Exemplar of a Non-Sacerdotal Appropriation of Sacred History," in *Grace upon Grace* (congratulatory volume for Lester J. Kuyper; Grand Rapids: Eerdmans, 1975).

It goes without saying that a publication like this reflects aid and inspiration willingly given by friends and colleagues. Most gratefully acknowledged is technical help provided by my former students Michael Casto, William Harper, and Hal Taussig, as well as by Mrs. Jean Campbell and my wife Betty. Scholars who have offered counsel or have read all or part of the manuscript are: Ronald Williams, John Giltner, and Everett Tilson of The Methodist Theological School in Ohio; Morgan Phillips of Ohio Wesleyan University; my teacher at Union Theological Seminary in New York, now deceased, James Muilenburg; Rolf Knierim of the School of Theology at Claremont; Alexander Bronkhorst of Utrecht; Ursula Niebuhr of Stockbridge, Mass.; Oscar Cullmann, professor emeritus of Paris and Basel; Max Wagner of Basel; Hendrikus Berkhof of Leiden; and Pieter de Boer, also of Leiden. I thank also the members of the English Seminar of the Ecumenical Institute for Advanced Theological Study in Jerusalem, who tested some of my ideas with me. Besides these I must mention the help of Peter Ackroyd of King's College, London, who gave helpful suggestions respecting the manuscript and assisted in making publishing arrangements, and especially another of my former teachers, Samuel Terrien of Union Theological Seminary in New York, who has honored this book with a Foreword.

Finally, an expression of appreciation is in order with respect to the editors and craftsmen of the William B. Eerdmans Publishing Company in Grand Rapids and the Society for Promoting Christian Knowledge in London, who have used all their skills in bringing this book into being.

Contents

Abbreviations

(additional to standard abbreviations customarily used in writing and publishing)

1. Books and commentary series

AB	*The Anchor Bible*, Garden City, N.Y.
ANET	*Ancient Near Eastern Texts Relating to the Old Testament*, ed. by J. B. Pritchard, Princeton, 2nd ed. 1955, 3rd ed. 1969
ATD	*Das Alte Testament Deutsch*, Göttingen
BDB	F. Brown, S. R. Driver, and C. A. Briggs, *A Hebrew and English Lexicon of the Old Testament*, Oxford, 1907
BH^2	*Biblia Hebraica*, 2nd ed. by R. Kittel, 1909
BH^3	*Biblia Hebraica*, 3rd ed. by R. Kittel, 1945
BHS	*Biblia Hebraica*, Stuttgart Edition, ed. by K. Elliger *et al.*
BK	*Biblischer Kommentar, Altes Testament*, Neukirchen
GHKAT	*Handkommentar zum Alten Testament*, Göttingen
GK	W. Gesenius and E. Kautzsch, *Hebräische Grammatik*, 29th ed. 1909
HAT	*Handbuch zum Alten Testament*, 1st series, Tübingen
IB	*The Interpreter's Bible*, New York and Nashville
ICC	*The International Critical Commentary*, Edinburgh
KAT	*Kommentar zum Alten Testament*, Leipzig, Gütersloh
KBL	L. Koehler and W. Baumgartner, *Lexicon in Veteris Testamenti Libros*, Leiden, 1953
KHCAT	*Kurzer Hand-Commentar zum Alten Testament*, Freiburg, Leipzig, Tübingen
KJ	The King James Version
NEB	*The New English Bible*, Oxford, 1971
RGG^3	*Die Religion in Geschichte und Gegenwart*, 3rd ed. by K. Galling, 1957-65.
RSV	*The Holy Bible, Revised Standard Version*, New York, 1952
SAT^2	*Die Schriften des Alten Testaments*, 2nd ed., Göttingen, 1921-25.
UGP	M. Noth, *Ueberlieferungsgeschichte des Pentateuch*, Stuttgart, 1948; ET *A History of Pentateuchal Traditions*, Englewood Cliffs, N.J., 1971
UGS	M. Noth, *Ueberlieferungsgeschichtliche Studien*, Tübingen, 2nd ed., 1957

2. Festschriften

Beer	*Festschrift für Georg Beer zum 70. Geburtstag*, ed. by A. Alt *et al.*, Stuttgart, 1933
Bertholet	*Festschrift für Alfred Bertholet zum 80. Geburtstag*, ed. by W. Baumgartner, O. Eissfeldt, *et al.*, Tübingen, 1950
Bultmann	*Zeit und Geschichte*. Dankesgabe an Rudolf Bultmann zum 80. Geburtstag, ed. by E. Dinkler and H. Thyen, Tübingen, 1964
Eissfeldt	*Von Ugarit nach Qumran. Beiträge zur alttestamentlichen und altoriestalischen Forschung Otto Eissfeldt . . . darge- bracht*, ed. by J. Hempel, L. Rost, *et al.* BZAW, 77, Berlin, 2nd ed. 1961
Miller	*Miscellanea biblica et orientalia A. Miller oblata, Studia Anselma*, 27-28 (1951)
Muilenburg	*Israel's Prophetic Heritage, Essays in Honor of James Muilenburg*, ed. by B. W. Anderson and W. Harrelson, New York, 1962
Nötscher	*Alttestamentliche Studien. Friedrich Nötscher zum 60. Ge- burtstag*, ed. by H. Junker and J. Botterweck. BBB, 1, Bonn, 1950
Procksch	*Festschrift Otto Procksch, zum 60. Geburtstag . . . über- reicht*, ed. by A. Alt *et al.*, Leipzig, 1934
Robert	*Melanges bibliques. Redigés en l'honneur de André Robert*, Paris, 1950
Rost	*Das ferne und das nahe Wort. Festschrift Leonhard Rost zur Vollendung seines 70. Lebensjahres am 30. November 1966 gewidmet*, ed. by F. Maass, BZAW, 105, Berlin, 1967
Thomas	*Words and Meanings. Essays Presented to D. W. Thomas*, ed. by P. R. Ackroyd and B. Lindars, London and Cam- bridge, 1968

3. Monograph series

AnBib	Analecta Biblica
ArTh	Arbeiten zur Theologie
ATA	Alttestamentliche Abhandlungen
ATANT	Abhandlungen zur Theologie des Alten und Neuen Testa- ments
AUNVAO	Avhandlinger Utgitt av Det Norske Videnskaps Akademi i Oslo
BBB	Bonner Biblische Beiträge
BEvT	Beiträge zur Evangelischen Theologie
BWANT	Beiträge zur Wissenschaft vom Alten und Neuen Testament
BZAW	Beihefte zur Zeitschrift für die alttestamentliche Wissen- schaft
EtB	Études Bibliques

FRLANT	Forschungen zur Religion und Literatur des Alten und Neuen Testaments
HSM	Harvard Semitic Monographs
SBS	Stuttgarter Bibelstudien
SBT	Studies in Biblical Theology
SOTSM	Society for Old Testament Study Monographs
SVT	Supplements to *Vetus Testamentum*
TB	Theologische Bücherei
TS	Theologische Studien, Zürich
WMANT	Wissenschaftliche Monographien zum Alten und Neuen Testament

4. Periodicals and Journals

AfO	*Archiv für Orientforschung*
AKG	*Archiv für Kulturgeschichte*
BASOR	*Bulletin of the American Schools of Oriental Research*
BibO	*Bibbia e Oriente*
BR	*Biblical Research*
BZ	*Biblische Zeitschrift*
CanJT	*Canadian Journal of Theology*
CB	*Cultura Biblica·*
CBQ	*Catholic Biblical Quarterly*
EE	*Estudios Eclesiasticos*
EvT	*Evangelische Theologie*
HTR	*Harvard Theological Review*
HUCA	*Hebrew Union College Annual*
IEJ	*Israel Exploration Journal*
JBL	*Journal of Biblical Literature*
JBR	*Journal of Bible and Religion*
JRT	*Journal of Religious Thought*
JSS	*Journal of Semitic Studies*
JTC	*Journal for Theology and Church*
JTS	*Journal of Theological Studies*
KuD	*Kerygma und Dogma*
NTT	*Norsk Teologisk Tidsskrift*
OA	*Oriens Antiquus*
OTS	*Oudtestamentische Studien*
PEQ	*Palestine Exploration Quarterly*
RB	*Revue Biblique*
RSO	*Rivista degli Studi Orientali*
RTP	*Revue de Théologie et de Philosophie*
TZ	*Theologische Zeitschrift*
VT	*Vetus Testamentum*
ZAW	*Zeitschrift für die alttestamentliche Wissenschaft*
ZDMG	*Zeitschrift der Deutschen Morgenländischen Gesellschaft*
ZKT	*Zeitschrift für Katholische Theologie*
ZTK	*Zeitschrift für Theologie und Kirche*

5. General

acc.	accusative case
comm.	commentary
Chr	the Chronicler
coh.	cohortative
D	Deuteronomic/deuteronomistic work in the Tetrateuch
Dtn	the Deuteronomic parenesis
Dtr	the deuteronomist(ic school)
E	the Elohist
Ep Barn.	the Epistle of Barnabas
ET	English translation
Heb.	Hebrew
hif.	hifil
hithp.	hithpael
impf.	imperfect
impf. cs.	waw-consecutive imperfect
impv.	imperative
inf.	infinitive
J	the (J)Yahwist
jus.	jussive
LXX	the Greek Septuagint ($^{A, B, L, \acute{O}, S, etc.}$, the ms. witnesses as listed in the standard critical editions)
mg	the marginal apparatus
ms., mss.	manuscript(s)
MT	the Massoretic Text
N.F.	neue Folge
nif.	nifal
OT	Old Testament
p.	plural
P	the priestly writer (school)
par.	biblical parallel
pf.	perfect
pf. cs.	waw-consecutive perfect
pi.	piel
ptcp.	participle
1QIs[a]	first Isaiah Scroll from Qumran Cave One
1QM	Milḥamot (War) Scroll from Qumran Cave One
s.	singular
Sam.	the Samaritan Pentateuch
2 En.	Second (Slavonic) Enoch
ser.	series
Syr.	the Syriac version
Tg.	the Aramaic Targum
III Mac.	Third Maccabees
Vg.	the Latin Vulgate
VSS	the ancient versions

Ug.   the Ugaritic literature, as published in Cyrus Gordon, *Ugaritic Manual*, Rome, 1955

Θ   Theodotion

(1), (2), (3) represent the first, second, and third occurrences within a verse.

1cs, 1cp, 2ms, 2mp, 2fs, 2fp, 3ms, 3mp, 3fs, 3fp indicate the grammatical person, gender, and number, as abbreviated in the standard grammars.

Raised numerals indicate the edition number.

6. Books of the Old Testament (Hebrew order) and Apocrypha

Gen., Exod., Lev., Num., Deut., Josh., Judg., I Sam., II Sam., I Kings, II Kings, Isa., Jer., Ezek., Hos., Joel, Amos, Obad., Jon., Mic., Nah., Hab., Zeph., Hag., Zech., Mal., Ps., Prov., Job, Song of Sol., Ruth, Lam., Eccl., Esth., Dan., Ezr., Neh., I Chron., II Chron., Tob., Judt., Sus., I Mac.

7. Books of the New Testament

Matt., Mk., Heb., II Pet.

Transliteration of Hebrew Script

(Daghesh and raphē are not represented)

1. Consonants: א ', ב b, ג g, ד d, ה h, ו w, ז z, ח ḥ, ט ṭ, י y, כ ך k, ל l, מ ם m, נ ן n, ס s, ע ', פ ף p, צ ץ ṣ, ק q, ר r, שׂ ś, שׁ š, ת t

2. Pointed vowels: ָ (long qāmeṣ) ā, ַ (pathaḥ) a, ֶ (seghol) e, ֵ (ṣērē) ē, ִ (ḥireq) i (short) ī (long), ֹ (ḥōlem) ō, ָ (qāmeṣ ḥatuph) o, ֻ (qibbuṣ) u

3. Vowels represented by points and vowel letters: הָ â, אָ ā', יֵ ê, אֵ ē', הֵ ēh, יִ î, וֹ ô, הֹ ōh, וּ û

4. Diphthongs: וָ āw, יָ āy, יֵו êw, יִו îw

5. Shᵉwas: ְ (silent) = nothing, ְ (mobile) ᵉ, ֳ ᵒ, ֲ ᵃ, ֱ ᵉ

List of Tables

YESTERDAY, TODAY AND TOMORROW

CHAPTER ONE

A Comprehensive Analysis of the Day as an Essential Clue in an Understanding of the Hebraic Concept of Time

1. The problem of time and history in biblical theology

EVERY PEOPLE HAS a special way of speaking about time, but not always is speech commensurate to thought, for each linguistic system imposes its own arbitrary strictures. The ancient Hebrews spoke about time in ways similar to those of their kinsmen of neighboring Semitic stock, employing the resources peculiar to the Semitic language family.[1] Yet, so much of what the Hebrews wrote has been preserved, and in so many varying forms and styles, that we get a much clearer idea of their notion of time than we do of that of other ancient Semitic cultures. Although we must be cautious of exaggeration,[2] we need to be impressed by the fact that the Hebrews had a very special awareness of their presence in time and in history. For them time was no empty form or meaningless continuum: it was a factor in their experience that—even more than space—gave definition and quality to their existence. Thus their way of speaking about time invites our attentive interest.

The only systematic study of the Hebrew language of time yet to appear suffered from the erroneous methodology of the so-called etymologizing school. This was Conrad von Orelli's book on the Hebrew synonyms for time and eternity, published in 1871.[3] Orelli paid no heed whatever to matters of grammar, syntax, and contextual exegesis; he was solely interested in the meaning of words, and this only as derived from their supposed etymology rather than from their actual semantic application. Each and every "synonym" for time corresponds to one or another logical aspect of the phenomenon of time as seen from a philosophical perspective. Thus it is possible to categorize all the Hebrew words for time conceptually. There is a limited time and an unlimited time (eternity). Limited time is named according to its manifestation or according to the degree of its determinedness; if the former, it is seen in terms of opposing, driving, unrestricted,

1. In spite of well-taken criticisms on the part of James Barr (*The Semantics of Biblical Language*, Oxford, 1961, chap. 4) and others, much truth remains in the thesis of Thorleif Boman (*Hebrew Thought Compared with Greek*, Philadelphia, 1960, pp. 129ff.) to the effect that important philosophical and psychological differences manifest themselves in a study of the Semitic-Hebrew time concept over against that of the Greeks.
2. Sweeping statements to the effect that the Hebrews alone among the peoples of the ancient Near East had any significant concept of historical existence are being increasingly discredited by such studies as Bertil Albrektson's *History and the Gods* (Lund, 1967). For a judicious assessment of the genuinely distinctive elements in Israel's view of history, see Albrektson's "Concluding Remarks," pp. 115ff.
3. *Die hebräischen Synonyma der Zeit und Ewigkeit genetisch und sprachvergleichend dargestellt.*

accelerated, instantaneous, repetitive, coincidental, and encircling movement (*Bewegung*), or in terms of rest—the lack of movement; if determinedness is the criterion, limited time is described as legally ordained for a
particular purpose, qualitatively defined, numerically identified, or narrowly delimited. For each of these modes of thought there is a special and
distinctive word. So also for the various aspects of unlimited time, which is
described in terms of the negation of limitedness, the continuation of
temporal motion, extension and lengthening, or upward graduation. It was
because the Hebrews were relatively advanced in their ability to analyze the
phenomenon of time that they were able to develop the Old Testament's
relatively extensive lexicography of time.[4]

Quite apart from the lack of any evidence whatever to show that the
ancient Hebrews were capable of the abstract thinking that is here assumed,[5] we are altogether justified in rejecting any method that proceeds
deductively on the basis of a psychological theory rather than inductively
on the basis of contextual evidence. This is not to deny that the researcher
needs to bring to his study of the biblical text a wide range of concern. He
must be at least somewhat acquainted with the philosophical, psychological, and scientific approaches to the phenomenon of time; he must be
familiar with the meaning of time in the history of religions; he must know
the importance of time as a problem for biblical and systematic theology.
But it is sound linguistic and exegetical method, rather than any of these,
that must dictate the way to proceed in coming to grips with the biblical
data.

The meaning of time has been a constant concern in philosophical
inquiry. We need no more than refer to the classical treatments of this
problem by such great men of old as Aristotle and Augustine; by such
modern giants as Kant, Hegel, and Bergson. How important a question it
remains in current discussion may be gathered from the collection of essays
in Richard M. Gale's book, *The Philosophy of Time*.[6] The leading existen-
tialist philosopher of our day, Martin Heidegger, has made it a major theme
in his *magnum opus*, *Sein und Zeit*.[7] Among the physicists and logicians

---

4. Orelli was dominated by the principles of Max Müller, who held that there is "a
petrified philosophy in language." The linguistic method of those who shared this
point of view was given classical statement in the words of W. von Humboldt; cf. his
Sprachphilosophische Werke, ed. Steinthal (Berlin, 1884). Unfortunately, numerous
students of theology, religion-phenomenology, and biblical exegesis have been
taken in by this approach. It has dominated such influential works as J. Pedersen's
Israel and (at least the first volume of) Kittel's *Theologisches Wörterbuch zum
Neuen Testament*. James Barr (in *op. cit.*) has done biblical science an important
service in exposing the fallacies of Orelli's approach.
5. Still valid is the assessment of H. Frankfort in his book, *The Intellectual
Adventure of Ancient Man* (Chicago, 1946). See especially his last chapter, which
compares Greek mentality with "pre-logical" (including the Semitic-Hebraic) ways
of thinking.
6. Garden City, N.Y., 1967. An exhaustive bibliography is included.
7. Halle, 1927; ET of 7th ed. by J. Macquarrie and E. Robinson, *Being and Time*,

who have recently dealt with time we may mention Adolf Grünbaum and Arthur H. Prior;[8] among the psychologists, there are such as Jean Guitton.[9] Theologians who have recently made important contributions to discussion about the meaning of time are Karl Barth, C. H. Ratschow, E. Voegelin, and Paul Tillich.[10]

It is a comparatively recent development that has brought the insights of religion-phenomenology into the discussion of time. It figured somewhat in the older scholars' analysis of folklore,[11] but it is Mircea Eliade who has focused attention on the regeneration of time in primitive thought, con-. trasting this with the biblical view which understands time realistically and creatively.[12] Some biblical scholars have made use of religion-phenonemo-logical insights in combination with insights from biblical theology; we may mention here especially Johannes Pedersen's important book, *Israel*, which was marred somewhat in allowing preconceptions concerning the supposed psychology of the ancient Hebrews to weigh more heavily than contextual evidence.[13] Much more helpful have been several brief but systematic attempts by a number of biblical scholars to evaluate the Hebraic conception of time from a more strictly textual method and a more theologically

---

New York, 1962. See especially Division Two, "Dasein and Temporality," V. "Temporality and Historicity"; VI. "Temporality and Within-Time-ness as the Source of the Ordinary Conception of Time."

8. See especially the important collection of lectures and essays in Prior, *Papers on Time and Tense* (Oxford, 1968)—essentially an analysis of the logic and grammar of time.

9. See his book, *Justification du Temps* (Paris, 1961), translated into English by A. Foulke under the title, *Man in Time* (Notre Dame and London, 1966). This is a moving and eloquent analysis of the meaning of human finitude as temporally experienced.

10. Barth, *Kirchliche Dogmatik*, III/2, 47; Ratschow, "Anmerkungen zur theologischen Auffassung des Zeitproblems," *ZTK*, 51 (1954), 360-87, where an attempt is made to clarify definitions in the conflict between Barth and Rudolf Bultmann concerning the meaning of history; Voegelin, "Ewiges Sein in der Zeit," *Bultmann Festschrift*, 1964, pp. 593-614; Tillich, *Systematic Theology*, III (Chicago, 1963), pp. 318-20, 419f., and the entirety of Part V: "History and the Kingdom of God." Cf. also E. C. Rust, "History and Time," *Studies in Memory of H. Trantham* (Waco, Tex., 1964), pp. 167-88; H. Richard Niebuhr, *The Meaning of Revelation* (New York, 1941); Reinhold Niebuhr, *Faith and History* (New York, 1949).

11. Cf. G. van der Leeuw, *Religion in Essence and Manifestation* (New York, 1963), II, 384ff., on sacred time; 388ff., on the festivals.

12. *Cosmos and History, The Myth of the Eternal Return* (New York, 1959); see especially chap. 2, "The Regeneration of Time," chap. 3, "Misfortune and History," chap. 4, "The Terror of History." Cf. also Eliade, *The Sacred and the Profane* (New York, 1961), chap. 2, "Sacred Time and the Myths." S. G. F. Brandon's recent book, *History, Time and Deity, A Historical and Comparative Study of the Conception of Time in Religious Thought and Practice* (New York, 1965), is critical of Eliade at the point of the latter's interpretation of Babylonian religion (chap. 4); Brandon enumerates five different views of time: (1) the negation of historical time in the ritual perpetuation of the past; (2) time as deity; (3) time as sorrow and illusion; (4) time and history as the revelation of the divine purpose; (5) time and history as divine teleology.

13. London-Copenhagen, 1926-40; cf. II, 486ff.

informed point of view. We make special mention of studies by H. Wheeler Robinson,[14] James Muilenburg,[15] and Henri Yaker.[16]

Unfortunately, theologians have at times been all too eager to misuse philological data for the purpose of a facile systematic arrangement. Not only have certain systematicians been guilty of this (T. Boman and J. Marsh);[17] some biblical scholars, such as Oscar Cullmann, G. A. F. Knight, and Edmund Jacob,[18] have been accused of it as well. With greater or with lesser justification, all have been criticized by James Barr,[19] Walther Eichrodt,[20] and others. Theological a prioris are scarcely more allowable than philosophical-psychological a prioris like that of Orelli.

Much is at stake in working toward a thorough and accurate analysis of the Hebraic view of time. Several crucial questions of biblical theology depend upon it. One of these is the problem of the interconnectedness between temporal event, history, and revelation. It has long been clear to biblical scholars that the Hebrews took history seriously—that they were, in fact, the earliest people to produce any extensive historiography.[21] If they

---

14. *Inspiration and Revelation in the Old Testament* (Oxford, 1946), chap. 8, "Time and Eternity"; chap. 9, "The Prophetic Interpretation of History"; chap. 10, "The Day of Yahweh."
15. "The Biblical View of Time," *HTR*, 14 (1961), 225-52; "The Biblical Understanding of the Future," *JRT*, 19 (1962-63), 99-108.
16. "Motifs of the Biblical View of Time" (unpublished dissertation, Columbia University-Union Theological Seminary, 1956). Mention may also be made of W. Vollborn, *Studien zum Zeitverständnis des Alten Testament* (Göttingen, 1951); M. Sekine, "Erwägungen zur hebräischen Zeitauffassung," SVT, 9 (1963), 66-82; G. S. Ogden, "Time and the Verb היה in O.T. Prose," *VT*, 21 (1971), 451-69; H. D. Preuss, *Jahweglaube und Zukunftserwartung* (BWANT, V, 7, Stuttgart, 1968), pp. 91-96.
17. Boman, *Hebrew Thought Compared with Greek* (see n. 1); Marsh, *The Fulness of Time* (New York, 1952). In chap. 3, "Out of Egypt," Marsh makes a superficial attempt to explain how the biblical understanding of history got its start. Appealing to Artur Weiser for details, he postulates the "historicizing" of myth, cult, law, etc., as this took place in Israel. From this he argues that the concept of history was fundamental and formative for Israel. The Hebrews got it from the experience of their deliverance out of Egypt. Marsh thinks he has proven this when he goes on to enumerate the passages that refer to the exodus as the foundational experience. He argues that both P and J in Exod. 14 represent God as acting in and through natural phenomena. But this is far from an adequate analysis either of the Pentateuchal traditions or of the origin of Israel's historiography.
18. Cullmann, *Christus und die Zeit* (Zollikon-Zürich, 1946; cf. rev. ed., 1962); Knight, *A Christian Theology of the Old Testament* (Richmond, 1959); Jacob, *Théologie de l'Ancien Testament* (Neuchâtel, 1955).
19. *The Semantics of Biblical Language* (see n. 1); *Biblical Words for Time* (SBT, 33, Naperville, Ill., 1962).
20. "Heilserfahrung und Zeitverständnis im Alten Testament," *TZ*, 12 (1956), 103-25. The main impact of Eichrodt's essay is to counteract the claim that chronological time has no significance in Hebraic thought. Aiming at an appreciative correction of the onesided claims of "the biblical-theological school" (Marsh, Boman, Ratschow), it does not enter into detailed philological considerations, as do Barr's books.
21. Cf. an important statement by A. Jepsen in *Die Quellen des Königsbuches* (Halle/Saale, 1953), pp. 110-14. Long before Herodotus and Thucydides the

took history seriously, it was because they understood time as meaningful. Time was for them the arena within which Yahweh acts purposefully; temporal event was the vehicle of his self-disclosure.[22] Some writers have exaggerated the importance of temporal event,[23] provoking other scholars into a counterbalancing insistence on the importance of the interpretive word as a mode of divine revelation.[24] A significant contribution to this discussion has been the interjection of comparative data from the Near East generally,[25] but the most helpful contributions have been a series of studies on the actual development of the Hebrew historiographic writings, bringing to light both the theological relevance of these writings and their view of the revelatory significance of temporal event.[26] By far the most important of these have been Leonhard Rost's analysis of the throne-succession document,[27] Martin Noth's analyses of the deuteronomistic history, the Chronicler's history, and the Pentateuch,[28] and Gerhard von Rad's treatment of Deuteronomy and the Deuteronomist.[29] It is von Rad himself who has made the most successful attempt thus far toward inte-

---

Hebrews were writing genuine historiography, including the throne-succession document (tenth century B.C.) and the deuteronomistic history (*ca.* 550).

22. Cf. Robinson, *Inspiration and Revelation*, chap. 9; Eichrodt, "Heilserfahrung und Zeitverständnis." See also J. Hempel, *Altes Testament und Geschichte* (Gütersloh, 1930).

23. G. E. Wright, *The God Who Acts* (SBT, 8, Naperville, 1952). The so-called Pannenberg school has gone so far as to claim that revelation occurs only in "history"—that is to say, the tradition about historical event; cf. W. Pannenberg *et al.*, *Offenbarung als Geschichte* (2nd ed., Göttingen, 1963).

24. Cf. C. Westermann, "Zur Auslegung des Alten Testaments," Westermann, ed., *Probleme alttestamentlicher Hermeneutik* (Munich, 1968); J. Barr, "Revelation Through History in the Old Testament and in Modern History," *Interpretation*, 17 (1963), 193-205.

25. Cf. Albrektson, *History and the Gods;* Brandon, *History, Time and Deity*, chap. 5; and especially H. Gese, "Geschichtliches Denken im alten Orient und im Alten Testament," *ZTK*, 55 (1958), 127-45; ET in *JTC*, 1 (1965), 49-64.

26. Cf. G. Hölscher, *Geschichtsschreibung in Israel* (Lund, 1952).

27. *Die Ueberlieferung von der Thronnachfolge Davids* (BWANT, III, 6, Stuttgart, 1926), reprinted in *Das kleine Credo und andere Studien zum Alten Testament* (Heidelberg, 1965), pp. 119-253. This is a solid essay in literary criticism establishing clearly the shape of the succession document. For a theological appraisal of its contents one should turn to G. von Rad, "Der Anfang der Geschichtsschreibung im Alten Testament," *AKG*, 32 (1944), 1-42 (reprinted as "The Beginnings of Historical Writing in Ancient Israel," trans. by E. W. T. Dicken in *The Problem of the Hexateuch and Other Essays*, New York, 1966, pp. 166-204). For a more recent theological evaluation of the succession document cf. R. N. Whybray, *The Succession Narrative, A Study of II Samuel 9-20 and I Kings 1 and 2* (SBT, 2nd ser. 9, Naperville, 1968).

28. *Ueberlieferungsgeschichtliche Studien, Die sammelnden und bearbeitenden Geschichtswerke im Alten Testament* (Halle/Saale, 1943); *Ueberlieferungsgeschichte des Pentateuch* (Stuttgart, 1948).

29. "Die deuteronomische Geschichtstheologie in den Königsbüchern," *Deuteronomium-Studien*, Teil B. (FRLANT, 40, Göttingen, 1947), pp. 52-64; ET by E. W. T. Dicken, "The Deuteronomic Theology of History in I and II Kings," *The Problem of the Hexateuch*, etc., pp. 205-21. Cf. also von Rad, *Theologie des Alten Testaments*, I (Munich, 2nd ed. 1958), 332-44 (ET, 334-47).

grating the significance of this type of analysis into a systematic interpretation of Israel's theology.[30]

Another problem in biblical theology that depends on an adequate understanding of time is that of Old Testament eschatology. How is prophecy related to Israel's sacral traditions, and how is apocalyptic related to prophecy? How is revelatory temporal event in the past related to revelatory temporal event in the present and in the future? Does the Hebraic perception of time begin to shift with the emergence of eschatological expectation, or is it essentially the same, modulated into a different key? These are questions for which current biblical scholarship is seeking a solution. We cannot outline the details of this discussion;[31] we shall mention only one crucial problem that still awaits solution and for which an analysis of time is essential: the day of Yahweh. No one has any doubt about the central importance of this concept as an eschatological theologoumenon within the Old and the New Testaments; what still vexes the scholars is the question of its origin. Did it emerge as a foreign importation (Hugo Gressmann)?[32] Did it originate as a mythological element in Israel's cultus (Sigmund Mowinckel)?[33] Did it arise through spontaneous internal

---

30. *Theologie des Alten Testaments*, II (Munich, 1960), 112-25. S. G. F. Brandon's book, *History, Time and Deity* (see n. 12), chap. 5, crediting the Hebrews with the first positive evaluation of history, attempts unsuccessfully to delineate how the Yahwist conception developed. Brandon is influenced by von Rad but performs none of that scholar's painstaking analysis of the biblical text. He is vague about J's date (pp. 110, 123), yet makes much of J's assumed remoteness from the events described (pp. 110f.). He wrongly supposes that J is the creative author of the entire body of literature subsumed under his siglum and that the history recited there was fabricated tendentiously (seen by Brandon *in bonam partem*, admiringly). Brandon makes other naive assumptions, such as that the Deut. 26 credo must have had the passover rather than the harvest festival as its *Sitz im Leben* (pp. 114f.), and that the deuteronomistic scheme of periodic apostasy and return reflects historical actuality, evoking the demand for a common interest or sense of unity for which the J history was expressly created (p. 121).
31. Of central importance regarding prophetic eschatology in relation to apocalyptic are H. Gressmann, *Der Ursprung der israelitisch-judäische Eschatologie* (FRLANT, 6, Göttingen, 1905); *Der Messias* (FRLANT, 43, 1929); G. Hölscher, *Die Ursprünge der judischen Eschatologie* (1925); S. Mowinckel, *Han som kommer* (Copenhagen, 1951; ET by G. W. Anderson, *He That Cometh*, Oxford, 1956); C. Steuernagel, "Die Strukturlinien der Entwicklung der jüdischen Eschatologie," *Bertholet Festschrift*, 1950, pp. 479ff.; Th. C. Vriezen, "Prophecy and Eschatology," SVT, 1 (1953), 199-229; C. von Rad, *Theologie des Alten Testaments*, II, 125-32; D. S. Russell, *The Method and Message of Jewish Apocalyptic* (Philadelphia, 1964), especially pp. 205-34; S. Herrmann, *Die prophetischen Heilserwartungen im Alten Testament* (Stuttgart, 1965). Regarding the background of prophetic eschatology a number of important studies have recently been published, e.g., H.-P. Müller, *Ursprünge und Strukturen alttestamentlicher Eschatologie* (BZAW, 109, Berlin, 1969), but few of these have entered specifically into the problem of the conception of time.
32. *Der Ursprung der israelitisch-judäische Eschatologie* (see n. 31).
33. *Psalmenstudien*, II (Oslo, 1922), 230-44; "Jahwes dag," *NTT*, 59 (1958), 209-29; cf. L. Černy, *The Day of Yahweh and Some Relevant Problems* (Karlovy, 1948). An early critic of Mowinckel's view was H. Wheeler Robinson (*Inspiration*

development (Meir Weiss)?[34] Or did it find its origin within the traditions of Israel's holy war (as von Rad and an increasing number of scholars have come to believe)?[35] This question is important not only as an historical problem; those with insight into the central issues of current theological dispute will perceive that it will make a great deal of difference whether biblical eschatology is seen to have originated out of cultic myth or as a genuine offshoot from the Hebraic understanding of history.[36] Yet it should be clear that we can have no adequate understanding of "the day of Yahweh" unless we understand what each and every day meant to the Hebrews.

While progress is going forward on many fronts in analyzing these important theological problems, it is clear by now that basic exegesis is the only tool that can really clear away the underbrush of misunderstanding and save us from repeating the same old sweeping errors. We need to come to grips with the textual material—biblical and extrabiblical—that speaks in one way or another about time. We need to analyze this textual material from every conceivable point of view. It will not suffice to tabulate passages; each passage must be analyzed in its own right before it can be placed in a meaningful scheme of correlation. Not only philological study in a narrow sense (comparative lexicography and syntax) must be brought to bear; our study of words and concepts must take into account such matters as literary history, formal structure, traditional background, and practical purpose.

A number of detailed studies of biblical words for time have appeared, but generally their compass has been narrow, either in subject

---

and Revelation, chap. 10). A few studies in comparative materials from Near Eastern texts have seemed congenial to Mowinckel's position; cf. G. Hölscher, NTT, 24 (1923), 129; R. Largement and H. Lemaitre, "Le jour de Yahweh dans le contexte oriental," Bibliotheca Ephemeridum Theologicarum Lovansiensium, XII (1959). Sacra Pagina, Miscellanea Biblica Congressus Internationale Catholice de Re Biblica, I, 259-66; F. C. Fensham, "A Possible Origin of the Concept of the Day of the Lord," Biblical Essays (Pretoria, 1966), pp. 90-97. A position midway between Mowinckel, Gressmann, and von Rad is occupied in studies by Frank Moore Cross, Jr., "The Divine Warrior in Israel's Early Cult," A. Altmann, ed., Biblical Motifs (Cambridge, Mass., 1966), pp. 11-30; and Patrick J. Miller, Jr., "The Divine Council and the Prophetic Call to War," VT, 18 (1968), 100-107.

34. "The Origin of the 'Day of the Lord' Reconsidered," HUCA, 27 (1966), 29-60.

35. Von Rad, Der heilige Krieg im alten Israel (Zürich, 1949); "The Origin of the Concept of the Day of Yahweh," JSS, 4 (1959), 97-108; Theologie des Alten Testaments, II, 133-37; K.-D. Schunck, "Strukturlinien in der Entwicklung der Vorstellung vom Tag Yahwes," VT, 14 (1964), 319ff.; J. G. Heintz, "Oracles prophétiques et 'guerre sainte' selon les archives royale de Mari et l'Ancien Testament," SVT, 17 (1968), 112-38. This is also the position to which H. W. Robinson (Inspiration and Revelation, chap. 10) inclined.

36. The entire Bultmannian program of "demythologizing" the New Testament— and hence Christian theology—depends on the identification of eschatology with myth, which in its primitive form is rooted in the cult.

matter or in methodology.[37] We may mention two that have been particularly helpful: Ernst Jenni's study of *'ōlām*[38] and James Barr's book, *Biblical Words for Time.*[39] Jenni's study is important because it pays careful attention to the textual data. Barr's study pays attention to the text, but has the wider purpose of correcting the defective methodologies of other scholars. We take note also of a recent Münster dissertation by John R. Wilch, *Time and Event;*[40] this fairly extensive analysis of the word *'ēt* offers little significant advance over previous studies because it imposes premature categorizations on the biblical data.[41]

　　We propose to make our own contribution to an understanding of the biblical concept of time by studying inductively a key set of adverbial expressions. These expressions have to do with the content and meaning of what the Hebrews understood to be the basic unit of time: the day.[42] They speak about the day as being past (*bayyôm hahû'*), as being present (*bᵉʿeṣem hayyôm hazzeh, bayyôm hazzeh, hayyôm hazzeh, hayyôm*), or as being future (*bayyôm hahû'*) from the point of view of the writer or speaker. These expressions speak about a particular day in relationship to other days or as something unique in itself. We intend to pay attention to the precise function of each individual occurrence of these expressions within the narrowly defined Canon of the Old Testament and to correlate our analysis with the experiential situation out of which each individual passage emerges. In this way we hope to discover not only how and when the ancient Israelites spoke of particular days, but also why. What was it in their temporal experience that prompted them to speak a word of interpre-

---

37. P. A. Munch, *The Expression Bajjôm Hahu': Is it an Eschatological Terminus Technicus?* (AUNVAO, II. Hist.-Filos. Klasse, 1936. No. 2), Oslo, 1936 (this monograph is to be discussed in Chaps. Two and Four, below); J. Schmidt, *Der Ewigkeitsbegriff im Alten Testament* (ATA, XIII, 5, Münster, 1940); E. Katz, "The Word *yom* in Holy Scripture" (Bohemian), *Židovská Ročenka* (Prague, 1960-61), pp. 11-27. Useful data appear in such works as those of Boman and Yaker (see above) concerning certain of the biblical words for time; helpful but restricted in coverage are such dictionary treatments as von Rad's essay on "ἡμέρα, OT," in Kittel-Friedrich, *Theologisches Wörterbuch zum Neuen Testament*, II.
38. "Das Wort *'ōlām* im Alten Testament," *ZAW*, 64 (1952), 197-248; 65 (1953), 1-35.
39. See n. 19. Barr is concerned chiefly with the Hebrew words *'ēt* and *'ōlām*, together with their Greek counterparts. His book is essentially a refutation of Cullmann. With some justification, Barr has been criticized as being the skillful dissector of other scholars' methods without himself participating sufficiently in fundamental, painstaking exegesis.
40. *Time and Event, An Exegetical Study of the Use of 'eth in the Old Testament in Comparison to Other Temporal Expressions in Clarification of the Concept of Time* (Leiden, 1969).
41. See my review in *JBL*, 89 (1970), 474-76.
42. The ancient Hebrews did not yet know the hour or the minute. The day, month, and year were recognized because they involved the circuit of the earth, moon, and sun. The week was also observed by the early Hebrews, but its origin remains obscure. On ancient methods of measuring time, cf. M. P. Nilsson, *Primitive Time Reckoning* (Lund, 1920).

tation about it? If we can get an answer to this question, we shall have a clue to their understanding of history.

2. Terms for the day within the Hebrew vocabulary of time

Like all peoples, the Hebrews had their own peculiar capabilities for expressing time relationships. In the biblical period their verbal system had ceased to emphasize tense differences in favor of modes of action;[43] thus their language depended mainly on temporal clauses of various kinds for placing events in their context of time. There were three main ways of expressing contemporaneousness between two events: using adverbially a time-word with the article (*hayyôm* "today", *hallaylâ* "tonight", *haššānâ* "this year", *happa'am* "this time"),[44] using the infinitive absolute to qualify the main verb,[45] and using genitive phrases (time-nouns in the construct with prepositions or infinitive constructs with prepositions).[46] Relational time (before or after the event) was generally expressed by a variety of prepositions and conjunctions preceding subordinate clauses.[47]

It is significant that, as the Hebrews had no word for abstract "time,"[48] they had no way of speaking about the abstract "past," "present," and "future." There were no specific terms to correspond to these nominal ideas. All they had were a variety of adverbial phrases and substantives referring to a specific aspect of time. The adverbial expressions themselves derive from primitive demonstratives (*'āz*, "then," "so")[49] or substantives (*ṭerem*, "earliness," hence "early," "before"; *qedem*, "in front of"; *lipnê*, "to the face of," "before"; *'aḥar*, "back," "behind," "after"; *hayyôm* "today"; etc.). Naturally, there were nominal expressions for the day, the night, and various parts of each, such as the morning, noontime,

---

43. Biblical Hebrew ranges in date from *ca.* 1250 B.C. to *ca.* 300 B.C. Pre-Hebrew Canaanite and most of the early Semitic languages reflected time differences in verbal inflection, but this is mainly lost in Biblical Hebrew. The verb with the conjunction remained as the main way of indicating a sequence of action. In post-Biblical Hebrew, preserved mainly in the Mishna and later Jewish writings, verbal forms again assume the function of tenses in the proper sense. Cf. C. Brockelmann, *Hebräische Syntax* (Neukirchen, 1956), pp. 37ff.
44. Brockelmann, § 21[a].
45. *Ibid.*, § 93[i].
46. *Ibid.*, §§ 47, 144, 162.
47. *Ibid.*, §§ 109[b], 145[b], 163[b].
48. This has been rightly emphasized by a number of writers on the subject. We fail to be convinced by James Barr's argument (*Biblical Words for Time*, pp. 98f.) that Qoheleth uses the word *'ēt* abstractly: he speaks not of "time" but of "a time."
49. Cf. *GK*, § 100[i]. The archaizing form *'ᵃzî* occurs in Ps. 124:3, 4, 5. This demonstrative is cognate to Ugaritic *'idk*, Arabic *'iddaka*, Biblical Aramaic *'ᵃdayin*, Yaodic *'z*. The form *mē'āz*, "since," is to be read in Lachish letter III, 7: KY 'BDK [D]WH M'Z ŠLḤK 'L 'BDK, "For the heart of thy servant [has been] sick since thou didst write to thy servant."

and evening; also for longer periods of time, including the week, month, and year.

For nonspecific units of time the Hebrews had several words. The most common of these is *'ēt*, which may usually be translated "a time" or "a situation."[50] The word *mô'ēd* (a participial form of the verb יעד) properly means an assemblage, hence either the place or time of meeting; it becomes a technical term for a religious festival. The word *z^{e}mān* is an Aramaic loanword deriving ultimately from Akkadian; occurring only in late portions of the Old Testament, it has much the same meaning as *mô'ēd*.

Some of the common Hebrew terms for time refer to relative rapidity of occurrence or its opposite, relative slowness or permanence. Among the former are several words that mean "quickly" or "suddenly": *peta'*, *pit'ōm*, and *rega'* (the last is related semantically to the Aramaic word *šā'â*), all of which may be used alone or in prepositional phrases as adverbial expressions. Another set of substantives used adverbially refer to long duration, permanence, or duration: *'ētān*, *neṣaḥ*, *'ēd*, *'ôlām*, and *tāmîd*.[51]

Linguistically speaking, the Hebrews seem to have been more two-dimensional than three-dimensional with respect to time. That is to say, many of their words for the past and for the future were essentially the same. Unspecified time either in the past or in the future could be referred to as *'āz* or by means of the prepositional phrase, *bā'ēt hahî'*. A particular time either in the past or future could be referred to by using *bayyôm hahû'*. Remote time either in the past or future could be *'ôlām*. Thus time does not move through a series of points from past through present to future; it simply diverges in two directions, past and future, from the present. Both are much alike in that they are more or less distant from where one now is. The difference is that a person knows the past, having experienced it (hence *qedem*, "in front of," *lipnê*, "in the face of," referring to what one can look at in past memory), but does not know the future, which is still hidden from him (hence *'aḥar*, "behind," for events yet to come).

Alongside the very familiar *bayyôm hahû'*, "in that day," which is to be a major object of our study, the parallel form *bā'ēt hahî'*, "in that time"

---

50. Cf. KBL, *s.v.*; Wilch, *Time and Event*, pp. 155ff. A Canaanite origin may be inferred from the presence of cognates in Phoenician/Punic; cf. Jean-Hoftijzer, *Dictionnaire des Inscriptions Semitiques de l'Ouest* (Leiden, 1965), *s.v.* The locutions 'T H'T HZH, "(acc.) this time," and 'T ṬB, "a good time," occur in Lachish letters VI, 2 and VIII, 2, respectively.

51. On the etymology of *'ētān* see KBL, *s.v.*, and N. Sarna in *JBL*, 74 (1955), 273. *Neṣaḥ* derives its meaning "everlasting" from its primary meaning "glory," "glorious" (LNSH occurs in Lachish letter III, 10). On *'ēd* see J. Barth, *Etymologische Studien* (1893), p. 64; G. R. Driver in *Welt des Orients*, I (1947), 142; J. Barr, *Comparative Philology and the Text of the Old Testament* (Oxford, 1968), p. 332 (no. 228). On *'ôlām* see Jenni's study referred to in n. 38 ("remoteness"). On *tāmîd* cf. G. R. Driver in *ZAW*, 52 (1934), 55.

(II Chron. 15:5 has the plural), occurs in a fairly extensive list of passages with reference to historical events in the past.[52] As with '*āz*, this phrase is generally employed either for making a synchronism or for establishing a temporal (not a logical) sequence, the main difference being that the reference of *bā'ēt hahî'* is more specific than that of '*āz*. In some instances, the '*ēt* with which a synchronism is made, or from which a sequence is established, is quite specific in itself; however, this is usually no more than the general period in which the mentioned event took place.

Both in oracles of judgment and in oracles of salvation, use is made of *bā'ēt hahî'* referring to the future. Because this expression appears to be synonymous with futuristic *bayyôm hahû'*, we need to observe carefully how and where it is used. We see that in all passages except Mic. 3:4 and Zeph. 3:19 it stands at the beginning of the sentence, being preceded in Jer. 33:15, 50:4, 20, Joel 4:1 by its formal equivalent, *bayyāmîm hāhēm(mâ)*, "in those days," an expression that precedes it also in Jer. 3:17, though in the first part of the foregoing verse. Occasionally *bā'ēt hahî'* may be identified as a redactional transition (Jer. 8:1, 31:1, Joel 4:1), but usually it serves to introduce a literary addition (Isa. 18:7, Jer. 3:17, 4:11, 33:15, 50:4, 20, Zeph. 3:20) or has been introduced into the text as a gloss (Mic. 3:4, Zeph. 1:12). In Zeph. 3:19 it is an integral part of a literary addition, rather than a gloss. Thus this expression is never part of an original composition when referring to the future. It is a mere artificial synchronism, functioning to attach supplementary material onto older texts. It is unable, for this reason, to tell us very much about the Hebraic understanding of time and history.

The word '*ēt* occurs with the demonstrative adjective, "this," in only one Old Testament passage, and it is a memorable one.[53] In Esth. 4:14, Mordecai warns his beautiful cousin not to keep silence "at such a time as this" (*bā'ēt hazzō't*), for "who knows whether you have not come to the kingdom for such a time as this" (*lᵉ'ēt kāzō't*).

When the ancient Hebrew wanted to say "now," "at this time," he had available a favorite expression from the '*ēt* root: '*attâ*. The number of its biblical occurrences is one hundred thirty-four. With the prefixed conjunction (*wᵉ'attâ*) it is even more frequent, appearing two hundred sixty-five times in the Old Testament.

When we look closely at how '*attâ* and *wᵉ'attâ* are used, we arrive inevitably at the conclusion that the root '*ēt* cannot have been the primary Hebrew term for expressing pure time relationships. By far the majority of

---

52. Cf. J. Marsh, *Fulness of Time*, pp. 47-49; Wilch, *Time and Event*, pp. 56ff.; J. G. Plöger, *Literarische, formgeschichtliche und stilkritische Untersuchungen zum Deuteronomium* (BBB, 26, Bonn, 1967), pp. 218-25.
53. It occurs in Lachish letter IV, 1-2 in the masculine gender: 'L 'DNY Y'WŠ YR' YHWH 'T 'DNY 'T H'T HZH ŠLM, "To my lord Yaosh, May Yahweh cause my lord to see *this time* in peace."

Old Testament occurrences use ʾattâ and wᵉ ʾattâ to express a logical and situational, rather than temporal, relationship. These words mean, first, "so," "hence," "accordingly"—and only by derivation, "now," "at this time." The root meaning of ʾattâ is therefore: "in this situation."[54] Extrabiblical documents firmly support this judgment.[55]

If ʿēt is not the primary Hebrew time-word, that honor must fall to the word often used as its synonym: yôm. Yôm is by far the most frequently occurring biblical expression for a unit of time. It is in fact the fifth most frequent substantive in the entire Old Testament. Its basic meaning is the period of light, i.e., from dawn till sunset, the opposite of the night. Thus it is often mentioned in contrast to the night (Gen. 8:22, Num. 11:32, etc.). A modified meaning arises when the days are counted; instead of using such a ponderous expression as "forty days and forty nights" (Exod. 24:18), it is simpler to say "forty days," which is understood to include the nights in between. In this expression the word yôm includes the entire period from sunrise to sunrise or—chiefly in late texts influenced by the lunar calendar—from sunset to sunset.[56]

The ancient Israelites, like many peoples, had a specific ideology of what was suitable activity for the day. In contrast to the night, day was the time for work, travel, worship, and warfare. Abraham's servant sets out on his journey in the morning (Gen. 24:54); David goes out to battle in the morning (I Sam. 17:20, 29:10f.; cf. II Sam. 11:14); in the morning Elkanah and his family depart homeward from the festival (I Sam. 1:19). The daytime is when Boaz carries out his business concerning Ruth (Ruth 3:18, 4:9). It is also when the king sits to hear his people's causes (Ps. 101:8; cf. II Sam. 15:2ff.)[57] and when the evildoer is sent to his punishment (Esth. 5:14).

---

54. This is recognized by Wilch, *Time and Event,* in connection with his examination of the Murubaʿat and Lachish letters (cf. pp. 131ff.). Strangely, Wilch offers no systematic study of ʾattâ and wᵉʾattâ—a shortcoming that may have contributed to his error of forcing the inappropriate meaning "occasion" on the word ʿēt.

55. See *ibid.*; also P. Tachau, *'Einst' und 'Jetzt' im Neuen Testament* (FRLANT, 105, Göttingen, 1972), pp. 21-52. A favorite locution of the Lachish letters (cf. II, 3, IV, 1, V, 2f., VII, 2, VIII, 2) is ʾT KYM (ʾattâ kᵉyôm), meaning "now, this very day."

56. On this question cf. H. R. Stroes, "Does the Day Begin in the Evening or Morning?" *VT*, 16 (1966), 460-75. Judg. 19:5ff. offers clear evidence that early Israel did count the days from sunrise to sunrise. In the great majority of passages where "day" and "night" are mentioned together, "day" comes first. (So also in ancient Near Eastern literature outside the Old Testament; cf. *ANET*, 90a, 91a.) As the importance of the lunar festivals (new moon, new year, passover) increased, it became common to count the days from the evening (so Gen. 1:5ff., Exod. 12:18, Lev. 23:32, Esth. 4:16, Isa. 27:3. This usage is especially apparent in Dan. 8:14, "two thousand and three hundred evenings and mornings." Karl Marti's article, "Day," in *Encyclopaedia Biblica* is one of the most helpful ever written on this subject. Cf. also the article "יום jōm" in E. Jenni and C. Westermann, *Theologisches Handwörterbuch zum Alten Testament* (Munich, 1971), where extensive statistics are provided.

57. In Zeph. 3:5 this royal prerogative is ascribed to Yahweh. Cf. J. Ziegler in

The day was also the time for Yahweh to perform his judging and saving acts, and it was such acts that were memorialized in Israel's *heilsgeschichtliche* tradition. The most common way to speak about one of these memorable days in Israel's past experience was to use the word *yôm*, qualified with a genitival phrase, an infinitive, or a relative clause introduced by *ᵃšer*.[58] Thus there was a *yôm* of salvation experienced in a variety of past events; this could be the day of Israel's election (Deut. 9:24, Ezek. 16:4f.), the day (and night) of the plague on Egypt (Exod. 10:13), the day (= night) of the crossing of the sea (Exod. 12:17), the day(s) of the giving of the quails (Num. 11:32), the day of the dedication of the tabernacle (Num. 9:15), the day of the giving of the law (Deut. 4:10), or the day of victory over the Amorites (Josh. 10:12). There arose, in tradition, a variety of stock expressions containing *yôm* and referring in a general way to what may be called the exodus experience: "on the day when I brought them up/out of Egypt," and the like (Judg. 19:30, I Sam. 8:8, II Sam. 7:6, Isa. 11:16, Jer. 7:22, 11:4, 7, 31:32, 34:13, Hos. 2:17, Ps. 78:42). From this model it became possible also to speak of a past new day of salvation, experienced in the return from exile (Hag. 2:15, 18, 19, Zech. 4:10, 8:9). Moreover, what had happened for Israel as a people could be celebrated, in the psalms of declarative praise, as a day of individual relief (Ps. 18:18, 20:2, 59:17, 77:3, 138:3, 140:8, Lam. 3:57). But the *yôm* to be remembered could also be a day of judgment; a general past day of judgment is referred to in Num. 32:10, Isa. 9:13, Ezek. 31:15, 34:12, Zech. 14:3 (cf. Hos. 10:14), Ps. 78:9, 95:8, Lam. 1:12, 2:1, 21f., II Chron. 28:6; the days when a specific people or city had been judged were "the day of Midian" (Isa. 9:3) and "the day of Jerusalem" (Obad. 11, 14, Ps. 137:7).[59]

There is a striking contrast between the singular and plural use of *yôm*. The plural is used not so much to memorialize a unique event as to identify and specify the duration of a period of time, whether this be limited or unlimited, definite or indefinite. The definite length of such a period could be stated by adding a specific number to the plural, *yāmîm*. An indefinite period might be *yāmîm* alone or *yāmîm 'eḥādîm* ("some days," "a few days") if it was short; if it was long it would be *yāmîm rabbîm* ("many days"). Thus *yāmîm* alone is used as a synonym for *šānā*, "year." If a duration was boundless or immeasurable, the expression generally chosen was *yᵉmê 'ôlām* ("the days of remoteness"), but occasionally we find *yᵉmê haššāmayim* ("the days of heaven"). Terms for the past are *yᵉmê qedem, hayyāmîm qadmōnîm* (both meaning "the former

Nötscher Festschrift, pp. 287f.; J. Hempel, "Die Lichtsymbolik im Alten Testament," *Studium Generale*, 13 (1960), 360ff.; P. Humbert, "La thème véterotestamentaire de la lumière," *RTP*, 99 (1966), 1-6.

58. Cf. A. Fischer, *ZDMG*, 56 (1902), 804.

59. Cf. also the plural with "Gibeath" in Hos. 9:9, 10:9.

days") and *hayyāmîm harî'šônîm* ("the beginning days"). The future is *hayyāmîm habbā'îm* ("the coming days"); hence the conventional eschatological expression *yāmîm bā'îm* (a verbal clause meaning "days are coming"), used frequently in the prophetic literature.[60]

A general period is also identified with the person or persons to whom it is attributed. Here the plural construct of *yôm* is often followed in the genitive relation by a proper name.[61]

Alongside this function of identifying a period and stating its duration, the plural of *yôm* may be constructed in one of several ways (relative clause with *'ᵃšer*, construct with infinitive, construct with nonpersonal noun) as a means for qualifying a certain time or stating its dominant characteristic. Here *yāmîm* is a virtual synonym of *'ēt*. In relative clauses, we find a past period (*yāmîm*) characterized as a time of cutting hair (II Sam. 14:26), traveling (Deut. 2:14), reigning (II Sam. 2:11, I Kings 2:11, 11:42, 14:20, II Kings 10:36, I Chron. 29:27), remaining (Deut. 1:46, I Sam. 27:7), being relieved (Esth. 9:22), abiding (Num. 9:18), and spying (Num. 14:34). With infinitives, we find days in the past characterized as a time of seeking Yahweh (II Chron. 26:5), being in a certain place (Judg. 18:31, I Sam. 22:4, 25:7, 16), going with someone (I Sam. 25:15), preparing to give birth (Gen. 25:24), coming out of a place (Mic. 7:15), being afflicted (Ps. 90:15), being destroyed (II Chron. 36:21), being watched (Job 29:2), and judging (Ruth 1:1). With nonpersonal nouns, days in the past may be characterized as times of mourning (Gen. 50:4, Deut. 34:8), worshiping the baals (Hos. 2:15), embalming the dead (Gen. 50:3), festival (Hos. 12:10) and feasting (Judg. 14:12, Job 1:5), beautifying oneself (Esth. 2:12), youth (Ezek. 16:22, 43, 60, 23:19), and harvest (Gen. 30:14, Judg. 15:1, II Sam. 21:9,[62] Job 29:4).

The present day is sometimes described by characterizations, particularly in laments, complaints, and salvation oracles. Laments speak of a *yôm ṣārātî* or *yôm ṣar lî*, "day of my distress" (Ps. 86:7, 102:3); also of a *yôm 'eqrā'* or *yôm qār'ēnû*, "day when I/we call(ed)" (Ps. 102:3, 20:10). All these refer to the suppliant's present day of suffering. So likewise the

---

60. See below. Spatial metaphors intermingle with temporal metaphors. It is said that days come (בוא); cf. Isa. 7:17, etc. It can also be said of a person that he "goes in days" (בוא בימים, Gen. 18:11, 24:1, Josh. 13:1, 23:1f., I Kings 1:1), i.e., grows old. Thus, literally speaking, days are seen as moving toward and past one, but also as something through which one moves. The first involves a qualitative, the second, a quantitative ideology.

61. The formal phrases, "the days of (the) years . . ." and "the days of (the) life . . ." imply the intensiveness (quality) as well as the extent (quantity) of a duration.

62. Here the expression *bîmê qāṣìr* is a formal parallel to *bayyôm hahû'*. Inasmuch as this is a tale regarding the curse of famine produced by the Saulides' sin against the Gibeonites, vs. 9 formed the original conclusion and vss. 10f. constitute a late addition (introduced along with vss. 7, 12-14). The saying, והם המתו בימי קציר, pleonastic after ויפלו שבעתים יחד, epitomizes the entire narrative, indicating that the Saulides' death produced its immediate effect.

complaint in Jer. 17:16-18, which speaks of the present *yôm 'ānûš*, "day of desperation," and *yôm rā'â*, "day of evil." The parallel passages, II Kings 19:3 and Isa. 37:3, speak of "this day" as a *yôm ṣārâ wᵉtôkēḥâ ûnᵉ'āṣâ*, "day of distress, rebuke, and disgrace." The hymn of Isa. 49:8 identifies the present as a *yôm yᵉšû'â*, "day of victory/salvation," while other passages (Isa. 61:2, 63:4) speak of the present as a *yôm nāqām*, "day of vengeance" (i.e., on Judah's enemies). As for the plural, Lam. 1:7 speaks of Jerusalem's present "days of affliction and bitterness" (*yᵉmê 'onyāh ûmᵉrûdêhā*); Hos. 9:7 refers to present "days of reckoning and recompense" (*yᵉmê happᵉquddâ . . . yᵉmê haššillum*); Ps. 49:6 has the prepositional phrase, "in evil days" (*bîmê rā'*); Ps. 102:4 has a simple *yāmāy*, "my days."

As we analyze the use of present *yôm*, we soon see that a basic distinction needs to be made between the day that is historically present in existential distinctiveness and the day that is present only in gnomic discourse or in cultic regulation. The latter refers to a "today" that is continually repeated and hence continuously present.

The gnomic present, using a form of *yôm* or of *'ēt*, is the present of various kinds of gnomic discourse: exhortations, proverbs, aphorisms. It is the present to which the wisdom sayings pertain, hence it is repeated and repeatable as long as the sayings are true. The cultic present is very similar: it is the ongoing present to which every sort of ritual and cult legislation pertains. These two kinds of present are, together, ideologically opposite to the historical present. The essential difference is that the historical present is always unique—an experience unto itself—whereas the gnomic and cultic present is everything but unique. If the historical present is disjunctive, even irruptive, the gnomic/cultic present is repetitive, cyclical, and institutional.

The substantive *yôm* occurs a few times in combined forms with reference to the gnomic present. Many of the passages involved are wisdom sayings, and, not surprisingly, the combinations in question borrow heavily from similar terminology with *'ēt*. What is very intense and particular in the historical present is here generalized as a dogma. Wisdom sayings speak of *yômô*, "his day," i.e., the wicked man's day of judgment (Ps. 37:13, Job 18:20); more specifically, of a *yôm 'appô*, "day of his (God's) anger" (Job 20:28), a *yôm 'ebrâ*, "day of wrath" (Job 21:30, Prov. 11:4), a *yôm 'ēd*, "day of distress" (Job 21:30), a *yôm qᵉrāb ûmilḥāmâ*, "day of battle and war" (Job 38:23), and a *yôm hᵃrēgâ*, "day of slaughter" (Jer. 12:3). Following in the wisdom pattern, an individual lament turns the historical present into the gnomic present ("day when I call," Ps. 56:10; cf. Ps. 20:10, 102:3, above). The expression *yôm ṣārâ*, "day of distress," becomes the gnomic present in Nah. 1:7 (hymn of theophany) and Jer. 16:19 (individual lament). The gnomic *yôm rā'â*, "day of evil," is mentioned in Ps. 27:5 (individual thanksgiving), 41:2, 50:15 (wisdom hymns).

The gnomic present is also referred to in many passages where the plural of *yôm* is used. There are days of youth, *bᵉḥûrôt* (Eccl. 11:19, 12:1), days of vanity, *hebel* (Eccl. 7:15; cf. 9:9), days of darkness, *haḥōšek* (Eccl. 11:8), days of vigor, *ᵃlûmîm* (Job 33:25), days of affliction, *'onî* (Job 30:16, 27; cf. Prov. 15:15, Lam. 1:7), days of service, *ṣᵉbā'* (Job 14:14), days of evil, *rā'*, *rā'â* (Ps. 94:13, Eccl. 12:1), days of famine, *rᵉ'ābôn* (Ps. 37:19), and days of hired service, *śākîr* (Lev. 25:50). When one reads this list, he is deeply impressed by the sorrowful realization on Israel's part of the tragic and mournful side of life. The list may be extended by noting the gnomic passages in which the qualifiers of *yôm*, plural, occur in the predicate position; one hears almost as a platitude that (all) one's days are "few and evil" (Gen. 47:9), "empty breath" (Job 7:16), "pain" (Eccl. 2:23), "like an evening shadow" (Ps. 102:12), "like a passing shadow" (Ps. 144:4), or "like a hireling" (Job 7:1).

What we call the cultic present is referred to in a considerable variety of technical and semitechnical expressions. Referring to the cultic present, singular *yôm* appears in construct with the following terms: *'āšēmâ*, "guilt offering" (Lev. 5:24); *bô' 'el haqqōdeš*, "entering the sanctuary" (Ezek. 44:27); *hēbî' 'et 'ōmer hattᵉnûfâ*, "bringing the sheaf for waving" (Lev. 23:15); *habbikkûrîm*, "first fruits" (Num. 28:26); *zebaḥ*, "sacrifice" (Lev. 19:6); *ḥag*, "festival" (Ps. 81:4), *mô'ᵃdîm*, "festivals" (Num. 10:10); *haḥōdeš*, "new moon" (Exod. 40:2, Ezek. 46:1, 6); *ṭeheret, haṭṭāhōr*, "cleansing" (Lev. 14:2, 57); *haṭṭāmē'*, "uncleanness" (Lev. 14:57), *(hak)-kippurîm*, "atonement" (Lev. 23:27, 28, 25:9); *māšaḥ, himmāšaḥ*, "anointing" (Lev. 6:13, 7:36, Num. 7:10, 84); *mᵉlō't*, "ordination" (Lev. 8:33); *hēnîp 'et hā'ōmer*, "waving the sheaf" (Lev. 23:12); *ṣôm*, "fasting" (Isa. 58:3); *qorbān, hiqrîb ('et zebaḥ)*, "presenting (the sacrifice)" (Lev. 7:15f., 35); *simḥâ*, "rejoicing" (Num. 10:10); *haššabāt*, "the sabbath" (Exod. 20:8 = Deut. 5:12, Exod. 20:11 = Deut. 5:15, Exod. 31:15, 35:3, Lev. 24:8, Num. 15:32, 28:9, Isa. 58:13, Jer. 17:22, 24 *bis*, 27 *bis*, Ezek. 46:1, 4, 12, Ps. 92:1, Neh. 10:32, 13:17). All these occurrences belong to cult legislation, torah, cultic oath, liturgy, ritual, or apodictic law; what appears superficially as a future is actually a permanent, idealized present, seen in terms of a perfect observance of the laws prescribed for the days involved. Some of the same cultic terms with *yôm* naturally appear in past narration (I Sam. 20:34, Jer. 36:6, Neh. 13:15, 19, 22), in laments with reference to the gnomic present (Lam. 2:7, 22), and in prophetic threats with reference to the future (Hos. 9:5, Zeph. 1:8).

Other frequently occurring expressions involving *yôm* are *bᵉyôm kᵉyôm* and *yôm yôm*, "each day"; also *dᵉbar yôm lᵉyômô*, "according to the daily routine." These are rigidly stereotyped, mainly priestly terms. A cultic term involving the plural is *zebaḥ hayyāmîm*, "the yearly sacrifice" (I Sam. 1:21, 20:6). Other frequently occurring cultic expressions have the plural of *yôm*; the following list all occur in cult legislation or cult narrative: the days of *zôb ṭum'â*, "unclean flowing" (Lev. 15:25f.); *heḥag*, "the festival" (Ezek. 45:23); *ṭāhār*, "cleansing" (Lev. 12:4, 6); *'ăšer han-nega' bô*, "when the disease is on one" (Lev. 13:46); *niddâ*, "uncleanness" (Lev. 12:2, 15:25); *nezer, hazzîr*, "dedication" (Num. 6:4, 5, 6, 8, 12, 13); *mᵉluʾîm*, "ordination" (Lev. 8:33); (*ham*)*miŝteh* (*wᵉśimḥâ*), "feasting (and rejoicing)" (Judg. 14:12, Job 1:5, Esth. 9:22); *hisgîr* (*bêt*), "a (house's) closing" (Lev. 14:46); *happûrîm* "Purim" (Esth. 9:28).

We refrain from entering into a description of the cultic-priestly practice of numbering days. Suffice it to say that certain numbers of days and certain numbered days had particular significance, especially the combinations three/third and seven/seventh. Various patterns of numbering days evolved within the secular, equally formal atmosphere of ordinary daily life; but it is clear that the cultic concern predominates. In the recurrent pattern of festivals and other cultically significant periods there was fertile ground, no doubt, for the imaginative combination of numbered days that came to create calendars and chronologies, proper concern for priests above all.

We conclude with the remark that in cult-legislation several time-designatives that seem to refer to a relative future in fact involve the cultic present. Thus it is with the terms *mimmāḥᵒrāt*, "on the morrow," *bōqer*, "morning," and *hayyôm haŝŝᵉlîŝî*, "the third day," occurring in Exod. 29:34, Lev. 7:11-15, 19:5-8,[63] and Deut. 16:7, as also with the calendrical terminus technicus, *mimmāḥᵒrāt haŝŝabbāt* (*haŝŝᵉbîʿit*), "on the morrow of the (seventh) sabbath," occurring in Lev. 23:11, 15f.[64] A seeming future is in fact also the gnomic/cultic present in a variety of passages where the expression *kol yôm* is used with the pronominal suffix: Jer. 35:8 (1cp) and 37:7 (2mp); Deut. 12:19 and 23:7 (2ms); Deut. 22:19, 29, Eccl. 2:23, 5:17 (3ms); the genres represented here are apodictic law, admonition, casuistic law, and wisdom aphorism. A similar situation prevails with respect to the apparent future in Deut. 17:9, 26:3, Josh. 20:6, where the expression *bayyāmîm hāhēm* appears.[65]

We come now to a consideration of the genuinely futuristic use of the word *yôm*.[66] It will be useful to indicate the intriguing variety of genitival,

---

63. Two forms of apodictic law, those of Exod. 23:18b and Exod. 34:25b, underlie the Leviticus passages. Cf. a similar law in Lev. 22:29f.

64. According to K. Elliger, *HAT*, 4, *in loco*, the original law in this passage made no mention of the day after the sabbath or of the seven sabbaths—only of the fifty days. Thus our expression appears to be very late.

65. Ordinarily this expression refers to the past or future. The passages mentioned are relatively late; they are, respectively, an expansion of casuistic law, an expansion of a torah, a gloss upon a late law code.

66. In prophetic parallelism the word *šānâ*, "year," is sometimes qualified as the synonym of *yôm*. Isa. 34:8 speaks of a "year of recompense" (*šillûmîm*), Isa. 61:2 of a year of Yahweh's favor (*rāṣôn laYHWH*), Isa. 63:4 of the year of redemption (*gᵉʾûlîm*), Jer. 11:23, 23:12, 48:44 of the year of accounting (*pᵉquddâ*). Cf. the gnomic-lyrical expressions, "year of drought" (Jer. 17:8) and "year of thy goodness" (Ps. 65:12). All other instances where *šānâ* is qualified genitivally are dates (so also Gen. 41:50, *šᵉnat hārāʿāb*, "the year of the drought") or cultic terms.

adjectival, and prepositional combinations that qualify it and give it color, showing how these combinations are related to particular genres. The combinations with 'ēt appear pale and pedestrian as compared with the combinations containing yôm.

A purely formal attribute is assigned in the combination yôm habbā', "the coming day" (Jer. 47:4).[67] Compare Mal. 3:19, where "coming" is ascribed predicatively to "the (eschatological) day," and Isa. 13:9, Mic. 7:4, where it is ascribed predicatively to a day that is qualified. Contrariwise, certain days are defined by a person's coming (Mal. 3:2, yôm bô'ô; Ezek. 38:18, yôm bô' gôg). Nah. 2:4 speaks of a yôm hᵃkînô, "a day prepared by him," while Ezek. 39:8 speaks of hayyôm 'ᵃšer dibbartî, "the day of which I spoke."

The person who acts on the future day is indicated predicatively in Isa. 61:2 and Zech. 14:1, but he is indicated attributively more often and in a variety of ways. This person is, of course, Yahweh. Thus it is his special day, i.e., his day to act. We find the divine name qualifying yôm by means of the prepositional possessive (yôm laYHWH, yôm laYHWH ṣᵉbā'ôt) in judgment oracles at Ezek. 30:3 (against a foreign nation) and Isa. 2:12 (against Israel).[68] We find this expressed also by the divine name in construct (yôm YHWH) in three oracles against foreign nations (Isa. 13:6, Joel 4:14, Obad. 15) and eight times in oracles against Israel (Ezek. 13:5, Joel 1:15, 2:1, 11, Amos 5:18 bis, 20, Zeph. 1:7). We find the construct form plus an attributive adjective in an oracle against a foreign nation (Isa. 13:9: yôm YHWH 'akzārî, "Yahweh's cruel day"), in an oracle against Israel (Zeph. 1:14, yôm YHWH haggādôl, "Yahweh's great day"), and in two apocalyptic passages (Joel 3:4, Mal. 3:23, yôm YHWH haggādôl wᵉhannôrā', "Yahweh's great and fearful day"). It is important to observe that there is no set technical term for the so-called "day of Yahweh."

The object of judgment is indicated by adding pronominal suffixes to yôm. Oracles against foreign nations have this with the 2ms suffix in Jer. 50:31 and with the 3mp suffix in Jer. 50:27 and Ezek. 21:34, while an oracle directed against Judah's "wicked prince" (Ezek. 21:30) has the 3ms. In the first two passages the expression "time of reckoning" is in parallelism, while "time of final punishment" is in parallelism in the latter two passages. A salvation oracle has yôm in construct with a proper name to indicate a symbolic place or event (Hos. 2:2: yôm yizrā''ēl, "the day of Jezreel").

The future day is qualified in various ways with respect to its essential action or purpose. This occurs with infinitive phrases in judgment oracles against foreign nations (Ezek. 31:15, yôm ridtô, "the day of its downfall"; Zeph. 3:8 LXX, Syr., yôm qûmî lᵉ'ēd, "the day when I arise as witness"),

---

67. Cf. BH³ mg.
68. Cf. also Jer. 46:10.

in judgment oracles against Israel (Ezek. 24:25, *yôm qaḥtî*, "the day when I take away"; Exod. 32:34,[69] Amos 3:14, *yôm poqdî*, "the day when I call to account"), in salvation oracles (Isa. 30:26, *yôm hᵃbōš YHWH*, "the day when Yahweh binds up"; Ezek. 36:33, *yôm ṭahᵃrî*, "the day when I cleanse"; Isa. 14:3, *yôm hānîᵃḥ YHWH*, "the day when Yahweh gives rest"; Jer. 27:22, *yôm poqdî*, "the day when I pay attention"), and in apocalyptic (Ezek. 39:13, *yôm hikkābᵉdî*, "the day when I honor myself"; Zech. 14:3, *yôm hillāḥᵃmô*, "the day when he fights"). This is also expressed by prefixing *lᵉ* to the infinitive; so in an oracle against a foreign nation in Jer. 47:4 (*hayyôm habbā' lišdôd . . . lᵉhakrît*, "the day that is coming to destroy . . . to cut off") and in a salvation oracle at Mic. 7:11 (*yôm libnôt gᵉdārayik*, "the day to build your walls"). Relative clauses figure in a salvation oracle at Jer. 31:6 (*yôm qārᵉ'û nōṣᵉrîm*, "the day when watchmen call") and in judgment/salvation oracles at Mal. 3:21, 17, where the phrase, *yôm 'ᵃšer 'ᵃnî 'ōśeh*, "the day when I act," appears.[70] The construct with genitival noun is used in three judgment oracles against Israel, Isa. 10:3 (*yôm pᵉquddâ*, "the day of accounting"), Mic. 7:4 (*yôm mᵉṣappêkā pᵉquddātᵉkā*, "the day of your watchman, of your accounting"), and Hos. 5:9 (*yôm tôkēḥâ*, "the day of punishment").

The future day is qualified also in familiar terms of pathos. Oracles of foreign judgment speak of a *yôm hᵃrôn 'appô*, "day of his (Yahweh's) wrath" (Isa. 13:13) and a *yôm nāqām, nᵉqāmâ*, "day of vengeance" (Isa. 34:8, Jer. 46:10), while oracles of judgment on Israel qualify the coming day in terms of its wrath (*zā'am*, Ezek. 22:24; *'ebrâ*, Zeph. 1:15), speaking of it also as the day of Yahweh's anger (*yôm 'ap YHWH*, Zeph. 2:3) or wrath (*yôm 'ebrat YHWH*, Ezek. 7:19, Zeph. 1:18). The royal decree in Ps. 110 likewise speaks of the coming *yôm 'appô*, "day of his (Yahweh's) anger" (vs. 5).

The quality or effect of the coming day of judgment is also indicated. Oracles against the nations speak of a *yôm 'êdām*, "their day of calamity" (Jer. 46:21), a *yôm ṣārâ*, "day of distress" (Hab. 3:16), and thrice of someone's "day of downfall" (*yôm mappaltēk*, Ezek. 26:18, 27:27, 32:10). Oracles against Israel also have the familiar *yôm 'êdām* (Deut. 32:35, Jer. 18:17); other expressions are *yôm maḥᵃlâ ûkᵉ'ēb 'ᵃnûš*, "a day of grief and incurable pain" (Isa. 17:11),[71] *yôm mar*, "a bitter day" (Amos 8:10), *yôm ṣārâ ûmᵉṣûqâ*, "a day of distress and anguish" (Zeph. 1:15), *yôm rā'*, "an evil day" (Amos 6:3), and *yôm šō'â ûmᵉšô'â*, "a day of ruin and devastation" (Zeph. 1:15).

The imagery of the coming day borrows occasionally from other realms. The analogy is drawn from nature in two verses from oracles against

---

69. Yahweh speaks to Moses within the framework of Pentateuchal narration.
70. Cf. Ps. 118:24, *zeh hayyôm 'āśâ YHWH*, "this (is) the day when Yahweh acts."
71. Emending the text; cf. BH³ mg.

the nations, Amos 1:14 (*yôm sûfâ*, "day of storm") and Ezek. 30:3 (*yôm 'ānān*, "day of cloud"), while two Israel-oracle passages, Zeph. 1:15 and Joel 2:2, contain the identical piling up of images, *yôm ḥōšek wa'ᵃpēlâ . . . yôm 'ānān wa'ᵃrāfel*, "day of darkness and gloom, day of clouds and thick darkness." Warfare provides the analogy in oracles of judgment against the nations (Amos 1:14, *yôm milḥāmâ*, "day of warfare")[72] and against Israel (Ezek. 7:7, *yôm mᵉhûmâ*, "day of tumult"; Isa. 22:5, *yôm mᵉhûmâ ûmᵉbûsâ ûmᵉbûkâ*, "day of tumult, trampling, and confusion"; Zeph. 1:16, *yôm šōpār ûtᵉrû'â*, "day of trumpet and outcry"), as well as in an apocalyptic passage, Zech. 14:3 (*yôm hillāḥᵃmô . . . yôm qᵉrāb*, "day of his fighting . . . day of approach"), and a royal decree (Ps. 110:3, *yôm ḥēlekā*, "day of your army").[73] Imagery is borrowed from the cult for judgment oracles against Israel (Zeph. 1:8, *yôm zebaḥ YHWH*, "day of Yahweh's sacrifice"; Hos. 9:5, *yôm mô'ēd . . . yôm ḥag YHWH*, "day of festival . . . day of Yahweh's feast") and for one oracle of salvation (Isa. 30:25, *yôm hereg rāb*, "day of great slaughter").[74]

   This brings us to the absolute use of *yôm* and related terms. Parallelism reveals the meaning everywhere to be: the eschatological day. It occurs in oracles against the nations with the demonstrative adjective (*hayyôm hahû'*, Jer. 46:10) or with the cardinal number "one," meaning "a certain day" (*yôm 'eḥād*, Isa. 10:17, 47:9). Oracles against Israel have the expressions *yôm* (Zeph. 2:2),[75] *hayyôm* (Ezek. 7:10, 12, Mal. 3:19; cf. Joel 1:15), or *hayyôm hahû'* (Jer. 30:7, Zeph. 1:15). Salvation oracles use only the forms *hayyôm (ha)hû'* (Mic. 7:11f.) and *yôm 'eḥād* (Isa. 66:8, Zech. 3:9), while *yôm* and *hayyôm hahû'* are found in apocalyptic passages (Ezek. 48:35[76] and 39:22, respectively).

   We must also mention that the plural, *yāmîm*, is qualified in various ways with respect to a future period. With the relative clause and the verb חיה "live (in the land)," it occurs in a few parenetical verses, Deut. 4:10, 12:1, 31:13, I Sam. 20:31. The future *yāmîm* is in construct with an infinitive phrase from שמם, "destroy," in two verses containing curses (Lev. 26:34f.). Gen. 27:41, belonging to a folk saga, has the construct plural with *'ēbel*, "mourning."

   Another eschatological expression involving the plural of *yôm* is *bᵉ'aḥᵃrît hayyāmîm*, "in the sequel of days," occurring in Gen. 49:1, Num. 24:14, Deut. 4:30, 31:29, Isa. 2:2, Jer. 23:20, 30:24, 48:47, 49:39, Ezek. 38:16, Hos. 3:5, Mic. 4:1, Dan. 10:14 (see similar expressions in Ps. 139:9, Dan. 8:19, 23). A familiar formula for introducing oracles of judgment (Isa. 39:6, Jer. 7:32, 9:24, 19:6, 48:12, 49:2, 51:47, 52, Amos 4:2, 8:11) or of

---

72. Here a literal prediction rather than a mere metaphor; see also Jer. 6:4f.
73. The text is doubtful; cf. BH³ mg.
74. Cf. also Ezek. 36:33.
75. Missing in the LXX; cf. BH³ mg.
76. See BH³ mg.

salvation (Jer. 16:11, 23:5, 7, 30:3, 31:27, 31, 38, 33:14, Amos 9:13) is *hinnēh yāmîm bā'îm*, "behold, days are coming," qualifying this further by a characterization in a dependent clause or similar construction.

Not only is *yôm* a unit of time; it is a unit of experience. It is true that for purposes of time reckoning it may be defined in relationship to other days. It may also be identified—ordinarily in terms of its place on the calendar—or it may serve to determine a synchronous or sequential relationship between events. But very frequently it is defined in terms of its own unique character and quality. This character and quality are, moreover, determined by way of the day's dominant event, so that in this manner time participates in history, receiving its meaning from it.

It is clear that the word *yôm* demands inspection beyond what we have thus far been able to give it. Actually, our study of *yôm* up to this point has been purely formal, showing how a day may be qualified but failing to show how and why a day comes to receive such a qualification. We are invited to turn, therefore, to a detailed study of the leading adverbial expressions with *yôm* in order to see how particular contextual data define this qualification. The choice of terms lies close at hand, indeed, thrusts itself upon us: so numerous are the phrases *bayyôm hahû'* and *ha(ba)yyôm (hazzeh)*, in comparison with other similar phrases, that we are compelled, if only by sheer numbers, to pay close attention to them.[77] With reference to the past, *bayyôm hahû'* occurs eighty-nine

---

77. Very briefly, we can get these expressions into formal perspective by surveying the stock of parallel terms in common use. It is not necessary to cite statistics, for these may easily be checked in the concordances; suffice it to say that *bayyôm hahû'* and *hayyôm* far outnumber all others.
A table will show the forms that are found in the OT:

(past)	(present)	(cultic/gnomic present, future)
hayyôm hahû', s.	*hayyôm (hazzeh)*, s.+p.	
bayyôm, s.		
bayyôm hazzeh, s.	*bayyôm hazzeh*, s.+p.	
beʿeṣem hayyôm hazzeh, s.	*beʿeṣem hayyôm hazzeh*, s.	
bayyôm hahû', s.+p.		*bayyôm hahu'*, s.+p.
beʿôd hayyôm, s.		
kayyôm hahû', s.	*kayyôm hazzeh*, s.	
	kehayyôm hazzeh, s.	
kol yôm, p.+ suffix	*kol yôm*, p.+ suffix	*kol yôm*, s.
kol hayyôm, p.	*kol hayyôm*, s.	*kol hayyôm*, s.
		kol hayyôm wekol hallaylâ, s.
kol hayyôm hahû' (wekol hallaylâ), s.		
	layyôm hazzeh, s.+p.	
lipnê hayyôm hahû', p.		
mēhayyôm hahû', s.		
min hayyôm hahû', s.		*min hayyôm hazzeh*, s.
'ad hayyôm hahû', s.+p.	*'ad ('eṣem) hayyôm (hazzeh)*, s.	
	'ôd hayyôm, s.	

times; with reference to the present, *hayyôm* and related forms occur two hundred seventeen times; *bayyôm hahû'* also refers to the future one hundred twelve times and to the cultic present six times.[78]

Are these terms original to the text? Are they synchronizers, time-identifiers, quality-definers, or what? How are they used: do they belong to the formal schema of any particular forms of literature? In which period of Israel's history, and in relationship to what kinds of events, are they employed? These and many others are the questions that we feel we need to ask in order to come to grips with the Hebrew conception of time.

An intriguing study lies ahead of us. We shall divide our investigation into three parts, corresponding to the three dimensions of time that we recognize: past, present, and future. This will involve us first in a study of historical narration in its various genres: legend, saga, historical report,

---

Two terms, *kayyôm hazzeh* and *kᵉhayyôm hazzeh*, call for a brief word of special comment. The expression *kayyôm* generally means "first" (Gen. 25:31, 33, I Sam. 2:16, 9:27, I Kings 1:51, 22:5 = II Chron. 18:4), but in one passage (Isa. 58:4) it means "like today"—comparing the present to the future. *Kᵉhayyôm* meanwhile means an emphatic "this very day" (I Sam. 9:13, Neh. 5:11). This is the meaning of the expanded form, *kᵉhayyôm hazzeh*, in Gen. 39:11, where it actually refers to the past, seen as present in the narrator's imagination. An emphatic "this very day" is also the meaning of the form *kayyôm hazzeh* in I Sam. 22:8, 13 (Saul's angry speech) and Dan. 9:7, 15, but in all the remaining passages the two forms *kᵉhayyôm hazzeh* and *kayyôm hazzeh* mean "like today," comparing the past to the present or the present to the future. One quickly notes that this is a characteristic Deuteronomic-Jeremianic locution, but different combinations are observed. *Kᵉhayyôm hazzeh* compares Yahweh's past saving act with a present good in Deut. 6:24, Neh. 9:10; a past sin on the part of Israel with a present evil in Jer. 44:22, Ezr. 9:7, 15. *Kayyôm hazzeh* compares a past saving act with present good in Gen. 50:20, Deut. 2:30, 4:20, 38, 8:18, 10:15, I Kings 3:6, 8:24 = II Chron. 6:15, Jer. 11:5, 32:20; it compares a past sin with present evil in Deut. 29:27, Jer. 25:18, 44:6, 23; it also compares a present virtue with future good in two passages, I Kings 8:61 and I Chron. 28:7.

78. The plural, *bayyāmîm hāhēm(mâ)*, "in those days," refers often to a past period of time. Of the twenty-five passages where it occurs, three in the book of Judges are glosses from a monarchistic editor who epitomizes the period in question in much the same manner as in many of the passages with *bayyôm hahû'* ("In those days there was no king in Israel; every man did what was right in his own eyes," Judg. 17:6, 18:1 (1), 21:25). Otherwise *bayyāmîm hāhēm(mâ)* referring to the past either is a synchronism or produces a sequence. In the early passages it appears as a gloss or redactional transition (Gen. 6:4, Exod. 2:11, Judg. 18:1 (2), 19:1, 20:27, 28, I Sam. 3:1); so also in the relatively late passages, II Kings 20:1 = Isa. 38:1 = II Chron. 32:24, Ezek. 38:17. In more sophisticated materials it provides a transition within the original composition (Exod. 2:23 P, I Sam. 28:1, II Sam. 16:23, II Kings 10:32, 15:37, Esth. 1:2, 2:21, Dan. 10:2, Neh. 6:17, 13:15, 23). There is also a futuristic *bayyāmîm hāhēm(mâ)*, but all twelve occurrences are identifiable as redactional or editorial synchronisms, introducing secondary materials into salvation oracles. Jeremiah has it the most often (3:16, 18, 5:18, 31:29, 33:15, 16, 50:4, 20), with other occurrences in Joel (3:2, 4:1) and Zechariah (8:6, 23). As has already been mentioned, *bayyāmîm hāhēm* refers also to a cultic present/future in Deut. 17:9, 19:17, 26:3.

The twenty-one passages in which the parallel term *ballaylâ hahû'*, "in that night," occurs use it regularly as a mere identifier of time when. It has no specific theological significance.

annals, and the like. It will involve us next in a study of various kinds of discourse in which some person (an authoritative interpreter) is represented as speaking about the meaning of "today." It will involve us thirdly in a study of prophetic and apocalyptic genres, in which the future is being defined from the present point of view. This will show us how some of those who were immediately involved in—or were at least intimately concerned about—historical events interpreted their meaning. Those who speak about the present (*hayyôm*, etc.) are there present as participants. Those who speak about the past (*bayyôm hahû'*) were either themselves actually there as participants or are there now in their imagination and concern. Those who speak about the future, whether immediate (*māḥār*, "tomorrow") or distant (*bayyôm hahû'*), likewise participate in it in their imagination and concern. Putting the meaning of a day into words, they give history its meaning and its purpose; for without the mind and heart of man—brought to expression in the interpretive word—history is nothing but a chain of occurrences, aimless, void, and futile.

CHAPTER TWO

The Day Past: *bayyôm hahû'*

IN PREPARATION FOR analyzing the eschatological bearing of the familiar phrase *bayyôm hahû'*, we shall do well to observe carefully how the writers of Scripture used it in other contexts. In a few cult-legislative passages it pertains to the cultic present.[1] The futuristic references are mainly in the prophetic books. Besides these there are a considerable number of occurrences in the narrative literature of the Old Testament, almost always referring to events that are past from the point of view of the speaker or writer.

In a monograph published in Oslo in 1936, Peter Andreas Munch subjected all futuristic references of this phrase to a minute criticism, arriving at the conclusion that "everywhere . . . the expression can be understood as a temporal adverb."[2] Munch's judgment depended to a large extent on the fact that, in his analysis, the phrase almost always constitutes a secondary literary element among the more than one hundred passages where it occurs, and is thus quite conventional and artificial. Munch meant to suggest that *bayyôm hahû'* has much the same function and meaning in passages where it refers to the past, but the fact is that he quite neglected to analyze these passages,[3] even though these total almost ninety references in the Old Testament—virtually as many as the number of futuristic passages. It would seem scarcely necessary, in view of the present status of biblical criticism, to argue that an understanding of futuristic usage depends at least in part on an understanding of past usage; and this to the same degree that prophetic prediction depends for its meaning on the historical tradition out of which it emerges.

The number of past occurrences of *bayyôm hahû'* by Bible book is as follows:[4] Genesis, 5; Exodus, 3; Numbers, 3; Deuteronomy, 2; Joshua, 11; Judges, 9; I Samuel, 22; II Samuel, 12; I Kings, 3;[5] II Kings, 1; Isaiah, 2; Jeremiah, 1; Ezekiel, 3; Zechariah, 1; Esther, 3; Nehemiah, 3; I Chronicles, 2; II Chronicles, 2. Thus fifty-four out of eighty-eight occurrences are found in the four books, Joshua, Judges, I and II Samuel—those that reflect the history of Israel in the early premonarchic and nation-building periods. The impression conveyed is that the predynastic period was the time when *bayyôm hahû'* was used in past reference the most frequently.

---

1. See Chapter Four.
2. *The Expression Bajjôm Hahû'*, p. 6 (publication data in Chapter One, n. 37). Cf. S. Mowinckel, *Prophecy and Tradition* (Oslo, 1946), p. 108, n. 89a.
3. He devotes no more than one and a half pages of his text to a discussion of this.
4. Excluding doublets in Chronicles (I Chron. 13:12 = II Sam. 6:9; II Chron. 18:34 = II Kings 22:35). Our statistics are based on the MT.
5. Excluding I Kings 13:3, which we read as futuristic; see in Chapter Four.

However, we know that documents do not necessarily emerge from the time concerning which they speak. In order to allow our impression from these statistics either to be corrected or to ripen into full understanding, we must apply a methodology to the analysis of this group of passages that will lay bare in the greatest possible detail exactly how, where, when, and by whom the phrase was used, and what shifts in its meaning may have come about in the process of literary development. We may not assume that the phrase is a mere temporal adverb, or has any other particular function in a given passage, without first examining that passage carefully. The phrase is not in itself a clue to secondary literary accretion, in spite of what Munch has suggested. On the contrary, literary criticism must first be independently applied, and this then becomes a basis upon which the phrase's formal function can be analyzed and its place in tradition determined.

We shall examine each occurrence of *bayyôm hahû'* in past reference in the sections that follow. Through this we shall discover that, more often than not, the expression is original (i.e., fifty-four out of eighty-eight times), and that there exist varying degrees of attachment on the part of the secondary materials in relation to their respective original contexts (i.e., some occurrences are glosses, some are redactional, some are parts of literary supplements, some are parts of clearly distinguishable oral supplements). We shall see, further, that the phrase appears in a variety of positions within a given pericope, whether in the original or in secondary materials, and that these positions are directly related to a number of distinct functions.

Although we have approached each passage without precommitment, it will no doubt prove more helpful to the reader if we discuss the individual passages according to categories and functions, rather than simply in their order of occurrence. First we shall treat those that involve a loose connection to original contexts (glosses, redactional additions, literary supplementation); next we shall discuss passages containing *bayyôm hahû'* as a concluding formula, taking first the secondary passages and then the original; following this we shall examine passages in which the phrase occurs as a transitional formula, again following the sequence of secondary-original; and finally we shall deal with a variety of special kinds of passages—which by that time, it is hoped, we shall be better able to understand in the light of all that has preceded. After we have done all this, we shall be in a position to judge whether various writers and documents have been consistent in their employment of this prase.

1. Glosses

The passages falling into the category of gloss may be surveyed rather quickly. They involve additions that have no integral relation to the internal structure of the pericopes into which they have been inserted. Unassociated glosses, i.e., those from an editor or scribe who introduced them in order to redirect the temporal bearing of the passage in question, outside the process of a systematic redaction, are the occurrences of *bayyôm hahû'* in Exod. 5:6,[6] Josh. 10:35 (both),[7] and I Chron. 16:7,[8] as well as the second occurrence in Num. 9:6.[9] To these we must add the occurrences of this phrase in Ezek. 23:38-39; it is missing in the LXX text of this passage and is without meaning or function.[10]

II Kings 3:6

Part of a redactional supplementation is *bayyôm hahû'* in II Kings 3:6. It has been recognized that the names of the kings in vss. 4ff. have been added secondarily to the text;[11] the ancient versions lack them in

---

6. Missing in LXX. It serves no authentic function in the original narrative.

7. Probably from the same hand as was responsible for "the second day" in vs. 31, attempting to interject a time sequence into a formidable series of encounters, but without sense or consistency. The LXX has no equivalent to the second occurrence in this verse.

8. ביום ההוא is superfluous before אז. The same glossator may have been responsible for adding בראש; he intended by these additions to emphasize the uniqueness and solemnity of the event recorded.

9. See the special discussion of this passage below, p. 61.

10. Cf. W. Zimmerli, *BK*, XIII, *in loco*. Four of the MT occurrences are missing in the LXX (Exod. 5:6, Josh. 10:35(2), Ezek. 23:38f. are glosses); Jer. 39:10 is missing in the LXX, along with the entirety of vss. 4-13 MT.

There are several passages where, with no counterpart in the MT, the LXX has the equivalent of *bayyôm hahû'* in past reference. In Deut. 31:10 this is an editorial gloss; in Deut. 32:44 it is part of an editorial expansion, copied from 31:22 and related passages; in Josh. 9:26 it is a gloss added under the influence of *bayyôm hahû'* in vs. 27; in Josh. 24:33a it belongs to a lengthy expansion not found in the MT; in I Sam. 14:45 its originality is suspect because of the immediately preceding *hayyôm*; in I Sam. 21:14 the schematic and syntactical pattern indicates the phrase to be a gloss; it comes at the end in I Kings 2:24, probably as a gloss making an emphatic synchronism in view of σήμερον in vs. 24, out of place for *bayyôm hahû'* as a concluding epitome; in I Kings 2:37 it has been added at the end, probably as a gloss intended to justify the harshness of Solomon's treatment of Shimei (the latter's reply in vs. 38 would be a pale anticlimax to an oath); in Dan. 5:1 it belongs to an introductory colophon; in I Chron. 10:6 the phrase occurs as a gloss, correcting the MT according to the reading of I Sam. 31:6. We may add that in I Kings 16:16, LXX^A has the phrase as a probable dittography, while in Judg. 13:10 this same manuscript wrongly adds *hahû'* to *bayyôm*.

The usual form for the LXX equivalent to the MT *bayyôm hahû'*, whenever normal, unemphatic word-order is involved, is (ἐν) τῇ ἡμέρᾳ (ἢ) ἐκείνῃ. However, Exod. 32:28, Num. 9:6(2), Deut. 31:22, Josh. 4:14, 14:9, Ezek. 20:6, I Chron. 29:22 have the form ἐν ἐκείνῃ τῇ ἡμέρᾳ, with emphasis on the demonstrative; but in fact, this emphasis is justifiable only in Josh. 4:14, where *bayyôm hahû'* stands at the beginning, and in Ezek. 20:6, where it connects back directly in poetic parallelism to *b^eyôm bāh^orî* of vs. 5. Esth. 8:1 and 9:11 LXX have ἐν αὐτῇ τῇ ἡμέρᾳ, as though reading ביום הזה, which, in the light of our argumentation concerning these verses (see below), is not likely to be original. Ἐκείνη is not attested in the oldest LXX mss. for I Kings 13:11, where MT *hayyôm* was apparently read.

11. For a discussion of the probable original setting, see J. Maxwell Miller, "The Elisha Cycle and the Accounts of the Omride Wars," *JBL*, 85 (1966), 446ff.; cf. J. D. Shenkel, *Chronology and Recensional Development in the Greek Text of Kings* (HSM, 1, Cambridge, Mass., 1968), pp. 92ff.

certain of these verses. The original quasi holy-war story involved four anonymous kings and a prophet who may also have been anonymous. Its purpose was to tell how the prophet's prediction (18f.) was fulfilled through Yahweh's intervention, coming to a conclusion in a statement recording the fulfillment of the prophet's word (25). In all likelihood vss. 26f. are supplementary; so also the time reference at the beginning of vs. 5, "But when Ahab died" (ויהי כמות אחאב).[12] *Bayyôm hahû'* in vs. 6, which creates an awkward word order (severing "from Samaria" from the verb)[13] and has little meaning apart from its redactional framework (could all Israel be mustered in one day?), has itself probably been added by the redactor, who used this phrase to emphasize the promptness of Jehoram's reaction to Moab's revolt.

Conclusion

It will be observed that in each of the passages falling into this category the synchronism created by the insertion of *bayyôm hahû'* is entirely artificial, and in the case of the Exodus, Numbers, and Chronicles passages is superfluous as well inasmuch as a time-designation is already present in the original text. Even though this phrase has no organic connection to the context into which it has been inserted, it is especially noteworthy that the passages concerned have to do with the cult or the holy war, with the possible exception of Exod. 5:6, and even that passage has been influenced by the holy-war tradition.[14] As will be seen, these represent a favorite *Sitz im Leben* for many of the passages in which *bayyôm hahû'* forms an original element.

2. Incorporating supplements

Apart from the above passages in which the phrase in question is nothing more than a late insertion, it is ordinarily found to possess, in one way or another, some kind of direct function within the context of which it is a part. We shall do best to discuss these according to literary types: i.e., first the ordinary kind of historical narrative and next the three special kinds of narrative material found in deuteronomistic parenesis and prophetic oracles. The first constitutes by far the largest group of passages, and among them we find many in which *bayyôm hahû'* incorporates supplementary material of one kind or another, many others in which it functions

---

12. Compare the deuteronomistic note at II Kings 1:1.
13. LXX[B] follows the word-order of the MT. An older reading may be preserved in LXX[L], which places the time-designative in front of the prepositional phrase.
14. The contest motif is independent of the holy-war tradition, but is plainly influenced by it in such passages as I Sam. 17.

as part of a concluding formula, and still others in which it serves as part of a transition to a following episode within the pericope.

We come first to those passages in which *bayyôm hahû'* forms part of an introductory formula, or in some way introduces supplementary material into a given context. As will be seen, such an addition may be one of several types. Sometimes it is no more than a brief explanatory comment, sometimes it consists of independent, preexistent material, and sometimes it constitutes a free expansion. But predominantly in all such passages, *bayyôm hahû'* functions as an artificial synchronism, joining the new material to the old material in point of time. We shall analyze each of the passages according to their order in the biblical text.

Num. 9:6

Num. 9:6 exhibits the third-mentioned manner of introducing supplementary material, i.e., as an expansion of the underlying text. This passage is generally acknowledged to belong to the P strand. However, it is not part of the original P document; it forms rather an artificial bridge between two sections that are themselves supplements to the original document.[15] In 9:1-5 we find a notice to the effect that Israel kept the passover at its appointed time at the beginning of the second year; this clearly comes to an end with the familiar formula: "according to all that Yahweh commanded Moses, so the people of Israel did." In vss. 10 and 13 we detect the elements of an ancient torah giving instruction concerning the keeping of the passover by persons who may have become unclean. This has been much elaborated by the elements surrounding it in its present context, and has been provided with a narrative introduction in vss. 6-10a, consisting of an account of how two men became unclean and a statement that Moses sought an oracle from Yahweh concerning their uncleanness. The entire section is attached to vss. 1-5 by the formula *way*^{e}*hî* (singular!),[16] followed by an indefinite plural subject and two relative clauses; the second of these is concluded by *bayyôm hahû'*. Vs. 6 continues with the narrative, "so they came (impf. cs.) before Moses and Aaron *bayyôm hahû'*." Since it is difficult to believe that the person who first composed this account would have used the phrase twice within the same sentence, it is more likely to have been original in the introductory narrative clause, where it performs the immediate function of creating an artificial temporal connection. Hence the identification, already made, of the second *bayyôm hahû'* as an unnecessary and functionless gloss.[17]

---

15. See Noth, *ATD*, 7, *in loco*.
16. See BH³ mg; the VSS attempt to emend a difficult reading.
17. P. 59.

Deut. 27:11

Next we mention one passage in which the phrase *bayyôm hahû'* introduces older material, Deut. 27:11.[18] Gerhard von Rad has shown us enough about the formal structure of Deuteronomy as a whole[19] for us to identify vss. 9f. with considerable confidence as part of the summons to covenant ratification; these verses are continued in 28:1ff., where the blessings of the covenant are set forth. 27:11-26 stands therefore by itself. This section contains an old decalogue expanded into a dodecalogue and provided with a narrative introduction. Since there is no reason to suppose that the temporal reference formed part of the original narration, we must assign it to an editor, probably to the deuteronomistic historian himself.[20]

Josh. 4:14

Josh. 4:14 exhibits the first-mentioned kind of supplement, i.e., an interpretive comment. Here the phrase *bayyôm hahû'* introduces an observation which the deuteronomistic redactor interjects into the narrative concerning the crossing of the Jordan without consideration to the structure of the narrative itself: "On that day Yahweh exalted Joshua in the eyes of all Israel so that they revered him, as they had revered Moses, all the days of his life." This statement is made with great solemnity and weight, specifically identifying Joshua as a new Moses; it is clearly programmatic to the theology of this redaction.[21] Here the phrase *bayyôm hahû'* has the function of epitomizing the deepest theological meaning of the crossing of the Jordan.

Josh. 6:15

Josh. 6:15 is the only example of *bayyôm hahû'* being used to introduce an interpretive comment in the oral stage of transmission. After stating that Israel's stylized marching around Jericho had come to a climax in the circuit of the city seven times on the seventh day, the text adds: "It was only on that day that they marched around the city seven times." Such an observation seems too self-conscious to have been part of the earliest form of this narrative, which was probably quite matter-of-fact in presenting its one-seven pattern. On the other hand, this notation antedates the literary supplementation responsible for the chronological confusion evi-

---

18. Similarly the phrase *bᵉ'eṣem hayyôm hazzeh* in Deut. 32:48; see below.
19. "The Form-Critical Problem of the Hexateuch," *The Problem of the Hexateuch and Other Essays* (New York, 1966), pp. 1-78; also *Studies in Deuteronomy* (SBT, 9, London, 1953).
20. Cf. M. Noth, *UGS*, p. 43.
21. Cf. N. Lohfink, "Die deuteronomistische Darstellung des Uebergangs der Führung Israels von Mose auf Josue," *Scholastik*, 37 (1962), 32-44; G. J. Wenham, "The Deuteronomic Theology of the Book of Joshua," *JBL*, 90 (1971), 145f.

dent in vss. 11 and 14, and is probably to be seen as originating at a stage when the narrative was still transmitted orally.

Josh. 10:28

Josh. 10:28 is clearly secondary within its context. The word order (ואת מקדה לכד יהושע ביום ההוא) places all stress on the object—the city being captured. The temporal phrase is intended as a mere synchronism. The verse as a whole represents the effort of a literary supplementer to include a report for the capture of the city of Makkedah (mentioned in vs. 10) according to the regular formulae for the capture of Libnah, Lachish,[22] etc., in the succeeding verses, making up for its omission in the preceding context, which speaks only of the episode at the *cave* of Makkedah.

Judg. 5:1

The introductory verse of Judges 5, containing the phrase under study, is clearly recognizable as an editorial device for connecting two originally independent sources of tradition concerning the battle at Kishon. Here *bayyôm hahû'* functions as an artificial synchronism between the two reports.[23]

Judg. 20:15

In Judg. 20:15 the phrase *bayyôm hahû'* comes in regular word order, following verb and subject, to introduce a redactional expansion to original materials narrating the purgative war against Benjamin. The redactor in question is particularly concerned about harmonizing the numbers provided in his sources and freely supplies imaginative figures of his own, as here. It is not certain that he was the Deuteronomist, though this is a distinct possibility.[24]

I Sam. 3:2

Most probably I Sam. 3:2-18 was connected to its narrative framework in the process of reducing it to written form.[25] Use was made of the unusual formula, *wayhî bayyôm hahû'*,[26] in an entirely artificial syn-

---

22. In vs. 35 the phrase is a gloss; see above.
23. See W. Richter, *Traditionsgeschichtliche Untersuchungen zum Richterbuch* (Bonn, 1963), p. 84.
24. For the complete literary analysis of this chapter, see below, pp. 79-82.
25. Like the rest of I Sam. 1—3, this section reflects a complex development within oral tradition. The original narrative, reworked in 3:12f. by the insertion of additional condemnations on the house of Eli, probably came to an end in vs. 18. The framework continues in vss. 19ff., legitimizing Samuel as a prophet before all Israel. For a fuller exposition of this pericope, see Chapter Four on I Sam. 3:12.
26. Only here, where it is followed by a noun-clause and circumstantial clauses

chronism. The phrase has no proper antecedent since vs. 1 contains only a noun clause with the participle, followed by a clause with היה and the temporal phrase *bayyāmîm hahēm*. In any event, the time designation of vs. 2, "in that day" (RSV, "at that time"), seems singularly unsuitable for introducing an episode that is reported to have taken place at night.[27]

I Sam. 14:18b

A late glossator is responsible for the archeological note appearing in I Sam. 14:18b, "For the ark of God went at that time with the people of[28] Israel." As will be shown when this chapter receives an extended analysis, the original holy-war narrative proceeds in a direct and unselfconscious fashion, with no attempt at correlating it with a larger historical context. It is only a glossator familiar with the more extensive complex of sacred literature into which this story came to be fitted who would have shown such a concern as is here manifested for harmonizing the reference to the ark in vs. 18a with the contradictory references of I Samuel 4ff., and II Samuel 6.[29]

---

with the perfect and imperfect, and in Gen. 26:32, where it is followed by the imperfect consecutive.

27. But see also Gen. 15:18, Exod. 14:30, I Sam. 14:37ff., II Kings 7:9, each of which will be analyzed below.

28. MT ובני cannot be read, hence must be emended as in the VSS; cf. BH³ mg.

29. See below, pp. 212ff. Many of the older commentaries (see now also K.-D. Schunck, *Benjamin, Untersuchungen zur Entstehung und Geschichte eines israelit-ischen Stammes*, BZAW, 6, Berlin, 1963, p. 93, n. 79) prefer to follow the LXX in substituting "ephod" for "ark" in both occurrences of vs. 18. It would be difficult to imagine, however, what could motivate an archeological statement about the ephod at this point; if a redactor or glossator had felt the need for such, he would have introduced it at vs. 3, where Ahijah is first mentioned as wearing (carrying?) it. The likelihood is, therefore, that MT ארון is original in 18b, and this would require that the redactor read the same word in the first half of the verse. Nevertheless, אפוד may originally have stood in 18a (surviving in the LXX's *Vorlage* and transferred through normalization to 18b). If there is any historical reality whatever in the tradition recorded in I Sam. 4 concerning the ark's capture—and there is every reason to believe there is—an early narrator such as we have to do with here would have been as aware of this as a later glossator.

As for the problem of this verse's tradition-history, we need to observe first that the Shilonite priesthood had lost its ascendancy with the capture of the ark (cf. R. Smend, *Jahwekrieg und Stämmebund*, Göttingen, 1963, pp. 56-70 [ET, *Yahweh War and Tribal Confederation*, trans. M. G. Rogers, Nashville-New York, 1970, pp. 76-97], for a plausible argument that the ark was the sole possession of the Shiloh shrine). Its representatives would scarcely continue to function as Saul's priest after they had been dispossessed, a fact confirmed by the observation that the Mizpah and Gilgal priesthoods are clearly identifiable as the major tradents of the Saul traditions (cf. Schunck, *Benjamin*, pp. 80-108), in spite of the arguments of Richter (*Traditionsgeschichtliche Untersuchungen zum Richterbuch*, pp. 177-86), who ascribes the basic tradition of I Sam. 14 to the Shiloh priesthood. There is reason to believe, furthermore, that the identification of Ahijah the son of Ahitub with the Shilonites in vs. 3 is a secondary development (cf. A. H. J. Gunneweg, *Leviten und Priester*, Göttingen, 1965, pp. 104-14). See also M. Tsevat in *HUCA*, 32 (1961), 209-14.

I Sam. 21:8 [E-7], 22:22

As will appear when we have opportunity to examine in detail the original account of Saul's confrontation with Ahimelech appearing in I Sam. 22:6-18,[30] the narrative of David's interview with the priest of Nob, contained in 21:2-10, is probably the later creation of the historian who prepared the story of David's accession. The twofold report of the presence of Doeg, 21:8, 22:22, is one of the surest clues leading to this assessment. To begin with, David's reply to Abiathar in 22:22 is plainly connected to 21:8; it even repeats some of its very language (שם דויג האדמי) to make the connection inescapable for those to whom the story was to be told. But in 21:8 the temporal phrase is not stressed as it is in 22:22. Rather, the adverb of place (*šām*) is put foremost, stressing the coincidence of locale; following in order are (1) the indefinite subject, "one of Saul's servants," (2) the temporal phrase,[31] then (3) noun-clauses stating this person's business at Nob, his name, and his occupation.[32] In 22:22 we are in the midst of a pericope concerning Abiathar's escape to David, expanding the report of the slaughter of the Nob priesthood. Here words are put in David's mouth to stress the temporal rather than the spatial coincidence of Doeg's presence; first comes the verb "I knew," then the temporal phrase *bayyôm hahû'*, then a qualifying noun-clause including *šām*,[33] and finally the clause of indirect discourse completing the main verb ("that he would surely tell Saul"). We detect a threefold purpose in the insertion of these two verses:[34] first, to make a place in the accession history for the compiler's material concerning Abiathar's presence in David's entourage;[35] second, to create a chronology for the several episodes which the writer understood to

---

30. See below, pp. 90ff.
31. Although receiving only secondary stress, *bayyôm hahû'* is inserted for the purpose of strengthening the coincidence. Its appearance in a noun-clause and in this position is highly unusual. Its sole function is that of a synchronism.
32. Not every detail agrees with the account given in 22:6-18.
33. The *kî* must be read as "when," in which case it would constitute a second temporal phrase reinforcing *bayyôm hahû'*; or less likely as "because," expressing the reason for David's misgiving, in which case *bayyôm hahû'*, standing alone, would hark back even more pointedly to the antecedent in 21:8.
34. Many would emend סבתי in vs. 22, following the lead of the VSS. P. A. H. de Boer's argument (*OTS*, 6, 43) in favor of retaining the MT, with the meaning with which its root occurs in vss. 17f., is weakened by the literary analysis of the present study, which separates 6-18 and 19ff. into distinct sources.
35. This pericope is intended as a legitimation for Abiathar as David's priest; the writer of the accession history has expanded an early tradition, of which the closing words of vs. 23 probably constitute the original core. Abiathar functions as the giver of oracles in 23:6, 9 (where the mention of him may be secondary) and 30:7, but his name does not appear in references to oracles occurring in 23:1-5, II Sam. 5:19ff., 23ff. Annalistic extracts (II Sam. 8:17, 20:25, I Kings 4:4) and the throne-succession history (II Sam. 15:24-29, 35f., 17:15f., 19:11, I Kings 1:7, 25, 42, 2:26f.) mention him alongside his rival Zadok.

have taken place during this particular period;[36] third, to put Saul in as bad a light as possible, for the benefit of David.[37]

I Sam. 21:11 [E-10]

Since I Sam. 21:11ff. has a doublet in 27:1ff. that is not connected to an equivalent of the Nob narrative,[38] it is altogether likely that the phrase *bayyôm hahû'* in 21:11 comes from the author of the Davidic accession narrative, who wove together at this place a series of originally independent narratives. In any case, we again observe the phrase being used to create an artificial synchronism.

II Sam. 5:8

It is possible that oral supplementation is responsible for the occurrence of *bayyôm hahû'* in II Sam. 5:8. In any event, the temporal phrase has a redactional purpose. The entire pericope concerning Jerusalem's capture by David, vss. 6-10, involves not only an attempt to report in a suitable place[39] the historical event, but also the significance of the event. Hence, to the report of the city's capture are appended two similar but originally unrelated sayings, "The blind and the lame will ward you off" (vs. 6) and "the blind and the lame shall not come into the house" (vs. 8).

Jerusalem had stood uncaptured for so long that the first saying, current in popular speech, seemed an apt characterization of anyone's prospects for taking it. So the narrator depicts it, putting the saying into the mouth of the Jebusites—adding laconically that nevertheless David *did* take the stronghold of Zion. At an early point in the transmission of this simple narrative, the second saying came to be associated with the first, giving rise to the explanatory words of vs. 8.[40] This is in every respect a primitive apodictic prohibition; it occurs in inverse order, i.e., with the double subject followed by the negative, the imperfect verb,[41] and the prepositional phrase. Like much apodictic law, it probably had an original cultic association, and as such was intended to ward off the unfit from

---

36. The erroneous impression is created that Doeg was at Nob at least several days before the confrontation at Gibeah; see the analysis of 22:6ff.

37. By making a sinister and bloodthirsty character out of Doeg, strong discredit is reflected on Saul. The writer injects nationalistic bias by stressing that Doeg was an Edomite, reported as a simple matter of fact in the original account.

38. The temporal connective is lacking in 27:1.

39. The responsible author/redactor of the David accession history overlooked that vss. 17ff. should have immediately followed the report of David's crowning in vs. 3; he apparently wanted to draw the report of Jerusalem's capture to the earliest point possible.

40. That they cannot have been part of the original narrative should be apparent in that David's instruction for capturing the city would scarcely follow the report of its capture. Vs. 8 has no close syntactical attachment to the preceding; it is not an explanatory clause, but a very loosely structured afterthought.

41. The singular verb following the double subject is noteworthy.

attendance at Yahweh's shrine.[42] The redactor composed words to be placed in David's mouth,[43] prefacing them with the prepositional phrase and connecting them by the formula *'al kēn yō'm^erû* to the apodictic saying he was seeking to explain. It is not clear why the Chronicler, in his version of this event (I Chron. 11:4-9), omits all reference to these circumstances.[44]

Neh. 12:44, 13:1

Two further passages where *bayyôm hahû'* occurs in the introduction to a literary supplement are Neh. 12:44 and 13:1. In the first, the phrase occurs in normal word order, but it is apparent from its anticlimactic nature and quite different content that it originally had no connection whatever with the preceding context.[45] It is very possibly a continuation of the Chronicler's own work, supplementing his abstracts from the Nehemiah memoirs. In 13:1 a very late insertion[46] begins with *bayyôm hahû'*; it is intended as sanction for an extreme policy of Jewish particularism. In both passages the temporal phrase is a mere conventionality.

Conclusion

We may now group these passages according to literary character and formal function, with the following results. Interjecting interpretive comment into original material by the use of *bayyôm hahû'* are three passages, Josh. 4:14, Josh. 6:15b, and I Sam. 14:18b. Neither form nor function is identical in all three. In the first, *bayyôm hahû'* stands alone at the

---

42. This early law may have applied to laymen as well as priests, even though such a restriction is applied specifically to priests in the cult legislation of Lev. 21:18. In any case, there can be little question but that "the house" (note the determinative!) has to be a shrine, whether specifically the Jerusalem temple or some other.
43. This leaves entirely open the question of just what was involved in getting up "the water shaft" (הצנור), about which the commentators continue to differ. Also undecided is the question whether David actually gave such an order. It may very well be an historical fact that he made reference to "the lame and the blind," with the current proverb in mind; nevertheless, it is the redactor, not the original narrator, who was responsible for reporting it.
44. An "etiology" for Joab's primacy has been substituted. The secondary nature of Chronicles' substitution should be apparent from the further reference to Joab in vs. 8b—a reference that the narrator in I Samuel would have had no motive for omitting, had it been original.
45. As will be shown below, p. 115, the phrase is firmly anchored as part of a formal conclusion in vs. 43.
46. So M. Noth, *UGS*, p. 131. The contrary arguments of W. Rudolph (*HAT*, 20, p. 202) ascribing 13:1-3 to Chr, fail to take account of the unusual syntax (*bayyôm hahû'* at the very beginning), differing from the regular word-order in 12:44, and of the unlikelihood that the same writer would use the expression twice within a few verses without apparent good reason. Rudolph's claim that 13:1-3 is best explained as an integral part of Chr's own work is countered by this consideration, by his own admission that it does not contain Chr's characteristic style and speech, and by the pericope's late and programmatic character.

beginning, in the second it is at the beginning with *raq*, and in the third it comes lamely near the end. The first *bayyôm hahû'* introduces an epitomizing evaluation whose purpose is to state emphatically the high theological significance of this one particular day from the view of the deuteronomistic history; the second *bayyôm hahû'* serves merely to identify and delimit the point in time when a striking event occurred;[47] the third *bayyôm hahû'* functions as a synchronism whose purpose is to give historical background for the understanding of the passage into which it has been inserted.

Introducing independent material are the occurrences of *bayyôm hahû'* in Deut. 27:11, Judg. 5:1, I Sam. 3:2, 21:11, and II Sam. 5:8. In none of these is the temporal phrase in the emphatic position; it regularly follows verb, subject, and object (wherever these are present), but in I Sam. 3:2 it follows immediately after the narrative link, *wayhî*. In all these passages the formula functions as a mere artificial synchronism.

Introducing, or otherwise incorporating (as in I Sam. 21:8, 22:22), secondary expansions of narrative materials is the phrase *bayyôm hahû'* in Num. 9:6, Josh. 10:28, Judg. 20:15, I Sam. 21:8, 22:22, Neh. 12:44, 13:1. In the first three of these, *bayyôm hahû'* occurs without emphasis in regular word order, following verb, subject, and object (as the case may be). The temporal phrase receives somewhat more emphasis in Neh. 12:43, where it intrudes between the verb and its object. In Neh. 13:1 it stands foremost, preceding a passive verb, thus receiving emphasis even though the synchronism is purely artificial. In the twin redactional verses, I Sam. 21:8 and 22:22, the temporal phrase first stands in a place of auxiliary emphasis (subordinate to the adverb of place) and second in a place of primary emphasis, thus performing the redactor's purpose of stressing the coincidence of time and place. In all seven of these passages, *bayyôm hahû'* functions as no more than a synchronism.

Here the formula under study is more firmly anchored into its context—i.e., the immediate context that constitutes the literary addition—than when it appears as a mere gloss. The supplementers, editors, and redactors who were responsible for these additions apparently found this phrase a ready device for connecting materials that they thought for some reason should be bound together. We may venture to suppose that they could make use of it in this way because it had already become familiar in some more basic and original function—one that will appear more clearly as we pass on to an investigation of this phrase as a concluding formula. Even so, these secondary materials remain essentially within the same general area of literary genres that received this formula as a gloss. This is the area

---

47. The restrictive *raq* performs essentially the same function as the ordinal number in the specification of dates, identifying precisely the day of the event in question in relationship to other (or all) days.

of the sacral—more specifically, the cultus, the holy war,[48] and now the covenant ceremony.

3. Concluding formulae

In the following we shall attempt to justify an analysis of seven occurrences of *bayyôm hahû'* as a concluding formula in secondary contexts, and of seventeen occurrences of this phrase as a concluding formula in original contexts.

a. Within secondary materials

Deut. 31:22

Taking the secondary passages first, we see that Deut. 31:22 comes at the end of a very late intrusion into the text of Deuteronomy.[49] The "song of Moses" in chap. 32, with its special introduction in 31:26b-30 and a conclusion in 32:44f., is itself secondary. 31:16-22 not only provides a superfluous double introduction to the song, but severs the two parts of a late addition regarding Joshua, 31:14f., 23. Prophetic influence is apparent especially in the invective-threat pattern of vss. 16f.;[50] late deuteronomistic influence is seen not only in the emphasis on Israel's apostasy but also in the theme of the song as a witness (vs. 19; cf. 28). Vs. 22 contains only the report that Moses did what Yahweh commanded (vs. 19); *bayyôm hahû'* stands here as a highly artificial synchronism, connecting the secondary command to write the song with the speaking of it (vs. 30).

Josh. 8:25

An entirely different process is involved in Josh. 8:25. This verse is secondary only in the sense that it represents an addition or expansion within the process of oral development. As a whole, this is a very early passage. Its internal inconsistencies are to be accounted for almost entirely

---

48. Even the apparently quite secular story of David's political difficulties has a sacral character from the point of view of the court historian who was its author. It was in effect a legitimation for the Davidic covenant. Cf. S. Amsler, *David, Roi et Messie* (Neuchâtel, 1963), pp. 23-32; A. Weiser, "Die Legitimation des Königs David: zur Eigenart und Entstehung der sogenannte Geschichte von Davids Aufstieg," *VT*, 16 (1966), 325-54.

49. For further discussion of the literary composition of this section, see in Chapter Four on vss. 17f. Although some commentators (e.g., Steuernägel in *GHKAT*) see vs. 22 as continuing in the following verses, many agree that vss. 16-22 is an isolated and very late section (cf. Driver, *ICC*). Very helpful is the analysis of Noth, *UGS*, p. 40. See now N. Lohfink, "Der Bundesschluss im Land Moab," *BZ*, N.F. 6 (1962), 52-55 ("ein authentischer Kommentar!").

50. Note the futuristic use of *bayyôm hahû'* in vs. 18.

on the basis of a complex tradition history preceding any literary fixation.[51] In all likelihood, the original account came to an end in vs. 22, where it is reported that Israel smote the men of Ai, "until there was left none that survived or escaped." This is an ending characteristic of a
• holy-war narrative (cf. Judg. 4:16, I Sam. 11:11, etc.),[52] and may originally have concluded a local account independent of any connection with the Ai tradition. It is probable that the transference to Ai was a secondary development. This was reflected not only in the etiological formula of vs. 28, but also in a resumption of the narrative in vss. 24-25,[53] where it is stated that Israel returned to smite Ai with the edge of the sword.[54] Vs. 25 stands in this expansion as a concluding casualty report, similar in form to other examples where it serves with *bayyôm hahû'* to form an epitomizing statement;[55] this once led directly to the statement in vs. 28 that Joshua also burned the city of Ai, followed by the etiological formula. Vss. 26f. again expand the narrative, reporting anew the total destruction of Ai's inhabitants; interest here in the application of the *ḥerem* ties this expansion to chaps. 6-7; it probably comes from a Benjaminite (Gilgal) stage of tradition-building. Vss. 23, 29 represent still another originally separate tradition, one that has arisen out of curiosity about the great heap of stones at the gate of Ai. The combination of all these stages of growth is reflected in the redactional introduction to the narrative at vss. 1aαb, 2a.

Judg. 20:46

The next example, Judg. 20:46, is part of a redactional addition harmonizing two conflicting original accounts.[56] Although the purgative war of the sacral union against Benjamin described in Judg. 20 was not strictly a holy war,[57] its stylized procedures reflect certain holy-war

---

51. Gressmann, *SAT*[2], I, 2, 148f., assigns vs. 25 to the E source, together with the note regarding the death of the king of Ai in vs. 29aαb. Noth, *HAT*, 7, *in loco*, recognizes only minor literary seams (in vss. 11-13), arguing for at least the following stages of preliterary development: (1) local, (2) Benjaminite, (3) Israelite.
52. Cf. Richter, *Traditionsgeschichtliche Untersuchungen zum Richterbuch*, p. 179.
53. Both vs. 24 and vs. 25 begin with *way*[e]*hî*; however, the first introduces a resumption of the narrative, using an infinitive phrase to establish contact with the preceding material, while the second introduces a new conclusion.
54. Only the theory of successive stages of tradition building can explain the internal contradictions that arise from the repeated statements concerning the annihilation of Ai's inhabitants (vss. 17, 22, 24, 26).
55. Cf. Exod. 32:28, Judg. 20:21, 35, 46, I Sam. 22:18, II Sam. 18:7. (See also the secondary report of mustering, using this formula, in Judg. 20:15.) It may be significant that all these examples with definite, though exaggerated, casualty figures are from accounts of warfare between various factions within Israel. The typical holy-war story, on the contrary, characteristically states total annihilation, without figures (but cf. Judg. 3:29 with *bā'ēt hahî'*).
56. For a complete analysis of Judg. 20—21, see below.
57. It is certainly excluded by the definition offered in von Rad, *Der heilige Krieg im alten Israel*, pp. 25-33, since this can hardly be construed as a war of defense.

features. Vs. 35 constitutes the conclusion of one of the original narratives. It states in the familiar pattern of the casualty report the number of Benjaminites destroyed. The original figure was very likely 100, and this was later altered to the fantastic figure of 25,100. In vs. 44, the second narrative reaches its climax in a statement that 18,000 Benjaminites fell; here the figure may be original to the narrative, though beyond all historical probability. A redactor whose hand is abundantly evident elsewhere in this chapter recognized the disparity between these two figures and sought, without complete success, to harmonize the two by the addition of vss. 45b-46. All we need to observe here is that vs. 46 follows the regular pattern of the casualty report, with *bayyôm hahû'* serving to epitomize the event of the day in question.

I Sam. 6:15

This brings us to I Sam. 6:15, part of the ark narrative. This verse, together with vss. 5-9, 17-18, represents a literary expansion to the Beth-shemesh episode, as is evident particularly from its repetition of the statement that sacrifice was made to Yahweh. Moreover, vs. 14 mentions a great stone (an etiological signal) in order to point to it as the place where the sacrifice was made; vs. 15 reinterprets this as the place where the ark was set down. Vs. 16 has *bayyôm hahû'* at the very end to indicate the conclusion to this episode (and to this particular day as a distant unit of experience). In the secondary vs. 15, *bayyôm hahû'* comes in more regular word-order, following the emphasized subject and the double verb-object (the so-called *schema etymologicum*), but preceding the indirect object, *laYHWH*, in order to place a secondary accent on it. The conclusion we draw is that vs. 15 uses *bayyôm hahû'* as a conventional and artificial synchronism; here it is not the day but the sacrificing that is important.

I Sam. 27:6

Critics have generally observed that I Sam. 27:5-7 disrupts its context. David's plea to Achish for the gift of a town seems to come too early, before he is said to have done anything to earn it. Moreover, vss. 9ff. indicate that David returned from his raids not to Ziklag but to Gath, which surely would not have been the case had Ziklag already been his. Hence, some assign 5-7 and 9-12 to different literary sources and place the former immediately after the latter. Although there would be fewer objections to this than to the suggestion that vss. 8-12 is a secondary interpolation,[58] any adequate solution must take into account the redactional methods employed by the author of the Davidic accession history, who was

---

58. This would leave unresolved the objection that David's plea has no basis in prior service to Achish.

no doubt the writer responsible for inserting chap. 30 into a context where it was not original and providing the editorial introduction at II Sam. 1:1.[59]

Taking note that I Sam. 27:7 employs the expression $ś^e d\bar{e}h\ p^e li\check{s}t\hat{i}m$, a phrase that appears also in vs. 11 (in contrast to '$ere\d{s}\ p^e li\check{s}t\hat{i}m$ in vs. 1), we may agree with Julius Wellhausen in viewing vs. 7 as the introduction to vss. 8-12.[60] Such an analysis would leave vss. 5f. standing in complete isolation. There is every reason to identify these two verses as a redactional interpolation, probably by the same writer of the accession history, attempting to provide a framework for chap. 30. It is entirely possible, however, that the geographical etiology contained in these verses[61] had an independent existence in tradition prior to being interpolated into this passage. The form, with $bayy\hat{o}m\ hah\hat{u}$' connecting David's plea and Achish's response, followed by the etiological formula, is scarcely typical.[62]

II Chron. 35:16

In II Chron. 35:16 the phrase $bayy\hat{o}m\ hah\hat{u}$' indicates the rather formal conclusion to a very late literary supplement. We must follow Kurt Galling[63] in judging references in this chapter to the performance of sacrifices as secondary expansions of the Chronicler's narrative. There are several arguments to support this conclusion. First, vs. 16, with the temporal phrase $bayy\hat{o}m\ hah\hat{u}$', clearly cannot be part of the same source as vs. 17, containing the parallel temporal phrase $b\bar{a}\ '\bar{e}t\ hah\hat{i}$'. Vs. 17 is the conclusion to the original narrative, indicating that preparations for the passover led to its actual celebration; it is integrally connected to vss. 18f., in which the Chronicler expands the statement of II Kings 23:21-23, to the effect that Josiah was the first of all the kings of Israel to keep the passover.[64] Vs. 17 mentions only the keeping of the passover—together with the feast of mazzoth—while vs. 16 includes the offering of burnt offerings along with the keeping of the passover. Thus vs. 16 belongs with vss. 1a, 6-9, 11-15, a reinterpretation in which elaborate preparations for

---

59. There can be little question but that 29:11, 31:1 belong together. II Sam. 1:2, introduced by the temporal phrase, $way^e h\hat{i}\ bayy\hat{o}m\ ha\check{s}\check{s}^e li\check{s}\hat{i}$, immediately followed the account of Saul's death and burial; vs. 1 figures artificially in that David had to remain in Ziklag two days after the battle against the Amalekites (30:17) in order to allow for the messenger's three days of travel.

60. *Der Text der Bücher Samuelis* (1871), *in loco.*

61. This passage receives special comment in B. S. Childs, "A Study of the Formula, 'Until this Day'," *JBL*, 83 (1963), 282f.

62. Compare Josh. 14:14, which lacks $bayy\hat{o}m\ hah\hat{u}$', with II Sam. 2:16f., 6:8f., in which $bayy\hat{o}m\ hah\hat{u}$' stands outside the etiology and within a redactional framework (see below, pp. 100f.).

63. *ATD*, 12, *in loco.* Rudolph, *HAT*, 21, *in loco,* assigns all to Chr.

64. It is impossible, in the light of this statement, to believe that Chr could have inserted the report of Hezekiah's passover, chap. 30, which must therefore be secondary.

sacrifices, together with a report of how these sacrifices were carried out,[65] have been added to Josiah's simple command in the original work of the Chronicler, to make arrangements for the passover.

This analysis is confirmed by an observation of the way in which the vocable לון is used in these two sections, respectively. In the original command of vs. 4 and original report of vs. 10, its reference is to the stations and roles assigned the priests and Levites in preparation for the ceremony,[66] but in vss. 6, 14 *bis*, 15, its reference is to the actual work of preparing the sacrificial victims, as undertaken by the Levites on behalf of the priests and other temple servants. Therefore the clause כל ותכון עבודת יהוה, though obviously modeled after vs. 10, means something entirely different. Followed as it is by ביום ההוא and infinitives of result, it is intended as a retrospective and epitomizing statement, to the effect that the sacrificial rites connected with the passover and, according to the supplementer, commanded by Josiah, had actually been carried out. In the eyes of the supplementer this was the essential part of the passover—quite at variance with the historical fact that sacrifices at the altar had no part whatever in the rite, as we know it from the earliest texts.

b. *Within original contexts*

Gen. 15:18

Next the original materials. We go back to Gen. 15:18 for the first example. There is no need to reenter the vexed question of this chapter's literary analysis, particularly in the opening verses. One of the most satisfying of such to appear thus far is that of Martin Noth;[67] we may well agree with him that at least vss. 7-11 and 17-18 belong to J, with a rather apparent literary supplementation in vss. 19-21. It is important to see that the divine address to Abram in vs. 7, "I am Yahweh who brought you from Ur of the Chaldeans, to give you this land to possess," is a thematic retrojection from the exodus and conquest traditions, deliberately drawing the patriarchal traditions regarding the promise of land into a position of subordination as a prototype to the fulfilment that Israel later experienced as a nation. This means that vs. 7 is programmatic to the J-writer's theme, not simply part of the saga and legend material with which he was working. The question in vs. 8, "How shall I know . . . ?" is, of course, J's device for

---

65. Vss. 11-16 anticipate the original report of vs. 17 concerning the carrying out of the passover rites.

66. Cf. 29:35b.

67. *UGP*, n. 85; see now also H. Lohfink, *Die Landverheissung als Eid, eine Studie zu Gen. 15* (Stuttgart, 1967); Ronald Clements, *Abraham and David, Genesis 15 and its Meaning for Israelite Tradition* (SBT, 2nd. ser. 5, Naperville, 1967); S. E. Loewenstamm, "Zur Traditionsgeschichte des Bundes zwischen den Stucken," *VT*, 18 (1968), 500-506.

incorporating the covenant of vss. 9ff. The latter derives from a very ancient theophany tradition. For the ritual involved here, we still lack any clear parallel in ancient Near Eastern records.[68] J himself unquestionably understands the ritual as part of a covenant. He has to supply the words himself, though. These are ready to hand in the lines of the traditional promise, "To your descendants I give this land, from the river of Egypt to the great river." Vs. 18a is the writer's link between these two bodies of received materials; the ritual and the promise together make up the covenant that Yahweh "cut" with Abram.

Precisely here occurs the phrase *bayyôm hahû'*, in emphatic position at the beginning of the sentence.[69] It is not a literal temporal designation since the ritual is described as taking place in the night (vs. 17);[70] it is not a synchronism since the ritual and the promise are not conceived of as being separate from each other. It serves rather as the introduction to an epitomizing statement with regard to the ritual; i.e., ביום ההוא כרת יהוה את אברם ברית explains what Yahweh was actually doing in this mysterious and awesome event, its meaning being made more explicit in the words of the appended promise. In any case, the forward position of *bayyôm hahû'* calls attention to this "day" as a moment of unique self-revelation on the part of Yahweh, intervening in Abram's life to shape it toward the fulfillment of his promises in the history of the people who should come forth from his loins.

Gen. 33:16

The analysis of Gen. 33:16 presents peculiar difficulties. First, it must be observed that this verse terminates the episode of Jacob's confrontation with Esau. Although the J document continues in vs. 17, an entirely different block of tradition is involved. Vss. 12 and 14 assume that Jacob would go to visit Esau in Seir, but no more is heard of such a visit, or, in the early sources of Genesis, of Esau himself. Martin Noth has argued quite cogently that the identification of Esau with Seir and Edom is secondary— his original home, like that of Jacob, being Gilead.[71] The early saga about the confrontation between the two patriarchs, preserved in connection with the Peniel legend,[72] lay completely outside an itinerary schema, which is

---

68. References in the Mari documents do not elaborate a ritual; cf. M. Noth, "Old Testament Covenant-making in the Light of a Text from Mari," *The Laws in the Pentateuch and Other Essays* (Edinburgh-London, 1966), pp. 108ff. Gen. 26, 31, Exod. 24, etc., suggest other forms. The ritual reflected in Jer. 34:18-20 may have been influenced by the present passage.
69. This is the only original context where this occurs. It is at the beginning in deuteronomistic comments at Josh. 4:14 and I Kings 8:64, in a gloss at I Chron. 16:7, and at the beginning of a literary addition at Neh. 13:1.
70. The preparations mentioned in vss. 9ff. occur during daylight; they may be included in the scope of *bayyôm hahû'*.
71. *UGP*, pp. 108-11.
72. See the pun on Peniel in the E confrontation scene, 33:10.

the creation of the J-writer or some other early narrator. Thus vs. 16 originally existed independently, not only of vs. 17 but also of vss. 12-15, the word "Seir" having been added in 16 as a secondary normalization.

It must furthermore be seen that the subject "Esau" in vs. 16 stands in a highly unusual word-order, following the verb and *bayyôm hahû'*.[73] Thus it is doubtful that it was original; it was probably added to make a contrast to vs. 17 when the two verses were brought into juxtaposition.[74] But the person responsible for combining these traditions may have put the wrong name here. The last person mentioned in vs. 15[75] is Jacob, hence he is the probable subject of vs. 16. If this is so, וישב ביום ההוא לדרכו originally recorded Jacob's final action after the confrontation with Esau.[76] The temporal phrase was used not as a synchronism, connecting the confrontation scene with a notice of Esau's return, but as an epitome, identifying and characterizing this particular day as one on which Jacob was able to return after a crucial encounter with a threatening antagonist.

Exod. 14:30

Our comments on Exod. 14:30 may be somewhat shorter. We shall not enter into the much-discussed question of the literary analysis of this chapter, save to indicate concurrence with the view that this verse is from the J document and connects back directly to vs. 27, where the "event" of the crossing comes to its dramatic conclusion. The clause וינער יהוה את מצרים בתוך הים in 27b states climactically what Yahweh did to the Egyptian army. Therefore we must understand vs. 30a as the interpreting and epitomizing conclusion, with its first clause referring back to the thematic declaration of vs. 14, "Yahweh will fight for you, and you have only to be still," and the second clause picking up the motif of witnessing featured in 13b, "for the Egyptians whom you see today, you shall never see again."[77] Here the phrase *bayyôm hahû'* is fraught with significance: this was the day of all days for Israel, a day to be remembered forever. Little wonder that as this tale was told again and again, probably in cultic celebration, new phrases were added on at the end (31) to drive home the theological lesson of this supreme act of divine revelation.[78]

---

73. LXX has the normalized order of verb—subject—temporal phrase.
74. ויעקב, followed by the perfect at the beginning, indicates that vs. 17 is a new pericope.
75. The text of vs. 15 is in some disorder; see the commentaries.
76. This conclusion was connected somewhere else in the narrative, according to the original tradition.
77. Vs. 30b is to be understood as irony: the promise was fulfilled in its not being fulfilled, i.e., Israel did see the Egyptians, but they saw them dead. Cf. 10:28f. J.
78. The conflation in vss. 30f. is to be understood not as literary duplication but as supplementation to the oral tradition.

Josh. 9:27

The technical formulae in Josh. 9:27 indicate that this verse has an etiological as well as an epitomizing function. The narrative of Gibeon's masquerade, its covenant with Israel, and the inevitable discovery of its deceit comes to a pointed climax in Joshua's curse of vs. 23, "Now therefore you are accursed, and a slave shall never be cut off from you."[79] All that is left to say is that the Gibeonites resigned themselves to Joshua's judgment (vs. 26), and that the curse was carried out (vs. 27). But the results of the curse continue "to this day"[80] —the very circumstance that gave rise to the narrative. Hence the concluding and epitomizing statement, "So Joshua appointed them on that day hewers of wood and drawers of water. . . ." This not only terminates the narrative, but summarizes the action and characterizes the lasting significance of the day for all time to come.

Josh. 24:25

In Josh. 24:25 a clause with *bayyôm hahû'* constitutes the original conclusion to the account of a solemn ceremony. The people are assembled at Shechem. Joshua addresses them, summoning them to covenant affirmation (vss. 2-15); in response, they revoke other gods and dedicate themselves to Yahweh (16-18). Their words are followed, in what is likely a secondary literary expansion,[81] by Joshua's warning (19f.) and by the people's emphatic reaffirmation of their purpose (21-24). With the discourse at an end, the narrator now reports, "So Joshua made a covenant with the people that day." This statement is to be understood not as adding something new to the action of the preceding discourse, but as summarizing or epitomizing its meaning. The discourse *is* the covenant; vs. 25a only states in abrupt, incisive language that this is what the words mean, at the same time placing all future generations—whoever should read and hear these words—under the authority of their witness.

Thus vs. 25a is a clear formal conclusion. It is followed, to be sure, by several further acts on Joshua's part (reported in a series of imperfect consecutives), the effect of which is to bind the law to the covenant. These

---

79. The words that follow in vs. 23, authentically preserved in MT (note the various versional efforts to emend!), have been secondarily supplied from vs. 27 without regard to syntax. Cf. Noth, *HAT*, 7, *in loco*.

80. Cf. Childs, *JBL*, 83, p. 283; J. Blenkinsopp, *Gibeon and Israel* (SOTSM, 2, Cambridge, 1972), pp. 106ff.

81. Assigned by M. Noth, *HAT*, 7, *in loco*, to a deuteronomistic supplementer. H. W. Hertzberg, *ATD*, 9, *in loco*, and Dennis J. McCarthy, *Treaty and Covenant* (AnBib, 21, Rome, 1963), pp. 145-51, acknowledge the secondary nature of this material but prefer to emphasize its prophetic affinities. Cf. also J. Muilenburg's study, "The Form and Structure of the Covenantal Formulations," *VT*, 9 (1959), 357-60, analyzing the structure of Josh. 24 while assuming its literary unity, and H.-J. Kraus, *Gottesdienst in Israel*, pp. 161-66.

probably result, however, from further expansion of the primitive tradition, perhaps at a comparatively early period.[82] In any case, they do not detract from the basic character of vs. 25a as the formal conclusion to the covenant narrative itself.

Judg. 3:30

The analysis of the function of *bayyôm hahû'* in Judg. 3:30 is specially difficult because it seems to parallel the preceding statement with *bā'ēt hahî'*. The duplication of time-designation is not to be taken as evidence of parallel literary strands,[83] nor is vs. 30a to be joined with 30b as part of the deuteronomistic redaction.[84] 30a is rather the formal conclusion to the entire holy-war account featuring Ehud as *môšî^a'*, vss. 15ff. As Wolfgang Richter's exemplary study has shown,[85] this pericope is compounded from a very primitive hero saga, vss. 15-26, and a holy-war narrative, vss. 27ff.[86] The casualty report in vs. 29, with its stated number of dead and the phrase *bā'ēt hahî'*,[87] is unique in this schema; we may assume that it concluded the original narrative. But the person who combined the report with the narrative must have felt it necessary to interpret the meaning of this event for Israel, hence he epitomized its consequence in the new closing formula of vs. 30a, "So Moab was subdued that day under the hand of Israel."

Judg. 4:23

The function of Judg. 4:23 is similar to that of 3:30; it is the formal conclusion to a combinational holy-war story,[88] but properly attaches

---

82. The complex tradition-history of this pericope has been emphasized, as by Noth, *HAT*, 7, p. 139. Muilenburg, *op. cit.*, believes that "what we have here is a precis or abridgement of what was once a much more elaborate account" (p. 359). Although whatever actual historical discourse underlay this report would indeed be presumed to have been more extensive, the likelihood is that our present text has been fleshed out from a bare outline. Götz Schmitt can hardly be right, however, in identifying vss. 1, 25-27, excluding the discourse, as the original core of the chapter (*Der Landtag von Sichem*, ArTh, I, 15, Stuttgart, 1964, pp. 8ff.); there is nothing left for the epitome with *bayyôm hahû'* to epitomize, and it is not likely that the parenesis of vss. 14ff. has been redactionally substituted for a now-missing apodictic code.

83. So O. Eissfeldt, *Die Quellen des Richterbuches* (1925), p. 20.

84. So most commentaries, e.g., Hertzberg, *ATD*, 9, p. 142.

85. *Traditionsgeschichtliche Untersuchungen zum Richterbuch*, pp. 1-29.

86. It is not uncommon for such reports to find a place in the broader framework of a holy-war narrative; e.g., the Jael episode in 4:17-22; cf. also I Sam. 14:1ff., II Sam. 23:9f. The verb כנע, "subdue," "vanquish," functions in the conclusion to holy-war narratives in three Judges passages, twice with *bayyôm hahû'* (Judg. 3:30, 4:23, 11:33). In addition, the nif. impf. cs. of כנע appears in final reports in two passages that are secondarily attached to holy-war narratives (Judg. 8:28, I Sam. 7:13).

87. A modification of the usual battle report.

88. Vs. 24 is a superfluous addition, possibly a deuteronomistic gloss. Note the repetition of "Jabin king of Canaan."

directly to the end of the battle-account, vs. 16, the Jael saga, vss. 11, 17-22, being only loosely related to the basic structure of the chapter. One should observe that Jabin is here called king of Canaan, as in vs. 2, rather than king of Hazor, as in the Jael episode (17). Here again the phrase *bayyôm hahû'* epitomizes the significance of the narrated event, stating the essential character of this day in Israel's history.

Judg. 6:32

In Judg. 6:32 *bayyôm hahû'* is part of the etymological formula that concludes the pericope, 25-32. Whatever unevenness may be present here is not to be explained as arising from literary interweaving. Nor are Richter's arguments that 31b-32 constitutes a secondary framework convincing.[89] In the first place, one should weigh carefully that the pun on the name Jerubbaal[90] is very strong and clear; the whole narrative reaches its climax in Joash's pointed questions, "will *you* contend (תריבון) for Baal? Or will *you* gain a victory (תושיעון) for him? . . .[91] If he is a god, let him contend for himself (ירב לו)." One would like to know to what other conclusion these questions could lead if not to the etymology; certainly there is no other in the context, and the narrative is left up in the air without one.[92] It is true that the explanatory words of the etymology do not correspond exactly to Joash's words as quoted in vs. 31:[93] it is also true that the threefold repetition of כי נתץ את מזבחו seems awkward and monotonous. However, the change from לו to בו creates an altogether appropriate adaptation from a general possibility (vs. 31) to a concrete actuality (vs. 32), while כי נתץ את מזבחו in 31b and 32 are to be taken as apodoses to what Joash and the narrator intend as conditional sentences: "Let Baal contend against him *if* he (or someone) has pulled down his altar!"[94] The repetition in altered syntax has the purpose of dramatic emphasis.

---

89. *Traditionsgesch. Untersuchungen*, pp. 157-68. It is very likely, however, that he is right in seeing secondary reworking in vss. 25-27a. Note particularly that Yahweh's command in vs. 25 features the vocable הרס rather than the root נתץ of vss. 28, 30, 31, 32.

90. The biblical writer has no scientific knowledge of the name's etymology. It is probably a combination of the theophoric element with the root רבב, "to increase."

91. Vs. 31a is a theologizing gloss.

92. Richter, *op. cit.*, p. 164, assumes that the ending has been left out by the writer who was responsible for adding vss. 31b-32. Richter identifies the *Gattung* as "Aussage-Erzählung," whatever that may be. Cf. C. A. Keller, "Ueber einige alttestamentliche Heiligtumslegenden, I," *ZAW*, 67 (1955), 162, identifying the story as an anecdote. Various critics wrongly identify the story as a cult legend. For the juridical procedures involved in the narrative, cf. H. J. Boecker, *Redeformen des Rechtslebens im Alten Testament* (Neukirchen, 1964), pp. 20, 23.

93. ירב בו instead of ירב לו. It is unlikely that the author of vs. 32 would be careless in repeating a key phrase. Rather, he varies it for the specific purpose he has in mind.

94. Cf. *GK*, § 159, indicating the function of the perfect in an apodosis. In Judg. 6:30 these words constitute the legal charge against Gideon, stated as a fact. The narrator uses the same words for presenting the terms of a challenge to Baal.

The above argument might seem to be in danger of running aground on the observation that the traditions featuring the name Gideon and those featuring the name Jerubbaal derive from different sources and are not satisfactorily integrated with each other in this narrative cycle.[95] The impact of this observation is not to be obscured. It does not drive us to conclude, however, that the Jerubbaal etymology has been redactionally added to 6:25ff. Rather, it leads to the conclusion that this pericope is late enough in origin to reflect the desire to combine two heretofore independent strands of tradition. We should note that only in this pericope is a sharp anti-Baalite polemic, characteristic of the time of Elijah, expressed in the narratives pertaining to premonarchical Israel.

To conclude: Judg. 6:32 is original in its context, part of an etymological formula,[96] and an epitome of the significance of the preceding account. The time-reference, "on that day," does not conflict with the placing of this narrative in a night-morning sequence because it points to the decisive event rather than to any particular period of time or point in time.

Judg. 20:35

Next in order is Judg. 20:35, where, alone among five occurrences of *bayyôm hahû'* in this chapter, an original concluding formula is involved. In vs. 15 and vs. 46 the phrase has been supplied by a redactor, in the first instance as an introductory formula (synchronism) and in the second instance as a concluding formula (epitome), as we have already seen.[97] This leaves vss. 21, 26, and 35—all part of original narrative material; however, the first two will prove to be transitional to successive episodes within the narrative, and will accordingly be listed under a different heading.

It is necessary to enter into a somewhat extensive analysis of Judg. 20. This is only part of a larger pericope constituting chaps. 19—21, one of two appendixes to the original collection in the book of Judges, but it contains the central and climactic materials. Most recent scholars are prepared to give up the Wellhausenian dictum that the account of the sacral league's attack upon Benjamin is late and unhistorical, agreeing that in spite of later expansions it goes back to actual events in the early life of Israel.

---

95. Cf. Richter, *op. cit.*, pp. 167f.; also H. Haag, "Gideon-Jerubbaal-Abimelek," *ZAW*, 79 (1967), 305-14. Jerubbaal is undoubtedly the original given name. If Gideon is the same person, this is probably a heroic designation (from גדע, "to drive," hence "the driver"; cf. "David" for Elkanah, "Maccabeus" for Judas ben Eliezer, etc.).

96. Cf. J. Fichtner, "Die etymologische Aetiologie in den Namengebungen der geschichtlichen Bücher des ATs," *VT*, 6 (1956), 372-96. Judg. 6:32 exhibits the nonetiological form usually used with respect to persons, rather than the form generally used for places; cf. Fichtner, pp. 378-85. Etymological name-giving is infrequent in the Former Prophets as compared with the Pentateuch (in Judges at 1:17, 2:5, 6:32, 15:17, 18f.).

97. See above, pp. 63, 70f.

We may mention in particular the incisive analysis of K. D. Schunck, who traces the development of these chapters to a rudimentary tradition in which Ephraim attempted to keep the emerging tribe of Benjamin under its control, appealing to an alleged crime on the part of the inhabitants of Gibeah as requiring the support of the other members of the sacral union; two times Benjamin's antagonists were defeated, but a third time Benjamin succumbed. It was in one of Benjamin's leading shrines (Gilgal) that this narrative was at first preserved.[98]

When one examines Judg. 20 carefully, one quickly discovers a considerable number of inconsistencies and contradictions. Two different shrines are mentioned, Mizpah and Bethel; in vs. 11 the Israelites are ready to attack Gibeah, while in vss. 17f. they need to be mustered before they can attack; twice it is reported that they prepare the attack of the second day (22, 24); most striking of all, it is said in vs. 36 that Benjamin was defeated, yet in the following verses the Benjaminites go out to attack. This evidence for diverse sources is strengthened by observation of linguistic variations from verse to verse, in particular the vacillation in the designation of the Israelites ($b^e n\hat{e}$ $yi\acute{s}r\bar{a}'\bar{e}l$, $'\hat{i}\acute{s}$ $yi\acute{s}r\bar{a}'\bar{e}l$) and of the Benjaminites ($b^e n\hat{e}$ $biny\bar{a}min$, $biny\bar{a}min$).

Scholars who have argued for continuing parallel sources throughout the book of Judges have notably failed to prove their case.[99] However, alternative solutions have likewise come short of satisfying all the requirements of this complex text. Martin Noth has posited for chap. 20 one basic primitive narrative expanded by a variety of literary alterations and supplements, the longest of which (vss. 36b-46) imposes the description of an ambush upon an original, straightforward battle account.[100] The failure of Noth's theory is mainly that without adequate explanation it identifies all references to Bethel as secondary, assigns the similar procedures in vs. 23 and vss. 26ff., respectively, to variant sources, and neglects to explain many of the more glaring linguistic inconsistencies. On the other hand, Schunck's complex theory of successive redactions, in which he attempts to reckon with linguistic variants, is not completely satisfying. He makes a major mistake in assigning the references to Mizpah to a late redaction and fails to deal consistently with the linguistic data.[101]   John Gray appears to be

---

98. K.-D. Schunck, *Benjamin*, pp. 69f. See also O. Eissfeldt, "Der geschichtliche Hintergrund der Erzählung von Gibeas Schandtat (Richter 19-21)," *Beer Festschrift* (1935), pp. 19ff.; R. Smend, *Jahwekrieg und Stämmebund*, p. 26 (ET, p. 34).

99. Cf. E. Bertheau, *Kommentar zum Buch der Richter* (2nd ed. 1883); R. H. Pfeiffer, *Introduction to the Old Testament* (rev. ed. 1941).

100. *Das System der zwölf Stämme Israels*, Exkurs IV, "Literarische Analyse von Ri. 19-21." According to Noth, the following are secondary in chap. 20: vss. 2b, 9b, 10a, 15-18, 23, 25b, כל העם and ויבאו בית אל in 26, 27b-28a, 29, 31aβ, 33b, 35b, 36b-46, 48. The fantastic numbers are redactional.

101. *Benjamin*, pp. 57-70. To R[1] he assigns 19:1-30a, 20:2aα, 3b-6, 8-9abα, 10-13a, 17a, 20, 22, 24-25a, 29, 33, 36b-43, 45, 47, 48, 21:1. To R[II] (= Dtr[I]) he

moving in the right direction as he identifies two originally separate traditions, preserved at the Mizpah and the Bethel shrine respectively, which in his view have been interwoven with each other and supplemented by a redactor.[102]

Refining somewhat Gray's analysis for Judg. 20:15ff., we would posit the following: (1) a Mizpah narrative, 20 ... 22 (without העם), 29, 31aβ ... bβ, 32, 33a, 36b-45a, 47, 48; (2) a Bethel narrative, 18a, 19, 21, 23-25a, 26 (without וכל העם), 27a, 28b, 30, 31aαbα, 34, 35; (3) redactional, 15-17, העם 22, 25b, וכל העם 26, 27b-28a, 33b, 36a, 45b-46. To the redactor is also to be assigned the probable expansion of the original numbers in vss. 21, 25, 34, 35. He omitted parts of the Mizpah document in favor of the Bethel tradition. The Mizpah narrative speaks of the antagonists as *'iš yiśrā'ēl* and *binyāmin* respectively,[103] uses ערך hif. with *hammilḥāmâ* as object, and conceives of the ambush as the clue to victory for Israel. The Bethel narrative speaks of *bᵉnê yiśrā'ēl* and *bᵉnê binyāmin*, uses ערך hif. without an object (vs. 29), makes no mention of an ambush, and conceives of victory as coming through an overwhelming military force (vs. 34), following repeated oracles. The redactor, in attempting to harmonize the two, has created more confusion than clarity.

We cannot dwell on further details except to outline the conflicting time sequences involved in these two narratives. It is only in the Bethel tradition that a three-day pattern of battle is involved. In the beginning, Israel prepares for battle by seeking an oracle at the Bethel shrine.[104] The Israelites go out on the first day, are defeated, and return to Bethel for a new oracle; they go out the second day, are defeated, and return to Bethel for still another oracle;[105] they go out the third day, appear at first to lose,[106] finally gain a resounding victory, perhaps through the late arrival

---

assigns 20:46, 21:5-14a; the expanded numbers. To R[III] (= Dtr[II]) he assigns 20:9bβ, 13b-16, 17b-19, 21, 23, 25b-27a, 28b, 30, 32, 34-36a, 21:2-4. Early traditions supplied by R[III] are in 21:15-24.

102. *Joshua, Judges and Ruth* (The Century Bible, New Edition, London & Edinburgh, 1967), *in loco*. To the Mizpah tradition (= document) he assigns 20:1-2, 14, 20, 22, 25a, 29, 33a, 34b, 36b-45a, 47-48. To the Bethel tradition (= document) he assigns 20:19, 21, 23, 24, 25b, 26, 27a, 28b, 35, 36a. The deuteronomistic redactor is responsible for 20:8-10, 12-13, 15-16, 17-18, 27b-28a, 45b-46, and his hand is apparent in vss. 1-6. He is also responsible for the expanded numbers. Compare Smend, *op. cit.*, who assigns 20:18, 23, 26-28, 21:2 to special Bethel traditions.

103. Except in vs. 32, where the individual Benjaminites are represented as speaking, and in vs. 48, where the effects of defeat are appropriately described as falling on individuals and their possessions.

104. The much-suspected oracle of vs. 18 (modeled after Judg. 1:1f.), if original, represents a meaningless conventionality since Judah plays no special role in the story.

105. The expanded details, together with the more precise oracle, prepare for the climactic event of the final day.

106. The expression *bᵉpa'am bᵉpa'am* (vss. 30, 31) is appropriate to this schema, not to that of the Mizpah tradition.

of reinforcements. By contrast, the Mizpah tradition reports that all Israel approached Gibeah "as one man" (vs. 11) and went out directly to the battle line. They were defeated (the report of which has been supplanted by the Bethel version, vs. 21), but took courage and reformed for battle on another day.[107] This time they drew Benjamin into an ambush,[108] sent men behind them to burn Gibeah, pursued them into the wilderness, and came back to harry the survivors. Here the sequence is simpler: initial defeat, subsequent victory. There can be little question but that this is closer to historical reality than the highly schematic pattern of the Bethel narrative.[109]

It is now clear that the phrase *bayyôm hahû*, in vss. 21, 26, 35 constitutes a special technical element in the Bethel narrative. Vs. 35 comes at the conclusion, epitomizing the final and decisive day, first by stating in summary form that Yahweh smote Benjamin before Israel,[110] then by combining a report of casualties[111] with the temporal phrase in the manner of Josh. 8:25. The same casualty-report pattern characterizes vs. 21, which very appropriately epitomizes the results of Israel's first attack. However, in order to suit the purposes of the three-day scheme, the content of this day is expanded by the additional activity of weeping and seeking an oracle "until evening," so that its function becomes transitional rather than concluding. An epitomizing *bayyôm hahû'* is missing from the casualty report of the second day. It occurs in vs. 26, but out of the regular word-order (following five verbs, subject, adverbial and prepositional modifiers), and is expanded by an indication of duration, "until evening," which occurs also in vs. 23. In this position it serves to prepare a transition to the third.[112] Thus the occurrence in vs. 35 is the sole original concluding formula in this chapter.

I Sam. 6:16

We may pass on, then, to a brief consideration of *bayyôm hahû'* in I Sam. 6:16.[113] This expression comes at the very end of the Beth-shemesh

---

107. *Beyôm hārî'šôn* (cf. *kebārî'šonâ*, vs. 32) indicates no more than a previous day of battle—not necessarily the first in a sequence of three successive days. Yahweh's oracular instruction, "Up, for *māhār* I will give him into your hand" (vs. 28), functions like an epitomizing *hayyôm*. It is only the three-day schema that defers the victory until tomorrow.

108. The influence of Josh. 8 is evident.

109. The OT offers no parallel elsewhere, although a similar climactic impact is apparent in Exod. 19:11, 15f., with reference to a solemn cultic event. A pattern of seven days occurs occasionally as an artificial time scheme in quasi holy-war narratives, e.g., Josh. 6:14ff., I Kings 20:29, II Kings 3:9.

110. The singular gentilics are appropriate in this closing summary, rather than the plurals of the preceding verses; here is stated the battle's consequence for the respective tribes, seen as units rather than as collections of individuals.

111. Again, the number of casualties is unhistorical, having been expanded by the redactor.

112. See below, p. 102.

113. See the preceding analysis of vs. 15, in which *bayyôm hahû'* appears secondarily as an artificial synchronism.

episode concerning the ark, which may at one time have stood as an independent narrative, though it now appears in expanded form as part of a *hieros logos* for the ark's entrance into Jerusalem. Very appropriately, vs. 16 epitomizes the entire narrative in its simple statement that the Philistines saw the Israelites accept the ark and returned to Ekron. *Bayyôm hahû'* is not intended as a synchronism, because the narrative has no interest in telling *when* the lords returned, only that the day of the ark's acceptance was the day when they relinquished their claim to it.

I Sam. 7:10

We must view I Sam. 7:10 in connection with vs. 6, where *bayyôm hahû'* also occurs but, as we shall see, as part of a transition within an episode. Martin Noth ascribed this entire chapter to the deuteronomistic historian,[114] but more recently Artur Weiser has argued that the materials in this pericope go back to the early Mizpah shrine.[115] While we may agree that Mizpah is the most probable place of preservation, it is apparent that vss. 3-6 and vss. 7ff. arise from quite different life-situations.

In vss. 3f. Samuel calls Israel to the ancient covenant ritual of renouncing foreign gods.[116] In vs. 5 he calls the people[117] to a sacrifice of contrition at Mizpah. The character of this particular day is made clear by the terms of Samuel's summons ("I will pray to Yahweh on your behalf") and by the statement of 6aβ, "so they fasted on that day and said,[118] 'We have sinned against Yahweh.' " To this is attached the narrator's concluding statement regarding Samuel's role: "And Samuel judged (= acted as covenant mediator for)[119] the people at Mizpah." This episode may originally have existed as an independent tradition. However, as it now stands it is transitional to the second and climactic episode in vss. 7ff. We shall accordingly list it under the following heading.[120]

The second episode follows a schema of the holy-war narrative.[121] Vs. 7aα is a combinational transition; then follows in 7aβ-9 a description of the situation (approach of Philistines; Israel's plea; Samuel's sacrifice of an

---

114. *UGS*, 54-56.
115. *Samuel*, pp. 5-24. Weiser views vss. 10ff. as a secondary expansion; the original narrative comprised vss. 3-9 and originated during the period of Philistine oppression. Even though this chapter may not have been composed by the deuteronomist, it did play an important part in his redactional arrangement, as has been argued by H. J. Boecker, *Die Beurteilung des Königtums in I Samuel 7–12* (Neukirchen, 1969), pp. 94-98. Cf. also F. Langlamet, *RB*, 77 (1970), 161ff.; J. T. Willis, *JBL*, 90 (1971), 289ff.
116. Cf. Gen. 35:4, Exod. 33:5, Josh. 24:14, 23f. See A. Alt, "Die Wallfahrt von Sichem nach Bethel," *Kleine Schriften*, I (Munich, 1963), 79ff.
117. The designations "Israel," "house of Israel," "sons of Israel," appear with seeming lack of discrimination in this pericope.
118. MT שׁם, missing in LXX, makes no sense here.
119. See Weiser, *Samuel*, p. 17; Noth, "Das Amt des 'Richters Israel,' " Bertholet Festschrift, 1950, pp. 404ff.
120. See below, p. 103.
121. Cf. Richter, *Traditionsgesch. Untersuchungen*, p. 181.

'ôlâ and cry[122] to Yahweh, with proleptic statement that Yahweh answered),[123] a statement in 10abα of the manner in which Yahweh defeated the Philistines (with foregoing circumstantial clauses restating the situation), and a statement of the result in 10bβ. Vs. 11 is a later expansion related to vss. 12-13a. This outline enables us to see that the phrase *bayyôm hahû'* appears at the climactic point in this episode, the moment of Yahweh's decisive intervention ("and Yahweh thundered with a mighty voice that day against the Philistines and threw them into panic"). This saving act is what above all characterized this particular day.

I Sam. 14:23 (24, 31, 37)

We come now to I Samuel 14, in which, among five occurrences of *bayyôm hahû'*, only vs. 23 contains it as a concluding formula in original narrative. Chap. 13 forms the background for the holy-war action of chap. 14,[124] which is introduced in vs. 1 with the connective phrase *way^{e}hî hayyôm w^e ...*, probably meaning no more than "and it happened on a certain day."[125] Forms with *yôm* continue to reappear at climactic points throughout the narrative: *bayyôm hahû'* in vss. 18, 23, 24, 31, 37; *hayyôm* in vss. 28, 30, 33, 38; *hayyôm hazzeh* in vs. 45.[126] If we are to gain a clear impression of the precise bearing of these temporal terms it will be necessary to establish the narrative sequence and to weigh carefully the literary relationships of the materials comprising this account.

Although the Wellhausen school attempted to divide chap. 14 into distinct literary strands, most modern scholars are inclined to ascribe the unevenness that appears here to the vicissitudes of oral tradition, identify-

---

122. One should observe the difference of verb in this reference (זעק) as compared with vs. 5 (פלל hithp).

123. Weiser's claim (*Samuel*, pp. 21f.) that this terminates the original account is not convincing. Surely the stage has been set for something beyond this laconic statement. A holy-war deliverance is quite in keeping with the period of Samuel, hence there is little ground for Weiser's attempt to relegate this to a later period. Vs. 13 belongs to a later stage of tradition-building than vss. 10ff.

124. G. von Rad, *Heilige Krieg*, p. 21, characterizes this account as based upon a genuine historical occurrence of the holy war. It is commonly recognized as being close to historical actualities, partly because of its sympathetic image of Saul, in contrast to the antipathetic, and presumably later image of 8:1ff., 10:17ff., 12:1ff., 13:7b-15a, 15:1ff. Recent discussions of the military-political situation are H. Seebaas, *ZAW*, 78 (1966), 160ff.; C. Hauer, "The Shape of Saulide Strategy," *CBQ*, 31 (1969), 153ff. See also A. Weiser, *ZAW*, 54 (1936), 18ff.

125. See G. R. Driver, *Notes on the Hebrew Text of the Books of Samuel* (2nd ed. 1913), *in loco*. Its occurrences in I Sam. 1:4, II Kings 4:8, 18, Job 1:6, 13, 2:1, show that it is a conventional introduction to a new narrative episode.

126. The LXX translates *hayyôm* as σήμερον, but in vs. 33 its reading ἐνταῦθα presupposes חלם (cf. MT in vs. 36; LXX in vs. 41). In vs. 45 the LXX adds ἐν τῇ ἡμέρᾳ ἐκείνῃ, the usual translation for *bayyôm hahû'*, probably under the influence of the preceding *hayyôm hazzeh*. Because vs. 46 provides the concluding rubric for this narrative, a concluding epitome with *bayyôm hahû'* is not likely in vs. 45.

ing only minor redactional elements, chiefly in vss. 47ff. [127] But those who argue for the literary unity of 14:1-46 have given scant attention to the problem of the time-sequences involved. [128]

No difficulty arises with regard to the term for Saul's oath in vs. 24: it is clear that the formula "until it is evening," parallel to "and I am avenged on my enemies," is intended to cover the entire day of battle against the Philistines. It is a more emphatic and expressive equivalent to *hayyôm* in vs. 28. That the text so understands it is clear from the report of the slaughter of captured animals (32ff.), which comes at the end of the final battle-report in vs. 31, "They struck down the Philistines that day from Michmash to Aijalon," and is explicitly placed at night in the MT of vs. 34. [129] It seems rather strange that an altar should be consecrated and sacrifices offered at night, [130] but the time appears to be confirmed by Saul's proposal in vs. 36 to pursue the Philistines all night, "until the morning light." The people, refreshed from their food, express willingness, but no approving oracle can be obtained "that day." Suddenly the time-references have become incommensurate with the situation; how can "that day" or "this day" in vss. 37, 41 LXX, 45 (not to speak of the MT's היום in vs. 33!) have any meaning if night has already fallen?

In working toward an adequate analysis of this narrative, we must acknowledge first of all that the altar episode (vss. 31-35) simply does not fit in. Not only does it destroy the time sequence; it splits in two the otherwise tightly drawn account of Saul's oath, Jonathan's transgression, the casting of lots, and the people's ransoming of their hero. This is the culmination of a popular hero saga which has been expanded into the holy-war narrative providing the present basic structure of the overall narrative. The intrusion of vss. 31ff. must be seen as the work of a redactor, who considered Jonathan's complaint in vss. 29f. to be a suitable place to introduce the account of an incident whose nature he did not understand.

---

127. So Noth, *UGS*, p. 63. Noth also seems doubtful of vss. 31-35 (p. 107). Schunck, *Benjamin*, p. 93, goes further in identifying vss. 2, 3a, 16, 18-19, 23b, 52 as also secondary. Seebaas, *ZAW*, *loc. cit.*, identifies parallel documents (see below). H. W. Hertzberg, *ATD*, 9, *in loco*, treats the entire section as a literary whole.

128. See J. Blenkinsopp, "Jonathan's Sacrilege, I Sam. 14:1-46: a Study in Literary History," *CBQ*, 16 (1964), 423-49; Blenkinsopp himself notes that "the time-factor is all important" (426), but fails to handle perceptively the materials relating to it.

129. This is a tendential gloss, intended for making clear that the people did not violate Saul's oath; it is missing in LXX[B]

130. Discounting the gloss in vs. 34, it is impossible to squeeze all the slaughtering of animals, preparing and consecrating of an altar, preparing and eating of meat, deliberation, consultation of an oracle, casting of lots, and public controversy involved in the account of vss. 31-46, between the termination of Saul's oath (*'ereb* is the ending of the day, the beginning of the night) and the onset of darkness. Blenkinsopp, *op. cit.*, p. 426, speaks of all this happening "as the shadows were lengthening." But this is an unjustified wresting of the accepted meanings of the words involved.

That it was not part of the original narrative seems doubly certain in that the casting of lots did not mark the people, recent violators of ritual taboo, as guilty. As various critics have observed, the altar story was originally concerned only with the consecration of a local shrine (thus a *hieros logos* whose historical connection has become lost),[131] and may have had no original connection with Saul or his wars.[132]

In vs. 36 the redactor provides a transition back to the hero saga by having Saul propose the pursuit at night, the shift in time having been made necessary by the consideration that the people's eating must not have violated Saul's prohibition, and hence must have taken place after the day was finished. Thus the redactor would expand, beyond all concern for realistic probabilities, the temporal as well as the spatial aspects of this battle: Saul's men would fight all night and would penetrate deeply into Philistine territory. But the redactor is also responsible for locating the preceding altar episode at the edge of Philistine territory (vs. 31). This too is unrealistic, involving a previous pursuit of about fifteen miles, from Michmash due west to Aijalon; moreover, it contradicts vs. 23b, which already places the pursuing Israelites "beyond Beth-aven," probably some miles to the north or northeast of Michmash.[133]

Thus *bayyôm hahû'* is redactional in vs. 31, where it does no more than provide a sequential link from the intrusive altar episode. But it is not the redactor who is responsible for *bayyôm hahû'* in vs. 24, any more than it is he who is responsible for the geographical notice of 23b. We observe that the time element and the spatial element are separate here. Both are, moreover, integrally related to the following narrative of Jonathan's transgression; that is to say, the battle had gone beyond the scene of Jonathan's exploit into a forest where there was honey; it was only here that, because of what Jonathan would do, the day could become a day of distress for Israel.[134]   Together, 23b and 24a constitute a sequential link, introducing

---

131. Unless the LXX's "Gittaim" is original; but this locality is geographically distant from the Geba-Michmash area. The *hieros logos* contained no reference to night; as a matter of fact, הַיּוֹם has every claim to originality in vs. 33 since it is used in various cultic contexts to signalize the sacredness of the occasion (cf. Exod. 34:11, Lev. 9:4, Ps. 95:7). The people were eating meat עַל הַדָּם, which means "profanely, away from the shrine, without sacrificial consecration"; hence the urgent consecration of an altar. That the redactor is solely responsible for the framework, vss. 31, 32a, is apparent from the differing designations of the sacrificial animals (צֹאן ובקר ובני בקר, vs. 32; שׁיהו . . . שׁורו, vs. 34).

132. In spite of references to Saul sacrificing (I Sam. 13:9f., cf. chap. 15), Saul is not elsewhere presented as the founder of a shrine. But cf. the role of Samuel in I Sam. 7:17, whose name may have appeared in the original legend here. 14:35b is secondary.

133. In I Sam. 7:1ff., geographical extensions of the battle scene are similarly part of a secondary expansion. The precise location of Beth-aven (mentioned also in Josh. 7:2, 18:12, I Sam. 13:5, Hos. 4:15, 5:8, 10:5) is uncertain, mainly because the name has been used as an invective substitute for Bethel. The reference in I Sam. 13:5 looks very much like a harmonizing redactional gloss.

134. The use of *hayyôm* in vss. 28, 30, in statements containing unmistakable

in summary fashion the situation that pertains to the end of the episode, vss. 23b-30, 37-46.

While it is scarcely possible to enter into an adequate analysis of this entire chapter, some estimate of the literary origin of vss. 1ff. is essential to an appreciation of the role of *bayyôm hahû'* here in vs. 24 and just previously in vs. 23a. A weak element in the argument for literary unity is that the episode of Jonathan's exploit clearly has two beginnings (1, 6) and two conclusions (14, 15, each with *watt^{e}hî* and summarizing clauses). Also, we are twice told that Saul had about six hundred men (13:15, 14:2), and that the main Philistine force was located at Michmash (13:5, 16). We see also that the references to the panic are overfull. On the other hand, 14:17 indicates that Saul learned by conducting a special muster that Jonathan and his armor-bearer were not with his troop, whereas 23b-30, 37-46 assumes that Saul had never been aware of Jonathan's absence. This all points to the interweaving of variant accounts.

We set aside such an analysis as has recently been offered by Horst Seebaas because it is too rigidly wedded to a hypothesis of parallel narratives extending throughout the Saul cycle. [135] Rather than parallel, ongoing narratives, we are dealing here with supplementation through the addition of originally isolated fragments. Besides such an early shrine legend as has been taken up by the redactor in 14:31-36 (33-34) and the late intrusion in 13:7b-15a, we identify two separate hero-saga/holy-war narratives, [136] both of which report the same historical event [137] but in different ways. One story (13:5-7a, 19, 23, 14:2-3a, 6-14, 16-23a) tells of Jonathan's exploit in vivid detail and with animated discourse, placing special emphasis on characteristic holy-war features; culminating in the epitomizing statement of 14:23a, "So Yahweh saved Israel *bayyôm hahû'* " (note the contrasting negative statement with *b^{e}yôm milḥemet* in 13:22), it does not continue

---

innuendos against Saul's severity, makes it likely that נגשׂ, "were hard pressed," should be read in vs. 24. Seebaas comments on this passage in *VT*, 16 (1966), 74-76, retaining נגשׂ in the sense of "approached (into battle)"; this accords with Seebaas' theory that the original document involved here approved of Saul and disapproved of Jonathan (see below).

135. *ZAW*, 78 (1966), 148-79. One document (13:4f., 7b-18, 14:1, 4f., 14-15aα, 16-19, 23a, 32-35, 36b) continues from 9:1—10:16, 11:1ff., and extends into 15:1, 11-12a, 16-19, 24-28. The second document (13:2-3bβ, 6-7a, 19-22, 14:2f., 6-13, 15aβb, 20-22, 23b-31, 36a, 37-46) continues from 8:1ff., 10:17, 19b-27, 12:1ff., and extends into 15:2a, 3-9, 12b-14, 20b-23, 29-30a, 31a, 32-35a; cf. also F. Schicklberger, "Jonathans Heldentat," *VT*, 24 (1974), 324-33.

136. 13:2-4, which may contain a variant report of the event narrated in chap. 14, may be independent of the two narratives.

137. Seebaas' argument, *ZAW*, 78, 161-68, to the effect that the parallel documents he has identified record two separate historical incidents, has little in its favor. It is hard to believe that Jonathan would be a hero at the pass of Michmash on two (three?) separate occasions. Even less likely is the theory of H. Stoebe ("Zur Topographie und Ueberlieferung der Schlacht von Mikmas, I Sam. 13 und 14," *BZ*, 21, 269-80) that a Saul story involving Gibeah and a Benjamin story involving Geba have been combined because of the similarity of the place names.

with an account of Jonathan's transgression. The second story (13:15b-18, 14:1, 3b-5, 15, 23b-30, 37-46)[138] recounts Jonathan's exploit more briefly because its main point of interest is Jonathan's innocent transgression of his father's unpopular oath,[139] the ensuing ordeal by lot, and the people's eventual intervention. The reference to Jonathan's deed of valor is needed to make meaningful the people's culminating affirmation of 14:45, "He has wrought with God this day," while the emphatic observation that neither Saul (vs. 1) nor the people (3b) were aware of Jonathan's absence is needed to explain how Jonathan would have transgressed Saul's curse.

Upon this analysis the functions of the various occurrences of *bayyôm hahû'* become clear. In 14:18 it is part of a gloss,[140] in vs. 23 it is part of an epitomizing conclusion to one of the hero saga/holy-war narratives; in vs. 24 it helps provide a sequential link to the central episode of the second hero saga/holy-war narrative; in vs. 31 it is part of redactional transition; in vs. 37 it helps provide a new sequential link, which at the same time characterizes the situation in which the ensuing episode transpires.

Only the occurrence in 14:23a, an epitomizing conclusion, is listed here; the other occurrences are listed below under the categories appropriate to them. A complete analysis of the time-designatives in I Sam. 14 must include the discussion of the functioning of *hayyôm* (*hazzeh*), which is to be taken up in the following chapter.

I Sam. 18:2

I Sam. 18:2 is the next passage in which *bayyôm hahû'* constitutes part of an original conclusion. The suggestion that this verse is the displaced conclusion to 16:14-23 scarcely commends itself.[141] How and why did it get severed from that context? Besides, at the end of chap. 16 it would be a feeble and superfluous repetition of vs. 22. 16:14ff. ends as it began: with reference to the evil spirit from Yahweh that came upon Saul.

It is apparent that 18:2 terminates David's interview with Saul, 17:55ff., in which the king learns his identity and takes him into his service. 18:1 intrudes with its report concerning Jonathan's fondness for

---

138. Material preceding vs. 15 and vs. 23 may have been omitted redactionally, as less descriptive than the corresponding material in the parallel account.

139. It may very well be that the final redactor, approving of Saul's zeal in making this oath, intended to censure him for not carrying through with the curse on Jonathan (so Seebaas), just as he censured him for failing to prosecute fully the *herem* on Amalek (chap. 15). But the pro-Jonathan tone of the original tale in 14:23b-30, 37-46 is unmistakable; if it intends to blame Saul for anything, it is for his excess of zeal rather than for any lack of it. As many present scholars agree, the Saul narratives were first heavily colored by pro-Davidic partisanship (cf. R. Knierim, "The Messianic Concept of the First Book of Samuel," F. T. Trotter, ed., *Jesus and the Historian*, Philadelphia, 1968, pp. 20-51), later by prophetic anti-monarchism, eventually by the deuteronomistic philosophy of history.

140. See above, p. 64.

141. So K. Galling, "Goliath und seine Rüstung," *VT*, 15 (1965), 150.

David. These verses, together with 17:12-31, 41, 48b, 50, 18:3-6a are lacking in the oldest manuscripts of the LXX, and are for this reason generally assigned to a separate and later literary source than that which appears in the Septuagintal text.[142] However, there is no proof that all this material is from a single author or that all of it is late.[143] There can be little doubt but that the LXX does contain a simpler and more cohesive account than does the MT.[144] But we have seen evidence in 18:1ff. for an ongoing process of accretion within the MT's additions, and this impression is strengthened when the materials at the beginning are similarly examined.[145] Out of the analysis of these materials emerges a simple, cohesive narrative that appears to be considerably more primitive than the highly stylized and heavily theological tale contained in vss. 32ff. The former, featuring an unknown shepherd-lad who comes to Saul's attention through a deed of great valor, is a simple hero saga; the latter, presenting David as a familiar champion who conquers in the power of Yahweh, is similar in form and conception to the legends told by and about the prophets.[146]

---

142. Recently, e.g., by G. B. Caird, *IB, in loco,* and pp. 857f.; G. Rinaldi, *BibO,* 8 (1966), 11-29, identifies 17:12-31 and 17:55—18:6a as late supplements.

143. The latter alternative depends for support on the former alternative; but if the non-Septuagintal material is not cohesive, there is no a priori argument against an early dating for certain elements within it. Taking a stand against early material is, among many others, H. J. Stoebe, "Die Goliath-pericope und die Form der Septuaginta," *VT,* 6 (1956), 397ff. (cf. especially p. 405).

144. See below; it has eliminated the primitive hero-saga and retained the hero-legend, combined in the MT. Previous doubts as to whether the LXX text of Samuel may at certain points stand closer to the original than the MT have been pretty well laid to rest by fragmentary Qumran texts, which in parts of Samuel generally represent a recension closer to the LXX than to the MT. (See now H. Orlinsky, "Qumran and the Present State of Old Testament Text Studies: The Septuagint Text," *JBL,* 78 [1959], 26-33.) But in this passage the LXX has eliminated material in its *Vorlage;* cf. H.-U. Nübel, "Davids Aufstieg in der frühe israelitischer Geschichtsschreibung" (dissertation, Bonn, 1959), pp. 17f.

145. E.g., David is twice introduced (12, 14); it is twice stated that the three eldest sons (named in 13 but unnamed elsewhere except in 28) followed Saul (13, 14); the Philistine speaks in vs. 23, but it is the *sight* of him that makes the men of Israel afraid (24f.); Saul learns of David in vs. 31 but does not know him in vs. 55; the phrase "spoke the same words as before" (23), with variants in vss. 27, 30, obviously comes from a secondary writer who wished to make a facile connection to foregoing material, without repeating its substance. Cf. Nübel, *op. cit.,* pp. 20-26.

146. H. Gressmann, *SAT²,* II, 1, *in loco,* calls the LXX material "Die Pagen-Erzählung" and the additional MT material "Die Hirten-Erzählung," dividing the latter into two parts at vs. 41, but not distinguishing a significant internal development. Cf. also O. Eissfeldt, *Die Komposition der Samuelisbücher* (1931), *in loco.* Nübel, *loc. cit.,* fails to identify these distinct sources. Von Rad, *Heilige Krieg,* pp. 47-49, does not characterize the two stories form-critically and dates them from approximately the same period, i.e., sometime after the reign of Solomon. For him, the combined story is "das Glanzstück" in the group of spiritualized holy-war stories developed in what he calls "die nachsalomonische Novellistik." Galling, *VT, loc. cit.,* speaks of the story (in particular vss. 31ff.) as a legend, dating it after the eighth century. Until the present, the legend's affinities with the prophet legends has been little noted.

Apparently, the recension underlying the Hebrew text made use of a very ancient saga still in circulation, expanding it by a variety of additions and adapting it to the legend that appears in the MT-LXX text. There is no need to draw on the hypothesis of a redactor in order to harmonize vs. 31 with the rest of the story—vss. 55ff. in particular; that verse is part of the midrashic expansion, while 55ff. belongs to the saga in its unexpanded form. Other elements adapting the saga to the legend appear to be in vs. 12a, the substitution of ודוד בן for a possible ויהי[147] and of שמנה for רביעה,[148] plus the addition of הזה מבית לחם יהודה; perhaps all of vs. 12b and vss. 13, 15, and 16; normalizations to vs. 4 of references to the Philistine antagonist in vs. 23aα, plus all of 23aβb; finally, vss. 26-31, enlarging upon a suggestion taken from vs. 25 to the effect that David might have had presumptuous designs on Saul's daughter.

The excision of this midrashic material reveals the outline of a simple tale, all of which survives in the present Hebrew text except for an account in the middle of how David accepted the Philistine's challenge (the legend's vivid narrative was more than adequate for this) and the alterations at the beginning. The saga had three parts: (1) an introduction in which the *dramatis personae* were presented (17:12a*, 14) and an account was given of how David came to the battle (17-22); (2) the climactic episode in which were depicted the threat posed by the appearance of a champion from the Philistine ranks (23a*, 24f.) and how David engaged the Philistine in battle (41, 48b, 50); (3) a concluding episode in which the conversations between Saul and Abner, then Saul and David, were recorded (55-58) and it was stated in final, summary form that Saul accepted David into his service (18:2). The structure of the saga indicates that it was completely independent of the legendary account. It may, as a matter of fact, have been close to the historical reality of the situation, stating no more than the simple facts of how an obscure shepherd lad from Judah came into favor with Saul, eventually to become the leader of his army. The phrase *bayyôm hahû'* again serves an epitomizing function in saga-like material dealing with a holy-war event.[149]

I Sam. 22:18

As I Sam. 22:18 stands in its present context, it does not appear clearly as a narrative conclusion; it seems rather to introduce an episode—not the final one—in which Doeg's murderous act takes place. Its present

---

147. For the form see, e.g., Judg. 13:2.
148. According to vs. 14, Jesse had only four sons. Vs. 12 has been normalized to 16:10.
149. For a more complete analysis of this passage see S. J. DeVries, "David's Victory over the Philistine as Saga and as Legend," *JBL*, 92 (1973), 23-36.

literary affinities are obscured by David's remark to Abiathar in vs. 22 indicating that he had taken note of Doeg's presence at Nob when Ahimelech had given him the holy bread and Goliath's sword (cf. 21:8); this draws 21:2-10 and 22:20-23 together and appears to make 22:6-19 part of a unified ongoing narration. There are several contradictions, however, between 21:2ff. and 22:6ff., such as that Doeg the Edomite is introduced in 21:8 as Saul's chief herdsman, but in 22:9 as one of his military retainers.[150] Especially striking is the fact that Doeg specifies three charges against Ahimelech in 22:10: inquiring of Yahweh, providing food,[151] and giving a sword (all of which is repeated by Saul in summary form in vs. 13); but in chap. 21 there is no mention of David's seeking an oracle, while in 21:7 the rations become the bread of the Presence and in 21:10 the sword becomes the sword of Goliath.[152] Noting the sly humor underlying 21:2ff., Hugo Gressmann designated it as an anecdote, imaginatively developed out of the earlier account in 22:6ff. The latter, according to Gressmann, stands close to historical reality, reflecting a situation in which Saul was forced to take stern measures against a very real conspiracy against him on the part of David, in collusion with the Nob priesthood.[153]

Supporting this analysis is a close study of the temporal sequence involved. The present arrangement of the text, with three independent pericopes (21:11-16, 22:1f., 3-5) intervening between 21:2-10 and 22:6ff., creates the impression that a considerable period must have passed between the time involved in these two passages. This impression, created by the writer of the Davidic accession-history, has been deliberately strengthened by that writer's synchronisms in 21:8 and 22:22.[154] In spite of this, 22:6ff. clearly proceeds from the point of view that the alleged crime, the trial, and the punishment all occurred on one and the same day. That is, when Ahimelech admits that he has given David an oracle he attempts to defend his action, first by reference to David's position of eminence, second by the claim that he has often done such things in the past. In the rhetorical question of vs. 15 Ahimelech deliberately places foremost the temporal adverb *hayyôm*, stressing that the oracle he has just given David follows a long practice. This means that David had shortly before been to Nob and departed, that Doeg also had just come from there. Evidently Nob

---

150. See above, pp. 65f., for an analysis of 21:8 and 22:22. 21:8 speaks of Doeg as *'îš mē'abdê šā'ûl*, further explicating his position as that of *'abbîr hārō'îm *ᵃšer lᵉšā'ûl*. 22:9 simply describes him as *niṣṣāb 'al 'abdê šā'ûl*.
151. Doeg speaks of *ṣêdâ* (10), Saul speaks of *leḥem* (13). For the civil process involved in this account see H. J. Boecker, *Die Beurteilung des Königtums*, pp. 87ff.
152. 22:10 has been normalized to the later form of the text. Note that in 22:13 Saul does not repeat the reference to Goliath, as he surely would have done if this had been in the original account, since it would make, in his eyes, the deed of Ahimelech even more culpable.
153. *SAT*, II, 1, *in loco*.
154. See above, pp. 65f.

was fairly close to Gibeah, close enough for Doeg first to have observed Ahimelech's actions and then to have been present for the summary confrontation that Saul demanded with his retainers on that very day (cf. *kayyôm hazzeh*, vss. 8, 13).

From these considerations we are able to proceed to the conclusion that 22:20ff. is an addition to the original story. The author of the Davidic accession-history, weaving all these materials together, puts as dark an aspect on Saul's deed as the tradition will allow. Certainly it is he who is responsible for adding the report of a *ḥerem* on the inhabitants of Nob (vs. 19), styled like I Sam. 15:3 and altogether beyond the range of historical probability.[155] This means that 22:18 is the original conclusion. Its form is that of the ancient casualty-report, summarizing the significance of this particular day of confrontation by stating the number of those who had been slain.[156]

II Sam. 3:37

The historian of David's accession to the throne has included in II Sam. 1–4 the record of a series of bloody deeds, manipulating his sources in such a way as to give the impression that David was quite guiltless, though he profited greatly. The phrase *bayyôm hahû'* appears in a verse that may be viewed as programmatic to this writer's entire point of view, II Sam. 3:37. Here it is said that "all the people" (i.e., David's supporters) and "all Israel" (i.e., the northern tribes) knew "on that day" that it had not been David's will to slay Abner the son of Ner. Coming at the conclusion of the story of Abner's murder, it would appear clearly to reflect the epitomizing form that we have been observing, except for the fact that more material follows, leading to another and different climax in David's call for divine punishment on the evildoers, at the end of vs. 39.

Many commentators on this passage seem content to attribute to the dynamic processes of oral development the unevenness that close scrutiny reveals, but we may well question whether this explanation is adequate. Flatly contradicting vs. 37 is the statement of 4:1, to the effect that "all Israel" were dismayed (נבהלו) at the report of Abner's death: if Ishbaal and his supporters were so convinced that David had not willed this murder there would have been little reason for their dismay. So 4:1 is suggesting the very opposite. It also suggests that, rather than there being bad feelings

---

155. The MT's "85" has been expanded to 305 in LXX. The accession-historian is particularly concerned to emphasize the enormity of an attack on the priesthood. He made the text read "priests of Yahweh" in vs. 17 (cf. 21), instead of an unspecified term as in vss. 11, 18, adding נשא אפוד בד for emphasis at the end of vs. 18.
156. Cf. Josh. 8:25, Judg. 20:35, 46, II Sam. 18:7. That Doeg, who witnessed to the crime, should be the executioner was more in accordance with amphictyonic law than the demand that Saul's *rāṣîm* (vs. 17) should do the bloody deed.

between Ishbaal and Abner, Abner had come to Hebron as his *bona fide* and trusted ambassador, suing for peace with David—a goal apparently desired by David too, but frustrated by the vengefulness of the sons of Zeruiah.[157] Such a situation appears to be presupposed in 3:14-16, which contain a fragmentary report of the negotiations that went on between Ishbaal and David, the former conceding a point of personal concern to the latter.[158] The narrative must have continued on to state that Ishbaal sent Abner to Hebron to conclude a treaty with David (cf. 20a), but this has been lost or obscured in the present form of the text.

The repetitions and inconsistencies[159] within II Sam. 3 witness to the combination of two separate literary sources. Carefully separating these two sources, we discover that the first had as its primary theme the menace created by the vendetta carried on by the sons of Zeruiah as they threatened the negotiations between the Saulides and the house of David. Its background is the account of Asahel's death in 2:18ff. It appears in fragmentary form in vss. 6, 14-16, and is combined with the second source in vss. 20-22a,[160] then continues virtually intact in 23-25, 26aβ, 30, 32, 38f., 4:1. It is structured in three episodes: (1) the negotiations between Ishbaal and David, with Abner as ambassador; (2) the stealthy murder of Abner by Joab and Abishai,[161] preceded by Joab's insolent reprimand to David; (3) Abner's funeral, followed by David's peroration and a summary of the consequences of this violent deed. Joab and his brother are in the forefront of interest throughout the climactic sections of this narrative.

The second source begins with 3:1, where it states emphatically that protracted warfare resulted in making David stronger and the Saulides weaker; this leads naturally to the statement of vs. 6 to the effect that Abner was making himself strong within the house of Saul.[162] This in turn serves as the introduction to vss. 7-13, 17-19, according to which Abner

---

157. This explains David's exclamation in vs. 39, "I am this day weak, . . . these . . . are too hard for me." Their harshness and bloodthirstiness had weakened David's policy for restoring normal conditions within Israel. The source involved here may have intended to depict David's motivation as no more than the wish to rebuild the nation through harmonious relations with the Saulides.

158. David's demand for Michal was made both to Abner (vs. 13) and to Ishbaal (vs. 14), according to the present text; evidently it appeared in each source. When Abner came to Hebron he apparently brought Michal with him, though this fact is not reported in vss. 20ff.

159. Joab arrives with *'abdê dāwid* in 22, with *kol haṣṣābā'* in 23; Abner is twice said to have been allowed to depart in peace (21, 23); this is again stated to Joab in 23; Abner is said to have been brought back (*wayyāšibû 'ōtô*) in 26, but he is said to have returned (*wayyāšāb*) in 27; his murder is twice described (27, 30); vs. 32 says the king wept, vs. 33 says he lamented; the people are twice said to have wept (32, 34); David twice utters Abner's obituary (33f., 38); in 29 he curses Joab, but in 39 he only invokes divine judgment on him.

160. Conflation is especially apparent in 22a, where וְהִנֵּה עַבְדֵי דָוִד ... מֵהַגְּדוּד וְשָׁלָל רַב עִמָּם may be from the second source, וַיּוֹאָב בָּא ... הֵבִיאוּ from this first source.

161. LXX reads, perhaps correctly, *'orbû.*

162. Vss. 2-5 are a secondary insertion, belonging originally with 5:13-15.

threatens Ishbaal and then proceeds to arrange betraying him to David. Vss. 20f. superimpose this story's account of the negotiations in Hebron upon the parallel event of the first source, the difference being that the first source spoke of Abner as Ishbaal's ambassador while the second source spoke of him as a conspirator against him. The conflation of sources continues in vs. 22a, but the second source emerges clearly in 22b, where Joab is represented as receiving the report of Abner's departure; it continues with the account of how Joab proceeds to murder Abner (26aαb, 27). Up until this point David has remained somewhat of a secondary figure in the narrative, but now he takes over completely. We read of his bitter curse upon Joab (28f.),[163] his call for public mourning (31a), his lament over Abner (33-34a), and his fast (35). The narrator reports the effect of all this upon the people (36a), concluding with the summarizing and epitomizing statement of vs. 37. The writer of the accession-history added vss. 31b, 34b, 36b as interpretive material when he combined this source with the first.[164]

This second source focuses its attention on Abner and David, rather than on the sons of Zeruiah. Its apparent concern is to make clear that though Abner died through treachery, this was not according to David's design. On the one hand, Joab was able to act without David's knowledge and consent, and is roundly cursed for his deed; on the other hand, Abner really got what he deserved since he was himself a ruthless and disloyal plotter, seeking to take advantage of his proper liege.[165]

Of these two narratives, the first seems less tendentious than the second, and appears accordingly to be earlier. It seems to be a report from David's court at Hebron, reflecting closely the external politics and internal intrigues of an early period. The second is legitimation propaganda from the Jerusalem court, at the same time establishing David's claims over the Saulides and reflecting the growing tension between the king and Joab that came to a head in the events of I Kings 1–2.

II Sam. 23:10

In II Sam. 23:9-10 we find a saga-like hero report concerning the second of David's champions, terminating in an assessment of his valor that

---

163. This is in striking contrast to parallel material in vs. 39, where David only commits "the evildoer" to Yahweh's judgment in recognition of the relative right in Joab's act.

164. The combination *hammelek dāwid* does not appear in this chapter except in 31b; it may have been added to accentuate David's innocence. 34b seeks to harmonize 33f. with 32. 36b is an interpretive addition; LXX lacks the preposition ב. In addition, the words בדם עשהאל אחיו in vs. 27 (abbreviating a parallel phrase in 30) appear to be from the redactor.

165. Subtle irony may lie in the words of David's lament in vss. 33f. Not only do they exculpate David, but they suggest that the treachery that brought Abner down was the deserved death of a fool.

includes the clause, "so Yahweh wrought (וַיַּעַשׂ) a great victory that day."
It is neither possible nor necessary to enter into a thorough analysis of the
text-critical problems involved in this difficult passage. Suffice it to say that
bayyôm hahû' is thoroughly attested in the versions, though, not surprisingly, it is missing from the parallel passage in Chronicles (I Chron.
11:12-14), which combines the report about Eleazar with the report
concerning Shammah (vss. 11f.).[166]

These two pericopes, together with the report about Josheb-basshe-
beth (vs. 8), appear to have belonged together in a single combinational
unit before being expanded by the addition of 13ff., 18f., 20f., 24ff. This is
to be deduced both from the references to "the three" in vss. 13, 16f.,[167]
19, 23,[168] and from the fact that only vss. 9 and 11 contain the connective
w^e '*ah*ᵃ*râw*. Thus the introductory formula at the head of vs. 8, "These are
the names of the mighty men whom David had," may have pertained
originally only to the three that immediately follow, although ultimately it
came to serve as the introduction to the entire collection of reports.[169]

We cannot understand vss. 9f. without some consideration to the
reports with which this section has been combined. Differences among
them, both in form and content, are such as to indicate that they derive
from diverse traditions, in spite of certain external similarities. An especially striking similarity is the statement, "so Yahweh wrought a great
victory (וַיַּעַשׂ יהוה תשׁועה גדולה), repeated in vs. 12 from vs. 10. It is
probable, however, that in vs. 12 this formula derives from the person who
combined the three reports. The pericope as such is the fragmentary
reproduction of a hero saga; the people have no part in the victory (it is
expressly stated that they fled, נָסוּ), hence the formula, turning it into a
holy-war narrative,[170] would have had no place in the early independent
tradition.

It is otherwise, however, in 9f. Here the victory formula, containing

---

166. Various critics favor Chronicles over Samuel, but it is difficult to understand
why, in the light of Chr's methods. Chronicles is eclectic, interpretive, and tendential; moreover, the MT of Chronicles is more corrupt than the LXX. Chronicles
attempts to identify Eleazar's victory with the encounter of I Sam. 17, an erroneous combination that has led commentators (e.g., Driver, *Notes on the Hebrew
Text of the Books of Samuel;* Hertzberg, *ATD*) to suppose that the former must be
interpreted on the basis of the latter.
167. Vss. 13ff. have generally been recognized as an anecdote of independent origin.
The three heroes mentioned here are not necessarily the same as the three of vss.
8ff.
168. Vss. 18f. and 20ff. give Abishai and Benaiah the first and second places,
respectively, among "the thirty." The phrase "but he did not attain to the three" is
clearly redactional in both instances, since the association of the three with the
thirty is a secondary combination.
169. For a survey of these materials, introductory to an acute analysis of 24-38,
see especially K. Elliger, "Die dreissig Helden Davids," *Kleine Schriften* (Munich,
1966), pp. 72-118.
170. Cf. I Sam. 14:23.

the phrase *bayyôm hahû'*, has been integrated into the saga at a very early stage. The process seems quite similar to that which was operative in the Jonathan-Saul narrative of I Sam. 14.[171] It is not at all clear, as many commentators have assumed, that ויעל in vs. 9 must be translated "withdrew," or something equivalent to it. Although there are passages in which עלה does indicate retreat or withdrawal (II Sam. 20:2, I Kings 15:19, Jer. 21:2),[172] other passages indicate advance or attack (Judg. 20:30, I Sam. 7:7, I Kings 20:2, Isa. 21:2). Hence the narrative in an early stage of its development may have intended to combine the report of Eleazar's exploit with the report of a victory in which the army had a part as the instrument of the divine working.[173] Working from the *lectio deficilior*, we may accordingly translate:

> And after him,[174] Eleazar ben Dodo the Ahohite[175] was among the three champions who were with David when they defied the Philistines. They were gathered there[176] for battle, and the men of Israel went up. He arose and smote ... so Yahweh wrought a mighty victory that day; and the troops returned (from) following him only to plunder.

The phrase *bayyôm hahû'* epitomizes this day of battle, stating in summary its basic character and its final effect.

II Chron. 15:11

In this verse *bayyôm hahû'* appears to serve as a synchronism, joining the account of a victory sacrifice to the immediately preceding (incomplete) date[177] for Asa's covenant assembly. But in terms of traditional Old Testament usage, the merging of a victory celebration with a covenant ceremony is equally as strange as a prophet's exhortation to courage (vss.

---

171. See above, pp. 84ff.
172. All with a combinational form with *min*.
173. The clause *wehā'ām yāšubû 'aḥᵃrâw 'ak lepaššēṭ* need not imply a previous retreat; it may simply mean that once Eleazar had done his killing, the people had to come back over the battlefield only to strip the dead. The final position of this statement makes it likely that the saga existed independently before its reinterpretation as a holy-war story.
174. ואחריו was added secondarily, as in vs. 11. The rest may be original, however, including the hero's name and the reference to the three champions, who in this context may have included others than the two mentioned in vss. 8, 11. This and the other stories may date from the earliest days of David's career, in spite of the lateness of the redactional process that introduced them into the text.
175. In respect to "Ahohite," here and in vs. 28, see Elliger, *Kleine Schriften*, pp. 87-89.
176. Driver, *Notes*, p. 365, argues that *šām* presupposes the naming of the battle's locale, hence he adopts the reading of Chronicles. The oral report, however, appears to be as vague about topography as it was about the general features of the battle in question, so the antecedent of *šām* is "the place where" David and the champions defied the Philistines. Chr's attempt to supply a place name is as tendentious, and as worthless, as that of certain late LXX manuscripts.
177. Since Asa is said to have enjoyed peace for the first ten years of his reign (14:1), Chr must have conceived of the war with Zerah as lasting five years, if the text is correct.

1-7) after the battle had already come to a successful conclusion (14:8-14). The Chronicler is here evidently working freely from his sources, some of which may be oral and some fragmentary. There is reason to believe that the war with Zerah of Gerar[178] may have an historical basis, but the Chronicler tells about it in the highly technical and highly idealistic terminology of the holy war, which has, by this time, long since ceased to exist as a living institution.[179] Quite appropriate, and possibly historical, is the concluding statement of chap. 14 that much booty was taken from the Gerarites before the army's return to Jerusalem. The army would have offered a sacrifice of thanksgiving at the temple[180] from the animals they had captured, which is the statement we find in 15:11.

Occurring with the phrase *bayyôm hahû'*, this last may have concluded the report of the war with Zerah as the Chronicler found it in his sources. As such, it functioned somewhat as an epitome, according to the traditional pattern so often found in holy-war accounts, characterizing the sacrifice as the culminating and typifying event of this momentous day. But the Chronicler felt moved to include a "sermon" by Oded according to his usual custom[181] —in however inappropriate a place[182] —together with his account of a covenant ceremony,[183] thus completely obscuring the original character of 15:11. His chronological note in vs. 10 is completely artificial, intended to bridge the way to it.

Conclusion

Looking back over this group of passages in which *bayyôm hahû'* occurs as part of a concluding formula, we realize a rather striking fact. Within three of the secondary passages (Deut. 31:22, I Sam. 6:15, 27:6) we found it functioning in familiar fashion as a synchronism, tying the secondary material of the passage in question to its context; but in four other secondary passages (one very early, one very late, two in between) we saw

---

178. The identification of Zerah with the Ethiopians is artificial and inappropriate. There is no hint that he is an Egyptian pharaoh, as some interpreters have suggested. In their counterattack, the Judahites plunder only Gerar. Chr probably is himself responsible for the fancy of making Zerah appear more formidable than he was historically.

179. Cf. von Rad, *Heilige Krieg*, pp. 79ff.

180. In the even more stereotyped and fanciful holy-war account of chap. 20, Jehoshaphat's army is said to have returned to "the house of Yahweh" after their victory (vs. 28).

181. Cf. G. von Rad, "The Levitical Sermon in the Books of Chronicles," *Problem of the Hexateuch*, pp. 267-80 (reprinted from Procksch Festschrift, 1934, pp. 113-24).

182. Oded's exhortation should have come before the battle account, cf. 20:14-17. But Chr wanted to use it for introducing his account of the covenant festival, so introduced it here instead.

183. The concluding phrase, "and Yahweh gave them rest round about" (15b), belonged to the battle account; cf. 20:30.

that it bore little self-conscious relation to the literary context, functioning instead to epitomize in a brief summary the decisive significance of the day in question, i.e., of the event that gave that day its particular character and importance.

And now, as we review our analysis of the seventeen passages that may reasonably be identified as original, we find that every one of them contains such an epitomizing summary with the formula *bayyôm hahû'*. Have we arrived at the bedrock of this formula's development? So it would seem. Here are holy-war stories and stories that reflect the pattern—though not the genuine essence—of the holy-war stories. Here we have, also, narratives of the cult—specifically, this time, of covenant ceremonies— etiologies, and tribal saga. The holy-war and quasi holy-war narratives predominate, but it is significant that they do not constitute the only narrative type containing the formula in this original function. The whole range of sacral activities is involved; whenever an act of God or of man—or of God and man together—is of special significance for the meaning of a particular day, this schema could be called into use. Interestingly, it is mainly, though not exclusively, the predynastic period of Israel's history that is reflected in these narratives. There can be little question but that this is also the period that produced most of them.

4. Transitional formulae between episodes

a. Within secondary materials

Having now analyzed those passages in which *bayyôm hahû'* serves to introduce new materials into a context and those in which it serves to conclude a pericope, we are in a position to evaluate a third sizable group of passages in which it provides a transitional link between episodes within a given passage. Among these, only a small number may confidently be identified as secondary from a literary point of view. They are Gen. 26:32, 48:20, I Sam. 14:24, 31, II Sam. 2:17. As we shall see, the first two have probably arisen in the process of oral supplementation, while the others may be ascribed to literary redaction. We shall examine these closely before going on to an analysis of the longer list of original passages. Interestingly, all these secondary occurrences involve *bayyôm hahû'* as a beginning formula.

Gen. 26:32

First, Gen. 26:32 J. It is part of the framework into which the original saga concerning Abimelech's treaty/covenant with Isaac, vss. 26-31, was placed. More precisely, it forms the transition to the concluding part of that framework. Both the treaty saga and the framework, which together with vss. 17, 19-23, 25b strings together a series of etiological well stories, are very old.[184] In any case it needs to be seen that the temporal phrase, in this instance immediately preceded by *way^{e}hî*, creates an artificial synchronism between the two.

Gen. 48:20

Similar is Gen. 48:20 E. Gunkel assigns all of vss. 15 and 16, together with the rhythmic material in vs. 20, to the E source, identifying the intervening words, including ויברכם ביום ההוא at the beginning of vs. 20, to J. He believed an editor to be responsible for the word לאמר which binds the two sources together.[185] It is not at all likely, however, that an editor would have proceeded in this fashion, arbitrarily dividing the patriarch's discourse into two sections. It is more probable, as Noth holds,[186] that Gen. 48:1f., 8ff. belong to a single literary source, with vss. 15f. as a literary supplement. If this is true, the introductory words of vs. 20 are not to be taken as the conclusion to vss. 17-19 (so Gunkel) but as a transition to the blessing formula of vs. 20. Actually, Israel's words to Joseph in vs. 19 constitute in themselves a powerful blessing; it seems likely that the original narrative ended with them. Vs. 20 represents, then, a supplementation, probably oral, incorporating the words of a blessing from another source. The same supplementer added the conclusion, "So he put Ephraim before Manasseh."[187] Because of the context of this verse, the temporal phrase both synchronizes and epitomizes, but the former is its primary function.

I Sam. 14:31

The entire fourteenth chapter of I Samuel, with its five occurrences of *bayyôm hahû'*, has been analyzed above in the search for concluding formulae.[188] It will be recalled that a redactor's hand was discovered in vs. 31, using this phrase to provide an artificial transition to supplementary material. The phrase stands at the beginning of the new material, providing a sequence from one episode to the next. This is the first instance in which the phrase has been found to provide such a function.

---

184. Cf. B. O. Long, *The Problem of Etiological Narrative in the Old Testament* (BZAW, 108, Berlin, 1968), pp. 22f., 34f. The best form- and tradition-critical analysis of this material is still Gunkel's; cf. his *Genesis*, 3rd (6th) ed., pp. 304f. The framework of well stories is lacking in the E version, chap. 21.
185. H. Gunkel, Genesis comm., *in loco*.
186. *UGP*, pp. 91f.
187. The blessing of vs. 20 does not have as its aim to exalt Ephraim over Manasseh. It comes, of course, from Ephraimite circles, where this precedence was taken for granted. Its aim is only to declare the blessedness of these two tribes together. The conclusion to vs. 20 draws from these lines an inference that is the major point of vss. 17ff., viz., that Ephraim, the younger, has been set ahead of Manasseh, the elder.
188. See above, pp. 84ff.

II Sam. 2:17

A similar process is involved in II Sam. 2:17. This verse forms a transition between two fateful episodes in the history of David's accession. Each episode displays the characteristics of heroic saga, having been built, no doubt, around an historical core but embellished with imaginative features beloved by soldiers at ease around their campfire or in their barracks.[189] As a matter of fact, each episode forms a little story in itself, most notably the first, with its etiological termination.[190] Nevertheless, the historian has worked skillfully to present the duel of vss. 12-16 as the logical and necessary introduction to the duel of vss. 18-23, and thence to the further hostilities recorded in the pericopes following.[191] Having recounted the surprising and tragic ending to the "play" of the twelve champions from each of the two sides, including as a parenthesis the etiological formula, he goes on to state in meagre words the consequence: "So the battle became very fierce that day." We might be curious to read more details of this "main event," but are told only its outcome: "and Abner and the men of Israel were beaten before the servants of David." This is then followed in greater detail by the Abner-Asahel duel, etc. So the phrase *bayyôm hahû'* forms a transition whose function is not so much to make a synchronism as to call attention to the overriding consequence of this fateful day as a whole, drawing the connection between the several events that gave it its momentous significance in terms of the history of Yahweh's dealings with his anointed, David.

II Sam. 6:9, I Chron. 13:12

In II Sam. 6:9 (par. I Chron. 13:12) *bayyôm hahû'* makes the initial impression of being intended as an epitome. Careful study reveals, however, that it comes from a redactor who inserted vss. 6-9 as a secondary intrusion,[192] and that it actually functions as a time-identifier. Standing in contrast to the "three months" of vs. 11, its purpose is to tie in vss. 6-9 as an explanation of an otherwise inexplicable delay.

---

189. Cf. K. Koch, *Was ist Formgeschichte?* (Neukirchen, 1964); ET, *The Growth of the Biblical Tradition* (New York, 1971), pp. 148ff.

190. It is difficult to determine whether this (quasi?) etymological etiology formed an original part of the narrative. There is no perspicuous paronomasia. The duel is said to have taken place at "the pool of Gibeon," not at a "field"; the meaning of *haṣṣurîm* is uncertain: if it means "enemies, opponents," it characterizes the event only in a very general way. The generally accepted change to *haṣṣidîm* does not commend itself as a *Vorlage* for LXX τῶν ἐπιβούλων, which elsewhere translates other OT words than this; cf. H. P. Smith, *ICC, in loco.*

191. Cf. Gressmann, *SAT²*, II, 1, 132.

192. See BH³ mg. LXX^B is a strong witness to the absence of this reference. The interpolator would have had good reason to make the insertion, though we would assume that he would have been active before the time of the Septuagintal translation.

There are a number of strong arguments for identifying vss. 6-9 as secondary. First, etiological formulae like that of vs. 8 normally come at the end of narrative episodes, hence the presumption is that vs. 8 is a conclusion here also.[193] Second, the reference to David's being angry is firmly tied to the etiological element by the connective *'al '*ᵃšer*; the following statement, indicating that he was afraid of Yahweh *bayyôm hahû'*, seems lame and aimless except as a redactional transition to vs. 10. Third, vs. 10 itself appears as an idle repetition of vs. 9, but as the original continuation of vs. 5 it performs an essential function.[194] Finally, there is a contradiction in the topology involved.[195]

The tale of Uzzah developed, probably imaginatively, as an explanation of the strange name, *Perez-uzzah*. The place itself may have been forgotten, while the story was remembered. Probably David came in secondarily, as the supplementer-redactor identified the place with the well-known threshing floor of Nacon (vs. 6)—evidently somewhere on the road between the "house" of Abinadab and Jerusalem—using the entire narrative as an explanation of the delay in bringing the ark to Jerusalem.

b. Within original contexts

We come next to an examination of a lengthier list of passages in which transitional *bayyôm hahû'* makes every claim to being part of the original narration. Here we shall find it as a beginning formula, as a concluding formula, and as a formula in the middle. We shall also find that its function is far from exclusively that of a synchronism or sequence.

Gen. 30:35

Bayyôm hahû' functions in Gen. 30:35 to establish a sequence. A transition is made between the account of Jacob's bargaining with Laban and the report of the measures the latter took to cheat the former.

---

193. See B. S. Childs, "A Study of the Formula, 'Until this Day'," pp. 281f.

194. The original narrator did not feel it necessary to explain why David would not take (הסיר, literally "turn aside," "divert") the ark into his city. The reason would have been sufficiently obvious: the "ark of God," though named after Yahweh Sebaoth of Shiloh, would have been potentially dangerous in a strange environment—perhaps as dangerous as it had proved to be in the temple of Dagon (I Sam. 5f.), so that David took an entirely understandable precaution in seeing first whether it would curse or bless the "house" (probably shrine) of Obed-edom.

195. There is a superfluity in the two names for the place where the Uzzah episode occurred; in the original etiological narrative, only the one being explained (Perez-uzzah) would have appeared. References to the house of Obed-edom have nothing to do with this episode; vs. 10, beginning with a verb in the perfect, followed by a sequence of imperfect consecutives, introduces its own new episode in the original account.

Exod. 32:28

In Exod. 32:28 the expression *bayyôm hahû'* concludes a narrative concerning the Levites' work of zeal in slaughtering three thousand of their neighbors; it functions here in the pattern of the casualty report familiar from other passages.[196] This verse is, however, transitional to the true climax of the pericope, vss. 25-29; this is, of course, the interpretive declaration of Moses, "Today they ordained you. . . ."[197] There is much to commend the argument of A. H. J. Gunneweg to the effect that the clause איש בבנו ובאחיו forms the original core of tradition in this passage.[198] The likelihood, accordingly, is that the story of the slaughter is a later development,[199] intended as an imaginative explication of the Levites' legitimization; certainly the pericope as a whole is a secondary addition to the golden-calf account.[200] Thus *bayyôm hahû'* serves here to epitomize the narrative in preparation for the programmatic words of vs. 29.

Judg. 20:21, 26

The phrase *bayyôm hahû'* occurs next as a transitional formula in the primitive Bethel narrative of Judg. 20.[201] We have seen that it occurs in vs. 21 to close off the opening encounter at Gibeah, epitomizing its outcome in the form of a casualty report. We have also seen that in vs. 26 the phrase occupies a place in the middle of an episode, preparing a transition to the climax (the seeking of an oracle preparatory to the victory of the third day), perhaps at the same time epitomizing the significance of this transitional activity in terms of its most characteristic cultic ceremony. Most likely the phrase is intended here as a synchronism and nothing more. It is not to be identified as a sequential link since the fasting was contemporaneous with, rather than successive to, the activities associated with it; nor could it be identified as an indication of duration, a function performed by the expression, *'ad hā'ereb*, "until the evening."

I Sam. 4:12

We look next at I Sam. 4:12. This can be seen only as an integral part of the narrative of the ark's capture; yet its function is to create a transition

---

196. Judg. 20:21, 35, 46, I Sam. 22:18, II Sam. 18:7. See below.
197. So MT, against the VSS.
198. *Leviten und Priester*, pp. 29-37. Gunneweg calls this an ancient "Levitenspruch" or "Levitenregel."
199. The original tradition may have had no reference whatever to zeal for taking the sword against apostates. We note that "his son and his brother" in vs. 29 has been broadened in vs. 27 to "his brother . . . his companion . . . his neighbor."
200. Although, as it now stands, it has an anti-Aaronite impact, there is no indication that this was its original intent; cf. Gunneweg, *Leviten und Priester*, p. 36, in opposition to Noth, *UGP*, n. 416, and others.
201. See above, pp. 82, 117.

from the account of the battle of Aphek, which comes to a definite conclusion in vs. 11, to the account of how the bad news of this battle affected the people remaining behind at the central amphictyonic shrine at Shiloh, and in particular Eli and the wife of the dead priest Phinehas. The phrase *bayyôm hahû'* follows the name of the place, Shiloh; hence the interest of the narrative is focused on the place rather than on the time. Nevertheless, the time is also important. In creating a vivid picture of the panic that the news of the calamity produced, the narrator speaks of "a man of Benjamin"—one of Israel's finest!—running all the way from the battle line at Aphek to Shiloh "on that day"—quite a feat in itself since the crow's-flight distance between the two places, as commonly identified, is about eighteen miles. Hence the temporal phrase is more than a conventional connective; it establishes the conceptual unity between the battle and its results. This was a day to remember and to lament, a day made up of a military disaster plus the shattering effects of that disaster on the sacral union. It was a day in which Yahweh did an evil thing in Israel, "at which the two ears of every one that hears it will tingle" (3:11).[202] The day of evil at Aphek and Shiloh was the ominous type of the day of evil that would someday come upon Jerusalem.

I Sam. 7:6

In our analysis of I Sam. 7:10 we discovered the transitional role of *bayyôm hahû'* in vs. 6. Its function in vs. 10 is very similar to its function in Judg. 20:26. It provided a synchronism for the fasting, which, as the most characteristic cultic activity of the day in question, may be intended as also having some epitomizing function.[203]

I Sam. 9:24, 10:9

Upon close inspection, the two occurrences of *bayyôm hahû'* in the narrative of Saul's anointing prove to have different formal functions. It is not necessary to enter here into a detailed critical analysis of I Sam. 9:1–10:16.[204] We need only observe that the pericope has a pronounced

---

202. A. Weiser, *Samuel*, p. 14, underscores the "Glaubenskrise" that resulted. There is no reason to believe however, that Shiloh itself was destroyed; see now the archeological report by M. L. Buhl and S. Holm-Nielsen; cf. R. A. Pearce, *VT*, 23 (1973), 105ff. From the point of view of the ark history with its bias toward the Jerusalem temple, there was, no doubt, inner satisfaction in recounting how Yahweh had rejected Shiloh (cf. Ps. 78:60ff.).

203. See above, pp. 83f. As in Judges, our expression does not indicate sequence or duration. This passage has strongly influenced I Mac. 3:46f., which similarly reports fasting at Mizpah "on that day" in preparation for warfare.

204. H. W. Hertzberg, ADT, 9, *in loco*, argues that I Sam. 9:1–10:16 is a literary unity but combines two different traditions, the first of which had Saul going to an unnamed seer at Zuph, seeking an answer regarding the lost asses, and the second of which had Saul going to Ramah to be anointed by Samuel. For a more elaborate

time structure involving two special days in sequence.[205] The first part of the narrative concentrates its attention upon the first day's encounter with Samuel, in which Saul is received by him at a cultic festival; the second part of the narrative moves climactically to the events of the second day, on which Samuel first anoints Saul and then appoints three confirmatory signs.

The events of the first day are narrated solely for the purpose of building dramatic suspense. The report at the end of vs. 24, "So Saul ate with Samuel that day," is intended therefore not as a statement of the day's essential character but simply as a conclusion to Day I, making way for Day II. It tells the last significant thing Saul did on that day. Its function is that of providing the essential sequential link between these two days. This is the first example we have encountered of the phrase being used in this particular function.

As for the phrase in 10:9, we must observe that here it comes at the beginning of a new episode. It is not sequence alone that it determines. This closing and climactic episode opens with a statement of the interior fulfillment of Samuel's words: "And it came to pass as he turned his back to depart from Samuel that God gave him another heart." It is followed by "and all these signs happened that day," which is meant to cover sequentially the occurrence of the first two signs promised by Samuel, but at the same time to epitomize the final result, of which Saul's prophesying, narrated in vss. 10ff., is the only concrete example given.[206]

I Sam. 12:18

Samuel's "farewell address" has commonly been assigned to the deuteronomistic redactor, being defined by Martin Noth as one of the programmatic speeches giving the deuteronomistic history its basic structure and defining its theological goal.[207] Artur Weiser has recently made a new analysis of its tradition history, concluding that it arose at the Gilgal shrine and was preserved among prophetic circles in the northern kingdom, but the likelihood remains that the Deuteronomist has played a part in

---

assessment of this narrative's place in the total complex of the Saul traditions, see Schunck, *Benjamin*, pp. 85-87, 107, 109f.; A. Weiser, *Samuel*, pp. 48-61; G. C. Macholz, "Untersuchungen zur Geschichte der Samuel-Ueberlieferungen" (dissertation, Heidelberg, 1966), pp. 137-46.

205. The narrative abounds in time-designations: *hayyôm* 9:12, 19, 10:2; *kā'ēt māhār* 9:16; *bōqer* 9:19; *wayyaškîmû . . . ka'ªlôt haššahar* 9:26. See also 9:9, 12f., 15, 24, 27, 10:5, 9.

206. Though it is necessary to read ויהי instead of ויהיה at the beginning of vs. 9 (see BH³ mg), there is no compelling reason to eliminate the reference to the changing of Saul's heart. Here is the final epitome of the entire narrative in an early form, prior to the addition of vss. 10-13, 14-16. Cf. the helpful analysis of B. C. Birch, "The Development of the Tradition on the Anointing of Saul in I Sam. 9:1—10:16," *JBL*, 90 (1971), 55-68; he, however, wrongly identifies 9:24, rather than 10:9, as an epitomizing statement (p. 60).

207. *UGS*, pp. 59f. So also Hertzberg, *ATD*, 9, *in loco*.

shaping this chapter.[208] Form-critical studies of this chapter have revealed the affinities of its basic structure to early covenant forms.[209] But the peculiar feature of this chapter is to be found not so much in the covenant discourse, which includes a kerygmatic review (vss. 6-12) and a call to obedience (13-15), as in Samuel's call to controversy (3-5), his call for the sign from heaven (16-18), and the concluding confession, reassurance, and admonition (19ff.), all of which serve to personalize this particular confrontation as a choice for or against Samuel as the duly-designated covenant mediator.

It is in vss. 16-18 that the narrative climax comes. Samuel's discourse as such is at an end; he dramatically calls the people to witness the great thing Yahweh will do to support and authenticate what he has spoken to them (the familiar pattern for the call of a charismatic-prophet: sign confirming word; cf. Exod. 3-4, Judg. 6, Isa. 6, Jer. 1, Ezek. 1-2, etc.). Samuel announces that he will call to Yahweh for thunder and rain—at a time (wheat harvest) when none is to be expected—and so he does; Samuel calls to Yahweh, and Yahweh sends the thunder and rain[210] "on that day," with the result that all the people greatly fear Yahweh and Samuel. The phrase *bayyôm hahû'* functions here as in the conclusion to other tales concerning Yahweh's mighty deeds, e.g., Exod. 14:30f., I Sam. 7:10, stating neither a synchronism nor a sequence but the experiential content of this decisive moment of confrontation.[211]

I Sam. 14:24, 37

In the foregoing analysis of I Samuel 14 the occurrence of *bayyôm hahû'* in vss. 24 and 37 has been identified as providing a transitional formula in the original hero saga about the vindication of Jonathan.[212]

---

208. *Op. cit.*, pp. 79-94; cf. H. J. Boecker, *Die Beurteilung des Königtums in I Samuel 7-12*, pp. 61-88. Literary affinities with chap. 7 and ideological affinities with chaps. 8 and 10 may argue for Mizpah rather than Gilgal as the more likely place of preservation. See below on I Sam. 12:5, 17.
209. J. Muilenburg, "The Form and Structure of the Covenantal Formulations," *VT*, 9 (1959), pp. 360-64; Dennis J. McCarthy, *Treaty and Covenant*, pp. 141-45.
210. The combination of *qōlôt* with *māṭār* occurs, together with *bārād* (hail), in the plague story at Exod. 9:34 J; this is close to the conceptual background of I Sam. 12:18; i.e., these are signs of Yahweh's power and wrath. Elsewhere *māṭār* is seen as a blessing.
211. So strongly do vss. 16-18 echo Exod. 14:13-31 (together with Exod. 9:22-24) that we must assume the narrator in Samuel to have been familiar with at least a primitive form of the deliverance-at-the-sea tradition. For I Sam. 12:16, see Exod. 14:13f., 30. Compare also the conclusion in I Sam. 12:18, "and all the people greatly feared Yahweh and Samuel," with, "And the people feared Yahweh; and they believed in Yahweh and in his servant Moses," in Exod. 14:31. Thus the affinities of the theophany in this passage are at least as close to the exodus tradition as they are to the Sinai tradition, emphasized by some recent critics (Weiser, Muilenburg) as the point of closest comparison.
212. See above, pp. 84ff.

The saga is in three episodes: the background exploit; Jonathan's offense; the discovery of the offense and its consequences (i.e., no favoring oracle, the casting of lots, the action of the people). *Bayyôm hahû'* appears as a technical element at the beginning of the second and third episodes, linking them sequentially together while epitomizing a central element within the respective episodes.

I Sam. 20:26

The RSV is in error in beginning a new paragraph with I Sam. 20:26. The purpose of this verse is quite clearly to state the outcome of the first day in a sequence of two (or three), i.e., that Saul did not find David's absence from his feast ominous because of hypothetical uncleanness. It concludes 24b-25, providing a sequential link in this crucial time series.[213]

I Sam. 31:6

Even a casual reading of I Samuel 31 leaves the impression that vs. 6 is climactic. A careful criticism of the text and an analysis of the tradition development in chap. 31 are required, however, to see clearly the function of *bayyôm hahû'* in this verse.

The LXX reproduces the entirety of vs. 6 except for the phrase "even all his men," a gloss added in consideration of vs. 1. I Chron. 10:6 has a strikingly altered version of this verse: not only does it lack the phrase omitted by the LXX but it omits also the reference to the armor-bearer and the phrase *bayyôm hahû'*,[214] substituting a new clause, וכל ביתו יחדו מתו. In view of the Chronicler's notorious arbitrariness in paraphrasing the text of Samuel-Kings, it would be hazardous to adopt these emendations. Omitting גם כל אנשיו, we find that the MT of I Sam. 31:6 employs a meaningful and appropriate word-order, with the singular imperfect-consecutive in first place, then the principal subject, Saul, with the three sons and the armor-bearer as subordinate subjects added, then our temporal phrase, and finally the adverb "together." The adverb is in emphatic place at the end and directly modifies the phrase *bayyôm hahû'*, by which arrangement the narrator wished to stress that the death of all the Saulides came on the same fateful day. Thus *bayyôm hahû'* powerfully epitomizes the narrative of 31:1-6—and, we might add, the entire tragic history of Saul as well.

There seems to be little reason to doubt that I Sam. 31 is a literary unity. This does not mean, however, that it all comes from a single

---

213. The narrative of David's escape from Saul is crowded with time-designations, providing clues to its essential structure. Unfortunately, the text is confused at some crucial places.
214. But the LXX of Chronicles restores it.

traditional source.[215] On the contrary, the chapter presents certain duplications, inconsistencies, and afterthoughts that can best be explained as due to the combining of traditions from more than one source. Vs. 1 reports proleptically the outcome of the battle; vs. 7 reports a result that could not have taken full effect for some while following the battle; vss. 9-10a break into an account of what happened at Beth-shan with a statement of how Saul's head and armor were displayed back in the cities of the Philistines. It is probable that these verses, together with the artificial transition *wayhî mimmāḥ°rāt* in vs. 8,[216] derive from a stage of oral transmission subsequent to an original narrative, probably from Jabesh-gilead, which told the simple facts of Saul's death and burial with none of the subtle innuendos of our present text. Although this narrative (2-6, 8aβ, 10b-13) is brief and soberly factual, it is almost epic in its conception. It tells in two episodes, first how Saul had the spirit to take his own life when defeated and cornered, second how those who had been the first beneficiaries of his charismatic power manifested some of that same power in delivering his dead body from contumely, burying it in a place of sacredness and honor.[217] The phrase *bayyôm hahû'* terminates the first, climactic episode in preparation for the second.

II Sam. 11:12

In this narrative from the throne-succession history the passage of time is of primary interest. David is trying to get Uriah to visit his wife, while on leave in Jerusalem, so as to make it possible to legitimize her pregnancy. But repeatedly Uriah repudiates the royal invitation. The statement at the end of vs. 12, "and Uriah remained in Jerusalem that day and the next," concludes one episode, the one involving David's interview with Uriah, and at the same time intends to introduce another, the one in which he tries to make him drunk.[218]

---

215. Cf. Schunck, *Benjamin*, pp. 95-107. Discrepancies apparent in II Sam. 1 may reflect a variant tradition or be due to the redactor-historian's imagination.

216. This temporal phrase is entirely conventional wherever it is used in the OT. In the present passage it may be factually erroneous, since stripping the dead was not ordinarily delayed to a second day unless darkness intervened; cf. II Sam. 23:10 (also I Sam. 14:31f.).

217. The tamarisk seems to have been especially numinous: Abraham planted one in Beersheba in honor of El Olam (Gen. 21:33); Saul sat under one at Gibeah (I Sam. 22:6) and was buried under one in Jabesh. That we are more in the conceptual area of the holy war in this passage than in that of primitive taboo is rightly stressed by Gressmann, *SAT*[2], II, 1, *in loco*.

218. There is little to commend the elision of וממחרת at the end of vs. 12, adding it, introduced by ויהי, to vs. 13 (so LXX[L], Syr, BH[3] mg, Driver, *et al.*). There seems to be a conflict between the two parts of vs. 12, but the conflict is not real. David promised that Uriah should depart *māhār*. This should have been the day designated by וממחרת, but since David renewed his blandishments, the departure did not take place until the day following (vs. 14). Wherever possible, Hebrew narrators summarize temporal designations in a sequence like this; cf. Judg. 19:1ff., I Kings 18:44 ("Go up seven times").

II Sam. 18:7f.

We come next to two further texts from the throne-succession narrative. The author of this narrative reveals an element of his distinctive style in the way he uses *bayyôm hahû'* as a transitional formula in each of these two passages.

The first is II Sam. 18:7f. The commentaries do not observe the transition here.[219] These two verses form the junction between separate episodes in the narrative of the battle of the forest of Ephraim, where Absalom's threat to his father's throne was definitively settled. In 18:1ff. we find an opening scene, involving lively discourse between David and his commanders; David is dissuaded from personally leading his troops, and thereupon gives strict orders to be lenient with Absalom; the scene concludes with a series of verbs in narration, together with *šām*, "there," our temporal phrase and a statement of the number of casualties, indicating the outcome of the battle. This epitomizing conclusion is needed as a preparation for the more central episode of Absalom's death that immediately follows. This commences in vs. 8 with a preparatory statement beginning with *watt^ehî*: "Now the battle at that place (*šām*) became spread out over the face of the entire countryside, so that the forest consumed more people than the sword *bayyôm hahû'*." This is the introduction to the story of Absalom's accident and subsequent death (vss. 8ff.), which would scarcely be understandable without this general explanation. It is specially significant that the narrator repeats both *šām* and *bayyôm hahû'*, establishing emphatically that "the here and now" of vss. 8ff. is the same as "the here and now" of vs. 7.[220] Thus the *bayyôm hahû'* of II Sam. 18:8 is a synchronism, introducing an account that is part of the greater narrative, just concluded, and contemporaneous with it.

II Sam. 19:3f. [E-2f.]

The second throne-succession passage is II Sam. 19:3f. Here the transition between two episodes is marked by the threefold repetition of *bayyôm hahû'*. Generally the new episode is marked at vs. 2[221] because here it is stated that Joab was informed of David's weeping—seemingly a proper introduction to the reprimand that he undertook to bestow in the sequel. Vs. 2 belongs with the preceding verses, however. Together with vs. 3 it concludes the account of how David received the news of Absalom's death: not only must we be told that David wept, but also that Joab,

---

219. E.g., Gressmann, *SAT²*, II, 1, 181, dividing between 6a and 6b.
220. Note also that vs. 7 ends, and vs. 8 begins, with clauses introduced by *watt^ehî*. The second *šām* in vs. 7 is to be eliminated, with the LXX, as an obvious dittograph.
221. E.g., Gressmann, *SAT²*, II, 1, 182, and RSV divide between vs. 1 and vs. 2. Smith, *ICC, in loco*, and Hertzberg, *ATD, in loco*, divide between 18:32 and 19:1.

directly responsible for that weeping, heard about it; and further that the troops' would-be victory celebration "on that day" was turned into mourning when and because they heard about it "on that day." This is an epitome of the preceding episode, while the following clause with *bayyôm hahû'* is a statement of a synchronous circumstance. The entire character of a victory day had been drastically altered.

A third *bayyôm hahû'* comes in vs. 4. We will surely get the impression of meaningless, monotonous repetition unless we perceive that this is intended as the introduction to the new episode involving Joab's reprimand. The narrator prepares for the main event beginning with Joab's approach (vs. 6) by stating first the ominous (at least in Joab's eyes) fact that on this should-be victory day the troops' demeanor was that of men who had fled from battle (imperfect consecutive, temporal phrase, infinitive phrase, comparative clause); second, the narrator sets forth the corresponding behavior of the king,[222] repeating in part the words of his lament. The two observations together form the necessary preface to the discourse that follows. We may admire the narrator's skill and sense of dramatic development more fully if we understand the way in which he has made use of *bayyôm hahû'*, here and in 18:7-8.

II Sam. 24:18

Our next passage is II Sam. 24:18, part of the *hieros logos* for the Jerusalem temple. There are three circumscribed narrative elements in this story: the account of David's census (vss. 1-9), the account of the pestilence, symbolized in the vision of a destroying angel (10-17), and the account of David's purchase of Araunah's threshing floor (18-24, 25b). Omitting a considerable amount of secondary accretion, we are able to trace through these elements a single cohesive narrative (2, 4b, 8, 9, 15, 17-19, 25) that designedly leads up to the climactic conclusion of vs. 25a, "So David built there an altar to Yahweh and offered burnt offerings and peace offerings."[223]

The episode of the purchase of Araunah's threshing floor is prefigured in vs. 16, where it is stated that the angel was there, legitimizing this site, according to the narrator's intention, as Israel's most holy place of worship. In vss. 18-19 the pestilence episode is cemented to the following threshing-floor episode, and preparation is made for the conclusion of vs. 25a, by the insertion of a brief reference to the intervention of the prophet Gad, commanding David to rear an altar at that place. Thus the prophet's command is the turning-point of the entire story, a point of which we are

222. Vs. 5 begins with a circumstantial clause in inverse word-order. The verb לֹאמֹ may have been intended as a participle in the pre-Massoretic text (cf. BH³ mg).
223. We follow here the painstaking analysis of W. Fuss, "II Samuel 24," *ZAW*, 74 (1962), 145-64. An independent Jebusite cult-ideology underlies vss. 16, 20-24.

made doubly sure when we find here the words *bayyôm hahû'*. The narrator intends a synchronism, of course; i.e., he wants it understood that the angel's appearance and the dedication of David's altar both took place on the same day. But the phrase's primary function is to provide a sequence. Very likely the writer was influenced by his linguistic and conceptual tradition favoring the designation of such a day of solemn dignity as this in this familiar and time-honored way.

I Kings 8:64

Bayyôm hahû' is found in I Kings 8:64 in a literary expansion, clearly that of the deuteronomistic redactor. We class this passage as original in the sense that the new episode is original to the redactor. It introduces an afterthought into the Deuteronomist's long expansion of the original report concerning the dedication of Solomon's temple. After putting an elaborate prayer into the king's mouth and adding the words of his formal blessing upon the people, the redactor returns in vss. 62f. to an account of the more material aspects of the event as he imagined it. He reports now that Solomon offered sacrifice before Yahweh—an altogether likely procedure as such—but then exaggerates, beyond any possibility of historical actuality, the number of animals offered. Thereupon he is forced to posit some facility for accommodating Solomon's twenty-two thousand oxen and one hundred twenty thousand sheep. So vast a number of animals could never have been sacrificed on a single altar.[224] Hence the Deuteronomist adds as a necessary afterthought, "On that day the king consecrated the middle (את תוך) of the court that was before the house of Yahweh," continuing with a detailed explanation. Here we have, then, another example of the phrase *bayyôm hahû'*, standing at the very beginning, being used to introduce an artificial synchronism within the body of a pericope.

I Kings 16:16

It has long been apparent to biblical scholars that such reports as are found in I Kings 16:8ff., 15ff., 21ff. are drawn from official court records or annals, while the deuteronomistic historian-redactor is to be held responsible for the interpolated chronological and genealogical data, together with the stereotyped theological assessments regarding the various kings.[225] It is remarkable that we have in I Kings 16:16 the only instance

---

224. Regarding the altar involved, see K. Galling, "Altar," *IDB; idem* in *RGG*[3]. Cf. also M. Noth's comm., *in loco* (*BK*, IX).

225. Cf. Noth, *UGS*, pp. 73ff.; J. Gray, comm., *in loco*, etc. See now Shoshana R. Bin-Nun, "Formulas from Royal Records of Israel and of Judah," *VT*, 18 (1968), 414-32, stressing the formal differences between the king-lists of the respective realms and pointing out that the formulas in question must have a predeuteronomistic origin.

in which an annalistic record from the divided kingdom contains the phrase *bayyôm hahû'*.

The reason for its appearance here does not become clear until we observe that the two reports concerning Omri's accession, vss. 15ff. and 21ff., respectively, are in contradiction with each other and must accordingly come from different sources.[226] Vs. 22 states that Omri became king only when Tibni died. We observe also that according to vss. 16f. "all Israel" crowned Omri and went up with him against Tirzah, whereas only half the people followed him according to vss. 21f.

The difference in terminology respecting the supporting armies is not to be resolved simply by pointing to the fact that the "all Israel" of 16f. is equivalent to *hā'ām (ha)ḥōnîm* of 15f. "All Israel" appears, on the contrary, to denote specifically the sacral union assembled (actually or symbolically) for the purpose of crowning a new king (cf. I Sam. 11:11, 12:1, I Kings 12:1, 16).[227] Its presence here is a sure indication that Omri's designation came by popular acclamation. "All Israel" represents the unanimous consent, reacting in a time of crisis to the need for new charismatic leadership.

Another observation strengthens this conclusion. Immediately following Omri's coronation it is said that he led "all Israel" to Tirzah in order to deal with Zimri and deliver the nation. Omri thereby demonstrated that he was indeed Israel's true king. It may very well be that this entire story, including vss. 9, 10a,[228] 15b-18 in their original form, was intended as a legitimation for Omri's kingship.[229] It copies the general structure of the story of Saul's legitimation in I Sam. 11, including, like that chapter, (1) the crisis, (2) the designation or acclamation,[230] and (3) the victory. It certainly is more partisan to Omri than is the report contained in vss. 21f., which may have been added to the record by a scribe from the post-Omride period.[231]

---

226. Noth, *UGS*, p. 82, speaks of vss. 21f. as an "Anhang" to vss. 16ff.

227. This is unquestionably a northern tradition. Such a strongly Judean document as the throne-succession narrative avoids this expression (cf. I Kings 1:39f.).

228. Not only are the chronological data and the theological evaluations secondary; so also are the statements in vss. 10b-12 that Zimri reigned as king and exterminated the house of Baasha. The original story was concerned with Zimri only as a villain and usurper, whose crime led to the charismatic call of Omri.

229. It is important to observe that Zimri and Omri are the only two "kings" whose parentage is not mentioned in the biblical text; that they appear together as such in this passage strengthens our analysis. Zimri is identified only as *śar maḥ^aṣît hārākeb*, Omri only as *śar ṣābā'*. It is a mystery why at least Omri's lineage is not given, since he founded a dynasty (Bit-Ḥumri in Akkadian documents) known the world over. Since he was acclaimed as king according to the traditions of the sacral union, it is not likely that he was a foreign mercenary, as some scholars have suggested.

230. In I Sam. 11, Saul is first designated by the Spirit, next leads Israel to victory, is finally crowned.

231. The synchronism in Asa's thirty-first year (vs. 23), even if supplied by the deuteronomistic historian, depends on the report of vss. 21f. rather than on that of

The temporal phrase does not surprise us when seen in this setting. It is of course a synchronism, joining in time the act of crowning and the preceding report of the assassination. Together with the designation of place, "in the camp," at the end of the sentence, it serves also to stress the spontaneity of this event, at the same time stating the more enduring significance of the day in question, i.e., the designation of a new king. As such it may echo a more primitive form of the narrative in which vs. 16 functioned as a concluding epitome.

I Kings 22:35, II Chron. 18:34

Our next example is from a prophetic legend found in I Kings 22:35 (= II Chron. 18:34). This is cast against the background of international warfare, but is not to be considered as primarily a political-military document. It is intended, rather, as a demonstration of the power of Yahweh through the fulfillment of a prophetic word in the doom of a rebellious king.

Although the narrative of I Kings 22 envisages procedures remaining from the holy war (particularly the request for a preparatory oracle, vss. 5ff.),[232] its basic purpose is to demonstrate how a true prophet's word was fulfilled in the death of an Israelite king.[233] All interest focuses on this point. It is developed in the controversy between prophets and prophet, between prophet and king, and especially in the central oracle, vs. 17. It is dramatically restated in Micaiah's repartee of vs. 28. All of this is preparation for vss. 29-34, which tell of the central occurrence in the battle at Ramoth-gilead, viz., the death of the king. One should note that the narration at this point has a single, clearly defined aim, to tell of the king's inescapable fate; in spite of his disguise, he is at last fatally wounded by a stray arrow (dispatched, we are to understand, under Yahweh's direction). What comes, then, in vss. 35ff. is anticlimax. The narrator turns aside for a brief moment to indicate the course of the battle around the king's chariot ("and the battle increased on that day"). But this interests him as little as what happens to Israel's army, recorded in the appendix-like statement of vs. 36. The narrator brings all to a quick conclusion: following a circumstantial clause indicating the king's posture as his life ebbed away,[234] the story ends with the sober statement, "and he died at evening."[235] Then

---

vss. 16ff. The following statement of the length of Omri's reign represents an apparent attempt to account for both episodes together.

232. Cf. G. von Rad, Heilige Krieg, p. 54. It will be argued in Chapter Four that vss. 2-37 constitute two originally separate narratives.

233. Commentators rather generally agree that the king of Israel in this narrative was not Ahab, any more than Jehoshaphat was originally the king of Judah. Cf. J. Maxwell Miller, JBL, 85 (1966), 441-54.

234. Kings' מֶעֳמָד ("was propped up") appears to be more severe than Chronicles' מֶעֳמִיד ("propped himself up").

235. Chronicles displaces the temporal references while omitting the reference to

comes the notice about the dispersal of the army (36), an epitomizing statement that the king died and returned to Samaria, and an indication of the disposition of the king's body (37).

The time-references in these closing verses demand careful investigation. The phrase "at sunset" ($k^eb\bar{o}'$ $ha\check{s}\check{s}eme\check{s}$) has no independent theological significance; it is styled as a narrative variant to "at evening" ($b^e'ereb$), adding emphasis through repetition with variation, while making clear a very important synchronism, i.e., that the army dispersed when (and because) the king died. There is greater significance to the phrase "at evening." It does two things: (1) as a stylistic device it skillfully brings a denouement to the climactic occurrence of the king's wounding, retaining suspense to the last; (2) it designates a termination to the time covered by the phrase *bayyôm hahû'*, underscoring that the central issue produced by this particular day was resolved on that same day.

Hebrew narrative—and holy-war narrative in particular—tends to depict everything holistically, i.e., it telescopes into one decisive "day" an event and its consequences. This is clearly evident here. This is not to say that there is anything forced or unnatural about our story: many unfortunates wounded in battle die within a few hours, if not immediately. But the statement that the king's death came precisely at evening makes clear that our present narrative views this day as finished and complete, i.e., as a day of special, final and decisive encounter.[236] The phrase *bayyôm hahû'* has been introduced not only to indicate a time relationship, for it is perfectly clear that a battle was being fought at the time when the king was wounded. Unmistakably, it is also a signal to theological meaning. It indicates that the issues raised in the confrontation between prophet and king have been resolved. In one day Yahweh has demonstrated the power of his word.[237]

Jer. 39:10

In Jer. 39:10, at the very end of the verse,[238] the phrase *bayyôm hahû'* acts as a synchronism, joining in time Nebuzaradan's act of leaving

---

the army's dispersal; its reading is hardly to be preferred, *contra* J. Gray, comm., p. 398. Likewise precarious is the LXX, followed in one of its recensional readings by H. Seebaas in *VT*, 21 (1971), pp. 380-83. Vs. 35 has the temporal indication of when the king died; vs. 37 has an epitomizing recapitulation.

236. Note also how anxious the Gospels are to make clear that Jesus died and was buried on the same day he was crucified; perhaps more is involved in this concern than mere fastidiousness concerning the sabbath.

237. We would do well to consider what influences this account of a day of judgment upon one of Israel's kings, narrated according to the analogy of the holy war, may have had on the emergence of the idea of a day of Yahweh against Israel as a people. This may be particularly relevant in that judgment oracles against the nation originated out of judgment oracles against individuals (cf. C. Westermann, *Grundformen prophetischer Rede*, pp. 120-26.

238. John Bright's suggestion (*AB, in loco*) that *bayyôm hahû'* is an editorial link to vs. 11 is unlikely, since vs. 11 begins with a waw-consecutive imperfect.

the poor behind and his act of giving them vineyards and fields. Although opinions differ widely regarding the redactional provenance of this verse,[239] there can be little doubt but that it comes ultimately from some kind of memoir or annalistic report. It may be that the phrase *bayyôm hahû'*, missing in the parallel verse, Jer. 52:16 (= II Kings 25:12), was intended as a legal record testifying to the ownership of certain lands; as such it would have been of practical importance in the postexilic period, when returnees would have wished to reclaim their ancestral property.

Esth. 5:9, 8:1, 9:11

Temporal sequence is of great importance in the development of the book of Esther.[240] The only three occurrences of *bayyôm hahû'* mark the three episodes in the narrative where Esther makes bold to enter the king's presence with her request.

The occurrence in 5:9 immediately follows the episode in which the king agrees to Esther's invitation to dinner. The writer, in his often astonishing artfulness, evokes in his readers' imagination a feeling for the solemn fatefulness of this incident by interjecting at this precise point the phrase *bayyôm hahû'*. This is as if to suggest by association all the divine saving acts of Israel's ancient tradition, as epitomized elsewhere by that phrase. From this moment onward, Haman's fate is sealed. Ominously, he goes out "on that day," joyful, yet angry at the presence of his nemesis Mordecai.

In 8:1 the phrase immediately follows the account of Haman's hanging. Here *bayyôm hahû'* introduces a statement that the king gave Esther Haman's house; but the succeeding clause, with Mordecai as subject, introduces the remaining unfinished business in which Esther's renewed imploration will be the crucial factor, *viz.*, removing the ban upon the Jews.

The phrase appears once again in 9:11. Again it immediately precedes Esther's imploration—but now with little of the stylistic effectiveness evident in the first two occurrences. Not only is the narrative more sparse and rigid; what Esther asks for seems both trivial and offensive alongside her previous concerns; she requests the hanging of Haman's ten sons.[241]

---

239. E.g., W. Rudolph, *HAT*[2], *in loco*, and A. Weiser, *ATD*[4], *in loco*, seem to agree that vss. 3-14 are a secondary synopsis of 52:4-16. On the contrary, M. Noth, *UGS*, pp. 86f., believes that the deuteronomistic historian responsible for II Kings 25 and Jer. 52 has abridged original Baruch memoirs in Jer. 39—41, omitting specific reference to the prophet. J. P. Hyatt, *IB*, V, 790, ascribes all of Jer. 39—40 except 39:3, 14, to a D-writer.

240. Cf. Hans Striedl, "Untersuchungen zur Syntax und Stilistik des hebräischen Buches Esther," *ZAW*, 55 (1937), 73-108, especially pp. 106f. The LXX ἐν αὐτῇ τῇ ἡμέρᾳ in Esth. 8:1, 9:11 presupposes *hayyôm* (*hazzeh*) in its *Vorlage;* nevertheless our analysis seems to support the MT; also in 5:9, where the LXX (except the Hexaplaric text) lacks an equivalent to *bayyôm hahû'*.

241. The references to Haman's ten sons in vss. 7-10, 12 must be secondary additions, in view of Esther's request.

Rather than suspect a literary expansion at this point,[242] we need perhaps to recognize a simple weakening of the narrator's imaginative skill as he employs an artificial device—one rapidly becoming a stereotype—for incorporating etiological material concerning the second day of Purim.

All three occurrences provide transitions within a sequence of a number of fateful days, but, as we have seen, only the first two of them can be called crucial.

Neh. 12:43

It has been noted in our previous discussion[243] that Neh. 12:44ff. and 13:1ff. are secondary expansions. The memoirs of Nehemiah arrive at their climax in 12:43.[244] According to them, Nehemiah's work has reached completion; the wall is finished. To dedicate it, two processions march in opposite directions around the top of the wall (vss. 31, 32, 37-39), coming together at the temple (vs. 40). There is only one thing left to do: offer sacrifices and rejoice in public service before Yahweh. Nehemiah is familiar with the traditional usage respecting the phrase *bayyôm hahû'*, and accordingly uses it in vs. 43 to mark this final act of dedication as climactic. But the clause with *bayyôm hahû'* functions less as an epitomizing statement than as a sequential introduction to the final Godward act that gives the entire narrative its ultimate meaning. This day is seen as something memorable, not in itself, but as containing the festive event to which the entire work of Nehemiah has been proceeding.[245]

I Chron. 29:22

In this verse the Chronicler is bringing to a climax his long and extremely fanciful account of David's last peroration as he prepares to hand over the kingdom to Solomon (28:1—29:30).[246] We must bear in mind the programmatic character of this material if we are to understand the meaning of the time references in this and the preceding verse. Following David's

---

242. A secondary writer would scarcely have recognized the author's subtle device so as to imitate it; more likely, the original author tries, but fails, to use it as heretofore.

243. Above, p. 67.

244. Nehemiah's memoirs appear to continue in chap. 13, together with editorial material from the chronicler, but this is all anticlimactic; cf. Noth, *UGS*, p. 131; Rudolph, *HAT, in loco*. Galling, *ATD, in loco*, considers all of 12:41ff. to be secondary, but vs. 40 continues to hold the action in suspense. What would be the meaning of a procession without a final act of worship in sacrifice and praise (cf. the procession liturgy of the Psalter)?

245. The phrase nevertheless plainly signals one of Yahweh's mighty acts, though now in strictly cultic and institutional terms. It is no longer Yahweh who acts *bayyôm hahû'*, but the people who serve him.

246. Rudolph, *HAT, in loco*, sees 28:1ff. as terminating at 29:20, overlooking the apparent purpose of the entire section, i.e., to make the transition from David's to Solomon's reign and prepare for an account of the building of the temple.

prayer, terminating in a petition that Solomon may prove worthy to build the temple (29:10-19), the Chronicler has David prepare for Solomon's investiture by calling on the assembly to worship God (20). He continues in vss. 21f. with the following:

> And they sacrificed sacrifices ($z^e b\bar{a}h\hat{i}m$) to Yahweh, and they offered burnt offerings to Yahweh on the morrow of that day ($l^e m\bar{a}h^o rat\ hayy\hat{o}m\ hah\hat{u}'$),[247] a thousand bulls, a thousand rams, a thousand lambs, together with their (appropriate) drink offerings and numerous sacrifices ($z^e b\bar{a}h\hat{i}m\ l\bar{a}r\bar{o}b$) for all Israel, and they ate and drink before Yahweh on that day ($bayy\hat{o}m\ hah\hat{u}'$) with great rejoicing, and they made Solomon, son of David, king for the second time,[248] and anointed him as prince before Yahweh and Zadok as priest.

The problem is, of course, to punctuate this more meaningfully than can be done with a series of commas, and this can be done only by appropriately interpreting the indications of time. Noting that $z^e b\bar{a}h\hat{i}m$ are twice offered, the second time with exaggerated emphasis, we can follow the Chronicler's intention best by joining the first three words of vs. 21 to the preceding verse and commencing the narrative concerning the second day with ויעלו עלות. This produces the following sequence for the second day: (1) the offering of burnt offerings and drink offerings; (2) the sacrificing of sacrifices for all Israel; (3) eating and drinking with great rejoicing; (4) the investiture. For a statement regarding the eating and drinking, the Chronicler uses a combination of words found elsewhere in his writings for the climactic event of worship (cf. Neh. 13:46), including the phrase $bayy\hat{o}m\ hah\hat{u}'$, which is intended in this instance not as an indication of the time ("on the morrow of that day" had already performed that function) but as a signal that this is climactic. The statement in which this phrase occurs therefore has an epitomizing function. It terminates the account of activities leading up to the actual investiture of Solomon, formally preparing for it.[249]

Conclusion

Looking back over the passages just analyzed, we may make a number of observations. First, that while all the secondary transitions occur solely as beginning formulae, the ones that we have identified as due to oral supplementation (Gen. 26:32, 48:20) both turn out to function as synchronisms, although Gen. 48:20 seems to function secondarily as an epitome. The passages that we have identified as due to literary redaction have all turned out to be sequential links rather than mere synchronisms, which is not strange in view of the fact that all three (I Sam. 14:24, 31, II Sam.

---

247. LXX, τῇ ἐπαύριον τῆς πρώτης ἡμέρας, is interpretive.
248. Cf. 23:1.
249. Apparently Chr thought the first day to be already too crowded for all that he conceived of as occurring. As he has arranged his narrative, the first day is David's special day, the second day, Solomon's.

2:17) occur in narratives of ongoing history composed out of a variety of originally independent episodes.

Transitional formulae with *bayyôm hahû'*, when occurring in original contexts, display a more varied functional pattern. Only one of the original beginning formulae (I Kings 8:64) is a synchronism, and this is an unusual case because the entire account of which it is a part is redactional. The great majority of beginning formulae function as sequential links and, except in Esther (5:9, 8:1, 9:11), the sequence involved takes place within a single day (Gen. 30:35, I Sam. 4:12, 10:9, 12:18, 14:37, II Sam. 18:8, 19:4, 24:18, I Kings 22:35).

Two passages that elude classification either as beginning or ending transitional formulae are Judg. 20:26 and I Sam. 7:6, both of which have *bayyôm hahû'* following the verb צוֹם and occur in cultic narrative. In both passages the phrase in question helps fill the gap between the introduction and the conclusion of the particular episode. In both passages the fasting and associated cultic activities are immediately preliminary to the climactic event of the episode in question. The phrase functions essentially as a synchronism, though there is some possibility that we should recognize some kind of epitomizing force as well, especially in the Judges passage.[250]

The greatest number of transitional formulae within original pericopes appear at the end of episodes (Exod. 32:28, Judg. 20:21, I Sam. 31:6, II Sam. 18:7, 19:3 (1), I Kings 16:16, Jer. 39:10, I Chron. 29:22), and not surprisingly the largest number of such emulate concluding formulae at the end of entire pericopes, functioning to epitomize the event therein narrated. Thus the favorite function of *bayyôm hahû'* at the end, either of individual episodes or of entire pericopes, is clearly that of epitome. In II Sam. 19:3(2) the phrase functions as a synchronism, while in Neh. 12:43 it functions merely as a sequential link, albeit at the end of a sequence and with discernible echoes of the traditional epitomizing function. In I Sam. 9:24, 20:26, II Sam. 11:12, the phrase functions as a transitional link within sequences of more than a single day, closing off the narration of a first day in preparation for that of a second.

5. Narrative elements in nonnarrative pericopes

Up to this point we have discussed the occurrence of *bayyôm hahû'* in the narration of past events solely in narrative pericopes. This leaves us with a very small number of passages which should be discussed separately because (1) they occur in first-person discourse rather than in objective, third-person narration, and (2) their immediately purpose is not the simple

---

250. In Samuel this function is performed primarily by the statement of Samuel's judging.

recollection of past events, as such, but exhortation and warning concerning the hearers' or readers' present or very recent past. *Bayyôm hahû'* is found to introduce or accompany narrative elements in two distinct kinds of discourse: deuteronomistic-parenetic and prophetic. The examples of deuteronomistic discourse are themselves embedded in narrative literature, whereas the examples of prophetic discourse form part of the oracular collection.

a. Deuteronomistic

Num. 32:10

Scholarly opinions have differed widely regarding the literary composition of Num. 32, which records the granting of lands east of the Jordan to the Reubenites and Gadites (along with the half-tribe of Manasseh in the closing verses). Rather than attempt here a detailed review of proposed solutions, suffice it to point out that (1) although there is no sufficient reason to deny that vss. 5-15 constitute a literary unity, this is obviously a late supplement to the introductory elements in the chapter; (2) this section is familiar with the primitive Pentateuchal story of Num. 13-14, but in the form known by the deuteronomistic historian (Deut. 1:26-45, Josh. 14:6-15).[251] It is not necessary to assume, with some writers, that this passage is familiar with P.[252] The passage as a whole exhibits the style and spirit of the deuteronomistic school,[253] as is particularly evident in the way it reviews Israel's past history as a basis for parenesis concerning the present. A careful examination of its content will also reveal the similarity of its form, apparent in spite of its peculiar point of view, to Ezekiel's great chapter on Israel's apostasy, chap. 20.[254]

Like a number of prophetic oracles, Moses' reply to the sons of Gad and the sons of Reuben in vss. 6-7 begins with denunciatory questions.[255]

---

251. The most striking item of affinity with the Deuteronomist is the expression מלא אחרי in vss. 11, 12, which occurs elsewhere only in Num. 14:24 (its apparent place of origin), Josh. 14:8f., 14, Deut. 1:36, I Kings 11:6. All these references except the last are to Caleb (with Joshua), as contrasted to rebellious Israel; the Kings passage refers to David in contrast to Solomon. We take particular note also of the name Kadesh-barnea, as in Deut. 1:19, Josh. 14:6f. For other details, see the commentaries.

252. E.g., G. B. Gray, *ICC, in loco*. The reference to Joshua alongside Caleb, here and in Deut. 1:38, may have influenced P, rather than the other way around.

253. Cf. M. Noth, *ATD*, 7, *in loco:* "Er gehört damit zu dem Stadium der Zusammenarbeitung von Pentateucherzählung und deuteronomistischen Geschichtswerk."

254. In Ezek. 20:1-4 the present generation is reproached by the question impugning their motive for seeking an oracle; in vss. 5-29 the "abominations of their fathers" are recounted in a pattern of threefold repetition; in vss. 30f. (the threat) this is applied in judgment on the present generation (see below). Cf. W. Zimmerli, *BK*, XIII, *in loco*.

255. Cf. Ezek. 34:2, Amos 9:7, Mic. 3:1, Nah. 3:8, Hag. 1:3, etc.

The first question insinuates that these tribes are shirking their duty of sharing in the coming warfare; it is calibrated to the preceding narrative context. This leads to the second, in which the reproach is focused more sharply as that of becoming a hindrance ("discouraging," נוא hif.)[256] to Israel's entering the promised land. Following this introductory denunciation, the address launches in the fashion of Ezek. 20:4 ("Let them know the abominations of their fathers . . .") into a statement of what the fathers and Yahweh did at Kadesh-barnea (vss. 8-13).[257] Their sin was the identical sin with which Gad and Reuben are now charged: keeping Israel from the promised land (8-9). The result was the kindling of Yahweh's wrath (twice repeated: 10, 13) "on that day," leading first to Yahweh's oath of purging (11-12) and next to the act of purging that generation (13), except for Caleb and Joshua, "who wholly followed Yahweh." Finally comes the charge to this present "brood[258] of sinful men" (vss. 14-15); it is very similar to the invective-threat pattern of the judgment oracle, such as appears at the end of the historical review in Ezek. 20:30f., except that it is still shaped predominantly by the concern for parenesis and hence takes the form of accusation-warning. Here we should observe especially the alliterative parallelism between *lispôt 'ôd* in vs. 14[259] (man's action) and *weyāsap 'ôd* in vs. 15 (Yahweh's action), emphatically reiterating the connection between God's act in the past and God's action in the present.

This seems more than idle literary embellishment. So pointed is the parenesis of this pericope, particularly in the closing words, "And so you will destroy all this people," that we yearn to know to which particular historical event it was addressed. Was the writer "preaching" to postexilic Transjordanians who would not cooperate in rebuilding Jerusalem? It is idle to speculate. Nor can we be absolutely sure how the phrase *bayyôm hahû'* was intended. That it establishes a transitional synchronism (and hence causal connective) between the sin at Kadesh and Yahweh's disastrous anger is apparent. We may doubt that the double reference to this anger, together with *bayyôm hahû'*, deliberately intends to epitomize the day in question as a day of divine wrath. If this were so, its occurrence as epitome at the beginning of a new element in the formal schema would have to be recognized as highly unusual, the only other approximate example occurring at the very beginning of the deuteronomistic intrusion in Josh. 4:14.

---

256. See the *qere*, also vs. 9. This verb is found elsewhere at Num. 30:6, 9, 12, Ps. 33:10. There is no direct denunciation of the spies in J (Num. 13−14); P (in Num. 14:36) accuses them of causing the people to murmur (לון hif.); Deut. 1:28, Josh. 14:8 speak of them as melting (מסס, מסה hif.) the people's heart.

257. There is a jarring gap between the "fathers" of Gad and Reuben on the one hand and the "fathers" in the wilderness (= all Israel of that generation except Caleb and Joshua). Since it is unlikely that the writer was intending to place the sole blame for the Kadesh apostasy on the ancestors of the Gadites and Reubenites, this strengthens the impression of this being a forced and artificial polemic.

258. תרבות, *hapax legomenon*.

259. Cf. BH[3] mg.

Josh. 14:9, 12

The pericope Josh. 14:6aβ-15, which shows strong affinities to Deut. 1:19ff., intrudes into the original literary framework of its immediate context; it is clearly identifiable as part of the deuteronomistic redaction.[260] This passage manifests, moreover, a doubly programmatic character: (1) it establishes the forty-year pattern for the chronological structure basic to the deuteronomistic history,[261] and (2) it creates a place in the Deuteronomist's late and historically artificial portrait of the conquest for the incorporation of the very primitive, heretofore unsuccessfully assimilated, Caleb traditions.[262]

It is the first of these purposes that draws the reader's attention. One is impressed by the threefold *bayyôm hahû'* and the repetition of other words for time,[263] but especially by Caleb's self-conscious references to his age, emphatically establishing the temporal connection between the "then" of Moses' promise and the "now" of Caleb's request. But it is the second purpose, that of accommodating the Caleb traditions to the normative view of the conquest, that is the more essentially dominant in determining the structure of this pericope.

There is no need to analyze this passage in great detail. The vehicle for expressing the chronological interest is the artificial form of the farewell address, in which the patriarch reviews the past and makes his last appeal. But of course, this is not the end for Caleb; he pointedly mentions his undiminished strength for war, in spite of his eighty-five years (vs. 11). Having established (1) his right to Hebron and (2) his ability to conquer it, he receives it as his inheritance. Thus it is the etiology of the Calebite claim to Hebron that in fact dominates the structure of this account. *Bayyôm hahû'* in vs. 9 is a synchronism connecting Yahweh's oath to Caleb's deed; it is merely echoed in the same function in the appeal of vs. 12a, where an explicit connection is drawn from the promise to its anticipated fulfillment. In vs. 12b the phrase serves again as a synchronism, now introducing the report of the unconquered Anakim as a supplementary motivation for Caleb's appeal.

It is extremely interesting that in this passage and in Num. 32:5ff. the phrase *bayyôm hahû'* has no special formal place, as it has in much of the original preexilic literature. We may say that in these two passages it is a mere temporal connective, but an emphatic one, employed to strengthen the contrast between the exemplary past and the challenging present. For some reason, both these passages draw from the Caleb-Kadesh tradition. In

---

260. Cf. M. Noth, *UGS*, pp. 24, 44, and comm., *in loco.*
261. Cf. *ibid.*, pp. 18-27.
262. Cf. S. J. De Vries, "The Origin of the Murmuring Tradition," *JBL*, 87 (1968), 51-58.
263. *Wᵉ'attâ*, 10, 12; *hayyôm*, 10, 11; *bᵉyôm...*, 11; *mē'āz ... 'āz*, 10, 11; *'ad hayyôm hazzeh*, 14; *lᵉpānîm*, 15.

the original Deuteronomic lawbook and parenesis (Deut. 5–30) the phrase *bayyôm hahû'* is lacking altogether,[264] even though it is there that the then-now pattern reflected in these two late passages is firmly established.[265]

b. Prophetic

Isa. 22:8, 12

Much of the confusion surrounding the interpretation of the judgment oracle in Isa. 22:1-14, and particularly such as has been created by Duhm's attempt to separate vs. 8a from vs. 8b,[266] has been effectively cleared away by Brevard S. Childs's analysis of this passage in his monograph, *Isaiah and the Assyrian Crisis.*[267] Childs has shown that vss. 1-4 introduce an invective in which the prophet reproaches the people for unjustified rejoicing (in which he himself refuses to participate, vs. 4); further, that the invective is made more specific in vss. 5-13, where the people's inappropriate response to "a day of tumult and trampling and confusion"—i.e., a day of military crisis lying in the immediate past—is dramatically described; and finally, that vs. 14 contains a threat in the form of a succinct *Auditionsbericht.*

This analysis is strengthened by a careful inspection of the way in which *bayyôm hahû'* is used at the beginning of successive strophes in vs. 8 and vs. 12. In both verses the temporal phrase follows a thematic verb. In vs. 8 the verb is *wattabbēṭ*, with the addressees (singular, immediately changing to plural) as subject; this is followed by a series of imperfect consecutives indicating the self-assertive actions undertaken by the addressees in defense of their city; the strophe concludes with the pointed reproach, "But you did not look to him who did it," etc., vs. 11. In vs. 12 the verb is *wayyiqrā'*, this time with "the Lord Yahweh of Hosts" as subject; now the contrast between God's intent and man's action is drawn, not by repetition of the verb as in 8b-11, but by the juxtaposition of Yahweh's summons to a fast on the one hand and the picture of uninhibited regalement on the other.

In both instances *bayyôm hahû'* functions as a synchronism, but the purpose of the double synchronism is anything but casual. It is to draw an emphatic contrast between what the situation called for and what the people did. "In that day" refers back explicitly to "the day of tumult, etc.," of vs. 5. We are misled when we too simplistically speak of this as "the day of Yahweh"—i.e., identify it as a mere metaphorical variant for a

---

264. Except in secondary passages, as 27:11.
265. See our discussion below concerning *hayyôm* in Deuteronomy.
266. *Das Buch Jesaja* (Göttingen, 1892), *in loco*, followed by the majority of modern interpreters; cf. RSV.
267. SBT, 2nd ser. 3, Naperville, 1967, pp. 22-27.

conventional concept.[268] We can get Isaiah's meaning better when we translate literally, "For the day of tumult and trampling and confusion is (belongs) to the Lord Yahweh of Hosts." The prophet means to interpret the just-experienced political-military crisis theologically, therefore he identifies it as belonging to Yahweh (whose role as Lord of history is emphasized in the sonorous title, purposely repeated in vss. 12, 15). In vss. 5b-8a (beginning with "in the valley of vision") he goes on to depict this "day of tumult, etc.," explaining it at the end as being due to the fact that *Yahweh* had taken away "the covering" of Judah, i.e., its own effective military defense. But the people understood neither the crisis nor its apparently temporary removal in a theological way, so they trusted in their defenses when they should have trusted Yahweh, and they reveled when they should have wept.

Ezek. 20:6

The only other passage in the prophetic literature where *bayyôm hahû'* appears within an invective is Ezek. 20:3ff. The important difference between the use of the phrase in this passage and the last is that Isaiah uses it in reference to the immediate past while in Ezekiel it refers to a past that is both remote and paradigmatic. It has been pointed out in our preceding analysis of Num. 32:10 that *bayyôm hahû'* in that passage shares with Ezek. 20:6 the peculiarity of pertaining to the divine oath of swearing. In Numbers this was in an oath of destruction; here in Ezekiel it is in an oath of promise.

The resemblance to Num. 32 should in itself be sufficient to alert us to the central significance of the divine swearing for analyzing the function of *bayyôm hahû'* in our present passage. This awareness is reinforced by the observation that the expression, "I raised my hand," occurs no fewer than three times in vss. 5-6 (twice as imperfect consecutive, a third time as perfect).[269] To the casual reader this repetition may seem boring and meaningless, but a sensitive analysis of the parallelism in these verses reveals that the repetition is both deliberate and effective. While it is true that the original oracle of Ezek. 20:1-31 seems to lack an absolutely regular meter,[270] a persistent parallelism does present itself as a sure indication of

---

268. Cf. G. von Rad, "The Origin of the Concept of the Day of Yahweh," *JSS*, 4 (1959), 97-108. See our analysis of *yôm* future in Chapter One.

269. The LXX text in vs. 5 reads וְאוֹדִעַ twice rather than וָאֶשָּׂא יָדִי. Our analysis of poetic structure does not favor the LXX over the MT. Num. 32:10 has the root שׁבע used for the divine swearing everywhere but in Num. 14:30 P, Ezek. 20:5f., 15, 23, where נשׂא יד is substituted. Because Num. 14:30 and Ezek. 20:15 clearly refer to an early tradition of divine swearing in the spy story, we are unable to accept the proposal of Johan Lust (*Traditie, Redactie en Kerygma bij Ezechiel*, Brussels, 1969) that נשׂא יד means "act powerfully (in salvation or judgment)."

270. Cf. W. Zimmerli, *BK*, XII, 440, *contra* Lust. The lack of unanimity in arranging this pericope will not justify treating it as simple prose.

the essentially poetic nature of this pericope. The Hebrew text of the divine oracle in vss. 5-6 should be arranged as follows:

כה אמר אדני יהוה

ביום בחרי בישראל   ואשא ידי לזרע בית יעקב

ואודע להם בארץ מצרים   ואשא ידי להם לאמר   אני יהוה אלהיכם

ביום ההוא נשאתי ידי להם   להוציאם מארץ מצרים

אל ארץ אשר תרתי להם   זבת חלב ודבש   צבי היא לכל הארצות

Here is a rather tight and complex pattern. The second stich of 5a offers alternatives for the verb and the object; this means that the imperfect consecutive *wā'eśśā' yādî* in 5a is parallel to the infinitive *bāḥ°rî*, so that both together must be taken as characterizing "the day when." But the pattern of imperfect consecutives continues in 5b, which balances 5a; *wā'iwwāda*ʿ and the second *wā'eśśā' yādî* are intended as parallel to each other and to the verbs in 5a. Thus *wā'eśśā' yādî* is twice repeated, the second time with a citation of the covenantal words by which Yahweh identified himself. The progression, then, is in the fullness and specificity with which the divine swearing is characterized: the first time only the object is identified; the second time the subject identifies himself; the third time, in vs. 6, the promise contained in Yahweh's oath is delineated, and it is this that constitutes the real goal of this recital of his ancient favors to Israel.

Functionally considered, *bayyôm hahû'* is a synchronism, joining in time the action of vs. 6 and the action of vs. 5. But since the parallelism indicates the divine oath of each verse to be the same, the intent of the text must be to make a temporal connection between the oath and the two saving acts of election and self-revelation. This combination of theologoumena is made also in the story of Moses' call, particularly the P version of it (Exod. 6:2-9).[271]

Zech. 11:11

A myriad of problems of various kinds still surround the interpretation of the enigmatic passage concerning the shepherd and the two staffs in Zechariah 11; it seems that some of the most recent analyses create almost as many difficulties as they resolve.[272] The safest course appears to be that

271. Although the prophet's conception of the primitive *Heilsfeiten* shows several peculiarities, it is clear that Ezekiel and P draw from the same source of tradition. P substitutes God's covenant with the patriarchs for the theologoumenon of Israel's election, but like the late form of JE (Exod. 3) and Ezekiel, joins this with the self-revelation and the promise.

272. See now especially Benedikt Otzen, *Studien Ueber Deuterosacharja* (Acta Theologica Danica, 6, Copenhagen, 1964), pp. 146-68. Otzen identifies vss. 11-13

of following such a sober, yet imaginative and suggestive treatment as that of Karl Elliger, [273] who on the one hand arrives through judicious text- and literary criticism at the point of delineating an understandable structure for the pericope as originally set forth, and on the other hand places the passage in an historical context that gives it some meaningful impact, namely the time (probably in the years immediately following the Greek invasion) when a final rupture was taking place, or had recently taken place, between Jerusalem and Samaria.

With respect to tradition-historical development, it is apparent that Zech. 11:3ff. has been strongly influenced by two Ezekiel passages, 34:1ff. (a denunciation of the shepherds who prey upon the sheep) and 37:15ff. (a symbolic act involving the uniting of the two sticks "for Judah" and "for Joseph"). Nevertheless, the present passage is neither a judgment nor a symbolic-act oracle. It is rather an extended allegory in which a prophet representing the Jerusalem cultus attempts to legitimize the break with Samaria. [274]

Although certain features of the allegory remain unclear, a close study of the form is helpful in revealing what the writer had in mind. The original pericope of vss. 3-14 (omitting 6 and 8a) breaks down into two main sections, each with two subsections. The theme of the first main section, vss. 4-7bα, is the establishment of the shepherding office, while the theme of the second main section, 7bβ-14, is the dissolution of that office. In the first main section we find first the divine summons (including a modified herald formula, 4a; the commission, 4b; and the motivation, 5);

---

as secondary; the "covenant" is the covenant with David; the three shepherds of 8a are the three kings of the United Monarchy; the breaking of the first staff is the fall of the northern kingdom, the breaking of the second staff is the fall of the south (cf. especially p. 158). The general trend of Otzen's argument is toward a date for Second Zechariah radically earlier than that generally held.

273. *ATD*, 24/25, *in loco*. In Elliger's analysis vss. 6, 8a, 15ff. are late additions to 4ff. He joins the majority of critics in assigning most of Second Zechariah to the early Hellenistic period.

274. This conclusion seems to justify itself over against the interpretation proposed in Magne Saebø, *Sacharja 9—14, Untersuchungen von Text und Form* (WMANT, 34, Neukirchen, 1969), pp. 234-52, to the effect that an actual symbolic prophecy of Zechariah has been recast into expanded form. The artificiality of the symbolic act is clear in that it does not actually proceed according to the formal schema of the symbolic-act oracle in classical prophecy (see G. Fohrer, "Die Gattung der Berichte über die symbolische Handlungen der Propheten," *Studien zur alttestamentliche Prophetie*, BZAW, 99, Berlin, 1967, pp. 92-112), and in that the sign and the thing signified are constantly intertwined. The "flock doomed to slaughter" seems to signify the Israelite worshipers of Ephraim whom Jerusalem was trying to bring within its cultic orbit during the postexilic period. Those who bought and sold them (identical to the ironically intended $k^e na'^a n\hat{e}\ hass\bar{o}'n$ in vss. 7, 11) are their cultic and political leaders, some of whom may have claimed prerogatives in, and perhaps jurisdiction over, the Jerusalem temple. Just exactly who "their own shepherds (who) have no pity on them" are, is not clear. Though the prophet himself poses as the new shepherd, it is likely that he is symbolizing the political-cultic leader of the temple community, i.e., the high priest.

this is followed by a report of the prophet's response, which includes the act of compliance (7a) and the taking and naming of the two staffs (7bα). The names signify the purpose of the shepherding, which is to establish (or reestablish) the covenant and brotherhood of Israel (cf. vss. 10, 14).

In the second main section the breaking of these two staffs constitutes the basic structural element, defining the two respective subsections. First the covenant is dissolved: we find the report of a falling out between the shepherd and his sheep (7bβ, 8b), a report of his reciting a formula of annulment (9), a report of the symbol of annulment (10),[275] and a climactic statement of the fact of annulment (11a). Next the brotherhood is dissolved: it is reported (11b) that *hakkᵉna'ᵃnê hassō'n*,[276] to whom the shepherd was ostensibly responsible, accepted the symbol of annulment as divinely sanctioned ("It was the word of Yahweh"); next comes the report of the payment of the shepherd's hire (12); next is a report of Yahweh's estimation of this payment, including the oracular command and the report of compliance (13);[277] finally there is the report of the prophet's symbolic act (14).

Since we have so little historical information upon which to judge the bearing of this pericope, it is difficult to say whether the breaking of the respective staffs is intended as parallel or sequential. The likelihood is that they refer to sequentially connected rather than identical occurrences. The first episode, leading to the breaking of the covenant, seems to have proceeded on the initiative of the Jerusalemite "shepherd" portrayed by the prophet. The second episode, leading to the dissolution of the brotherhood, appears to involve the spiteful response of those who stood over against him and to whom he was in some respect answerable. In any event, it is important to see that *bayyôm hahû'* in vs. 11a does not function as a synchronism between these two episodes. If this were so, it would have modified the verb "knew" rather than the verb "was annulled." Thus *bayyôm hahû'* functions in what is essentially an epitome, stating the final result and purpose to which the entire episode had been proceeding. That the phrase is present here and absent at the end of vs. 14 may express the prophet's realization that the theological issue involved in the dissolution of the covenant was more portentous than the political-cultural issue involved in the dissolution of the "brotherhood." In any event, he seems to have been aware, even at his late date, that *bayyôm hahû'* was a suitable linguistic

---

275. Here and in vs. 14, the infinitive with ל expresses the purpose, not the result, of the symbolic act. Only in vs. 11a is a result stated.
276. Cf. LXX and BH³ mg, adopted by most modern interpreters. This group seems to have been responsible for supervising the "shepherd," interpreting divine oracles, and managing the public finance (unless the reference to the wages remains entirely within the scope of the shepherding allegory).
277. There can be no mistaking the sense of derision and outrage suffusing the terms of payment and the prophetic reaction to it. Matt. 26:14 is not obtuse to the intended irony (cf. Matt. 27:9).

vehicle for identifying and characterizing a day [278] of more than ordinary decisiveness in the history of God's people.

Conclusion

Thus the four deuteronomistic occurrences and the three occurrences within prophetic invective function as synchronisms, yet with an unmistakable awareness that *bayyôm hahû'* has been hallowed by Hebrew tradition as a term specially suitable for connecting events associated with some special day of God's revelatory action. The epitome of Zech. 11:11 is an astounding reincarnation of this ancient usage. Indeed, it may be said that these late non-narrative passages, few as they may be, show this awareness of the revelatory significance of God's day of action much more clearly than do a great many of the early passages in which *bayyôm hahû'* is seen to function as no more than a casual connection of events. In other words, this phrase is moving in late biblical tradition toward becoming a fixed theological *terminus technicus*—at any rate when it refers to the past. Whether this is also true when it refers to the future remains to be seen.

6. Interpretation: The day past as a moment of revelatory confrontation

Having arrived at the end of examining independently each occurrence of *bayyôm hahû'* where this refers to the past, we may draw together some major conclusions and attempt to suggest important consequences for a new assessment of the biblical understanding of time.

It may be helpful to the reader to present first a tabular summary of the formal functions of *bayyôm hahû'* as this occurs in the various passages. We have indicated these functions in Table 1, arranging them in five separate columns to indicate respectively: mere synchronism (I), sequence of one or more days (II-A, II-B), identification (III), and epitome (IV). Each passage, listed according to its literary character, structure, and/or purpose, has been placed in its proper column to indicate the primary function of *bayyôm hahû'*. This table, interpreted in the light of our extensive preceding discussion, speaks largely for itself. We are immediately struck that most passages of a secondary character use *bayyôm hahû'* as a synchronism, though its use in this function is not restricted to such passages; also that its use as an indicator of sequence occurs almost exclusively in original materials; and especially that when it is used as an

---

278. Certainly *bayyôm hahû'* means far more than "then." The prophet had in mind one particular fateful day when all efforts at cooperation between Ephraim and Judah came to a final and decisive end.

Table 1
The Expression *bayyôm hahû'* in Reference to the Past:
Formal Function in Relation to Literary Character, Structure, and Purpose

Formal Function				
Synchronism[a]	Sequence: one day	Sequence: more than one day	Time-identification	Epitome
I	II-A	II-B	III	IV

Literary character, structure, purpose
1. Gloss
   a. Unassociated (editorial or scribal):

Exod. 5:6[b]				
Num. 9:6(2)[b]				
Josh. 10:35 *bis*				
Ezek. 23:38, 39				
I Chron. 16:7[b]				

   b. Redactional:

II Kings 3:6				

2. Incorporating supplements to original material
   a. Interpretive comment:

				Josh. 4:14
			Josh. 6:15	
I Sam. 14:18				

   b. Independent material:

Deut. 27:11				
Judg. 5:1				
I Sam. 3:2				
I Sam. 21:11				
II Sam. 5:8				

   c. Narrative expansion

Num. 9:6(1)[c]				
Josh. 10:28				
Judg. 20:15				
I Sam. 21:8[c]				
I Sam. 22:22[c]				
Neh. 12:44				
Neh. 13:1				

3. Concluding formula
   a. Within secondary materials

Deut. 31:22				
				Josh. 8:25
				Judg. 20:46
I Sam. 6:15				
I Sam. 27:6				

continued

Table 1 (continued)

Synchronism[a] I	Sequence: one day II-A	Sequence: more than one day II-B	Time- identification III	Epitome IV
			II Sam. 6:9	
				II Chron. 35:16

b. Within original contexts:

				Gen. 15:18
				Gen. 33:16
				Exod. 14:30
				Josh. 9:27
				Josh. 24:25
				Judg. 3:30
				Judg. 4:23
				Judg. 6:32
				Judg. 20:35
				I Sam. 6:16
				I Sam. 7:10
				I Sam. 14:23
				I Sam. 18:2
				I Sam. 22:18
				II Sam. 3:37
				II Sam. 23:10
				II Chron. 15:11

4. Transitional formula between episodes
   a. Incorporating secondary material as a separate episode:
Gen. 26:32
Gen. 48:20

	I Sam. 14:31			
	II Sam. 2:17			

   b. Original to the context:
      (1) At the beginning of new episodes

	Gen. 30:35			
	I Sam. 4:12			
	I Sam. 10:9			
	I Sam. 12:18			
	I Sam. 14:24			
	I Sam. 14:37			
II Sam. 18:8				
	II Sam. 19:4			
	II Sam. 24:18			
I Kings 8:64				
	I Kings 22:35			
		Esth. 5:9		
		Esth. 8:1		
		Esth. 9:11		

continued

Table 1 (continued)

Synchronism[a] I	Sequence: one day II-A	Sequence: more than one day II-B	Time- identification III	Epitome IV
(2) In the middle of episodes Judg. 20:26 I Sam. 7:6				
(3) At the end of episodes				Exod. 32:28 Judg. 20:21
		I Sam. 9:24 I Sam. 20:26		I Sam. 31:6
		II Sam. 11:12		II Sam. 18:7 II Sam. 19:3(1)
II Sam. 19:3(2) I Kings 16:16 Jer. 39:10				
	Neh. 12:43[d]			I Chron. 29:22
5. Narrative elements in nonnarrative pericopes a. Deuteronomistic Num. 32:10 Josh. 14:9 Josh. 14:12 *bis*				
b. Prophetic Isa. 22:8 Isa. 22:12 Ezek. 20:6				Zech. 11:11

[a] All artificial except I Sam. 10:9, I Kings 16:16, Isa. 22:8, 12, Jer. 39:10, Ezek. 20:6.
[b] Superfluous as well as artificial because of original time-designation in the text.
[c] Narrative introduction to independent materials.
[d] End of sequence.

epitome it occurs most often in original material and at the end of the pericope in question.

The greatest benefit may be derived from the study of Table 1 when the respective passages are listed in a separate table according to their order of occurrence and with reference to the formal genre of the structures in which they are found, together with the probable individual, group, or institution responsible for originating or transmitting the passage in question. This we have done in Table 2. Again, the table pretty well speaks for itself.

Table 2
Bayyôm hahû' Past:
Analysis of Form and Tradition Background[a]

Literary character		Primary func-tion[b]	Genre: individual (and contextual)	Originator/tradent: primary (and secondary)[c]
Original	Secondary			
Gen. 15:18		IV	promise (covenant narrative)	Abraham tribe (J history)
	Gen. 26:32	I	local etiology (ethno-logical saga)	Beersheba shrine (J history)
	30:35	II-A	ethnological saga	Jacob tribe (J history)
33:16		IV	ethnological saga (itin-erary narrative)	"
	48:20	I	blessing (ethnological saga)	Shechem shrine
Exod. 14:30		IV	deliverance narrative	central shrine
32:28		IV	legitimation narrative	Levitical circles
	Num. 9:6(1)	I	cult narrative	P supplementer
Num. 32:10		I	quasi parenesis	Dtr redaction
	Deut. 27:11	I	editorial connective (covenant ceremony)	"
	31:22	I	editorial connective	D supplementer
	Josh. 4:14	IV	interpretive comment (legitimation narrative)	Dtr redaction
	6:15	III	interpretive comment (holy-war narrative)	Gilgal shrine (central shrine)
	8:25	IV	casualty report (holy-war narrative)	"
Josh. 9:27		IV	ethnological saga (holy-war narrative)	" "
	10:28	I	holy-war narrative	central shrine (early redaction)
14:9		I	quasi-farewell address	Dtr redaction
14:12 *bis*		I	"	"
24:25		IV	covenant narrative	Shechem shrine
Judg. 3:30		IV	hero saga (holy-war narrative)	Benjamin tribe (Gilgal shrine)
4:23		IV	holy-war narrative	Tabor shrine? (central shrine)
	Judg. 5:1	I	editorial connective (holy-war narrative)	early redaction
6:32		IV	etymological etiology (holy-war narrative)	northern shrine
	20:15	I	editorial expansion (quasi holy-war nar-rative)	early redaction
20:21		IV	casualty report (quasi holy-war narrative)	Bethel shrine (central shrine)

continued

Table 2 (continued)

Literary character		Primary func-tion[b]	Genre: individual (and contextual)	Originator/tradent: primary (and secondary)[c]
Original	Secondary			
20:26		I	ritual narrative (quasi holy-war narrative)	"
				"
20:35		IV	casualty report (quasi holy-war narrative)	"
				"
	20:46	IV	"	early redaction
	I Sam. 3:2	I	theophany narrative (legitimation narrative)	Shiloh shrine (prophetic circles)
I Sam. 4:12		II-A	hieros logos	Jerusalem shrine
	6:15	I	cult etiology (hieros logos)	Bethshemesh shrine? (Jerusalem cult-history?)
6:16		IV	hieros logos	Jerusalem shrine
7:6		I	ritual narrative (holy-war narrative)	Mizpah shrine (central shrine)
7:10		IV	holy-war narrative	"
9:24		II-B	legitimation narrative	Gilgal shrine
10:9		II-A	"	"
12:18		II-A	sign narrative (covenant narrative, farewell address)	Gilgal/Mizpah shrine (Dtr redaction)
	14:18	I	interpretive comment (holy-war narrative)	late redaction
14:23		IV	holy-war narrative	Gilgal shrine
14:24		II-A	hero saga (holy-war narrative)	Saul's army (Gilgal shrine)
	14:31	II-A	hieros logos (holy-war narrative)	local shrine (Gilgal shrine)
14:37		II-A	hero saga (holy-war narrative)	Saul's army (Gilgal shrine)
18:2		IV	hero saga	Saul's army (court)
20:26		II-B	accession history	David's court, Jerusalem
	21:8	I	editorial connective (accession history)	"
	21:11	I	"	"
22:18		IV	casualty report (accession history)	Saul's court (David's court, Jerusalem)
	22:22	I	editorial connective (accession history)	David's court, Jerusalem
	27:6	I	local etiology (accession history)	David's court, Hebron (Jerusalem)
31:6		IV	casualty report (charismatic legend, accession history)	Jabesh shrine (David's court, Jerusalem)
	II Sam. 2:17	II-A	hero saga (accession history)	David's army (court, Jerusalem)

continued

Table 2 (continued)

Literary character		Primary function[b]	Genre: individual (and contextual)	Originator/tradent: primary (and secondary)[c]
Original	Secondary			
II Sam. 3:37		IV	legitimation narrative (accession history)	David's court, Jerusalem
	5:8	I	battle report, cult etiology (accession history)	David's army, Jerusalem shrine? (David's court, Jerusalem)
	6:9	III	cult etiology (hieros logos)	local shrine (Jerusalem shrine)
11:12		II-B	throne-succession narrative	Solomon's court
18:7		IV	casualty report (throne-succession narrative)	David's army (Solomon's court)
18:8		II-A	throne-succession narrative	Solomon's court
19:3(1)		IV	"	"
19:3(2)		I	"	"
19:4		II-A	"	"
23:10		IV	hero saga (holy-war narrative)	David's army (Jerusalem shrine)
24:18		II-A	hieros logos	Jerusalem temple
I Kings 8:64		I	expansion to temple-consecration narrative	Dtr redaction
16:16		I	legitimation narrative (annalistic extract)	Omri's army (court records)
22:35		II-A	battle report (prophet legend)	northern army (prophetic circles)
	II Kings 3:6	I	quasi holy-war narrative	Dtr redaction
Isa. 22:8		I	judgment oracle	Isaiah school
22:12		I	"	"
Jer. 39:10		I	annalistic report	Baruch memoirs
Ezek. 20:6		I	judgment oracle	Ezekiel school
Zech. 11:11		IV	symbolic act, allegorical legitimation oracle	postexilic prophet school
Esth. 5:9		II-B	folk history	late Jewish
8:1		II-B	"	"
9:11		II-B	"	"
Neh. 12:43		II-A	ritual narrative	Nehemiah memoirs
	Neh. 12:44	I	secondary expansion	Chr redaction
	13:1	I	"	"
I Chron. 29:22		IV	ritual narrative (accession narrative)	Chr history/redaction
II Chron. 15:11		IV	ritual narrative (quasi holy-war narrative)	Chr source
35:16		IV	ritual narrative	Chr history/redaction

[a] Includes all passages except unassociated glosses.
[b] As in Table 1.
[c] Tentative and hypothetical, although based largely on predominant current opinion. The secondary tradents do not necessarily correspond to the contextual genres.

The term "individual" in reference to genre is intended as the equivalent of what Klaus Koch calls "Gliedgattung," as distinct from "Rahmengattung." Koch has argued that the science of form criticism is at the point where further progress demands the distinction between formal structures to which a particular element has a primary and intimate relationship, and formal structures enclosing this primary unit.[279] The larger, broader units, whether surrounding the primary unit in an original form, or coming to surround it in subsequent literary adaptation, is what we mean to designate by our term "contextual" genre. In some instances there are more than one layer of such "contextual" genres.

It is with this distinction in mind that we have attempted to list primary and secondary tradents. Often, but not always, the primary tradents correspond to the individual genres, and the secondary tradents to the contextual genres. We have not labored at this equation because the table is intended as suggestive rather than definitive. We have indicated tradents that are generally accepted or that have seemed the most likely to our own thinking, making no attempt to extend the argumentation to the point of justifying each identification in minute detail, because the eventual profile which we are aiming to construct will not depend on minor variations.

The main impression one gets from scanning Table 2 is that of the considerable variety of forms and tradents, most of which focus upon patterns and institutions of the predynastic and early monarchic periods. This strengthens, and to an extent clarifies, our initial impression, based upon the observation that a predominant number of occurrences are found in the four books, Joshua, Judges, I and II Samuel. Digesting statistically our listing of probable tradents, we may clarify our impression even further by arranging these in approximate chronological order, with the number of occurrences for each. The following image results:

1. *Primary tradents:* presacral union tribes, 4; sacral union shrines, 22; Saul's army and court, 6; David's army and court, 12; Jerusalem shrine and temple, 3; Solomon's court, 4; early redaction, 4; Omri's army, 1; Ahab's army, 1; Levitic circles, 1; preexilic and exilic prophetic schools, 5; unidentified late redaction, 1; deuteronomistic history/redaction, 5; D supplementer, 1; P supplementer, 1; postexilic prophetic school, 1; Nehemiah memoirs, 1; Chronicler's source material, 1; Chronicler's history/redaction, 3; late supplementer, 1; folk history, 3.

2. *Secondary tradents:* sacral union shrines, 16; Saul's court, 1; David's court, 6; Jerusalem shrine and temple, 3; Solomon's court, 1; Yahwistic history, 3; preexilic prophetic schools, 1.

One further thing may be done to interpret the data before us; that is, list the various oral and literary genres systematically in combination with our analysis of function. This we have done in Table 3, preserving the

---

279. *Growth of the Biblical Tradition*, pp. 23ff.

Table 3
Bayyôm hahû' Past:
Statistical Analysis of All Forms

(secondary forms in parentheses)

Formal function[a]	In original contexts		Incorporating secondary materials		Totals
	I-III	IV	I-III	IV	
I. *Elemental forms from oral tradition*					
ritual narrative	2				2
hieros logos			1		1
cult etiology			3		3
local etiology			2		2
promise		1			1
blessing			1		1
sign narrative	1				1
casualty report		5			5
totals	3	6	7	0	16
II. *Complex forms from oral tradition*					
theophany narrative			1		1
hieros logos	1	1	(2)		2(2)
covenant ceremony			(1)		(1)
covenant narrative	(1)	1(1)			1(2)
legitimation narrative	3	2	(1)	(1)	5(2)
ethnological saga	1	2	(2)		3(2)
hero saga	2	3	1		6
holy-war narrative	(3)	3(4)	1(3)	(1)	4(11)
deliverance narrative		1			1
battle report	1		1		2
itinerary narrative		(1)			(1)
farewell address	(1)				(1)
charismatic legend		(1)			(1)
prophet legend	(1)				(1)
judgment oracle	3				3
totals	11(6)	13(7)	4(9)	(2)	28(24)
III. *Literary forms*					
quasi accession narrative		(1)			(1)
quasi parenesis	1				1

continued

Table 3 (continued)

Formal function[a]	In original contexts		Incorporating secondary materials		
	I-III	IV	I-III	IV	Totals
quasi farewell address		3			3
quasi holy-war narrative	(2)	(3)	1(1)	(1)	1(7)
cult/ritual narrative	1	3	1		5
hieros logos	1				1
etymological etiology		1			1
annalistic	1(1)				1(1)
accession history	1	(3)	(6)		1(9)
throne-succession narrative	4	1(1)			5(1)
allegorized symbolic act		1			1
folk history	3				3
secondary expansion	1		3		4
editorial connective			6		6
gloss			7		7
totals	13(3)	9(8)	18(7)	(1)	
Grand totals	27(9)	28(15)	29(16)	(3)	

[a] As in Table 1.

distinction we have made all along between passages where *bayyôm hahû'* is an original element in the context and where it has been introduced by the writer in connection with (and in many cases specifically for the purpose of) the introduction of secondary materials. In this table any one of our three types of forms may be found in either of these two literary categories; the listing of formal types identifies the source and character of the type as such, however it may have been used from a literary point of view. Thus we list: I, elemental forms derived from oral tradition; II, complex forms derived from oral tradition; III, literary forms.

We have recorded the number of primary and secondary forms in each category, as derived from the preceding data. The table is structured in such a way as to exhibit the respective functions of *bayyôm hahû'* within the various formal types, combining functions I-III in one column and function IV (epitome) in another. It will be seen that within the elemental oral forms the phrase functions more often as synchronism-sequence than as epitome, although most of the passages involved are literarily secondary. It is the casualty report that employs *bayyôm hahû'* the most often as part of an epitome. Among the complex forms derived from oral tradition, the occurrences with synchronism-sequence are slightly more frequent than those with epitome, now with the original passages predominating over the secondary passages; as in the simple forms, *bayyôm hahû'* never occurs with an epitome in secondary passages. Among the literary forms, synchronism-sequence occurs much more frequently than epitome, with secondary passages having the preponderance.

After all has been said, the fact that surprises us the most is that *bayyôm hahû'* is used as often as it is in an epitome, i.e., a summarizing characterization concerning a particular day in which Israel's God was in some way seen to be active in crucial confrontation with his people. It hardly seems strange that the period when this usage enjoyed its greatest spontaneity and vitality was the period which Gerhard von Rad has characterized as the time of "pan-sacrality"—the time when the sacral union and the holy war were still more than hallowed stereotypes. In this age Israel still lived in naive belief that Yahweh was immediately present in their life, ever ready to manifest himself on some new and special "day" of his own choosing. When he did reveal himself, it was more often through the charismatic acts of men acting under his overpowering guidance than through the structures of cultic ceremony.

The time came when the institution of kingship made this awareness little more than a pious fiction; the kings in their wars still acted on the theory that Yahweh was fighting for and with them, and they tried to justify their rise to power according to the patterns of pan-sacrality, but the reality was gone. It returned to a measure of new vitality in the preaching of the prophets, who spoke of a "day"—mainly future, but sometimes seen as already past—when Yahweh would manifest his presence once again in the events of Israel's history.

This is the setting for an understanding of *bayyôm hahû'* in futuristic reference. The prophets used a hallowed phrase to describe the future in terms of the past. Was there more than grammatical similarity in their application of this phrase to the future?[280]

---

280. Based on probable Hebrew or Aramaic originals, the following passages from the Greek text of the Apocrypha appear to read *bayyôm hahû'* in a variety of functions with respect to the past.

 Synchronism: Tob. 3:7, 11:17, Judt. 7:2, I Mac. 3:37, 5:67 (also epitome in negative evaluation, with the subject other than the Maccabees/Hasidim), 10:50 (also epitome, with other subject than Maccabees/Hasidim), 11:47 (also epitome), 48 (also epitome).

 Sequence: Tob. 3:10, 4:1.

 Identification: I Mac. 4:54 (SV).

 Epitome: Sus. 62 (Θ), I Mac. 5:34, 60, 9:49, 11:74 (these last four have the form of the holy-war casualty report and pertain to the battles of Bosora, Jamnia, Jordan, and Kedesh, respectively; the epitome respecting Jamnia is negative, recording, as it does, a defeat).

Based on a probable Greek original is, in addition, the occurrence in III Mac. 7:15, which epitomizes in casualty-report form the victory over Ptolemy Philopator, while identifying the day of a festival.

The sole occurrence of *bayyôm hahû'* in the Qumran material thus far published is at 1QM 18:5, where it apparently functions as a synchronism.

CHAPTER THREE

The Day Present: *hayyôm* and Its Equivalents

IT IS SCARCELY POSSIBLE to leap directly from the past into the future; we must pause to look carefully at the present. Not only the historian, whose work it is to record and study the past, and the seer, who tries to glimpse the future, but every person—he who thinks at all about the phenomenon of time, as well as he who does not—stands in the onward rushing moment of the present. As the philosophers have reminded us, the past is none other than a present that is subsiding into memory, while the future is none other than a present that is ever coming forward to meet us.

This proves to be as true linguistically as psychologically and philosophically. We have explored the functions of the expression *bayyôm hahu'* in reference to the past, with the aim of discovering the roots of its meaning when it refers to the future. But we shall not be entirely ready to appreciate its meaning as future unless we first examine its equivalent in present usage. We must ask whether the ancient Hebrews were able to speak of their present experience in ways analogous to their speech about the experiences of the past. We need especially to inquire whether their epitomizing usage with *bayyôm hahû'*, qualifying the essential meaning of memorial days in the past, had its counterpart in discourse regarding the essential meaning of the moment in, and about which, the speaker was presently speaking.

As we discovered in our introductory chapter, the Old Testament very frequently uses *'attâ*, from the common word for "time," *'ēt*, in speaking of the present. However, it likewise makes frequent use of various constructions with *yôm*, the primary word for time. *Keḥayyôm* and related forms sometimes mean "right now," "this very day." The closest morphological equivalent to *bayyôm hahû'*, past and future, is *bayyôm hazzeh*, "on this day," referring to the present. For this expression we find an emphatic variant, *beʿeṣem hayyôm hazzeh*, "on this very same day"—which does not, however, generally refer to the present, as we shall see. Neither of these is a frequent equivalent of the expression *bayyôm hahû'*, in spite of the similarity of form. The ancient Hebrews preferred to use *yôm* with the simple determinative: *hayyôm*, "this day," i.e., "today." Very often *hayyôm* stands alone in adverbial usage, equivalent to our "today" (i.e., indicating time when, rather than identifying the present day by name), though in a sizable number of instances the demonstrative adjective is added (*hayyôm hazzeh*), sometimes to produce a special effect, sometimes not.

We shall carefully examine the occurrences of these four forms of expression[1] with a view to learning more about the Hebrews' insight into the meaning of the present. More than a strictly philological analysis is needed. We must indeed look carefully into questions of grammar and syntax, but more importantly, we must look into the formal functions these expressions perform within the particular contexts where they occur. Do they identify the present moment? Do they create a synchronism or a sequence? Or do they qualify and epitomize, like the expression *bayyôm hahû'*?

1. Bayyôm (b^e'eṣem hayyôm) hazzeh

It is best to treat the two expressions *bayyôm hazzeh* and *b^e'eṣem hayyôm hazzeh* together, because, in spite of morphological differences, they function in much the same way, the longer form being nothing other than an emphatic variant of the shorter.

---

1. The following are the LXX correspondences to these expressions:
σήμερον: *hayyôm hazzeh* adverbial, I Sam. 17:46(1), 24:20, 25:32, 33, 26:24, Jer. 1:10; *hayyôm* adverbial, Gen. 4:14, *passim*, except as below; omitted, Deut. 4:1, 2 *bis*, 6:2, 7:9, 9:6, 11:7, 22, 12:11, 14, 13:1, 30:16, Josh. 7:19, 22:16(2), 24:27, Judg. 6:17 (LXX^A), I Sam. 12:5, 14:41, 44, 16:5, 17:36, 21:3, 24:12, 19(2), 25:34, II Sam. 19:8, I Kings 2:31, 8:15, 56, Ezek. 8:9, Esth. 5:4(2), II Chron. 6:19, 10:7; *taḥat hayyôm hazzeh*, I Sam. 24:20.
τὸ τῆς σήμερον: *hayyôm*, Exod. 5:14.
τῇ σήμερον ἡμέρᾳ: *hayyôm*, Josh. 22:29.
ἐν τῇ σήμερον: *hayyôm hazzeh*, I Sam. 26:21; *hayyôm*, Exod. 13:4.
ἐν τῇ σήμερον ἡμέρᾳ: *hayyôm*, Josh. 5:9, Jer. 1:18.
ἡμέρας: *hayyôm*, Hos. 4:5.
τῇ ἡμέρᾳ ταύτῃ: *bayyôm hazzeh*, Gen. 7:11, Exod. 19:1; *hayyôm hazzeh*, Judg. 9:19, 12:3, I Sam. 28:18, II Sam. 16:12, I Kings 1:30.
τὴν ἡμέραν ταύτην: *b^e'eṣem hayyôm hazzeh*, Lev. 23:21; *hayyôm hazzeh*, I Sam. 14:45.
ἐν τῇ ἡμέρᾳ: *hayyôm*, I Kings 13:11 (LXX^BA).
ἐν τῇ ἡμέρᾳ ταύτῃ: *bayyôm hazzeh*, Lev. 8:34, 16:30, I Sam. 11:13, I Kings 2:26; *b^e'eṣem hayyôm hazzeh*, Gen. 7:13, Exod. 12:17, Deut. 32:48; *hayyôm hazzeh*, Deut. 2:25, 5:24, 26:16, 27:9, Josh. 3:7, 22:22 (LXX^A), Judg. 10:15, I Sam. 12:5, 17:10, 46(2), 24:11, II Sam. 3:38, 18:20 *bis*; *hayyôm*, I Kings 12:7; omitted, I Sam. 14:45, II Sam. 3:9.
ἐν ταύτῃ τῇ ἡμέρᾳ: *b^e'eṣem hayyôm hazzeh*, Josh. 5:11.
ἐν αὐτῇ τῇ ἡμέρᾳ ταύτῃ: *b^e'eṣem hayyôm hazzeh*, Lev. 23:28, 29, 30.
ἐν τῇ ἡμέρᾳ ἐκείνῃ: *b^e'eṣem hayyôm hazzeh*, Exod. 12:51, Ezek. 40:1.
ἐν τῷ καίρῳ τῆς ἡμέρας ἐκείνης: *b^e'eṣem hayyôm hazzeh*, Gen. 17:23, 26.
Substantially different from MT: *b^e'eṣem hayyôm hazzeh*, Josh. 7:25, Ezek. 24:2; *hayyôm hazzeh*, II Sam. 4:8, Ezek. 24:2; *hayyôm*, I Sam. 9:12, 14:33, Isa. 38:19, Jer. 42:19, 21, Ezek. 24:2, Zech. 9:12, Job 23:2.
Omitted: *b^e'eṣem hayyôm hazzeh*, Exod. 12:41; *hayyôm hazzeh*, Jer. 44:2 (= LXX 51:2); *hayyôm*, Exod. 16:25(3), 32:29(2), 34:11, Deut. 15:15, 29:12, 17, Josh. 22:31, 23:14, I Sam. 9:9, 18:21, II Sam. 3:8(1), Jer. 40:4, Prov. 22:19.

a. In past narration

Although this chapter directly concerns only expressions for the present, it is necessary to mention, first of all, that in a number of passages these two phrases refer to events in the past. The day referred to is actually long gone at the time of writing, even though, for the writer, the day may still be very real and present. To speak of an event remote from present time as though it were present reveals a considerable power for abstract reconstruction, and anyone acquainted with biblical criticism will not be surprised to learn that most of the passages reflecting this peculiar usage must derive from the priestly writer (P), or from others closely sharing his mentality.

Gen. 7:11, 13

First of all are two occurrences in the P account of the flood. The priestly writer not only dates the flood[2] according to the years of Noah's lifetime, but provides the precise month and day (Gen. 7:11):

> In the six hundredth year of Noah's life, in the second month, on the seventeenth day of the month, on this day (*bayyôm hazzeh*) all the fountains of the great deep burst forth, and the windows of heaven were opened.

This is followed by a verse in which he tells how long the rain fell; then the writer makes a precise and emphatic synchronism between the beginning of the flood and Noah's act of entering into the ark,[3] using now the longer expression *bᵉ'eṣem hayyôm hazzeh*, "on this same day" (vs. 13).

Gen. 17:23, 26

The P story in Gen. 17, concerning the institution of circumcision, has two concluding reports, each containing the expression *bᵉ'eṣem hayyôm hazzeh*. The interest of the first occurrence (vs. 23) appears to be to provide a date, judging from the fact that the temporal expression comes

---

2. Since the earliest days of modern criticism, a strong interest in chronology has been recognized as a hallmark of P. This is apparent in the creation story (Gen. 1), in the genealogies (especially chaps. 5, 11), and in the story of the flood. P not only provides a date for the flood but tells also how long the rain fell (7:12), how long the waters remained on the earth (7:24), when the ark came to rest on Ararat (8:3-5), and when the waters were dried from the earth (8:13f.). On possible affinities with the Jubilees-Qumran calendar, see A. Jaubert, *The Date of the Last Supper* (New York, 1965), pp. 33ff. On dating as a structural feature in P, see now S. E. McEvenue, *The Narrative Style of the Priestly Writer* (AnBib, 50, Rome, 1971), pp. 56ff. Without warrant, McEvenue ascribes a vaguely defined cultic innuendo to P's use of *bayyôm hazzeh* and *bᵉ'eṣem hayyôm hazzeh* (pp. 61f., n. 55).

3. This is in jarring contradiction to J, who expressly states (vs. 10) that the flood came seven days after Noah entered the ark.

in unemphatic position at the end of the main clause[4] and that it is followed in vss. 24f. by statements of Abraham's and Ishmael's respective ages at the time of their circumcision. *Be'eṣem hayyôm hazzeh* in vs. 26, in emphatic place at the beginning, is a synchronism connecting back to vs. 22, its intent being to stress the promptness of Abraham's compliance with the divine injunction.[5]

Exod. 12:41, 51

In P material occurring toward the end of Exod. 12, we find two instances of *be'eṣem hayyôm hazzeh* introducing statements that Israel departed or was brought out from Egypt (vss. 41, 51). The first of these verses follows a characteristic P chronological notice (vs. 40), to the effect that Israel dwelt four hundred thirty years in Egypt; the phrase *wayehî miqqēṣ*, plus the number, intends to date the departure according to this period. Awkwardly, the text adds a synchronism with a certain unnamed day—evidently the day of the passover[6]—repeating the imperfect consecutive before *be'eṣem hayyôm hazzeh*.[7] The repetition of this identical phrase in vs. 51 must be explained as part of a redactional attempt to incorporate the new passover ordinance of vss. 43-49; it makes a feeble synchronism between a new report of the passover celebration in vs. 50 and this second report of the departure.

Exod. 19:1

The last example from P is Exod. 19:1, where *bayyôm hazzeh* makes an emphatic identification of the date when Israel appeared at Sinai, i.e., the third *ḥōdeš* (new moon)[8] since departing from Egypt. So important was this date to the P-writer that he inserted it before the itinerary information of vs. 2a.

---

4. The concluding phrase, "as God had said to him," modifies not the temporal reference but the main verb.
5. Since the phraseology of vss. 23-25 is more elaborate than that of vss. 22, 26f., and an interest in precise dating is likely to be later than the making of a simple synchronism, vss. 23-25 probably represent the latter of the two conclusions, and are hence to be identified as a secondary expansion to the text.
6. The reference is to vs. 28, where it is reported that Israel performed the command concerning the passover. The date when this occurred cannot be the twenty-first day of the month mentioned in vs. 18 (so Noth), since this belongs to a late torah for the mazzoth; it must be the fourteenth day mentioned in vs. 6, or, if Rolf Rendtorff's analysis is correct (*Die Gesetze in der Priesterschrift*, FRLANT, N.F. 44, 2nd ed., Göttingen, 1963, pp. 56ff.), the tenth day of vs. 3.
7. The MT definitely has the *lectio deficilior;* the LXX omits this entire phrase, perhaps because it was simply at a loss as to how to translate it.
8. So RSV and most commentators. "Month" is an unlikely meaning, without a reference to a specific day.

Deut. 32:48

It is not likely, as von Rad claims,[9] that the occurrence of *b^e 'eṣem hayyôm hazzeh* in Deut. 32:48, where it introduces a second command to Moses to ascend Mount Nebo, is from P; probably the pericope, vss. 48-52, is late redactional, combining as it does extracts from Num. 21:22ff. and 27:12ff. in preparation for P's displaced notice of Moses' death in Deut. 34:1ff.[10] In any event, it is clear that it creates a synchronism, though an artificial one, since the relationship to the preceding context is entirely arbitrary.

Josh. 5:10

In two other Old Testament passages *b^e 'eṣem hayyôm hazzeh* creates an explicit dating. First we mention Josh. 5:10, where it occurs as a late gloss. Martin Noth is probably right in identifying both the date provided in vs. 10 and *b^e 'eṣem hayyôm hazzeh* in vs. 11 as secondary intrusions on the part of a priestly glossator, one who was not content with the original text's simple synchronism between the passover at Gilgal and the cessation of manna, hence had to make sure that the date was right.[11]

Ezek. 40:1

B^e 'eṣem hayyôm hazzeh is unquestionably original to its context in Ezek. 40:1—though perhaps not from the reputed author of the book.[12] Here two dates are given for the new-temple vision. The first appears in characteristic Ezekielian form,[13] with year, month,[14] and day, figured according to the era of Jehoiachin's exile. The second date is a reference to the years since Jerusalem's capture, omitting mention of a month or day. The phrase *b^e 'eṣem hayyôm hazzeh* can hardly refer to the latter date

---

9. *ATD*, 8, *in loco*.

10. Cf. Noth, *UGS*, pp. 190f.

11. Noth, *HAT*, 7, *in loco*. For an illuminating discussion of the tradition-critical and *religionsgeschichtliche* background of this passage, see H.-J. Kraus, *Gottesdienst in Israel*, pp. 190f. The LXX omits ממחרת from vs. 11 and vs. 12, reading בעצם היום הזה as the beginning of vs. 12; although ממחרת in vs. 12 is both difficult and suspicious, there is no reason to question its originality in vs. 11, once בעצם היום הזה has been recognized for the late intrusion that it is.

12. See the commentaries for a discussion of the problems surrounding the authorship of chaps. 40—48. The consensus of recent criticism favors attributing an original core in these chapters to the prophet or his intimate circle of disciples.

13. It is true that an initial *way^e hî*, usually in Ezekiel's genuine dates, is lacking; the form in this respect is more similar to that of P. However, the LXX, καὶ ἐγένετο, presupposes *way^ehî*, though it may have supplied this out of familiarity with Ezekiel's form in other passages.

14. It is unlikely that בראש השנה should be emended to בראשון, according to the LXX reading, ἐν τῷ πρώτῳ μηνὶ, which may only have been attempting to interpret, according to the usual pattern of Ezekiel's dates, a form it did not understand.

since, according to II Kings 25:8ff., the city was captured on the seventh of the fifth month. Hence it is to the tenth day that the phrase refers, though the precise reason for this identification remains obscure.[15] In any event, it is clear that the temporal phrase does provide a date.

b. In reference to the cultic present/future

Next we consider four late cult-legislative passages that use *bayyôm hazzeh* or *be'eṣem hayyôm hazzeh* in reference to a present that is no more historically actual than the past that has been made present in the passages we have just considered. In order to find the means for distinguishing this kind of present from the real historical present, we must take the pains to give each some special attention. As will be seen, each instance of the temporal phrase identifies, dates, or synchronizes.

Exod. 12:17

The passover ordinance of Exod. 12:1-14 has drawn to itself a complex series of expansions (vss. 15-20); dealing, as these do, with the mazzoth, they were evidently added to the text after the passover and the mazzoth festivals had been combined. It will be seen that this series of *toroth* is structured with the verb in the imperfect, except for vs. 17 and in apodoses following the participle in the grounding formulae of vss. 15 and 19. Rendtorff's suggestion, to the effect that in vs. 17 the LXX and Sam. should be followed in reading "(this) ordinance" instead of "the mazzoth," and that this verse is to be understood as an echo of vs. 14 (originally referring, like it, to the passover),[16] is called into question by the following observations: (1) it is not attached to the passover ordinance, but to those ordinances that have to do with the mazzoth; (2) II Chron. 30:21, 35:17 use the verb שמר with *ḥag hammaṣṣôt* as object; (3) the phraseology of vs. 17b differs significantly from that of vs. 14b (שמר יום instead of חגג חג). That the mazzoth feast, a seven-day festival, is seemingly spoken of here as a one-day observance, is perhaps to be explained by the late identification of the first day of the mazzoth with the passover. In any event, this usage, together with the syntactical pattern involving perfect-consecutive verbs, is

---

15. Scholarly opinion remains divided over whether *berō'š haššānâ* should be taken to mean the first month (Nisan, in the spring), in line with the meaning of Exod. 12:2 (so recently Galling, Kraus), or should be taken to mean the fall new year's day, as in later Jewish usage, in which case *be'āśôr laḥōdeš* would be epexegetical, referring, as in Lev. 25:9, to the tenth day of the seventh month (so recently Gese, Zimmerli). The apparent special emphasis on dating this restorative vision may be taken as an argument for the latter position. If a new year's day in the fall is meant, we can understand why specific mention of a seventh month was omitted from the text, since it seems certain that Ezekiel counted his years from a (Babylonian) new year in the spring.

16. *Die Gesetze in der Priesterschrift*, p. 58.

evidence that this verse probably represents a very late expansion to the entire mazzoth section.

On its face, *b^e'eṣem hayyôm hazzeh* seems to create a synchronism between the *heilsgeschichtliche* event of the deliverance from Egypt and the annual observance of the festival. What is in fact happening is that the saving act of the past is being made recurrently present in the cultic "now." Here is a vivid example of what Martin Noth has called the "Vergegenwärtigung" of the past.[17] The present is being repeatedly contemporized with a past moment of salvific experience, as epitomized in the divine declaration, "I brought your hosts out of the land of Egypt."[18]

Lev. 8:34

The cult narrative in Lev. 8:34 puts into Moses' mouth the words, כאשר עשה ביום הזה צוה יהוה לעשות לכפר עליכם, "As has been done today, Yahweh has commanded to be done, to make atonement for you." One of the considerations that marks this verse and vss. 33b and 35 as secondary intrusions is that the comparison, using the perfect verb, "as it has been done today," comes too soon, in front of the concluding rubric of vs. 36, "And Aaron and his sons did all the things which Yahweh commanded by Moses."[19] As it stands, vs. 34 is somewhat elliptical, lacking in its main clause a temporal expression to correspond to *bayyôm hazzeh* in the comparative clause. But it is nonetheless clear that a comparison is being made between the one day of the ordination ritual that is the main concern of the bulk of this chapter and the six days specified here for atonement.[20] The function of *bayyôm hazzeh* is, accordingly, simply to identify the one day that is being contrasted and compared with the six that follow it. *Bayyôm hazzeh* represents the cultic present.

---

17. "Die Vergegenwärtigung des Alten Testaments in der Verkündigung," *EvT*, 12 (1952/53), pp. 6ff.; cf. J. M. Schmidt, "Vergegenwärtigung und Ueberlieferung," *EvT*, 30 (1970), 169-200; also B. S. Childs, *Memory and Tradition in Israel* (Naperville, 1962), especially pp. 74ff.
18. The sole occurrence of divine speech among these expansions.
19. Cf. Noth, *ATD*, 6, *in loco*. K. Elliger, *HAT*, 4, *in loco*, relegates the entirety of vss. 33-35 to his Pg², but vs. 33b hangs loosely, repeats the "seven days" of 33a, and shares with 34a the unusual indefinite subject (מלא, 33; עשה, 34). Klaus Koch, *Die Priesterschrift von Exodus 25 bis Leviticus 16* (FRLANT, N.F. 53, Göttingen, 1959), pp. 102f., assigns Lev. 8 to his Pe ("exekutive Schicht").
20. Although Elliger, *loc. cit.*, may be right in identifying the extension of the ordination ritual to seven days as a late development (from which it may follow that vs. 33a is a late addition in chap. 8), a more striking development appears in the concept of needing to use this period to atone (לכפר) for the priests. No mention of atoning is made in references to priestly ordination (Exod. 29:1, 9, 33, 35, 44, 40:12-15, Lev. 8:10-12, 22, 28, 30, 33; though cf. the Levites in Num. 8:5ff.), except in a verse that may be dependent on the present passage, *viz.*, Exod. 29:36 (cf. atoning for the altar, Exod. 29:36f., Lev. 8:15; the ritual for the day of atonement, Lev. 16). It is not clear whether our interpolator expected the entirety of the ordination to be repeated; likely, he intended the reference to be only to remaining at the sanctuary in a sanctified condition and eating the sacrificial food.

Lev. 16:30

Lev. 16:30 employs *bayyôm hazzeh* to introduce a clause explaining the theological purpose of the day of atonement. The entire section, vss. 29-34a, is a parenesis from the final redaction of the material in this chapter.[21] The intent of the temporal phrase is not primarily to make a synchronism with the immediately preceding prohibition against work, but to identify the essential cultic purpose of the tenth day of the seventh month. Its main function is, accordingly, that of dating the day when atonement is to be made.

Lev. 23:21, 28, 29, 30

Four times within Lev. 23, *b^e 'eṣem hayyôm hazzeh* appears, referring, like *bayyôm hazzeh* in 16:30, to the cultic present. In vs. 21 the day in question is the festival of weeks; in the rest it is the day of atonement. It is likely that all four verses come from the same hand and represent a redactional stage of development. The function of the temporal phrase in each instance is to provide a synchronism between various activities appointed for the cultic day.[22]

c. In discourse referring to the historical present

Finally we come to a small group of passages in which *bayyôm hazzeh* or its emphatic variant is used with reference to the real historical present. In each instance the temporal phrase stands in a declaration that epitomizes the essential meaning of the momentary experience, in a way analogous to the epitomizing function of *bayyôm hahû'* observed in the preceding chapter.

Josh. 7:25

The first occurrence of this usage, in Josh. 7:25, is from the earliest materials in the Old Testament, in all likelihood having been preserved in oral tradition before being reduced to writing. In this verse a climax to the Achan episode is reached in Joshua's words to Achan, מה עכרתנו יעכרך יהוה ביום הזה, "Why did you bring trouble on us? Let Yahweh bring trouble[23] on you this day."

---

21. Cf. Elliger, *HAT*, 4, *in loco*.
22. Cf. *ibid.*, *in loco*.
23. This is the meaning of עכר in Middle Hebrew; so RSV, BDB. KBL overtranslates in following Schwally: "zum Taboo machen, für den Verkehr mit anderen unmöglich machen"; though several passages (Josh. 6:18, Judg. 11:35, II Sam. 14:29) identify this with an evil consequence connected with a vow, as here, other passages where it occurs (e.g., I Kings 18:17f.) prevent the meaning of "taboo" except in an extremely attenuated sense.

Joshua 7 contains three distinct literary elements:[24] (1) an etiological legend concerning a *gal* in the vale of Achor, concluded by the formula, "Therefore to this day the name of that place is called . . . ;[25] (2) the narrative of Achan's ordeal by lot; and (3) redactional materials connecting these two with the account of Ai's conquest. It is clear that the etiology was originally independent from the Achan narrative.[26] One should note especially that the legal confrontation that takes place between Joshua and the culprit in vs. 25 assumes that the interview of vss. 19-21 had never occurred. Thus vs. 25 belongs to the etiological legend rather than to the normalizing Achan narrative. "Why did you bring trouble on us?" is, in succinct form, the charge; "Let Yahweh bring trouble on you this day" is the sentence of condemnation, immediately carried out by the people. But the clause with *bayyôm hazzeh* characterizes the essential upshot of the entire event while pointing emphatically to the time—the immediate present—when the verdict was to be carried out.

I Sam. 11:13

The next example of *bayyôm hazzeh* referring to the real present occurs in a passage of unquestionable historical authenticity, I Samuel 11, the narrative of Saul's victory over the Ammonites and acclamation as king. We agree with Artur Weiser that 10:27 originally had nothing to do with the immediately preceding account of Saul's acclamation at Mizpah (10:17-26), but provides, together with 11:12ff., a setting for the holy-war narrative of 11:1-11.[27] Certain *bᵉnê bᵉliyya'al*, "worthless fellows," oppose Saul because there is no sign that he is able to save Israel, in spite of

---

24. Cf. M. Noth, *HAT*, 7, *in loco*.

25. Cf. B. S. Childs, "A Study of the Formula, 'Until this Day'," *JBL*, 83 (1963), 285f.

26. It is apparent that the paronomasia between עכר and עכן is superficial (cf. the harmonization in I Chron. 2:7). Folk-etymologizing has produced the identification of Achan, in what may once have been an independent ordeal story (note that vs. 15 mentions only burning as a penalty, while vs. 25 adds stoning), with the unnamed culprit of the etiological saga. (It is difficult to explain why the name should have become "Achan" if the ordeal story developed secondarily from the etiological saga.) In effect, the ordeal story absorbed the etiological saga, evidence for which is especially clear in vs. 25bβγ, where the stoning (root, סקל) element, germane only to the etiology, is added to the burning required by the ordeal story (the stoning of vs. bα [root, רגם], with כל ישראל as subject, is probably secondary [so Noth], in spite of the reading of LXX[B A]). Cf. B. J. Alfrink, "Die Achan-Erzählung," A. Miller Festschrift (1951), pp. 114-29; C. H. W. Brekelmans, *De Herem in het Oude Testament* (1960), pp. 92-98.

27. *Samuel*, pp. 71-79. The combination of holy-war elements with motifs of a legitimation narrative results from tradition development in the oral stages of transmission, not from literary supplementation. However, vs. 14b is redactional, combining this composite narrative with that of 10:17-26. That the opponents say other words in 11:12 than in 10:27 may be an indication that an original introduction to this story has been lost or deliberately omitted. See also M. Tsevat, *Tarbiz*, 36, 99ff., separating the narrative of 11:12—12:25 from 11:1-11.

his already having been put forth as *môšîaʿ*, "a deliverer." In answer to this resistance, the power and "dread" of the *rûaḥ ʾelōhîm* fall upon Saul (11:6; cf. 7b), empowering him to lead Israel to a spectacular victory. [28] The narrator goes on to his intended climax, telling of the people's impulse to slay Saul's opponents (12), Saul's[29] declaration forbidding this revengeful action (13), Samuel's summons to a festive ceremony at Gilgal (14), and a succinct statement of the actions that followed (15).

The main clause in Saul's declaration of vs. 13, "No man shall die *bayyôm hazzeh*," epitomizes the central issue concerning Saul's acclamation as king, and hence of the narrative as a whole; as we learn from such passages as II Sam. 19:23, I Kings 2:26, such a decree of amnesty was not only customary and appropriate to the occasion of a king's investiture, but vividly symbolizes all the power and authority that needed to be in his hands in order to allow him to make so grand a gesture.[30] The grounding clause of vs. 13, "for today Yahweh has wrought victory in Israel," is an epitome of the holy-war episode in vss. 1-11.[31]

II Sam. 3:9 LXX

We have previously shown[32] that II Sam. 3 has been drawn from two separate literary sources. Vss. 1, 6-13, 17ff. belong to a source that tells of Abner's nefarious behavior toward Ishbaal and subsequent murder. In his complaint to Ishbaal in vs. 8, Abner uses *hayyôm* initially in an identifying characterization, then again in an epitome;[33] in vss. 9f. he openly declares his intent to transfer Ishbaal's power to David. His statement is in the form of an oath, concluding, according to the MT, with a summary apodosis, "so shall I do to him." Here LXX[BA] adds the equivalent of our temporal expression.[34] Inasmuch as the LXX translates rather literally in this section, and the time-designative seems to have an authentic function in identifying this day as the day when Yahweh's oath to David would be fulfilled, it may very well represent the original text.[35]

---

28. For an analysis of the schema of this holy-war story, see Richter, *Traditionsgeschichtliche Untersuchungen zum Richterbuch*, pp. 177ff.

29. Weiser's argument (*Samuel*, p. 74, n. 60), supporting LXX[B] in reading "Samuel" instead of "Saul," is weakened by the consideration that it was the *king's* prerogative to proclaim amnesty.

30. The form is a negation of the יומת מות variant of the apodictic prohibition; cf. A. Alt, "Die Ursprünge des israelitischen Rechts," *Kleine Schriften*, I, 311f.; H. Schulz, *Das Todesrecht im Alten Testament* (BZAW, 114, Berlin, 1969).

31. Cf. below, in connection with *hayyôm* in various epitomizing functions.

32. Above, pp. 92ff.

33. See below, pp. 209f.

34. ἐν τῇ ἡμέρᾳ ταύτῃ. Since σήμερον translates היום in vs. 8 (*bis*), there can be little doubt but that the LXX reads היום הזה here (*contra* BH³ mg).

35. A similar structure and function occurs with *hayyôm hazzeh* (LXX, τῇ ἡμέρᾳ ταύτῃ) at I Kings 1:30.

I Kings 2:26

In I Kings 2:26 *bayyôm hazzeh* seems to identify and epitomize at the same time. Here the throne-succession history draws to a conclusion as Solomon disposes, one by one, of his most serious remaining enemies. The king is expelling Abiathar. Nothing is told of any special offense against the king's indulgence on the latter's part, as in the cases of Adonijah and Shimei. In vs. 26 we find first Solomon's command, "Go to Anathoth, to your estate," then the clause grounding this command, "for you deserve death, but *bayyôm hazzeh* I will not put you to death," and finally the clause giving the grounds for a commutation of the death sentence, "for you bore the ark of Yahweh, etc."

Puzzled by the position of the temporal phrase, many commentators have followed the LXX in reading "for you deserve death on this day, and (but) I will not put you to death . . ."; but the LXX has itself misunderstood. The first *kî*-clause states a death sentence that has already been nullified by the command of expulsion. The temporal phrase following it, in emphatic position at the beginning of the clause, expressly commutes that sentence. There is special stress on *bayyôm hazzeh*. A clue as to why may possibly be found in the policy of clemency effective upon the occasion of the royal accession, seen to be in force in the case of Saul in I Sam. 11:13. To be sure, we fail to receive the impression that this was still Solomon's actual accession day; but the policy appropriate to it may have still been in effect, extending, as it were, the day of clemency. Probably Abiathar's closeness to David was a factor. We may doubt whether his being a priest would in itself have kept Abiathar safe from Solomon's vengeance.[36]

Thus the statement with *bayyôm hazzeh* may contain an echo of the epitomizing function that it would have had in such a declaration as is found in I Sam. 11:13. However, its emphatic forward position requires us to recognize that this day is being contrasted with future days when Abiathar might still transgress and be punished. That is to say, the amnesty holds only for now, not for the future. *Bayyôm hazzeh* thus identifies time when, as in II Sam. 3:9 (LXX).

Ezek. 24:2

Our last passage offers the sole example of the emphatic phrase *be'eṣem hayyôm hazzeh* being used in an epitome. This passage, Ezek. 24:2, presents a number of textual difficulties. In the first place, there is the date (vs. 1), which may not be original.[37] Next, there are three

---

36. As is suggested by M. Noth, *BK*, IX/1, *in loco*. We need think only of what Saul did to Abiathar's father, according to I Sam. 22:6ff. Zadokite rivalry was surely an important element in the banishment of Abiathar.

37. It fails to reflect the rather standardized form of other dating formulae in

temporal phrases in the Hebrew text of vs. 2, but the Syriac and Vulgate lack anything to correspond to the second of these. Finally, the LXX of vs. 2 is either deliberately periphrastic or sadly confused, offering little basis for emending the difficult MT,[38] in which the locution, את שם היום, seems especially strange.[39]

Little progress can be made toward resolving these difficulties until we recognize that either את שם היום or את עצם היום הזה is secondary. Most probably it is the latter phrase, which may have been added, along with the date, to make an emphatic identification of the specific time when the attack upon Jerusalem began, as remembered from later experience. This leaves as original the divine command to write down (cf. Isa. 8:1, Hab. 2:2) the name (month and number?) of the day, followed by an explanation to the effect that the king of Babylon "has leaned on" (perfect)[40] Jerusalem *b*ᵉ*'eṣem hayyôm hazzeh*, "on this very day." All this is by way of introduction to a *mashal* in which Jerusalem under siege is compared to a pot set on the fire (vss. 3-5); in customary fashion, Ezekiel offers an interpretation of this metaphor in the words of woe found in vss. 9-10a.[41]

There is, of course, a synchronizing of Nebuchadrezzar's action with the prophet's writing; furthermore, it is the first that occasions and explains the second. The major emphasis falls upon this correlation, not on the temporal quality of the day as such, which happens to be important only because it provides the bond between these two actions. Nevertheless, we detect an epitomizing force in vs. 2b. The declaration that Nebuchadrezzar has "leaned on" Jerusalem gives meaning not only to the *mashal* and its interpretation; it symbolizes the dire fulfillment of the outpouring of divine wrath that Ezekiel has been continually warning his people about from the beginning of his ministry. The "name" of this very day is to be inscribed because this is that dread day of all days, from which there is no escape, beyond which there is no hope.[42]

Ezekiel; cf. W. Zimmerli, *BK*, XIII/1, *in loco*. It is the supposition of the originality of such things as this date that has created the mistaken notion that Ezekiel was some kind of clairvoyant; but the date probably is, in effect, a *vaticinium ex eventu*.

38. There is much confusion among the ms. families. The LXX scarcely supports the conjecture, עצם for שם (BH³ mg).

39. It does support the *qere*, *k*ᵉ*tab* (imperative), over against the *kethibh*. For the expression KTB ŠM HYM in a contemporary Palestinian inscription, see Y. Aharoni, "Hebrew Ostraca from Tel Arad," *IEJ*, 16 (1966), 1ff.

40. Heb. שמך has the opposing meanings, "support" and "lean on." RSV, "lay siege," is interpretive. The experiential stimulus for this statement may have been merely a report reaching the prophet that Nebuchadrezzar's army had set out to attack Jerusalem.

41. Zimmerli, *BK*, XIII/1, *in loco*, is probably right in identifying all the rest of vss. 3-14, involving reinterpretations of the kettle metaphor, as secondary.

42. This does not prevent the hope in God's new creative possibilities that emerges in the period after this immediate day of wrath is past; cf. especially 33:10ff.

d. Conclusion

We have seen that when *bayyôm hazzeh* refers to the past, it serves only to date an event, whereas the longer form, *b^e 'eṣem hayyôm hazzeh*, may provide a date or a synchronism; it never functions like *bayyôm hahû'* to make an epitome. In passages referring to the cultic present/future, *bayyôm hazzeh* provides a date (Lev. 16:30) or a simple identification (Lev. 8:34), while the longer temporal phrase serves in one passage to make a synchronism (Lev. 23:21, 28, 29, 30) and in one other to provide something like an epitome (Exod. 12:17). It is important to observe that this word, spoken by Yahweh himself, concerns the foundational saving act in Israel's past experience (the deliverance at the sea). Among the passages with *bayyôm hazzeh* that refer to the real historical present, Josh. 7:25 uses it in an appeal for decisive action, I Sam. 11:13 uses it in a royal decree that in effect epitomizes the day's central significance, while II Sam. 3:9 (LXX) and I Kings 2:26 use it for identification of time when. The emphatic form, referring in Ezek. 24:2 to the historical present, occurs with an epitomizing function.

An attempt to make a comprehensive interpretation of this data must be deferred until it can be correlated with the results of our survey of the companion expressions, *hayyôm hazzeh* and *hayyôm*.

2. Hayyôm hazzeh and hayyôm

The adverbial expression *bayyôm hazzeh*, with its emphatic variant, involves the inseparable preposition *b^e*, "on", "in." It is thus structurally analogous to *bayyôm hahû'*. But a functional equivalent that is apparently closer to *bayyôm hahû'* is the adverbial *hayyôm hazzeh*, performing the role that the simple dative or ablative plays in certain other languages (specifying time when an action occurs). This functional equivalence is reflected in the ambivalence inherent in the alternative LXX translations, ἐν τῇ ἡμέρᾳ ταύτῃ and τῇ ἡμέρᾳ ταύτῃ.

Thus we need to extend our preceding study to an analysis of *hayyôm hazzeh*. But a fourth, more common term likewise offers itself for study at this point. It is the adverbial *hayyôm*, which often functions identically to *bayyôm hazzeh* and *hayyôm hazzeh*, though sometimes with significant nuancing. Morphologically, *hayyôm* is a noun with the determinative, though its meaning may be "today" in an adverbial sense.

a. Substantival use

First we need to note briefly a relatively small number of passages in which *hayyôm* and *hayyôm hazzeh* occur not as adverbs but as substantives, i.e., in the nominative or accusative position. Here we find that the substantive sometimes has a striking similarity to the adverbial usage.

Hayyôm hazzeh is found as a substantive in festival proclamation:

> This day shall be for you a memorial day, and you shall keep it as a feast to Yahweh (Exod. 12:14).[43]

It is also found in cult legislation:

> And you shall observe the festival of Mazzoth, for on this very day (*b^e'eṣem hayyôm hazzeh*)[44] I brought your hosts out of the land of Egypt; and you shall keep this day (*hayyôm hazzeh*) throughout your generations as an everlasting ordinance (Exod. 12:17);

> Remember this day, in which you came out of Egypt . . . (Exod. 13:3).

In all these passages the reference is to the cultic rather than the historical present. The historical present of individual experience is envisaged, however, in two prophet-legend passages, first designating victory, then defeat:

> This day is a day of good news (*yôm b^e sōrâ hû'*) (II Kings 7:9).

> This day is a day of distress, of rebuke, and disgrace (II Kings 19:3).

The simple *hayyôm* occurs as a substantive in a variety of ways. Sometimes it is employed in qualifying relative clauses or infinitival phrases, but only a few times in reference to the historical or cultic present. Those referring to a victorious present are the following:

> Arise, for this is the day when Yahweh gives Sisera into your hand (Judg. 4:14);

> Behold, the day concerning which Yahweh has said to you, "Behold, I will give your enemy into your hand!" (I Sam. 24:5);

> Ah, this is the day we have longed for; we have found it, we see it! (Lam. 2:16).

One passage refers to the cultic present, the day of liturgical proclamation:

> This is the day when Yahweh has acted! (Ps. 118:24).[45]

Each of these passages will be seen to epitomize the central issue of the pericope in which they occur; hence they are closely analogous to the passages with epitomizing *hayyôm* adverbial.

Apart from these occurrences, substantival *hayyôm* generally refers to the daytime in distinction from the nighttime (Judg. 19:9 *bis*, Jer. 6:4, 33:20,[46] Ezek. 30:18, Mic. 3:6). Once it occurs as an explanatory gloss (I Kings 14:14),[47] once as a date (Ezek. 24:2).[48] It occurs in the fixed

---

43. We have noted the plural (*hayyāmîm hāhēm*) in late (secular) festival proclamation, Esth. 9:31; cf. 26, 27, 28 *tris*.

44. Cf. above, pp. 144f. In 16:29 the LXX has ἴδετε ὁ γὰρ κύριος ἔδωκεν ὑμῖν τὴν ἡμέραν ταύτην τὰ σάββατα, but this makes poor syntax and poor sense within the context.

45. *Zeh hayyôm 'āśâ YHWH*.

46. Emended from MT *yômām*; cf. BH[3] mg.

47. The best LXX witnesses omit MT, 14:1-20. The passage in the LXX corresponding to this passage is 12:24, where anything to correspond to זה היום וגם עתה ומה is lacking. The expression disrupts the syntax in the speech of the prophet to Jeroboam's wife.

48. Cf. above, pp. 148f.

phrase *way*ᵉ*hî hayyôm w*ᵉ . . . , "and the day came when . . . ," found in I Sam. 1:4, 14:1, II Kings 4:8, 11, 18, Job 1:6, 13, 2:1. Finally we mention that substantival *hayyôm* occurs without a modifier in cult legislation and liturgical proclamation, similarly to *hayyôm hazzeh* in Exod. 12:14, 17, 13:3:

Today is a sabbath unto Yahweh! (Exod. 16:25);

Today is holy to Yahweh your god . . . ! (Neh. 8:9, 10; cf. 11).

b. Adverbial use

We turn now to the lengthy list of passages using *hayyôm* and *hayyôm hazzeh* adverbially. The list is long: 14 passages in Genesis, 11 in Exodus, 3 in Leviticus, 60 in Deuteronomy, 13 in Joshua, 7 in Judges, 42 in I Samuel, 24 in II Samuel, 11 in I Kings, 5 in II Kings, 1 in Isaiah, 7 in Jeremiah, 1 in Hosea, 1 in Zechariah, 3 in Psalms, 2 in Proverbs, 1 in Job, 6 in Ruth, 1 in Esther, 3 in Nehemiah, 1 each in I and II Chronicles. Thus we have: from the Tetrateuch, 28 occurrences; from Deuteronomy, 60; from the Former Prophets, 102; from the Latter Prophets, 10; from all the Writings combined, 17.[49]

How many of these passages involve our time-designatives in epitomizing statements will appear from the detailed analysis in which we are about to be engaged. Much depends on the position of *hayyôm* and its equivalents within a given pericope. As we shall see, when the position is climactic, the tendency is toward epitomization. This may be directly in the form of an epitomizing statement, summarizing the central significance of a particular event and of the day in which it occurs. Or it may be in the form of a command or appeal, in which one party, confronting another party, addresses the latter in the second person, moving him to decisive action. Again, the statement may turn out not to occupy the climactic position within the pericope, but to provide a crucial characterization of one of the parties, or of the circumstances characterizing the confrontation. It is better to call this usage an identifying characterization rather than an epitome—reserving the latter term for similar statements in climactic position. Nevertheless, the close interrelatedness of these three functions will become sufficiently apparent.

Then again, we shall see that in many passages referring to the present day the time-designative serves mainly the purpose of telling time when, as often with *bayyôm hahû'* in passages referring to the past. The precise function may vary: synchronism, sequence, time-identification; but the important difference is that the time-designative serves in some way to

---

49. The apocrypha lacks this expression except in the book of Judith, where it is represented by the Greek translation, ἐν τῇ ἡμέρᾳ ταύτῃ. All occurrences appear in present discourse: 6:19 and 13:7 have it in prayers for deliverance and strength, echoing the OT appeal; 8:11 and 12:13 have it in synchronizing time-identifiers.

define the temporal element determining the action, rather than the action defining the day. The latter is the case with the epitome, the appeal, and the identifying characterization.

With these distinctions in mind, we turn now to an analysis of the individual passages with *hayyôm* and *hayyôm hazzeh*. There are many dozens of passages to be studied. Nothing is to be gained from oversimplification; the reader's patient attention to our detailed discussion of each passage is required.

Since only rarely does *hayyôm* (*hazzeh*) occur as a gloss, and almost never as part of a redactional transition, it will not be helpful to arrange the passages according to literary relationships, as in the previous chapter, but rather we shall treat them seriatim as they appear in the Hebrew text, combining *hayyôm* passages with those having *hayyôm hazzeh*. The only exception to this way or arranging passages will be in treating Deuteronomy, and that for reasons that will become apparent.

(1) Tetrateuch

Gen. 4:14

The folk saga featuring Cain and Abel is really about the people known as Kenites and has etiological significance. Two things were especially remarkable about these people: they were rootless wanderers, and they were known by some kind of protective mark (*'ôt*). The narrative of Gen. 4:1-16 is concerned in its present form to explain especially the latter, but the interview between the deity and the murderer seems to have been originally focused on the former. The interview begins with the inquiring question and defiant answer (9), the accusing question and statement of evidence (10), and the curse, banishing the murderer from the ground and making him *nā' wānād*, "a wanderer and a fugitive," in the land (11f.).[50] Vss. 13-15 contain the murderer's complaint of excessive punishment and the deity's mitigation of that punishment,[51] aiming at the climactic narrative statement of 15b, "And Yahweh put a mark on Cain, lest any who should come upon him should kill him"; but Cain's own words stress the curse of wandering rather than the danger of being slain. These words reflect the parallelistic structure of poetry:[52]

---

50. The last is introduced, in characteristic form, with *wᵉ'attâ*.
51. There is no compelling reason to emend MT לבן to לא כן, in spite of versional support for the latter (cf. BH³ mg). The function of *lākēn* is especially understandable if Yahweh's mitigating speech be recognized as an element of later reshifting.
52. What Cain is really complaining about is his being uprooted, and this is all that is actually reflected in the paronomasia of the concluding statement, which may reflect some of J's rephrasing in its present form (16): "Then Cain went away from the presence of Yahweh, and dwelt in the land of Nod (נוד), east of Eden." Careful attention to the parallelistic structure of vs. 14 makes it seem likely that the final stich of that verse, והיה כל מצאי יהרגני, is part of the later expansion directed toward the protective sign.

מעל פני האדמה   הן גרשת אתי היום

והייתי נע ונד בארץ   ומפניך אשתר

Here *hayyôm* concludes a stich introduced by the deictic particle and the perfect verb with object, followed by a prepositional phrase in the balancing stich and a second distich with parallel elements in a chiastic structure. The two lines epitomize the entire effect of the narrative in its original form.

Gen. 21:26

In a folk saga embodying elements of a Beersheba legend, Abimelech professes guiltlessness in the matter of Abraham's complaint, stating that Abraham had not told him, nor had he heard of it (i.e., from others) *biltî hayyôm*, "except for today" (Gen. 21:26).[53] Here *hayyôm* serves no other purpose than to provide a negative characterization of Abimelech's situation, contrasting this day to all previous days.

Gen. 22:14

At the end of what was probably the original E version of an etiology for a shrine whose real name may subsequently have been forgotten (more likely deliberately than by inadvertence),[54] Abraham is said to have bestowed a name upon it. However, the phrase that now appears in Gen. 22:14a seems to be an artificial reconstruction, together with the archeological statement in the relative clause that concludes the verse, אשר יאמר היום בהר יהוה יראה.[55] *Hayyôm* simply identifies the narrator's time in contrast to the time of the event narrated.[56]

Gen. 24:12, 42

It is generally recognized that Genesis 24 is a programmatic composition of the J-author, created to bridge the gap between the Abraham cycle and the Isaac cycle as he had them in his sources. Abraham's servant comes to the well in Nahor. Explicit time-designatives in vs. 11 set the scene. The

---

53. This combination occurs only here. It is not functionally equivalent to *ad hayyôm* which indicates the duration of a period related to the present.

54. It may have been the place known as *hammōriyyâ* (vs. 2), perhaps the famous Jebusite shrine (cf. II Sam. 24:18). The original E narrative ends with vs. 19, vss. 15-18 being a secondary expansion, while vss. 20ff. belong to J. On vss. 13f., cf. R. Kilian, *Isaaks Opferung* (SBS, 14, Stuttgart, 1970), pp. 57f.

55. Some versional readings add הזה. The saying, "which is called today, 'On the mountain Yahweh is seen'," implies that at one time the name may have been somewhat different.

56. The present narrator (E) has no genuine interest in the cultic site and is apparently rephrasing the story's original conclusion. He is responsible for reshifting the pun from seeing and being seen to the theme of "providing" a substitute (cf. vs. 8).

servant makes a prayer for success, setting a sign by which to test Yahweh's purpose (vss. 12-14). Following the vocative, the prayer puts in first place a succinct petition for success: "Prosper me *hayyôm* and perform fidelity to my lord Abraham." Although *hayyôm* is not emphatic, the appeal of which it is a part does express the cruciality of the encounter. Not needed as an indication of time when, it is defined by the nature of that encounter. It is not strictly epitomizing since it looks forward to the immediate present/ future. Yet the function is similar to that of the epitome. We shall apply to this occurrence, and to others belonging to prayer and exhortation, the term "decisive appeal."

The situation is somewhat different in vs. 42, where again it is the servant who is speaking. Having recounted to Rebekah's relatives the charge that Abraham laid on him (vss. 34-41), he begins to tell the events of the immediate present: "I came *hayyôm* to the spring, etc." All that follows the account of this day's happenings (vss. 42-49) is denouement. Although, strictly speaking, it is not necessary for the servant to designate the time of his coming to the spring (his hearers would have known that he had not been there the day before), the time-designative in fact simply identifies the present day in contrast to all previous days.

Gen. 30:32

In Gen. 30:25ff. Jacob is bargaining with Laban for his wages. The narrator (J) intends to emphasize his characterization of a man who enjoyed mightily the protection of a benign deity, guaranteeing the effectiveness of this man's own consummate craftiness. What Jacob proposes in vs. 32 seems to lay him open to Laban's deprivations (cf. 35f.), but all the while Jacob has in mind the clever scheme of vss. 37ff. *Hayyôm* in vs. 32 is contrasted to the unusual locution $b^e y\hat{o}m\ m\bar{a}h\bar{a}r$ ("hereafter") in vs. 33, identifying the immediate present in distinction from the future. The emphasis lies on this time-identification, rather than on the activity that is proposed.[57]

Gen. 31:43, 48

The Laban cycle comes to a conclusion in the pericope of which Gen. 31:43 and 48 are a part. Each of these verses features a declaration by Laban containing the word *hayyôm*. Source-analysis is vitally imperative at this point. Not only have the two narrative strands, J and E, been combined, but there is also some evidence of further literary supplementation.

Although the question of source-analysis could well be argued at

---

57. Jacob uses the impf. 1cs and the hif. inf. (cf. the impvs. of the Vulgate), thus this is no command or appeal, but a simple statement of fact. Note the pf. and impf. of vs. 33.

greater length than will be feasible here, a consideration of formal structure enables us to suggest the following as a likely solution.[58] To E belong vss. 43-45, containing Laban's invitation to a treaty and the report of his[59] act of erecting a *maṣṣēbâ*; vs. 44b is secondary supplementation.[60] E continues in vs. 50 with Laban's admonition and his appeal for divine adjudication, then in vss. 53b-54 with a report of Jacob's response. To J belong vs. 46, containing reports of Jacob's summons to the erecting of a *gal*, the making of the *gal*, and the eating of a covenant meal; also vs. 48, where Jacob[61] makes a declaratory statement, establishing the etiology for the name *gal'ēd*. Although vs. 47 may contain authentic historical information, it is in fact a literary supplement to this J account, as is also vs. 49, in which is contained an etiology for the name *miṣpâ*.[62]

Returning now to the first occurrence of *hayyôm*, we discover that it functions in an identifying characterization essential to the main issue of the material derived from an ethnological saga. Laban is concerned for his daughters; he declares his readiness for a covenant with Jacob by renouncing any intent to harm them: "But what can I do *hayyôm* to these my daughters, or to their children whom they have borne?"[63] This concern is further explicated in the covenant condition laid on Jacob (vs. 50).

The second occurrence of *hayyôm* comes in a noun-clause that provides the climactic declaration of a primitive covenant legend. "This heap is a witness between you and me *hayyôm*." This is an identifying characterization that also epitomizes the account by stating the essential quality of the day's occurrence, along with the significance of the archeological object memorializing that day.[64]

---

58. Cf. Noth, *UGP*, pp. 100-103; Gunkel, *Genesis, in loco*. The LXX, putting MT vs. 48a at the end of vs. 46, and substituting MT vss. 51, 52a, for vs. 48a, is hardly to be relied upon as a basis for emendation; it was most likely making an effort to improve a difficult Hebrew text, but the MT, as *lectio deficilior*, would be hard to account for as a deviation from the LXX *Vorlage*.

59. "Jacob" was substituted for "Laban" by a redactor who wished to avoid crediting the patriarch's adversary with imposing such an arrangement upon Israel's ancestors (cf. von Rad, *Genesis, in loco*), and to harmonize vs. 45 with vs. 46. He likewise was responsible for changing "Jacob" to "Laban" in vs. 48 in order to make it conform to vss. 49-50.

60. The reference to "covenant" as antecedent for "witness" can hardly be original, although such loose speech is often characteristic of later rephrasing.

61. Redactional; cf. n. 59.

62. Although the possibility exists that there was a shrine-site called Mizpah east of the Jordan, the identification with the Galeed of the original J account is artificial. The RSV's harmonistic "and the pillar" is scarcely justified since the Samaritan reading on which it relies is itself merely a harmonistic reading based on vs. 45.

63. It is commonly recognized that in the original folk-saga these "daughters" were descendant tribes or clans. The loose attachment of the reference to their children suggests that these were added as narrative embellishment at a subsequent stage.

64. Cf. Gene M. Tucker, "Witnesses and 'Dates' in Israelite Contracts," *CBQ*, 28 (1968), 42-45, suggesting that *hayyôm* functions as a date in vs. 48. But whatever the formal background of the witnessing formula may have been, the function here is not to date the event, which would have been appropriate only to a written

Gen. 40:7, 41:9, 42:13, 32

In Gen. 40 the redactor of the early Pentateuchal documents introduces his first extensive extract from the E version of the Joseph novella,
suppressing a presumed J parallel.[65] At this point the E story has the
object of depicting Joseph as an *'îš nābôn weḥākām* (41:33, 39; = *'îš 'ašer
rûaḥ 'elōhîm bô*, 41:38), i.e., one who can discern the times and the
seasons.[66] Hence the great interest in time sequences, seen especially in the
references to the three days (40:12f., 18f., 20) and the seven years
(41:26ff.). Characteristically, E emphasizes surprises and coincidences, such
as those of 40:5, 20, 41:11, 42:13. Sequence is of great importance;[67] this
is really all that accounts for *hayyôm* in 40:7 and 41:9. The noun-clause
question of 40:7b provides an identifying characterization as background
for the seemingly casual, yet portentful conversation that is to transpire
between Joseph and the two officials. The participial construction in 41:9
provides a similar identifying characterization as a device for interjecting
the chief butler's unanticipated recollection of his indebtedness to Joseph,
a key transition to the latter's subsequent elevation.

In 42:13b the brothers make a seemingly inconsequential reference,
one regarding Benjamin (repeated in somewhat altered form in their report
to Jacob in vs. 32): "And behold, the youngest is *hayyôm* with our
father. . . ." This is in fact nothing but another identifying characterization,
but one that throws out an important hint as to the central issue of the
forthcoming confrontation episode.

Gen. 41:41 LXX

In an extract from J, the episode of Joseph's elevation reaches a
climactic point in Gen. 41:41, where Pharaoh first declares to Joseph,
"Behold, I have set you over all the land of Egypt" (MT), and then bestows
the tokens of his office. The LXX offers the equivalent of *hayyôm* in
meaningful syntactical place in this declaration, following the verb and
object. Since this declaration of appointment has an epitomizing effect
similar to what is found in Ps. 2:7,[68] and is paralleled by Joseph's

---

document, but solely to epitomize the central meaning of the entire event, according to the J narrative. Tucker recognizes that the Ugaritic expression *ištu ūmi
annīm*, and the Akkadian formulae *ana dāri dūri* and *ana dārīti*, contain no precise
designation of date, but are similar in function to the Hebrew expression, *mē'attâ
we'ad 'ôlām*, a formula for permanent validity.

65. The E parallel to J's introductory formula in vs. 1 is *yāmîm* together with
belaylâ 'eḥād in vss. 4f.

66. A concern characteristic of wisdom tales; cf. G. von Rad, "Josephs geschichte
und ältere Chokma," *Gesammelte Studien zum Alten Testament* (2nd ed. 1958),
pp. 272ff., stimulating a lively new discussion of the origin of wisdom in current
literature.

67. Cf. Esther's similar preoccupation with time sequences.

68. See below, pp. 246ff.

declaration in 47:23 (J), to be analyzed below, there is reason to favor the originality of the LXX reading.

Gen. 47:23

A striking epitome with *hayyôm* occurs in Gen. 47:23, where Joseph makes a climactic declaration, "Behold, I have bought you *hayyôm*, and your land,[69] for Pharaoh." This is intended as the formal legal basis for the etiology appearing at the end of the pericope (vs. 26), where Joseph makes a statute "to this day" that "Pharaoh should have the fifth (לפרעה לחמש)."

The pericope about the Egyptians selling themselves for food (Gen. 47:13-26) is generally ascribed to J, although the possibility remains that it is a later composition, redactionally inserted into the combined JE account.[70] It should be apparent that the original account has been heavily interpolated. Vs. 13b, a doublet to 13a, mentions "the land of Canaan" alongside "the land of Egypt," as twice again in vss. 14f. "The land of Egypt" is mentioned also in vss. 20a, 26, while in vss. 19 and 23a the reference is to "our" or "your" land, in vs. 18 to "our lands," and in vss. 13, 20b and 23b to "the land." The statute that Joseph makes (26) is that a fifth of the produce is due as an annual tax to Pharaoh (so his declaration in vs. 24), not that a fifth (or all) of the land has been sold to him. This is the practical effect of the people's offering of themselves as slaves (19, 26), and the apparent meaning of Joseph's contractual declaration in vs. 23. The addition of vss. 13b-15aα, 19aα א, two further occurrences of אדמתנו in vs. 19, vss. 20-22, אדמתכם ואת in vs. 23, and vs. 26b turn the Egyptians' selling of themselves into a selling of their land.[71]

---

69. So the Hebrew word-order, making difficult syntax (which the LXX improves), showing that originally only the people were mentioned (*contra* Gunkel, *Genesis, in loco*). *Hayyôm* does not date the declaration so much as epitomize its intent and effect (cf. our observations in n. 64 regarding the witnessing formula in connection with a covenant).

70. It is apparent that our story, structured on a simple two-year famine pattern (cf. vs. 18), cannot belong to the E document with its seven-year famine cycle. Donald B. Redford, *A Study of the Biblical Story of Joseph (Genesis 37-50)* (SVT, 20, Leiden, 1970), arguing for a late date for the Joseph story, identifies 47:13ff. as an insertion by the Genesis editor (pp. 180-86). Redford's general conclusion, to the effect that the Egyptian background of the Joseph story is that of the Saite period, affects our pericope in making its artificiality very probable (see his treatment of Joseph's agrarian reforms, pp. 236-39).

71. On the legal background of Joseph's declaration, see R. Yaron, "Redemption of Persons in the Ancient Near East," *Revue internationale des droits de l'Antiquité*, 6 (1959), 16ff. L. Ruppert, *Die Josephserzählung der Genesis, Ein Beitrag zur Theologie der Pentateuchquellen* (Munich, 1965), pp. 154-61, assigns vss. 13-15aα to the J redaction, but it is likely that 13a is the original introduction, leading to mention of the suppliant Egyptians in 15aβb.

Exod. 2:18

A question with *hayyôm* introduces the climactic discourse in the folk saga concerning the encounter of Moses with the priest of Midian (Exod. 2:15bβ-22), used by J to incorporate his tradition about the close liaisons between Moses and the Midianites, as well as to establish the genealogy of Gershom, Moses' son.[72] As in the J stories of Genesis 24 and 29, this well encounter serves to introduce the protagonist of the narrative to his prospective in-laws. Although the seven daughters come early into the story, it is not upon them that the main interest focuses, but on their father, the priest. It is his question, "How is it that you have come so soon *hayyôm*?" that draws the scene from the well to the tribal dwelling. "Today" is apparently being contrasted to all previous days, when the daughters would come home later. Thus this verbal clause with *hayyôm* provides an identifying characterization sequential to the narrative climax.

Exod. 5:14

Hayyôm establishes a similar identifying characterization in Exod. 5:14, where the Egyptian taskmasters demand to know of the Hebrews why they have not made as many bricks *hayyôm* as formerly.[73] The only apparent purpose of the phrase *gam tᵉmôl gam hayyôm* is to underscore the more desperate situation of the Hebrews that has followed from Moses' first appearance before Pharaoh, intensifying the conflict and challenge between Moses, as Yahweh's spokesman, and this archenemy of the Hebrew people.

Exod. 13:4

There is little reason to doubt that the deuteronomistic school is responsible for the parenetic materials found in Exod. 13:3-10 concerning the passover-mazzoth. This passage juxtaposes stipulations for this combined festival in a notably less-successful amalgamation than in that of Deut. 16:1ff., where the seams are scarcely so visible as here. Here, in vss. 5ff., the parenesis addresses the second person singular concerning the historicized mazzoth festival, lasting seven days.[74] But in vss. 3f. it ad-

---

72. Cf. Gressmann, *Mose und seine Zeit* (Göttingen, 1913), pp. 19f.; Noth, *UGP*, pp. 151, 202f.; G. Fohrer, *Ueberlieferung und Geschichte* (Berlin, 1964), pp. 21-25.
73. The Hebrew text makes poor syntax as it stands, apparently contrasting גם תמול גם היום, "both yesterday and today " to "formerly" in the phrase כתמול שלשם. Rather than follow the LXX in eliminating גם תמול, we should perhaps identify the one temporal phrase as a literary doublet to the other (so Fohrer, *op. cit.*, p. 57, assigning גם תמול גם היום to E and כתמול שלשם to the dominant document in this passage, J), in which case the temporal contrast would be redactional. Cf. כתמול שלשם in vs. 7. ביום ההוא is a gloss; see above, p. 59.
74. Vs. 6 may have been added in view of Lev. 23:8b.

dresses the second person plural, and requires the commemoration of the single day of Yahweh's saving act. In all likelihood, vs. 3 was first a separate formula for the passover.[75] Vs. 4 appears to provide the bond between it and what follows, placing *hayyôm* in emphatic position at the beginning so as to draw the day of the passover into the mazzoth parenesis, at the same time using the participial form to describe the worshipers as in the very act of departing from Egypt.[76] The day to which *hayyôm* refers is, of course, the day of the cultic present, relived in festival observance, as well as the historical day of the exodus. This parenetical declaration epitomizes the day's significance according to the remembered historical and actual present liturgical situation.

Exod. 14:13

A high and solemn appeal for decisive behavior is involved in the use of *hayyôm* at a climactic point in J's narrative concerning the deliverance at the sea. We have noted that this narrative uses epitomizing *bayyôm hahû'* in its closing summation of this event, vss. 30f.[77] In vs. 13, where Moses confronts the Israelites with the revelatory meaning of the happening they are about to witness, he uses *hayyôm*, repeating it for special effect. Moses' command to the terrified Israelites is: "Fear not, take your position (*hityasṣᵉbû*),[78] and see the salvation of Yahweh, which he will perform for you *hayyôm*, for Egypt, which you see *hayyôm*, you will not see again anymore forever (*'ôd 'ad 'ôlām*)." The *'ᵃšer*-clause with the first *hayyôm* directly characterizes the Godward side of this event; the *'ᵃšer*-clause with the second *hayyôm* is an identifying characterization which, with the rest of the *kî*-clause to which it belongs, depicts the event's manward side. This day is emphatically a day when Yahweh will work Israel's salvation and when Israel's witness to that work is to lead to belief.

Exod. 16:25

Three times *hayyôm* appears in Exod. 16:25, once as a substantive and twice adverbially. This verse occurs at the climax of P's etiological narrative connecting the giving of manna with the origin of the sabbath. The manna story is told for the sake of the sabbath legislation which it contains. There seems to be little reason to quarrel with Noth's identification of a J sabbath-story in vss. 4f., 29-31, 35b;[79] one will observe that the

---

75. See above, p. 152.
76. The liturgist-redactor scarcely notices that the fictional background of vss. 5ff. is the plains of Moab, while that of vss. 3f. has to be Egypt.
77. See above, p. 75, and below on Deut. 11:2.
78. Cf. W. Harrelson, "Worship in Early Israel," *BR*, 3 (1958), 1-14.
79. *ATD*, 5, *in loco*. Noth identifies the rest as P, except for deuteronomistic glosses in 4bβ and 28. We should weigh the possibility that vss. 20 and 27 belong

P account is so much in the nature of a running commentary on these verses that at the very least it seems clear that P was familiar with J. In vs. 22, P reports an unmotivated detail, to the effect that on the sixth day the people gathered twice as much bread as usual, using this as a device for getting the *nᵉśî'ê hā'ēdâ*, "community leaders," before Moses to receive the sabbath command. All emphasis falls on the time element: Moses announces that "a day of solemn rest, a holy sabbath to Yahweh, comes *māḥār*," instructing the people to lay by the extra portion '*ad habbōqer*. The people comply (23f.). Then comes Moses' command (25), "Eat it *hayyôm*, for a sabbath is *hayyôm* to Yahweh; *hayyôm* you shall not find it in the field."[80] This in turn is followed by the torah-like command of vs. 26, with a narrative sequel in vss. 27ff.

The P account is interested in the motif of the marvelous preservation as a token of the divine will concerning the sabbath's special sanctity. The central purpose seems to be the negative one of differentiating this day from the other six. The first and third occurrences of *hayyôm* in vs. 25 emphatically identify and distinguish this day, first specifying it as the day for eating the extra portion, then characterizing it as the day when no other food is to be found. The intervening *kî*-clause, amounting to a liturgical proclamation, epitomizes the narrative's central concern; *hayyôm* is, however, almost certainly substantival in this clause.

The most unusual aspect of this passage is that it places in the foreground not the event that characterizes the day but the day itself. The day is inherently sacred; it determines the event appropriate to it. This is in striking contrast to the viewpoint of Israel's historiographic literature, where the event determines the day.

Exod. 19:10

The special solemnity of the Sinai confrontation is underscored by the time sequence involved in preparing for it, according to Exod. 19:10f., 15, 16 (J). The theophany is scheduled for *hayyôm haśśᵉlîśî*; "today" and "tomorrow" are to be spent in getting the people ritually prepared for it.[81] The reference to *hayyôm* in vs. 10 serves to establish this sequence, but the combination of time-designatives determines the temporal setting for the definitive command within this pericope.

---

with 4bβ, 28 as part of the late Pentateuchal redaction. How the sabbath tradition came to be associated with the manna tradition is not clear; the latter is still independent in the very early passage, Josh. 5:12 (cf. Exod. 16:35).

80. The Vg. lacks the second occurrence of *hayyôm*, while the LXX lacks the third. The second can be read either as a substantive or as an adverb.

81. It seems likely that the narrative grew out of a ritual or was designed to accompany a ritual. Cf. W. Beyerlin, *Herkunft und Geschichte der ältesten Sinaitraditionen* (Tübingen, 1961), pp. 10ff.

Exod. 32:29

Hayyôm occurs twice in Exod. 32:29, immediately following vs. 28, which contains a casualty report with *bayyôm hahû'*. As has been shown in our previous analysis,[82] the episode about the Levites' purge developed as the narrative expansion of a primitive *Levitenspruch* in vs. 29, being combined redactionally with the golden-calf story. Here in vs. 29 Moses says: "They have ordained[83] you *hayyôm* to Yahweh, for 'Each one against his son and against his brother'—[and] bestowing on you *hayyôm* a blessing." The repetition of *hayyôm* may have been occasioned by the intrusion of what was once a motto of the primitive Levites.[84] Both clauses serve to epitomize emphatically the day's memorial event.

Exod. 34:11

Yahweh's word to Moses, "Observe what I am commanding you *hayyôm*,"[85] introduces (vs. 11) the apodictic code that comprises the so-called J decalogue of Exod. 34. This is probably the earliest example of a formula—the so-called promulgation clause—that occurs frequently in Deuteronomy. One must work through to an understanding of the function of this appeal for decisive action not only by way of careful literary analysis, such as identifies most of vss. 10, 11b-13 as part of a deuteronomistic expansion, but especially by way of attention to the formal structure of the probable original. Everything points to the ritualistic background of vss. 1-9 (cf. Exod. 19).[86] Following the theophany described in those verses, Moses is told that Yahweh is about to make a covenant (10). Next comes the introductory rubric constituting vs. 11a; then the specific individual commands, commencing with לא תשתחוה אל אחר in vs. 14;[87] and finally Yahweh's instructions to "write these words" (27). The relative clause in vs. 11a is a summarization of the action which produces the commands; together with the imperative which it modifies, it clearly constitutes the climax of the entire narrative framework as well.[88] The relative clause with

---

82. Above, p. 102.
83. Reading a perfect in place of the MT's imperative. For the versional deviations, see BH[3] mg; the second *hayyôm* is missing in the LXX and Vg.
84. Cf. Gunneweg, *Leviten und Priester*, pp. 29-37.
85. The LXX lacks anything corresponding to *hayyôm*.
86. Cf. Beyerlin, *Sinaitraditionen*, pp. 90ff.
87. See the commentaries; also E. Nielsen, *Die Zehn Gebote, eine traditionsgeschichtliche Skizze* (Copenhagen, 1965), *in loco*.
88. From the point of view of tradition development, it seems quite likely that the apodictic code, with the introductory rubric in vs. 11a, once existed independently. The theophany may similarly go back to independent tradition, but in its present form (referring to the preparation of the two tablets) it has been shaped as a narrative framework for the apodictic code. The beginning of vs. 10, "And he said, 'Behold, I make a covenant'," forms the transitional link between the two; it may not be as old as the interpretive formula at the end (vs. 27).

hayyôm is in itself an identifying characterization; the sentence as a whole is a central parenetic appeal.

Lev. 9:4

Having given instructions for the sacrifices pertaining to the ritual of priestly ordination, Moses adds the explanatory motivation clause of Lev. 9:4b, "for today Yahweh is to appear[89] to you." The foremost position of *hayyôm* draws an emphatic connection to the report of a sanctioning theophany in vs. 23 (cf. vs. 6). But it seems impossible to defend the originality of all these references to Yahweh's appearance: either vs. 4b must be part of the early P narrative, and the references in vss. 6 and 23 late additions,[90] or the latter are early and vs. 4b is an intrusion.[91] The second choice is probably the right one, for the self-conscious use of *hayyôm* in itself makes the originality of vs. 4b quite suspect. In any case, the temporal term sits loose from any lively tradition, serving here to prepare an entirely artificial sequential connection between the ritual and the theophany.[92]

Lev. 10:19

Twice *hayyôm* appears in Lev. 10:19, first in reference to the sacrifices performed by Eleazar and Ithamar, second in reference to a hypothetical performance of the ritual by Aaron. Commentators agree that this is a very late addition to an already composite text.[93] Aaron is presented as remonstrating with Moses about his severity in dealing with a minor priestly infraction (vss. 16ff.), but with a view to the fierceness of God's anger as shown in the episode of vss. 1ff. In effect, Aaron is saying that not even if he should be the officiant would God's favor be guaranteed. Together, the two occurrences of *hayyôm* serve to provide a contrasting characterization of the actual and hypothetical personages involved in this complaint.

(2) Deuteronomy

Passing by Numbers, where *hayyôm* and *hayyôm hazzeh* do not appear in adverbial usage, we come to the concluding book of the Pentateuch. In sheer number of occurrences, Deuteronomy by itself far out-

---

89. The MT's perfect is hard to justify, in spite of support from the Vg. The reference is plainly futuristic, hence LXX ὀφθήσεται (reading a nif. ptcp.), followed by RSV.
90. So Elliger, *HAT*, 4, *in loco*.
91. So Koch, *Priesterschrift*, *in loco*; Noth, *ATD*, 6, *in loco*.
92. From the interpolator's point of view, vs. 4b epitomizes what is considered to be the ultimate meaning of the narrative, i.e., Yahweh's approval of, and blessing on, the ordination ritual.
93. Elliger, *HAT*, 4, *in loco*, speaks of it as a priestly midrash.

weighs the total provided by the rest of the Pentateuch. Not counting the frequent use of *hayyôm* in such set phrases as `*ad hayyôm hazzeh*, we identify no fewer than fifty-nine occurrences of adverbial *hayyôm* and *hayyôm hazzeh* in the MT of Deuteronomy. Besides these the versions read these terms in seven passages where they are lacking in the MT.

Not all the occurrences of *hayyôm* or *hayyôm hazzeh* fall into the same pattern. We find, for instance, that as many as twenty-five passages (MT) involve the stereotyped formula, "the commandments which I am commanding you today," or something very similar to it. If we look carefully, we can see that the various sections of Deuteronomy have each their own characteristic way of employing *hayyôm* or *hayyôm hazzeh*; there is a distinctive difference of usage in the original lawbook, the introductory and concluding parenesis, the deuteronomistic introduction, and the editorial supplementation. The lawbook uses these phrases the least, the parenesis uses them the most.

This is, of course, what we should expect in light of the general situation to which Deuteronomy as a whole addresses itself. That is to say, the essential program of the book in its present form is to confront Israel in a late moment of its preexilic history with a command from Yahweh that is modeled on the past but is validated for this particular moment of challenge and confrontation.[94] Inasmuch as it is particularly the parenesis that aims to close this existential circle between the past and the present, it is quite naturally the parenesis that also makes the most frequent use of *hayyôm* and *hayyôm hazzeh*, sometimes with emphasis, sometimes not. The deuteronomistic redaction, on its part, typologically extends this *hayyôm* of present confrontation, doing something analogous to what the Epistle to the Hebrews later does when it calls upon the Jewish-Christian community to "exhort one another every day, as long as it is called 'today' " (3:13).[95] Thus the deuteronomistic extension of the original parenesis likewise contains a sizable number of passages with *hayyôm* (one passage has *hayyôm hazzeh*). But the original lawbook, not so sharply focused upon a present moment of decisive encounter, contains only a few occurrences of *hayyôm*, and none at all of *hayyôm hazzeh*.

Without making the above discriminations, Gerhard von Rad has distinguished himself among commentators on Deuteronomy in the recognition he has given to the clear central importance of *hayyôm* as one of the leading theologoumena within this book. He offers the following insight into the significance of the situation in which the Israel addressed by Deuteronomy found itself:

. . . Dieses Israel, das faktisch in nichts mehr zu vergleichen ist mit dem Israel, das ehedem am Horeb stand, das von dem Horeb-Ereignis durch eine sehr lange und

---

94. See A. Alt, "Die Heimat des Deuteronomiums," *Kleine Schriften*, II, 250-75.
95. Cf. 3:7−4:13.

überaus belastende Geschichte getrennt ist, dieses Israel der späten Königszeit in seiner ganzen politischen und religiösen Fragwürdigkeit—ist es denn noch Jahwes Volk? Die Antwort ist hell und eindeutig: Diesem Israel, und zwar dem ganzen empirischen Volk, wird vom Dt. die Erwählung und die Heilsverheissung Jahwes zugesprochen. Somit stehen wir vor folgendem Phänomen: sechs in Sünde und fortgesetztem Abfall vertane Jahrhunderte werden durchgestrichen und Israel wird noch einmal an den Horeb gestellt, um Jahwes Heilswort, das noch nicht hingefallen ist, zu hören. Dieses Heilswort lautet: "Heute bist du zum Volke Jahwes, deines Gottes, geworden." Besonders eindringlich durch das in allen dt. Aussagen sich findende "heute" ist die Betonung des Präsentischen dieser göttlichen praedicatio impii. Die hohe Aktualität der Erwählung steht nun hinter dem Versuch des Dt. das schon in starker innerer Auflösung begriffene Israel noch einmal als das heilige Volk Jahwes zusammenzufassen.[96]

The analysis of the audience and life-situation to which the Deuteronomic parenesis addresses itself has been considerably advanced in Norbert Lohfink's monograph, *Das Hauptgebot*,[97] which, while restricting itself to chaps. 5–11, makes sharp distinctions between the way the original "Verfasser" presented the situation and the way it was modified by an "Ueberarbeiter."[98] Lohfink characterizes the parenetic situation in the following words:

So verschieden die Einzelaussagen sind . . . es gibt eine alles durchziehende Konstante: die Situation selbst, in der Dtn 5-11 geschieht, und die auch immer wieder ins Wort tritt: die Linie von Gott über Moses zum angeredeten Volk, dieses reine Gegenüber in der Einheit von Vergangenheit, Gegenwart und Zukunft. . . . Daher möchten wir die These vertreten, dass Nivellierung durch Ueberladung, Verarmung durch Reichtum bewusst gesucht werden, um den Hörer hinter all dem langsam immer deutlicher im eigenen Innern den Grundsinn seiner Existenz verstehen zu lassen.[99]

Biblical scholars generally recognize that Deuteronomy constitutes something of a monument in the development of Hebraic covenant theology, drawing together the traditions of the past for an address to the hazardous present and the problematical future. As it undertakes to simplify Israel's choice in a highly confused and complex situation, it draws diverse elements together, arranging them typologically according to the pattern of the renewed day of divine-human confrontation.

---

96. *Deuteronomium-Studien* (FRLANT, N.F. 40, Göttingen, 1948), pp. 49f. (ET by D. Stalker, *Studies in Deuteronomy*, London, 1953, pp. 70f.). Cf. also von Rad, *Theologie des Alten Testaments*, I (Munich, 1958), 230 (ET, p. 231), and *Das Formgeschichtliche Problem des Hexateuchs*, p. 28.
97. Norbert Lohfink, *Das Hauptgebot, Eine Untersuchung literarischer Einleitungsfragen zu Dtn 5-11* (AnBib, 20, Rome, 1963). See especially Part V, "Der paränetische Vorgang," pp. 261ff.
98. Lohfink identifies the covenant cult as the *Sitz im Leben* for the "Verfasser," leaves open the possibility that the work of the "Ueberarbeiter" may have been purely literary. In spite of the considerable attention paid to an analysis of the parenetic situation, Lohfink is not sufficiently impressed by the function of *hayyôm* (*hazzeh*) as to make any special analysis of it.
99. P. 284.

We must examine the individual passages in Deuteronomy that use *hayyôm* (*hazzeh*), but rather than treat them simply seriatim, we will do well to depart from our regular pattern and arrange them according to the literary strands that have come to be rather widely recognized in present-day critical analysis. Proceeding from the beginning of the book, but in retrograde with respect to the order of actual historical development, we take first the passages that are redactional (deuteronomistic) or editorial; next, passages that von Rad and others have identified as framework parenesis (preparatory in chaps. 5—11, applicatory in 26:16ff.); after this, the lawbook of 12:1—26:15 (including its own internal parenetical recasting); finally, the set phrases occurring in relative clauses—referred to by Lohfink as "die Promulgationssätze"—distributed throughout the various sections of the book.

We do not intend to involve ourselves directly in the vexing question of the vacillation between singularistic and pluralistic second-person address in the various sections of the parenesis. The majority of recent scholars appear to have been moving toward a literary explanation of this phenomenon (so recently G. Minette de Tillesse and E. W. Nicholson),[100] assigning the individual singularistic and pluralistic passages to separate literary strands or documents. Lohfink proposes, however, to solve this problem mainly on the basis of form and stylistics.[101] We intend to take up these two groups of passages separately, first the pluralistic and then the singularistic, as a means of keeping this question before us. It is conceivable that the use of *hayyôm* in these two groups of passages will offer useful data toward the solution of this problem.

(a) Redactional and editorial

More and more, the consensus of modern scholarship identifies the bulk of the first four chapters of Deuteronomy, together with most of the material in the last several chapters of the book, as a product of the so-called deuteronomistic school. It is closely akin to, and possibly a part of, a "deuteronomistic history book" extending through Joshua to the end of II Kings. Martin Noth, whose work, *Ueberlieferungsgeschichtliche Studien* (1943), has been influential in propagating this view, has gone so far as to identify Deut. 1 as the actual beginning of the history-book, having, in his view, been designed by the author as part of a framework for incorporating the entire Deuteronomic parensis and lawbook as a model for the subsequent historical account.

In the first three chapters of Deuteronomy, Moses confronts the

---

100. Tillesse, "Sections 'tu' et sections 'vous' dans le Deuteronomome," *VT*, 12 (1962), 29-87. Nicholson, *Deuteronomy and Tradition* (Oxford, 1967), pp. 22-36.
101. *Hauptgebot*, pp. 237-58. Cf. also H. Cazelles, "Passages in the Singular within Discourse in the Plural of Dt 1—4," *CBQ*, 29 (1967), 207-19.

Israelites encamped on the plains of Moab, offering them a review of the way Yahweh has led them through the wilderness from Horeb to the very border of the promised land. Von Rad identifies this address form-critically as a "Memoirenbericht."[102] Although geography is prominent, the time element likewise claims attention. A variety of time-designatives are used for providing transitions between the successive episodes of Moses' account,[103] but, alongside *hayyôm*, the phrase *bā'ēt hahî'* appears to predominate.

The latter expression introduces new narrative episodes in 1:9, 2:34, 3:12, 18, 21, and 23. Always its sole function is to provide a sequential transition.[104] The anxious repetition of *bā'ēt hahî'* in 1:16 and 18 suggests that the entire pericope, 1:9-18, is secondary to the context—a conclusion that is supported by the observation that this section breaks into the journey narrative. In 4:14 *bā'ēt hahî'* introduces a preparatory explanation rather than a new historical episode.

It is different with the seven occurrences of *hayyôm* (*hazzeh*) in Deut. 1–4: in only one passage does this provide a simple sequence, serving in the remaining passages in epitomes or identifying characterizations. We shall examine these seven passages seriatim, following this with a study of three passages from redactional or editorial additions at the end of the book.

Deut. 1:10

In Deut. 1:9ff., Moses rehearses to Israel at the conclusion of the wilderness journey what he had said to them before departing from Horeb. His discourse at that time had to do with the appointing of judges. The pericope is introduced by *bā'ēt hahî'*, similarly to other episodes in this section but, as we have just observed, this pericope is probably a secondary intrusion into the text.[105]

---

102. *ATD*, 8, p. 14; cf. his comm. *in loco*. See now also the extensive study of Deut. 1:6–3:29 in J. G. Plöger, *Literarkritische, formgeschichtliche und stilkritische Untersuchungen zum Deuteronomium* (BBB, 26, Bonn, 1967), pp. 1-59.

103. *'attâ*, 2:13; *we'attâ*, 4:1; *'āz*, 4:41; *'ad hayyôm hazzeh*, 2:22, 3:14; *kayyôm hazzeh*, 2:30, 4:20, 38. Cf. also temporal indications of a less formal nature at 1:45, 2:1, 14, 4:9, 10, 15, 32, 40, 42.

104. Cf. Plöger, *op. cit.*, pp. 218f., "In jener Zeit—ein Form-kriterium?" (covering *bā'ēt hahî'* in the entire OT)—to which the answer is given that this is not a fixed formula belonging to any particular *Gattung*. From a philological point of view, nothing can seem more frivolous than the attempt of John Marsh in his book, *The Fulness of Time* (New York, 1952), p. 49, to explain the frequent occurrence of *bā'ēt hahî'* in Deut. 1–10 as an indication that the events referred to were taking place, in the Deuteronomist's retrospective point of view, at one and the same time "because they were all part of the one activity in history whereby God constituted his people Israel." This is sheer nonsense; *bā'ēt hahî'* is only a transitional device in chaps. 1–3, quite without the epitomizing and typological function that we will find to belong to *hayyôm*. See the discussion of Marsh's book in Chapter One, n. 17.

105. See Plöger, *op. cit.*, pp. 25-31, for more extensive argumentation.

Vs. 10 intends to explain Moses' complaint of vs. 9: he cannot bear Israel alone because they are *hayyôm* "as the sand of the sea for multitude."[106] Now, the interpolator certainly must have been aware that this hyperbolic form of the father-promise scarcely could have found its fulfillment in the tradition regarding Israel's condition at the time of the Sinai experience.[107] This is why the text has Moses immediately add, "Yahweh, the god of your fathers, make you a thousand times greater than you are, and bless you, as he has promised you!" (11). Could the interpolator inadvertently have been thinking of the Israel of his own time—to which, he could have been quite aware, the book was in fact addressed? In any event, *hayyôm* functions here simply as part of an identifying characterization.

Deut. 1:39

Without attempting to discuss the complex problem of the divergences between the deuteronomistic version of the spy-murmuring narrative and that of the J-P combination in Num. 13–14, it is important for an understanding of the function of *hayyôm* in Deut. 1:39b to recognize that the section that immediately precedes it must be a literary addition; in the place of the references to Caleb's posterity found in Num. 14:24 (J), an interpolator has inserted a statement exempting all the underaged from the divine decree of annihilation.[108] Because *hayyôm* has been set forward, it is evident that special emphasis has been placed upon the time element as an especially crucial element in the identification of the new generation that is to be saved. Thus *hayyôm* serves as an essential part of an identifying characterization, as in vs. 10.

Deut. 2:18, 25

In the pericope containing Moses' recollections concerning the conquest of Transjordan (Deut. 2–3), *hayyôm* occurs once at 2:18, while

---

106. On Moses' office of *nāśîʾ*, see now H. Cazelles, "Institutions et Terminologie en Deut. i, 6-17," SVT, 15 (1966), 97-112. One should observe that the reference to Israel as the sand of the sea is lacking in the independent form of the tradition regarding Moses' complaint appearing in Num. 11:14 (J). Cf. Plöger, *op. cit.*, pp. 31-35.

107. One can only speculate whether the writer was familiar with J's figure of more than 600,000 (Exod. 12:37f.), or, if he were, whether this might fulfill, for him, the promise of becoming like the sand of the sea.

108. Plöger, *op. cit.*, takes the generally held position that all of vss. 36-39a is secondary (pp. 43, 49). It may very well be possible that the Deuteronomist did not know the Caleb tradition, so central to the early spy-murmuring narrative of Num. 13f., but the likelihood lies altogether in the opposite direction. If the introduction to Deut. 1:36 appears as an afterthought, this may only reflect a hesitation to record an embarrassing tradition, since in the deuteronomistic scheme of things Caleb was supposed to have got claim to Hebron only through Joshua's appointment (cf. Josh. 14). On the various problems surrounding the spy and the holy-war traditions in Deuteronomy, see H. Lohfink, "Darstellungskunst und Theologie in Dtn 1, 6-3, 29," *Biblica*, 41 (1960), 105-34.

hayyôm hazzeh occurs once at 2:25. Although both of these verses are within singularistic expansions to the original text,[109] the function of the time-designative is different in each. Moses' instructions in 2:16ff. originally had to do only with Sihon, therefore the true content of Yahweh's address in vs. 17 is to be found in 24aα. Vss. 18f., which intend to explain why Ammon was not attacked (cf. vs. 9b), employ *hayyôm* in nonemphatic order; the noun-clause to which it belongs is another identifying characterization, whose purpose is to connect temporally the crossing of Moab's boundary and the crossing of the boundary of Ammon, overlooking the fact that Israel did not immediately proceed on its way, as assumed in the original text in vss. 26ff.

The interpolation in vss. 24aβ-25, on the other hand, proleptically contemplates the conquest of Sihon as an occasion by which Israel's enemies will be put in deep dread. Although both the cause and the effect are envisaged as no more than incipient (החל רש ... אחל תת),[110] the foremost position of *hayyôm hazzeh* produces a striking synchronism between the two. The statement of the effect, introduced by *hayyôm hazzeh*, identifies the time as equivalent to that of its cause, viz., possessing the land of Sihon. Even though this verse epitomizes the central meaning of this event, the essential purpose of the time-designative is to emphasize the equivalence of time.

Deut. 4:4

All the commentators call attention to the highly complex process of literary composition that has produced chap. 4 of Deuteronomy.[111] The only materials that may be identified with any degree of confidence as a continuation of the historical review in chaps. 1–3 would have to be 4:1f., 5-8, since the theme of Moses teaching (למד hif.) the "statutes and ordinances"[112] in order to impart true wisdom to Israel marks these verses as the original deuteronomistic transition to the verses that introduce the decalogue in chap. 5 (cf. 5:1, with למד qal). These begin with w^e'*attâ*, a formal term marking an abrupt departure from the historical prologue and introducing this, the first formal parenesis of the book of Deuteronomy.

Hayyôm occurring in the promulgation formula, "which I set before you this day," as at the end of vs. 8, is to be discussed further on in our

---

109. Cf. Plöger, *op. cit.*, pp. 54ff.
110. For a close parallel to the syntax involved, cf. the deuteronomistic passage Josh. 3:7, where *hayyôm hazzeh* is similarly used (see below).
111. So, e.g., von Rad, *ATD*, 8, *in loco.* Cf. Noth, *UGS*, pp. 14f.
112. Note the combination, *(ha)ḥuqqîm* ... *w^eham(û)mišpâtîm*, in 4:1, 5, 8, 14, 5:1. It is possible that the original parenesis continues in at least parts of vss. 9-14, 21-23a. We leave open the question whether the writer was also responsible for the framework of the decalogue in chap. 5.

analysis. This is the only original occurrence of *hayyôm* within the section, vss. 1-8, since vss. 3f., also containing *hayyôm*, are probably secondary.[113]

We observe that the parenesis introduced in vss. 1f. suddenly breaks off as Moses returns in historical retrospect to the fate of those who "followed the Baal of Peor," and then as abruptly turns back again to his listeners, those who, he says, held fast to Yahweh, who "are alive this day" (vs. 4). The formulation is strikingly reminiscent of the deuteronomistic phraseology in 1:39, where *hayyôm* was likewise used in an identifying characterization of the group exempted from the decree of judgment. In our present passage all emphasis is on the equation between the two participles *hadd*ᵉ*bēqîm* and *ḥayyîm*, but *hayyôm*, coming at the end, is also important because it temporally defines those who are alive and are being addressed.

Deut. 4:26

Hayyôm occurs next at Deut. 4:26, in a witnessing oath invoking a curse upon those who provoke Yahweh with graven images. The entire section, 4:9-28, appears to be a secondary polemic against idol-worship, structured according to an abbreviated form of the familiar Deuteronomic *Bundesformular*. Vss. 9-14 constitute a historical preamble, calling on Israel not to forget Horeb, where it heard Yahweh's voice but saw no form. This is the basis for the central command of vss. 15-24, where Israel is forcefully prohibited from making and worshiping images. There is no blessing except for what is implicit in the references to Israel's possessing the good land (21f.), but the curse is powerfully emphatic in the entire concluding section, vss. 25-28. This striking imbalance between blessing and curse identifies this addition as dating from the exile. Both its locution and its tenor are similar to the late addition in Deut. 31:28f. (cf. 30:19, 32:1).[114]

So solemn is the oath of vss. 26ff. that Moses summons as witnesses none other than the very heaven and earth (cf. 8:19). The present day is not only a day of parenetic appeal but also one of solemn attestation. What is attested to—in fact, invoked in a curse—is what is to come in the future as a consequence of sin. The witnessing occurs *hayyôm;* the curse will come quickly (*mahēr*). It is in order to serve the contrast between these two temporal situations that the time-designative has been added to the solemn words of warning. Thus it is essentially a time-identification.

---

113. It is difficult to imagine that the writer who left Israel at "Beth-peor" in 3:39 would immediately use another name for this shrine site, the "Baal-peor" of 4:3. The manuscripts and versions that read לבעל for בבעל may offer a way out of this literary difficulty, but the likelihood is that 4:3f. is secondary. The interpolator simply used a form of this place name that was more familiar to him (cf. Hos. 9:10).

114. Cf. the expression HNH ŠLḤTY LH'YD BKM HYM, in a contemporary Palestinian inscription; Y. Aharoni, "Three Hebrew Ostraca from Arad," *BASOR*, 197 (1970), 16ff.

Deut. 4:39

Hayyôm occurs again in Deut. 4 at vs. 39 (also in the promulgation formula of vs. 40), recognizable as the climactic verse of the section, vss. 32-40. The greatest likelihood is that this section is a continuation of the new addition beginning with vs. 29, the clear purpose of which is to counteract the dread judgment of vss. 26-28. Accordingly, vss. 29ff. must be very late. Though mostly in the form of second person singular parenesis, these verses show the influence of the wisdom tradition and the oracles of restoration.

The special role of *hayyôm* in vs. 39 can best be seen when we observe that key time-designatives set the outline for this entire pericope. The first subsection, vss. 29-31, is identified timewise by the phrase $b^e{}^{\flat}ah^a r\hat{\imath}t\ hayy\bar{a}m\hat{\imath}m$, pointing to the time of the future return—future, i.e., from the vantage point of the apostasy and judgment envisaged in the underlying material, vss. 25ff. A second subsection, vss. 32-38, begins with phrases pointing to the time of Yahweh's past mercies ($y\bar{a}m\hat{\imath}m\ r\hat{\imath}^{\prime}\check{s}\bar{o}n\hat{\imath}m$ $^{\prime a}\check{s}er\ h\bar{a}y\hat{u}\ l^e p\bar{a}n\hat{e}k\bar{a}$, "the first days that were before you" = $l^e min\ hayy\hat{o}m$ $^{\prime a}\check{s}er\ b\bar{a}r\bar{a}^{\prime}\ {}^{\prime e}l\bar{o}h\hat{\imath}m\ {}^{\prime}\bar{a}d\bar{a}m$, "from the day when God created man"), referred to now as the theological basis for the expectation of blessing expressed in vss. 29-31; this second subsection concludes with *kayyôm hazzeh*, extending the time of Yahweh's past mercies to the very moment of present confirmation. A third subsection, vss. 39-40, contains the new parenesis, calling on Israel to acknowledge Yahweh (וידעת and parallel verbs in waw-consecutive perfect) *hayyôm*, in order that future blessing may be assured (pleonastic: $l^e ma^{\backprime}an\ ta^{\prime a}r\hat{\imath}k\ y\bar{a}m\hat{\imath}m$ with *kol hayyāmîm*).

The *hayyôm* of vs. 39 functions as part of an appeal for decisive action. Israel is challenged anew with the moment's central concern. It is most remarkable that this pericope seems entirely aware that this new *hayyôm* must be very late, a moment of renewed possibility following a period of severe judgment. Yet it maintains the fiction of a Moses speaking at the moment of Israel's birth. This is typology in the fullest sense: the *hayyôm* of the distant past repeats itself in the *hayyôm* of God's new age.

Deut. 31:2

The redactional framework that introduces Deuteronomy draws it to a new conclusion in chaps. 31ff. [115] At the beginning of chap. 31 it depicts Moses as preparing for his departure, handing over his authority to Joshua. He makes a farewell speech. As do Caleb in Josh. 14:10 and Barzillai in II Sam. 19:36, Moses mentions his age (one hundred twenty years!) as of this

---

115. So Noth, *UGS,* pp. 39f.; von Rad, *ATD,* 8, *in loco.* N. Lohfink takes Deut. 29—32 as a distinct redactional unit; cf. "Der Bundesschluss im Land Moab," *BZ,* 6 (1962), 32-56.

moment (*hayyôm*), then his physical condition with reference to the situation. The noun-clause with *hayyôm* is an identifying characterization, designed to set the scene for this last encounter between Moses and Israel.

Deut. 31:21, 27

The occurrences of *hayyôm* in Deut. 31:21, 27 belong to late editorial supplementations, which severely censure Israel for future apostasies, already seen as incipiently present (cf. 4:26ff.). In both verses (cf. vs. 29) Moses says that he knows the present conduct and proclivities of Israel as portents for the evil future.[116] The main function of *hayyôm* in each case is to aid the temporal contrast and to establish the identifying characterization.

(b) Pluralistic parenesis

We come now to the immediate parenetic framework of the Deuteronomic lawbook, taking up first the occurrences of *hayyôm* (*hazzeh*) that fall within pluralistic passages. Five such passages are scattered through the preparatory framework at 5:3, 24, 8:19, 11:2 and 11:26, while those belonging to the framework at the end are closely concentrated in two series of verses (29:9, 11, 12, 14 *bis*, 17; 30:15, 18, 19). This does not include occurrences of *hayyôm* in the promulgation formula, which we shall continue to ignore in this part of our analysis.

Deut. 5:3

Hayyôm appears in Deut. 5:3, one of the crucial passages for an understanding of the typological *double entendre* of this book. Here Moses states, with more emphasis than one would expect, "Not with our fathers did Yahweh make this covenant, but with us, even us, those here today, all of us living" (לא את אבתינו כרת יהוה את הברית הזאת כי אתנו אנחנו אלה אלה פה היום כלנו חיים).[117] From the vantage point of Moses addressing the Israelites at the plains of Moab, the "fathers" are the patriarchs, or possibly the generation that died in the desert, while "all of us living" are his listeners; from the vantage point of the seventh- or sixth-century redactor, these are, respectively, the Israel of early times and the Israel of the present.

This recognition of a self-conscious typological shift is confirmed by the probability that vss. 3-5 (except for the final word, לאמר) constitute an

---

116. In vs. 27 *hayyôm* does nothing but reinforce בעודני חי עמכם, with which it should be read ("while I am alive with you today"), rather than with the following ממרים חיתם עם יהוה, as in the RSV.
117. The LXX rearranges vs. 3b paraphrastically, attempting to avoid the unusual, seemingly awkward Hebrew.

expansion of the original introduction to the Deuteronomic version of the decalogue.[118] לאמר is syntactically awkward, not to say impossible, at the end of vs. 5; the style of 1:6 suggests that it originally belonged at the end of vs. 2. Furthermore, the ideology of vss. 3ff. scarcely accords with that of the undoubtedly original, patently programmatic transitional framework found at the end of the decalogue, vss. 22ff. In 22ff. nothing is said about Moses interposing himself between Yahweh and the people while Yahweh was speaking; this comes only subsequently, as the leaders appoint Moses henceforward to be the interpreter of the law that they have already heard and that has been inscribed on tablets (vs. 22). Thus the statement in vs. 5 has to be an addition, whether by the same or by another writer—though probably by the latter.

Coming back to *hayyôm* in vs. 3: its function is that of an identifying characterization, as in 1:10, 39, 4:4. But here the conditions of place and condition are added to that of time. The addressees are all those "here," "now," and "alive."

Deut. 5:24

In the transitional framework at the conclusion of the decalogue, *hayyôm hazzeh* occurs at vs. 24, where the leaders report, "We have seen Yahweh our god—his glory and his greatness—and his voice we have heard in the midst of the fire; *hayyôm hazzeh* have we seen that God may speak with man and he may live."[119] We shall not be detained by discussion of the formal structure of the pericope to which this verse belongs (vss. 22-33, with 6:1-3),[120] except to remark that it leads to the seemingly illogical proposal that Moses should agree to serve as mediator because, if the people hear the voice of Yahweh anymore, they will die. The point seems to be that this one time they had endured the risk of the *mysterium tremendum*, but should not ever again presume to risk it (cf. vs. 26). This consideration explains both the unusually long form and the forward position of the temporal phrase. Although in itself the clause with *hayyôm hazzeh* summarizes the preceding theophany episode, its function in this context is to draw a stark contrast between the "once" of that episode and the "from

---

118. The preponderant majority of critics erroneously separate only vs. 5 as secondary. The recent analysis of Lohfink (*Hauptgebot*, pp. 145-48) identifies vss. 3-5 as secondary (perhaps as an addition by the original writer), but Lohfink's separation of two distinct "Parenthesen" on the basis of stylistic differences is questionable.

119. There is no reason to suspect literary intrusion here; the writer seems merely to be struggling to reconcile competing ideologies (cf. Lohfink, *Hauptgebot*, *loc. cit.*).

120. Cf. *ibid.* Lohfink, combining Deut. 5 and 6 as an original unit, identifies 5:23 as a "Vertrag über die künftige Wortvermittlung" (23, Notiz; 24-27, Antrag des Volkes wegen Wortvermittlung; 28, Notiz; 28-31, Annahme des Antrags durch Jahwe).

now on" of what follows. It serves therefore as an emphatic identification of time.

Deut. 8:19

Hayyôm occurs in 8:19, here again as an element of the witnessing-cursing formula. Literary critics have often identified vss. 19f. as secondary, along with vs. 1, on account of the pluralistic formulation of these verses within a singularistic context. Recent form-critical studies, particularly those of Lohfink, have put some doubt upon this assessment.[121] The curse of 19f. is expected in the covenant schema following the blessing promised in the parenesis of vs. 18. Moreover, the witnessing formula in vs. 19 is probably the model for the more elaborate formula in 4:26, rather than a weak, stereotyped extract from it, as some critics have implied. At any rate, *hayyôm* functions here much as in 4:26. The witnessing formula essentially epitomizes the negative aspect of the present confrontation, yet *hayyôm* is introduced mainly to distinguish this present day of witnessing/warning/cursing from the coming day of judgment. Thus, within the context as a whole, its function is again identification of time.

Deut. 11:2

Hayyôm occurs next in pluralistic parenesis at Deut. 11:2, immediately following a section in the singular. Lohfink's painstaking analysis identifies 10:10—11:17 as the conclusion to the second phase of the original composition in chaps. 5—11. In Lohfink's opinion, this material goes back to early liturgies used in the covenant ceremony.[122] We note that even in its present, much reworked form, 11:1-17 itself follows the schema of the *Bundesformular* in its internal structure: historical review, 2ff.; command, 8ff.; blessing, 13ff.; curse, 16f. What is especially striking is that Israel is being called on in vss. 2ff. to confess or acknowledge the mighty acts of Yahweh which it has witnessed. As we shall see, similar constructions with ידע hif. occur in the singularistic passages, 7:9 and 9:3; but we have already found it in 4:39—a passage probably much later than the one we are dealing with here.

Two things in particular seem very strange about 11:2. One is the syntax. Do the object nouns, "the discipline of Yahweh your god, etc.,"

---

121. *Ibid.*, pp. 189-99. Lohfink sees chap. 8 as the work of the "Ueberarbeiter," who, by ending chap. 8 with this curse, has shaped a distinct unity of chaps. 5—8 according to the pattern of the "Bundesformular": chap. 5, Vorgeschichte; chap. 6, Gebotsteil; chap. 7, Segen; chap. 8, Fluch. Whatever validity there may be in this reconstruction, one observes that the switch to pluralistic formulation in 8:19f. is not adequately explained. Perhaps it is a hand later than that of Lohfink's "Ueberarbeiter" that has added these verses.

122. See *ibid.*, especially pp. 219-31. Cf. von Rad, *ATD*, 8, p. 15; K. Baltzer, *Das Bundesformular*, Neukirchen, 1960 (ET *Covenant Formulary*, Philadelphia, 1970).

belong with the two verbs in the circumstantial clause modifying "your children," or with the main verb, *wîda'tem?* If the former, the main verb is left curiously dangling, and we cannot help wondering whether certain words following it have dropped out. In this case, the *kî*-clause takes over until a following *kî*-clause in vs. 7, where the opposite is affirmed: "your eyes (emphatic) have seen." But the latter alternative seems more likely. It would involve the recognition that the *kî*-clause constitutes a kind of parenthetical explanation, leaving *'et mûsar YHWH 'elōhêkem* as the proper syntactical continuation of *wîda'tem*.[123]

But something else is strange here. The audience who are being addressed are ostensibly the new generation about to enter the promised land. Moses emphatically affirms that it is they, not their children, who saw the *Heilsfeiten*. Are we to think that the writer of these verses was not aware of the tradition that the generation who witnessed the saving acts also perished in the wilderness? Apparently so, and this seems to be the situation also with regard to 6:20ff., where Israel in Moab is instructed to tell succeeding generations about the deliverance from Egypt that it itself had experienced. Perhaps the recognition that such passages as these originate from liturgical formularies will explain why nothing is made of the lost-generation tradition, since each new generation of worshipers was called on to confess that they too had participated in the experience of Yahweh's saving acts.[124] But we still wonder why 11:2 makes so emphatic the disjunction between those who are being addressed and their children. This can only be for the purpose of sharpening the parenetic appeal to those who were the responsible confessors within the covenant community.

When we get down to the problem of identifying the function of *hayyôm* in vs. 2, we may be helped by the observation that when it was used with ידע hif. in 4:39, the clause of which it was a part served, in effect, to summarize the entire parenetical demand. That this is also its function here is made all the more likely by a recollection of how *hayyôm* serves with the vocable ראה in Exod. 14:13 (cf. vss. 30f.) to point up the central significance of the entire narrative concerning the deliverance at the sea.

Exod. 14:31 has a summary conclusion to the effect that "Israel saw the great work which Yahweh did . . . and feared Yahweh and believed (אמן hif.) Yahweh and his servant Moses." This is liturgical language, declaring how witnessing Israel was led to the act of faith to which the Moses of Deuteronomy is continually summoning the Israel of a later generation. Undeniably, it is this same liturgical tradition that manifests

---

123. See Lohfink, *op. cit.*, p. 221, n. 12, acknowledging the possibility of the former while preferring the latter. The את before בניכם has to be explained either as marking an emphatic subject (cf. Brockelmann, *Hebräische Syntax*, § 31[b]) or as implying an omitted verbal clause governing it as object.
124. Cf. Lohfink, *op. cit.*, p. 264.

itself here in Deut. 11:2ff., where ראה is a catchword alongside ידע and where *hayyôm* occurs not only in the initial summons to confession but repeatedly, in a variety of combinations (vss. 4, 7 LXX,[125] 8, 13).

Deut. 11:26

Hayyôm occurs next in pluralistic parenesis at Deut. 11:26, where Moses solemnly declares, "See, I am setting before you (confronting you with) *hayyôm* blessing and curse." In the verses that follow, *hayyôm* recurs three times as part of the promulgation formula (vss. 27, 28, 32). The similarity of this section to the eloquent concluding parenesis in 30:15ff. is most impressive. Lohfink identifies 11:26-32 as a "Proömium" to the lawbook beginning in 12:1.[126] *Hayyôm* in vs. 26 is unemphatic, all stress being placed on the action of Moses, as he announces the choice between blessing and curse. The function of the verse is clearly to epitomize a situation leading to an appeal for decision, showing the close relationship between these two functions of the time-designative.

Deut. 29:9, 11f., 14, 17 [E-10, 12f., 15, 18]

Hayyôm is employed with impressive frequency in the chapters that contain Moses' address to Israel as he makes a covenant with them in the land of Moab (29:1), *viz.*, Deut. 29–30. Gerhard von Rad has shown that these chapters exhibit in themselves the complete pattern of the *Bundesformular* (29:1-7, "Vorgeschichte"; 29:8, "Grundsatzerklärung"; 30:16-18, "Segen und Fluch"; 30:19f., "Zeugenanrufung"). These are the elements that presumably constitute the original core of these chapters; the materials standing between them are to be viewed as secondary expansions.[127]

Deut. 29:9-14 contains *hayyôm* five times. Lohfink has described this pericope as a kind of protocol, an enumeration of the distinct groups and generations who are involved in the covenant confrontation.[128]   It begins with a characterization of the general situation, "You are standing *hayyôm* all of you before Yahweh your god" (9a); then follows a detailed explication of the content of "all of you" (9b-10); next comes a clause stating why Israel is standing before Yahweh (לעברך בברית יהוה אלהיך ובאלתו), which in turn is specified in a relative clause containing *hayyôm* (11);[129]

---

125. The LXX reading may have arisen from the influence of היום connected with ראה in vs. 3. This reading is hard to justify syntactically or functionally.
126. P. 234.
127. Cf. von Rad, *ATD*, 8, *in loco*. The tradition of a covenant with Israel in Moab is unique to this passage. Lohfink, "Der Bundesschluss im Land Moab," *BZ*, 6 (1962), 32-56, argues that chaps. 29–32 constitute an eventual redactional unity, but recognizes that chaps. 29–30 alone constitute the original core of this redactional block.
128. Lohfink, "Bundesschluss," p. 38.
129. Cf. 4:23a. The formulation is modeled after, but not equivalent to, the promulgation formula.

this leads then to a purpose clause introduced by *l^ema'an* with the infinitive and containing *hayyôm* [130] in a nonemphatic position (12a). Whether this purpose clause refers back to the relative clause or the main clause of the preceding verse, it is certain that it constitutes the climax of the pericope, characterizing as it does the meaning of the entire confrontation: "that he may appoint you *hayyôm* as his people, and he may be your god."[131]

But this repetition of familiar traditions does not as such account for the presence of these verses in this particular text. What is new is the affirmation made in vss. 13f., to the effect that Israelites not present *pōh* and *hayyôm* are included. This is to be seen as a programmatic effort, similar to that of 5:3, to aim the parenesis at the late generation experiencing the covenant confrontation anew in liturgical celebration. Here in vss. 13f., *pōh* and *hayyôm* function as elements in identifying characterization, as in 5:3 (cf. 1:10, 39, 4:4).

Hayyôm occurs also in 29:17.[132] Von Rad has pointed out that the secondary pericope of which this is a part, vss. 15ff., is again modeled after the *Bundesformular*, with vss. 15f. as "Vorgeschichte," vs. 17 as "Grundsatzerklärung," and vss. 18ff. as "Androhung des Fluches."[133] Though we may perhaps modify this with the observation that the curse element actually begins with the clause introduced by פֶּן יֵשׁ in 17b, we are helped by the realization that 17a does constitute the central element in the pericope. Although *hayyôm* appears in a relative clause, the temporal element which it expresses is an essential part of the situation embraced by the parenesis. It is therefore more than an element of identifying characterization. "Today" qualifies as much the parenetical appeal as the evil it seeks to set aside.

Deut. 30:15, 18f.

Within the pericope marking what may be the conclusion to the original Deuteronomic parenesis, 30:15-20, *hayyôm* appears three times—not counting one occurrence in the promulgation formula at vs. 16.[134] The occurrences in vss. 15, 18, and 19 appear at points of special stress within the formal framework. It has been recognized that also this pericope reflects the structure of the *Bundesformular*, this time somewhat modified to suit the peculiar function of the pericope within the book. Lohfink's analysis of the schema is: 15, "deklaratorische Ankündigung"; 16, "Segen";

---

130. Missing in LXX; but, in light of the climactic function of this verse, the MT reading is probable.
131. Cf. 27:9.
132. Missing in the early LXX text.
133. *ATD*, 8, *in loco*.
134. The form requires the reading of the LXX text at the beginning of this verse; cf. BH³ mg and the commentaries.

17-18, "Fluch"; 19a, "Anrufung . . . zu Zeugen . . . mit Rekapitulation";
19b-20, "Schlussparänese."[135]

The announcement of vs. 15, "See, I have set before you[136] *hayyôm*
that which is life and that which is good, also that which is death and that
which is evil," epitomizes not only the present pericope but the entire
Deuteronomic parenesis. This is a deduction based on form as well as
content. This verse begins with *reʾēh* and the perfect of נתן, as compared
with the participial form of נתן following *reʾēh* in the introductory proem
to the lawbook (11:26). What was about to be given, according to chap. 11,
is seen in chap. 30 as given already, so that Israel must now make its final
and irrevocable choice.

Hayyôm in vs. 18 forms part of a curse formula—as a matter of fact,
part of the apodosis to the protasis beginning in vs. 17. The similarity to
the way *hayyôm* is used within the curse formula in 4:26 and 8:19 is
impressive; but most striking is that in those passages the verb was not
higgadtî, as here, but *haʿîdōtî*, the verb that governs *hayyôm* in 30:19,
where heaven and earth are summoned as witnesses, as also in 4:26 (cf.
31:28). Vs. 19 constitutes a final summation, introducing the moving
appeal to choose life with which the pericope (and the section) concludes.
We may summarize by stating that vs. 15 is an epitome, while vss. 18 and
19 are epitomes in which *hayyôm* is defined in terms of its content, but
also in terms of the future time against which it is contrasted, and functions
therefore basically as a time-identifier, as in 4:29 and 8:19.

(c) Singularistic parenesis

We analyze next the passages containing *hayyôm* which are singularis-
tically styled. Even including 30:15, which we have seen to be form-
critically inseparable from pluralistic elements in the pericope, the number
is strikingly small. As a matter of fact, there are only six occurrences in the
MT if we do not count 30:15; but this number may be expanded to seven if
we include one probable occurrence in the presumed *Vorlage* of the LXX.

Deut. 7:9 LXX

Deut. 7:9 is a singularistic passage, but the LXX has the verb in the
plural (γνώσεσθε). This is followed in the original hand of Codex B by
σήμερον, representing *hayyôm*. As in 9:6, this Septuagintal reading may
have arisen through the influence of the Hebrew text of 4:39, 9:3, and
11:2, where *hayyôm* follows the perfect consecutive of ידע; but the great

---

135. "Bundesschluss," p. 42.
136. Although this verse is styled in singularistic address, the formal unity of the
pericope indicates that it should be discussed in connection with the occurrences
that follow in pluralistic address (18f.). This weighs in the balance against any
simplistic documentary explanation.

similarity in the formal functioning of these verses forces us to acknowledge the probability that the LXX reading is original here. Regularly the verb has the force of a command, enjoining to confession; although in 9:3 the verb has more the force of an announcement, even there the confessional appeal is not wholly lacking.

We may follow Lohfink[137] in identifying 7:6ff. as a secondary element in this chapter. To some extent, this section follows the schema of the *Bundesformular*. Vs. 6a is a transitional introduction; vs. 6b is a kind of historical preamble stating Yahweh's elective act; vss. 7f. are a parenthetical—and perhaps supplementary—explication of the meaning of this act. Vss. 9-11 constitute the covenant requirement, taking place in two further acts, those of acknowledging/confessing (9f.) and of obeying (11).[138] A blessing follows in vss. 12ff. It is clear that the confession required in vss. 9f. is based on such a liturgical formulation as is to be seen in Num. 14:18 and Exod. 34:6f. The command, "So know (acknowledge) that Yahweh your god is God," has the central appeal of the entire section.

Deut. 9:1, 3

Deut. 9:1-7, in which *hayyôm* twice occurs, is another secondary expansion to the original parenesis, according to Lohfink.[139] A careful analysis of this pericope indicates that vs. 6 is its point of major stress. Here the parenesis comes to a head in the instruction to Israel that the "good land" would come into their possession not through any righteousness of their own but through the failure of the people now in possession of it. The parenesis of this section reflects that of the juridical confrontation; even the fictional holy-war setting is to be seen as no more than the arena in which Yahweh executes his judgment on the nations.[140]

The two *hayyôm's* in vss. 1 and 3 serve to point up contrasting aspects of the contemplated warfare.[141] Vss. 1f. contain a summons to battle in which Moses announces the plan of action and then reminds Israel how formidable the enemy are.[142] Vs. 3 informs Israel that Yahweh will

---

137. *Hauptgebot*, pp. 167-88. On pp. 185f. two different theories of literary development are offered.
138. One should observe the promulgation formula with *hayyôm* in vs. 11.
139. *Hauptgebot*, pp. 200-204. Von Rad, *ATD*, 8, pp. 14, 55, includes vs. 7 in the following "Memoirenbericht."
140. Cf. G. von Rad, *Deuteronomium-Studien*, pp. 30-41 (especially pp. 40f.), regarding the warlike setting of Deuteronomy; see also von Rad, *Heilige Krieg*, p. 68ff.
141. For *hayyôm* in the summons to battle, cf. Deut. 2:18, 25, 20:3. Influential in the underlying tradition is the "Uebereignungsformel" typical of holy-war stories, as in Judg. 4:14, etc.
142. Although the Anakim were an historical people, known in Egypt during the Middle Kingdom period (cf. *ANET*, p. 328), other biblical texts mentioning them (Num. 13:28, 33, Deut. 2:21), except perhaps the deuteronomistic passage, Josh. 11:21f., treat them as legendary figures. The reference here is conventional and figurative.

subdue these enemies. The *hayyôm* in vs. 1 is part of a characterization of Israel as it stands in this situation of insuperable challenge; they are certain to be defeated if they trust in their own resources. The *hayyôm* in vs. 3 stands in striking contrast; this verse is an appeal, calling on Israel to confess (ידע, pf. cs.) what the situation becomes once the initiative of Yahweh is taken into account. Since the "righteousness" of the respective combatants is the essential factor that determines the outcome of the holy war,[143] all this prepares the ground psychologically for the parenesis of vss. 4ff., reaching its climax in vs. 6.[144]

Deut. 26:16, 17, 18

It has generally been recognized that the Deuteronomic lawbook that commences in chap. 12 comes to an end in chap. 26, but discussion continues regarding the precise relationship of 26:16-18 to that corpus.[145] 12:1 furnished the introductory rubric: אלה החקים והמשפטים אשר תשמרון לעשות... To this 26:16a clearly harks back: היום הזה יהוה אלהיך מצוך לעשות את החקים האלה ואת המשפטים. Although 26:16ff. certainly now serves to provide the concluding framework to the lawbook, it likely originated from a redactional process subsequent to that which produced the introductory rubric in 12:1. Evidence for this may be seen in the way the demonstrative *hā'ēlleh* has been picked up from 12:1, where it served as predicate nominative to both *hahuqqîm* and *hammišpāṭîm*, but here is allowed to function as an attributive adjective modifying *hahuqqîm* alone. Further evidence lies in that 12:1 and the laws which it introduces contemplate no particular temporal situation, whereas 26:16ff. contemplates a very specific situation of confrontation, in which Yahweh calls on Israel to make a decisive commitment to obey his laws. It seems certain that 26:16ff. embodies the same parenetic purpose that we have seen at work in the sections previously studied. It belongs, accordingly, not to the editorial rounding-off of the lawbook, but to an early stage of its parenetic application.

We discover a striking difference in.function between the *hayyôm hazzeh* here in vs. 16 and the two occurrences of *hayyôm* in vss. 17 and 18. Not only does the difference in form demand our attention; we observe that vs. 16 has *hayyôm hazzeh* foremost, in emphatic position. This has

---

143. Cf. Judg. 11:27.
144. In 9:6 the originality of the LXX reading is improbable because the parenesis seeks to instruct Israel as to the juridical basis of Yahweh's saving act rather than call them to confession. The LXX has added σήμερον after καὶ γνώσῃ under the probable influence of vs. 3 (also 4:39, 9:3, 11:2).
145. Widely accepted is G. von Rad's analysis ("Das Formproblem beim Deuteronomium," pp. 23ff. in *Das formgeschichtliche Problem des Hexateuchs* [ET, pp. 26ff.]) identifying the redactional arrangement of "Urdeuteronomium" into the following pattern: geschichtliche Darstellung ... und Parenäse, 1-11; Gesetzesvortrag, 12—26:15; Bundesverpflichtung, 26:16-19; Segen und Fluch, 27-30.

been its position in 2:25 and 5:24, where time-identification was of central concern. Stress is clearly on the time element (time when) rather than immediately on the content or quality of the day. The intent is to mark the present day as the day to which Yahweh's command pertains. The commands have been written down (in 12:1–26:15); *now* is when they are intended to be in force.

This declaration with *hayyôm hazzeh* is followed by an appeal to obey. Together, this declaration and appeal constitute the heart of the Deuteronomic parenesis, corresponding in ideology to the often-repeated promulgation formula, which we have yet to study.

Although it is immediately apparent that *hayyôm*, repeated in parallel constructions in vss. 17 and 18, serves in an epitomizing statement, close inspection reveals that these words go back to a stage of textual development prior to that in which the *hayyôm hazzeh* of vs. 16 came into the text. The parenesis is throughout making conscious use of traditional materials derived from the covenant liturgy. We observe, first of all, that the declaration and appeal of vs. 16 are themselves repeating traditional covenantal formulations;[146] and furthermore that the references in vss. 18f. to Yahweh designating Israel as his peculiar possession (*'am s^egullâ*), setting them above the nations and making them holy to himself, borrow heavily from the liturgical language of Exod. 19:4-6,[147] a formulation that was evidently so well known that it is being directly referred to in the twice-repeated phrase, *ka'^aser dibber (lāk)*.

The parallel phrases, את יהוה האמרת היום להיות לך לאלהים (17) and ויהוה האמירך היום להיות לו לעם (18), are likewise borrowed from the traditional formulations of the covenant liturgy. They constitute original independent elements, embellished by the pareneticist with a number of, at times, ill-fitting phrases that shape the entire pericope as a strongly one-sided admonition, requiring obedience of Israel while omitting further reference to Yahweh's obligation.[148]

In the liturgy from which the original formulations of vss. 17f. have been borrowed, the covenant mediator solemnly declares—probably directly at the conclusion of certain sacrificial or symbolic acts—what each party has caused the other to say: "Yahweh thou hast caused to say today,

---

146. This verse may be directly echoing the introductory formula to the Sinaitic covenant in Exod. 34 (vs. 11, שמר לך את אשר אנכי מצוך היום), but the difference in phraseology makes it likely that both passages go back independently to traditional usage.

147. Cf. J. Muilenburg, "The Form and Structure of the Covenantal Formulations," *VT*, 9 (1959), 357ff.; N. Lohfink, "Dt 26:17-19 und die 'Bundesformel'," *ZKT*, 91 (1969), 517-53.

148. Cf. von Rad, *ATD*, 8, *in loco*. The often noted syntactical difficulties have been created by these embellishments, the most jarring of which is the series of infinitival phrases expressing Israel's obligation, awkwardly attached to the end of Yahweh's declaration of intent in vs. 17.

that he would become thy god"; "Yahweh has caused thee to say today that thou wouldst become his people."[149] In this manner the significance and effect of the covenant ritual is formally stated. These declarations powerfully epitomize all that has to be said about the essential structure of the covenantal relationship.[150]

Deut. 27:9

It has been widely supposed that the same hand that composed Deut. 26:16ff. shaped an extension of it in 27:9f., rounding it off with a recitation of blessings and curses in chap. 28. היום הזה נהיית לעם ליהוה אלהיך seems clearly to refer to the declarations contained in 26:17a, 18a, while the phraseology of 28:1 repeats that of 27:10. 27:9f. is to be seen either as the concluding element in the central summons to covenant decision or as the introduction to the blessings and curses. Inasmuch as the covenant mediator is specifically mentioned here, it seems plausible to connect vss. 9f. more closely with the following than with the preceding element.[151]

There is another consideration that underscores the relative divergence of 27:9f. from 26:16ff., namely, the use of *hayyôm hazzeh*, again in foremost position. Elsewhere in Deuteronomy this construction has regularly been used for emphatic time-identification, hence there is much probability that special stress is being placed on the time element here.

---

149. The reason for the forward position of the forms with אמר is not clear, unless it is to emphasize Yahweh's priority in the relationship. The unique hifil form has occasioned much discussion, leading to various proposals for textual or philological solutions. None is much worth considering except the suggestion to assign the meaning "proclaim" to this hifil form, in which case Israel speaks in the first declaration, Yahweh in the second.

150. The two-sided declaration reflects liturgically what has often been called the Sinai covenant formulation, "I am Yahweh your god and you are my people," or the like. Cf. R. Smend, *Die Bundesformel* (TS, 68, Zürich, 1963), where it is argued that this formulation is relatively late. Unlike many scholars, Smend is not at all confident that Josiah's covenant, narrated in II Kings 23:3, is the historical event to which "this day" of Deut. 26:16 refers.

151. See the commentaries. There is wide agreement that 27:1-8 and 27:11-26 are secondary intrusions, incorporating independent materials. The editorial introduction in vs. 11, referring to "that day," clearly presupposes vss. 9f. Counteracting the hypothetical possibility that the introductory rubric in vs. 9 may also be editorial is the observation that the addressee ("all Israel") closely corresponds to the vocative ("Israel"), and is different from the addressee in vss. 1 and 11 ("the people"). Nevertheless, the mention of the "Levitical priests" alongside Moses is suspicious: the verb is singular, followed by "Moses" and then these words; nowhere else do *hakkōheⁿnîm hallⁿwiyyim* figure as covenant mediators (cf. 17:9, 18:1, 24:8, Josh. 3:8, 8:33—all containing legislation concerning their role; cf. *hakkōheⁿnîm bⁿnê lēwî* in Deut. 21:5, 31:9). One would suspect, in light of the role they play in the Ebal narrative of Josh. 8:30-35, that the mention of them has been introduced into 27:9 by the same editor who inserted the legislation for Ebal contained in 27:1ff. On the place of the Levites in the Deuteronomic/deuteronomistic ideology, cf. Gunneweg, *Leviten und Priester*, pp. 126-38.

Being preceded as it is by a summons to hear (cf. 5:1, 6:4, 9:1, 20:3) and an unparalleled command to be silent,[152] this solemn declaration marks a striking new beginning, in which both the unique time and the unique event are stressed. *Hayyôm hazzeh* may therefore function less as time-identification than as part of an epitome—the epitome of all epitomes, stating the central fact of covenant existence before God.[153] Certainly it is a hand later than that which composed 26:16ff. that has given it its present position in the covenant structure of the book as a whole.

(d) The lawbook

We turn now to the remarkably few occurrences of the time-designative within the original lawbook collection.[154] Apart from verses containing textually uncertain promulgation clauses, we are concerned only with four passages, 12:8, 15:15, 20:3, and 26:3, all of which have *hayyôm* rather than *hayyôm hazzeh.*

Deut. 12:8

Hayyôm occurs in Deut. 12:8 in a prohibition that characterizes the situation in which the addressees currently find themselves, i.e., one in which every man is "doing whatever is right in his own eyes."[155] We may wonder whether vss. 8ff. constitute a secondary expansion of vss. 1ff., inasmuch as these preceding verses presuppose a situation of relative innocence on the part of Israel as it crosses over into the land and is called upon to destroy every temptation to idolatry lying in its path. The likelihood is that the writer/speaker has momentarily forgotten his fictional situation and begins to think of the chaotic conditions actual to his own time. Together, vss. 1-12 constitute a (pluralistic) parenetic refocusing of the original, singularistic law of centralized worship contained in vss. 14-19, but

---

152. The meaning of this hifil imperative of a verb סכת is to be conjectured from cognate usage and the context. It may be linguistically related to the *has* of Judg. 3:19, etc.
153. In any event, no synchronism is apparent; we are not apprised on any point of equivalence except the day's content. One should observe also the occurrence of *hayyôm* in the promulgation formula in 27:10 and 28:1. For further discussion of this crucial passage, see below, p. 261.
154. On literary problems cf. Th. Oestreicher, *Das deuteronomische Grundgesetz* (Gütersloh, 1923).
155. Judging from the deuteronomistic passages, Judg. 17:6, 21:25, this phrase has specific application to compromising with idolatry. This evaluation explains Israel's failure to possess "until now" the "rest" and the "inheritance" which Yahweh had promised (cf. G. von Rad, *Gesammelte Studien*, pp. 101-108; *Theologie*, I, 223). But even the deuteronomistic school ascribed the deferment of this fulfillment to Israel's refusal to go up from Kadesh rather than to their falling into idolatry (so Deut. 1:19–2:2); hence here again the writer betrays his real existential situation within the period of the kingdom's downfall. He envisages a resolution through the centralization of worship, which is the central point toward which he aims his parenesis (vss. 10-12).

this refocusing is probably earlier than the general Deuteronomic redaction.[156]

Deut. 15:15

In Deut. 15:12-18 we encounter the parenetic reworking of an old law regulating the release of Hebrew slaves, a more primitive form of which is found in the Covenant Code at Exod. 21:2ff. (cf. Lev. 25:39-46). Vs. 15 intrudes into the legal stipulations with a *heilsgeschichtliche* motive-clause whose content parallels that of Deut. 5:15 and terminates with the locution, על כן אנכי מצוך את הדבר הזה היום, which is identical to the closing formula used in 5:15, except that the latter uses the perfect verb with an infinitival phrase and has Yahweh as subject, and "the sabbath day" as object. The similarity is close enough to indicate that 5:15 and 15:15 are probably from the same hand. Here the parenesis is styled as a speech of Yahweh. The *hayyôm* in which Yahweh speaks has to be the situation of the general redaction (cf. 12:8, 20:3, 26:3), hence this entire verse must derive from the redactor.

Deut. 20:3

Deut. 20 is a conglomerate of rules and exhortations concerning the conduct of the holy war. Vss. 2-4, in the form of a battle sermon similar to that found in 7:1ff., 9:1ff., and 31:3ff., purports to issue from the mouth of the priest as he encourages the people to go forward to victory in Yahweh's strength. Although the pluralistic styling marks these verses as relatively late, the tradition underlying such a battle sermon is very old, being rooted in such a summons to battle as is found in Judg. 4:14. We see from that passage that the reference to the time, *hayyôm*, occurs in Deut. 20:3 as a standard element in the traditional formulation; this verse provides an identifying characterization preparatory to an appeal for faith.

Deut. 26:3

The last passage in the lawbook containing *hayyôm* is Deut. 26:3, which, in spite of its parenetic styling, clearly reflects actual ritual practice. Here is legislation for the offering of the firstfruits, but the parenetical recasting in 26:1-11 has combined two distinct reports of the ritual. Much recent scholarly attention has been concentrated on the second report (vss. 5-11) because of its *heilsgeschichtliche* resumé. We pass this by, observing merely that this resumé has its formal parallel in the epitomizing declaration of vs. 3. The worshiper's present moment is fraught with experiential fullness. He stands here professing that the oath to the fathers has come to

---

156. Cf. von Rad, *ATD*, 8, *in loco*; F. Horst, *Gottes Recht* (Munich, 1961).

reality, that he is here in Yahweh's land. And thus the *hayyôm* of grace becomes the *hayyôm* of gratitude and worship.[157]

(e) The promulgation formula

We have now surveyed all the passages in Deuteronomy with *hayyôm hazzeh* and all those with *hayyôm* except those that occur in what Lohfink calls "der Promulgationssatz"—a relative clause with *'aŝer* modifying one or more of the synonyms for the divine revelation, usually *hammiṣwâ* or *hammiṣwôt*.[158] Its function is to identify the revelation in question. It is remarkable because of its frequency of occurrence and because of its tendency toward a stereotyped phraseology. As the noun *miṣwâ*, singular or plural, is the favorite substantive in the antecedent phrase, the favorite verbal form is the piel of צוה ("command"), from which this substantive is formed. Thus there is a marked redundancy in the formula: the revelation in question is identified only by itself and by the fact that it is occurring *hayyôm*. Wherever the revelatory act is allowed to slip into the past, as happens in about twenty passages,[159] this time-designative is dropped and the verbal form, still from the piel of צוה, changes from the participle to the perfect.

The purpose of the promulgation formula with *hayyôm* is to provide an identifying characterization of the general parenetical situation. Identifying characterization has already proven to be the predominant use of *hayyôm* in Deuteronomy, occurring in 1:10, 39, 2:18, 4:4, 5:3, 9:1, 12:8, 15:15, 20:3, 29:9, 11, 12, 14 *bis*, 17, 31:2, 21, 27. But now it becomes part of a set pattern of expression, reflecting the fact that the unique situation of divine confrontation has been reduced to a ritual of constant repetition. That which is unique has now been generalized; the lawgiver continues to confront Yahweh's people, laying upon them and challenging them ever and again with the requirements of the covenant. In every individual passage the promulgation formula with *hayyôm* remains subsidiary to the central appeal (4:40, 6:2, 6, 7:11, 8:1, 11, 10:13, 11:8, 27:1, 4, 10) or the

---

157. R. P. Merendino, OSB, analyzing Deut. 26:1-11 on pp. 346-71 of his monograph, *Das deuteronomische Gesetz. Eine literarische, gattungs- und überlieferungsgeschichtliche Untersuchung zu Dt 12—26* (BBB, 31, Bonn, 1969), assigns vss. 2a, 3aαb, 10bα to the earliest of five literary strands, observing its form as a liturgical formulary without taking note of the function of *hayyôm*.

158. See his chapter on this in *Hauptgebot*, pp. 59-63, and Tables I and II at the end of the book. For our own complete analysis, see S. J. DeVries, "The Development of the Deuteronomic Promulgation Formula," *Biblica*, 55 (1974), 301-16.

159. 1:3, 4:13, 23, 44, 45, 5:33, 6:1, 17, 20, 9:12, 16, 13:6, 26:13, 14, 28:45, 69, 31:5, 29. To these Lohfink adds similar formulae which actually authenticate the past revelation rather than identify the act of its promulgation (4:5, 5:12, 16, 32, 6:25, 12:21, 18:20, 20:17), plus two passages that authenticate a present or future revelation (5:31 and 18:18).

wider characterization (11:13, 22 LXX, 27, 28, 13:19, 15:5, 19:9, 28:1, 13, 14, 15, 30:2, 8, 11, 16) to which it happens to be attached.[160]

This ends our study of passages in Deuteronomy, for which we shall defer a definitive summary and interpretation until the end of the present chapter.

(3) The Former Prophets

Our just-concluded study of *hayyôm* (*hazzeh*) in Deuteronomy has, for the greater part, taken us into a moderately late period in the development of Israel's sacred literature. Going on now into the so-called Former Prophets, we are in effect turning back in time because the large majority of passages with the time-designative are earlier than Deuteronomy and the work of the deuteronomistic school. We have been impressed by the large number of passages with *hayyôm* in Deuteronomy; yet the impression of frequent use has been diminished by the realization that most of the Deuteronomic passages employ *hayyôm* in the standardized promulgation formula, and that almost everywhere the situation to which *hayyôm* refers is one and the same, i.e., the situation of parenetical appeal in covenant confrontation. We shall be much more impressed, therefore, when we examine the passages in this new section of the Old Testament and discover that *hayyôm* and *hayyôm hazzeh* are even more frequent here—though nowhere so highly concentrated as in Deuteronomy—and that they reflect a very wide variety of specific situations.

Taking *hayyôm* and *hayyôm hazzeh* together, we have counted 13 occurrences in Joshua, 7 in Judges, 66 in I and II Samuel, and 17 in I and II Kings, a total of 103. But often the occurrences are piled together in particular passages. The count for individual passages containing these time-designatives is: Joshua, 6; Judges, 5; Samuel, 27; Kings, 10. This is leaving aside 14 questionable occurrences in the Septuagintal text, apparently added through familiarity with this usage elsewhere.[161] As with

---

160. Of seven passages where the LXX or other VSS read *hayyôm* in a participial promulgation clause (4:2 *bis*, 11:22, 12:11, 14, 28, 13:1) its presence in the condition of a blessing makes the occurrence in 11:22 the only one where the time-designative is meaningful, and hence probably original.
161. The LXX has σήμερον where *hayyôm* is lacking in the MT in a number of passages where we consider the time-designative to be original, as will be indicated in the discussion of the specific passages concerned; but it is a certainly or probably inferior reading in the following passages: Josh. 7:19, where the usage would be unparalleled if the LXX text were correct; Josh. 24:27, where the LXX has been influenced by the Deuteronomic pattern (esp. Deut. 27:4—cf. vs. 1) in spite of the fact that the Hebrew text has no precise parallels in Deut.; Judg. 6:17, where LXX[B] substitutes a reading based on a scribal error (σήμερον for σημεῖον) for the meaningful reading of the MT; I Sam. 4:7, where the LXX insertion, ἐξελοῦ ἡμᾶς κύριε σήμερον, a cry for help modeled after Judg. 10:15, breaks apart the woe cry and its grounding; I Sam. 14:44f., where σήμερον has been twice added through the

bayyôm hahû', the greatest concentration proves to be in the books of Samuel.

Josh. 3:7

The early narrative of the crossing of the Jordan has been heavily interpolated by a deuteronomistic redactor, one of whose chief concerns at this point was to authenticate Joshua as the successor of Moses (cf. the concluding rubric of Josh. 4:14, with *bayyôm hahû'* in emphatic place). In Josh. 3:7 he puts *hayyôm hazzeh* in emphatic position, at the beginning of Yahweh's declaration, to specify the moment of preparation for the crossing as leading to Joshua's authentication.[162]   Although the verse epitomizes the day's central significance from the redactor's point of view, the essential function of the temporal adverb is to draw an equivalence of time when. This is a usage characteristic of the deuteronomistic writers (cf. Deut. 2:25, 5:24, 26:16, 27:9).

Josh. 5:9

The first occurrence of *hayyôm* in Joshua is at 5:9, where Yahweh's declaration to Joshua, "*Hayyôm*[163] I have rolled away (גלותי) the reproach of Egypt from you," provides the basis for the immediately following etymological etiology for Gilgal.[164]   The circumcision etiology, vss. 2ff.

LXX's tendency to proliferate time-references (cf. ἐν τῇ ἡμέρᾳ ἐκείνῃ, 45), and is completely inappropriate in the people's speech of vs. 45; I Sam. 16:5, where the LXX's free and explanatory rendering of the MT (cf. P. A. H. de Boer, *Research into the Text of I Samuel i-xvi*, Amsterdam, 1938, p. 67; *contra* S. R. Driver, *Notes on the Hebrew Text of the Books of Samuel*, p. 133) seems very dubious in light of our study of the functioning of *hayyôm*; I Sam. 21:3, employing the time-designative in a fashion uncharacteristic of the Hebrew usage; I Sam. 24:12, 19 second, which offer further evidence of the LXX proclivity to insert extra time-designatives; I Sam. 25:34, where the LXX has apparently been influenced by translation equations in the immediately preceding verses; II Sam. 19:8, where σήμερον is a pure indication of time (in contrast to νύξ) within a context where *hayyôm* consistently epitomizes; and I Kings 8:15, 56, adding the time-designative to ascriptions of praise in a fashion uncharacteristic of Hebraic usage (see below on I Kings 5:21, 8:28). σήμερον appears in a meaningful position in I Kings 18:24, according to the Lucianic LXX text, but the weak attestation makes its originality improbable.

162. Identical syntax in Deut. 2:25 (*hayyôm hazzeh 'āhēl ...*) indicates that the redactor who was at work there wrote this. In the underlying narrative, Joshua announces the miracle that is to take place on the morrow, immediately after the ark has arrived at the Jordan from Shittim (vss. 1, 5, 11ff.; cf. Noth, *ATD*, 7, *in loco*). But the redactor has interpolated a three-day interval, including the ceremony of parading the ark before the people mentioned in vs. 6; this is why he has Yahweh telling Joshua that "this day" he is only "beginning" to exalt him. The words *kî ... 'eheyeh 'immāk* are taken directly from Exod. 3:12.

163. LXX ἐν τῇ σήμερον ἡμέρᾳ is an equivalent found elsewhere only at Josh. 22:29 (LXX[B] has the plural).

164. Cf. B. S. Childs, "A Study of the Formula, 'Until This Day,'" *JBL*, 83 (1963), 285. The argument of Jack M. Sasson, "Circumcision in the Ancient Near East,"

(of which only vss. 2f., concluding with the Gibeath-haaraloth formula, are original, vss. 4-7 being a detailed deuteronomistic explanation), has been artificially attached to the preceding crossing story by the use of *bāʾēt hahîʾ* and *šēnît*. Vs. 8, with הגוי instead of בני ישראל, is an early addition to this circumcision etiology, being designed to incorporate the declaration and Gilgal etiology of vs. 9. Yahweh's saying in 9a looks like a liturgical formula derived directly from the Gilgal shrine, which has here succeeded in assimilating the earlier Gibeath-haaraloth tradition to itself. The foremost place of *hayyôm* underscores the emphatic equation of these two traditions. Artificial as the declaration may be, it clearly functions as an epitome of the ritual's meaning from the point of view of the dominant Gilgal tradition.

Josh. 14:10f.

Twice in the deuteronomistic insertion at Josh. 14:6aβ-15, Caleb speaks of himself as he is at the time of speaking, *hayyôm*. In both instances the time-designative calls attention to itself, breaking apart syntactical continuities. This is entirely in line with the overall character of this pericope, whose frequent time-designatives are all emphatic. For a statement of the general purpose of this pericope, our preceding discussion, involving an analysis of the function of *bayyôm hahûʾ* in vss. 9 and 12, must suffice.[165] We observe only that the Deuteronomist has Caleb speak like Moses in Deut. 31:2 and like Joshua in Josh. 23:14 (farewell-address form), and that *hayyôm* functions in an identifying characterization rather than as part of an epitome.

Josh. 22:16, 18, 22, 29, 31

It seems difficult to quarrel with the judgment that the narrative of the altar at the Jordan, found in Josh. 22:10-34, may derive its materials from a very early tribal tradition, but in its present form reflects extensive late recasting.[166] The reader is struck not only by the patent artificiality of the altar's function and of Phinehas' performance, but also by the awkwardness and repetitiousness of the discourse. This is especially apparent in the way time-designatives are used. *Māḥār*, appearing in vs. 18 in contrast to the *hayyôm* of vs. 29, has the highly unusual meaning of a generalized "in the future."[167] The two occurrences of *hayyôm* in vs. 16, the first

---

JBL, 85 (1966), 474, to the effect that the "rolling away" of "the reproach of Egypt" refers to recircumcision, is brought into serious question by the consideration that vs. 9 and vs. 2 derive from separate traditions.
165. Above, pp. 120f.
166. The style is similar to that of P rather than to that of Dtr. Cf. Noth, *ATD*, 7, *in loco*.
167. See Chapter Four, n. 5.

occurrence in vs. 18, and the occurrence in vs. 29 have the function of identifying characterizations. The second occurrence in 18 produces a contrasting identification of time, which in turn provides the conditional structure for a warning: "If today . . . then later. . . ." In vs. 22, *hayyôm hazzeh* appears in an awkward syntactical construction that constitutes a negative appeal for decisive action;[168] it is a summary statement of what the situation would be like for the two and a half tribes if they were in fact guilty of the apostasy renounced in their self-adjuration. The only clear and simple epitomizing declaration comes in Phinehas' speech in vs. 31, introduced by *hayyôm* and continuing with a statement concerning the happy situation that now exists.[169]

Josh. 23:14

The deuteronomistic redactor has inserted a farewell address by Joshua in chap. 23; its content is little more than a summary of typical Deuteronomic parenesis. All emphasis falls upon the addressees, rather than on Joshua, who speaks of himself only in vss. 2bβ and 14a. The identifying self-characterization with *hayyôm* in vs. 14 no doubt reflects a popular locution (cf. Deut. 31:2, Josh. 14:10f., II Sam. 19:36).

Josh. 24:15

We have previously remarked about the structure of the Shechemite covenant discourse in Josh. 24:2ff.[170] As *bayyôm hahû'* functions in the epitomizing summation at vs. 25, so *hayyôm* functions as part of an appeal for decisive action in the climactic declaration of vs. 15. Joshua has reviewed the *Heilsfeiten* (vss. 2-13). He commands Israel to respond affirmatively by fearing and serving Yahweh, negatively by putting away other gods (vs. 14). So as to leave no room for temporizing or vacillation, he continues here in vs. 15 with a supplementary command for those who are unwilling to serve Yahweh to choose whom they will serve—and to choose him *hayyôm*. Since Joshua goes on to declare that he and his house will serve Yahweh, intending this to elicit the response that the people in fact make in vss. 16ff., it is clear that vs. 15's command with *hayyôm* concerns the essential matter of this entire confrontation.

---

168. Vs. 22ba is the protasis of a condition which, in effect, continues in vs. 23, leaving the jussive in 22bβ as the apodosis. The LXX has ἐν ταύτῃ, reading *bazzeh*; throughout this pericope the versional readings conflict with those of the MT.

169. It is unquestionably a sign of late origin that this pericope must make use of the emphatic forms of the time-designative to perform the epitomizing function, for which the simple *hayyôm* in unemphatic position characteristically serves in the early literature. See below, p. 276.

170. See above, pp. 76f.

Judg. 9:18f.

Judg. 9:16b-19a is a fairly late intrusion into the Jotham-Abimelech narrative. It contains both *hayyôm* and *hayyôm hazzeh*. It breaks apart the protasis (16a) and the apodosis (19b) of the positive condition which, together with the negative condition contained in vs. 20, constitutes the original writer's carefully constructed application of the fable told by Jotham in vss. 7-15.[171] Originally the application intended to express the probability that the king whom the Shechemites had chosen would turn out to be not only worthless to them, but positively dangerous. The interpolation turns this into a specific charge of disloyalty to the house of Jerubbaal and ingratitude for the saving deeds that Jerubbaal/Gideon had performed on their behalf—an image superimposed on the Abimelech episode from the composite cycle.[172]

The *hayyôm* that appears in vs. 18 is the interpolator's device for turning the report of Abimelech's crime in vss. 4f. into an epitomizing charge against all the Shechemites; the artificiality of the construction he uses is especially apparent in that vs. 18 repeats vss. 4f. almost word for word, yet the interpolator is concerned not so much to make a temporal equation[173] as to characterize the situation of the Shechemites in the familiar language of confrontation. It is somewhat the same with *hayyôm hazzeh* in vs. 19a, where the protasis of 16a is repeated in anticipation of the apodosis in 19b: the more emphatic form of the temporal designative underscores the contrary-to-factness of the original "if," as seen in the light of the interpolated charge; as such, it too has an epitomizing function, though again one quite foreign to the intent of the original narrative.

Judg. 10:15

Hayyôm hazzeh appears in a plea for deliverance in Judg. 10:15. This verse belongs to a clearly recognizable deuteronomistic section, vss. 6-16, where the characteristic cycle of sin-punishment-repentance receives programmatic restatement. Inasmuch as the entire pericope covers a long

---

171. For a detailed analysis of Judg. 9 see W. Richter, *Traditionsgeschichtliche Untersuchungen zum Richterbuch*, pp. 246-318. Vss. 16b-19a, together with vss. 22, 55, have been added to put the entire narrative cycle into a pan-Israelite framework (Richter, p. 316).

172. See *ibid.*; also H. Haag, "Gideon-Jerubbaal-Abimelek," *ZAW*, 79 (1967), 305-14.

173. The original narration involves a consciously stylized diatribe somewhat similar to what we find in I Sam. 24:8ff., 26:13ff. The setting is imaginatively staged, the summit of Gerizim being in actual fact too far from Shechem (Tell Balaṭa) for Jotham to have been heard (cf. Deut. 27:11ff.). In any case, there is no indication that the original writer envisaged the Jotham episode as occurring on the very day of his brothers' murder. The interpolator assumes the contrary; for him the temporal equation is important because the crime and its denunciation are seen as characterizing one and the same situation.

period of time and includes various events, the appeal to Yahweh, his reproach, and the people's plea are intended as no more than typical and representative. *Hayyôm hazzeh* scarcely identifies one unique day in history; yet any occasion when the plea would be uttered would always be on some particular day, like each of the particular days in the past. It is this underlying element of time correspondence that explains the more emphatic form.

Judg. 11:27

Hayyôm appears within the Jephthah cycle (Judg. 10:17–12:6) at 11:27, where the hero responds to the accusation of the king of the Ammonites (vs. 13) by transferring the attributed guilt from himself to the latter, and then appealing to Yahweh for arbitration.[174] Jephthah's words, "Let Yahweh decide, the one who is judging today between the Israelites and the Ammonites,"[175] point to the central issue of the entire confrontation, preparing the way for the denouement of vss. 29, 32f. However, several considerations, among them the fact that the early tradition identifies Jephthah as a local Gileadite hero rather than as a pan-Israelite leader (cf. 11:1ff.), lead one to the conclusion that vs. 27 belongs to a redactional framework.[176] Perhaps the nearest affinities of this characterization of a day of battle as a day of judgment are with the equation found in Deut. 9:1ff.[177]

Judg. 12:3

The Jephthah cycle has *hayyôm hazzeh* at Judg. 12:3, where it constitutes part of the hero's protest to the threatening Ephraimites. Since few details are provided in the probably late pericope to which this verse belongs (vss. 1-4a),[178] there is little possibility of determining the place of this expression within the narrative schema. There is no apparent reason for the longer form of the temporal adverb. The most that can be said is that it is concerned to characterize the threatening aspect of the confrontation, rather than to create an emphatic temporal connection or identification.

---

174. Regarding Yahweh as arbiter, cf. Gen. 16:5, I Sam. 24:13. For the legal forms involved, see H. J. Boecker, *Redeformen des Rechtslebens im Alten Testament*, pp. 50ff.

175. To take *haśśōpēt* as an attributive, constituting a divine appellative, seems undesirable because it would create an awkward break between the jussive and *hayyôm*; besides, this usage is understandable in terms of what appears to be the redactor's rather sophisticated theology.

176. See the exhaustive analysis of the Jephthah cycle by W. Richter in *Biblica*, 47 (1966), 485-556; on 11:27, pp. 522ff.

177. See above, pp. 180f.

178. Richter, *op. cit.*, pp. 520-22, identifies this as an artificial narrative whose aim is to draw Jephthah into the pan-Israelite orbit and expand his role. Nevertheless, the recollection of conflict between Gilead and Ephraim may rest on solid tradition from the premonarchic period.

Judg. 21:3, 6

There can be little question but that Judg. 21 continues the same literary sources as were found in chap. 20. As we indicated in our analysis of the latter part of that chapter,[179] a redactor combined a Mizpah account and a Bethel account of Israel's punitive action against Gibeah into a single pan-Israelite quasi holy-war story. Already in the common tradition underlying these separate accounts, what was originally the defeat of a single town had been expanded into the defeat and virtual annihilation of the entire tribe of Benjamin. It is this circumstance that gave rise to the incorporation of two originally independent traditions dealing with Benjaminite raids on Jabesh-gilead and Shiloh, respectively. To all appearances, these separate traditions were drawn independently into the two sources; all that the two have in common at this point is the concern to explain the ultimate survival of the tribe.

A number of apparent doublets, especially in the introductory framework, lead initially to the suspicion that the two sources may have followed a common schema throughout. Immediately we are struck by the repetition of *hayyôm* in statements about the tribe being lacking, or cut off, from Israel (vss. 3, 6); cf. the similar statement without *hayyôm*, in vs. 15. We note also that the oath is mentioned in both vs. 1 and vs. 18. Also, the question as to which tribe failed to appear before Yahweh at Mizpah (vs. 5) is repeated in a less elaborate form in vs. 8a; a second question concerning what was to be done to provide wives appears in vs. 7 and in vs. 16; the conclusion, stating that the Benjaminites returned, is found in vs. 14 and in vs. 23.

However, only the first two and the last of these are actual parallels, and the last is scarcely remarkable as the kind of standardization conclusion that one would expect to find at the end of any such narrative. Vs. 5, which asks substantially the same question as is asked in vs. 8, is part of a redactional transition from the Bethel account in vs. 4 to the resumption of the Mizpah account in 6b. Vs. 16, which repeats the question of vs. 7, but with a different reason for the question, is a redactional interpolation into the Bethel account, explaining why further measures needed to be taken to supply the Benjaminites with wives.[180] Following the same criteria as in our analysis of chap. 20, we may isolate the following literary strands: Mizpah account, 1, 6b-8 (except אל הקהל), 9-10, 12-14a; Bethel account,

---

179. Above, pp. 79ff.
180. Neither the Mizpah account (1, 7) nor the Bethel account (18) goes so far as to state, with the redactor, that all the Benjaminite women had been destroyed; the redactor assumes this without warrant from 20:48. He borrows the question form from the Mizpah account, repeating לנותרים rather than the פליטה of vs. 17. The reference is, of course, specifically to the six hundred men at Rimmon, whereas in the Bethel account it is general.

2-4αb, 15, 17-24; redactor, 5-6a, אל הקהל in 8, 14b, 16; probably later additions, 4aβ, 11, 25.[181]

All that the two early accounts really have in common, therefore, is (1) the report of the oath not to give wives to Benjamin and (2) the epitomizing statement with *hayyôm* regarding the effect of this oath in terms of threatening the ideal twelve-tribe pattern. In vs. 3 the people (*hā'ām*, = Israel) weep at the Bethel shrine, lamenting to Yahweh, God of Israel, that *hayyôm* one tribe is missing (from פקד hif., "to muster"). In vs. 6b the "men of Israel" (*'îš yiśrā'ēl*, vs. 1) simply declare that *hayyôm* one tribe is cut off (גרע nif.) from Israel. In both instances, this epitome serves as the fulcrum upon which the respective independent narrative sequels are structured.

Together with the strikingly self-conscious way in which epitomizing *bayyôm hahû'* is applied in the early strata of chap. 20, this primitive use of epitomizing *hayyôm* furnishes important evidence of an early development of the time concept that lends itself to this manner of expression. This is especially important in that up to this point most of the occurrences of *hayyôm* in Joshua and Judges have proven to belong to fairly late literary strata.

I Sam. 4:3, 16

The story of the capture of the ark in I Sam. 4 has *bayyôm hahû'* at vs. 12 and *hayyôm* in vss. 3 and 16. As our analysis of vs. 12 has shown,[182] the narrative intends to emphasize that the disastrous battle and the arrival of the report of it in Shiloh occurred on one and the same day, marking this day as the heavy day of judgment that 3:12f. had predicted. There is no general epitomizing statement to this effect, but the lament with *hayyôm* in vs. 3 does epitomize the situation following the first battle at Aphek, leading to the bringing of the ark into battle and its capture on this new day of disaster. Following an identifying characterization in vs. 16aα, the messenger's report with *hayyôm* in vs. 16aβ synchronizes the capture of the ark and the report of it, like *bayyôm hahû'* in vs. 12 binding together the two most significant constituents of this day of gloom.

I Sam. 9:9

Hayyôm occurs within an archeological note in I Sam. 9:9, where it has no other function than to identify the time of the narrator in contrast to the time of the narrative.[183]

---

181. In this analysis, variations of terminology regarding the respective contending parties are meaningfully applied, being determined by whether the reference is to the unit or the individuals comprising the unit. For other literary analyses of this chapter, see the commentaries and the works of Noth, Schunck, and Gray mentioned in our previous discussion of chap. 20.
182. Above, pp. 102f.
183. In light of the narrator's excessive fondness for time-designatives (see below),

I Sam. 9:12, 19f., 10:2

The legitimation narrative concerning Saul, I Sam. 9:1–10:16, has received previous comment in connection with the two occurrences within it of *bayyôm hahû'*; it was pointed out not only that this passage abounds with time-designatives, but also that it is self-consciously structured according to a two-day sequence.[184] None of the occurrences of *hayyôm* functions in an epitome, but instead each lends itself in one way or another to establishing this sequence. The first occurrence in 9:12 is forward for emphasis because it aims to explain the command to hurry,[185] but together with the second occurrence in this verse (in itself an identifying characterization), its essential function is to synchronize Samuel's coming and the people's feast. The occurrences of *hayyôm* in 9:19 and 10:2 establish a sequence. The occurrence in 9:20 identifies the present day with reference to an event three days previous.[186]

I Sam. 10:19

One cannot get a clear understanding of how *hayyôm* is used in the next passage, I Sam. 10:19, without coming to grips with the overall tradition-critical and redaction-critical problems surrounding the pericope, 10:17ff. Although we may agree with Artur Weiser's study in identifying this as deriving ultimately from an early, independent Mizpah tradition, we must not be misled into severing it redactionally from the deuteronomistic revision that has previously made its appearance in chap. 8.[187] It is quite true that the story of Saul's choice by lot (10:20-26) lacks any ostensible evidence of antipathy toward Saul; quite on the contrary, the whole tone of this account seems to be enthusiastically approving, apart from the redactional words of introduction found in vss. 18-19a.

The compiler-redactor added this narrative of popular acclamation to his collection, not because he considered it necessary as a corrective to the narrative of private designation found in 9:1–10:16, but simply because it existed. He was not willing, however, to leave it in its original form. He put words into Samuel's mouth that make him sound like a prophet, bringing a reproach upon the people strikingly similar to that of chap. 8. Yet 10:18-19 lacks the authentic form of a prophetic denunciation. In spite of the

---

the temporal references in this verse would tend to argue against assigning this note to a glossator.

184. Above, pp. 103f. It is worth noting that the time-sequence pattern is not germane to the lost-asses anecdote (9:20 being probably an artificial harmonization), which may be taken as support for the view that it arose independently from the tradition of Saul's legitimation.

185. LXX reads כהיום for MT כי היום.

186. Cf. 30:13.

187. See Weiser, *Samuel*, pp. 62-69; H. J. Boecker, *Die Beurteilung des Königtums in Samuel 7-12*, pp. 35-61; M. Buber, "Die Erzählung von Sauls Königwahl," *VT*, 6 (1956), 594-608; H. Seebaas, "Traditionsgeschichte von I Sam. 8, 10:17ff. und 12," *ZAW*, 77 (1965), 286-96.

herald formula at the beginning, Samuel speaks here the language of covenant confrontation, in particular such as challenges the people for their unwillingness to renounce other gods (cf. Deut. 32:15ff., Josh. 24:19ff., Judg. 5:8). Following "you," which is placed forward to contrast with "I," *hayyôm* occupies the emphatic foremost position. It is as if, by demanding a king, the covenant people were choosing other gods—and this is indeed what the redactor's Samuel/Yahweh intends to charge them with: "But you have *hayyôm* rejected your God!" But if this were part of the original narrative, we could scarcely expect to go on, as we do, and find Yahweh choosing Saul and the people behaving in a perfectly normal fashion, as though they were Yahweh's people without question.

Thus vss. 18-19 are fashioned on the tradition of the covenant ritual—but evidently in such a form as was known to periods much later than the time of Samuel and Saul. The declaration with *hayyôm* suggests the language of Deuteronomy—in this case such as accompanies the covenant curse (cf. Deut. 28:15). The epitomizing reproach reflects the general parenetic situation typical of Deuteronomy, only artificially qualifying the historical event of Saul's acclamation. The emphatic *hayyôm* is primarily a time-identifier, contrasting this day of confrontation with the former times of Yahweh's saving acts mentioned in vs. 18.

I Sam. 11:13

Saul's declaration in I Sam. 11:13b, "*Hayyôm* Yahweh has wrought victory in Israel," eloquently epitomizes the outcome of the holy-war story of which it is a part. But, as we have shown in our preceding discussion concerning the *bayyôm hazzeh* that occurs in vs. 13a, this is subsidiary to the ultimate purpose of this narrative in its present form.[188]

I Sam. 12:5, 17

Hayyôm hazzeh occurs in I Sam. 12:5, where Samuel solemnly calls upon the "anointed one," Saul, to bear witness to his foregoing deposition; *hayyôm* occurs in vs. 17, where Samuel introduces his declaration regarding the great sign that he is about to call for by asking the rhetorical question, "Is it not wheat harvest today?"

It will not be necessary to enlarge upon the observations we have previously made concerning this chapter in connection with our analysis of *bayyôm hahû'* in vs. 18,[189] except to add that the work of the redactor (late prophetic or deuteronomistic) is especially evident in the first five verses, where *hayyôm hazzeh* occurs. We observe that Samuel's statement in vs. 2, "And now, behold, my sons are with you," certainly assumes a

---

188. Above, pp. 147f.
189. See above, pp. 104f.

more favorable attitude toward these persons than is implied in the Deuter-onomist's stern censure of 8:3-5; also that the statement that "the king walks (מתהלך) before you" hardly makes sense within the same original context as the statement that immediately follows, "And I have walked (התהלכתי) before you"; also that the original text of vs. 5 evidently identified the king alone as witness. [190] From this we conclude that vss. 2-5 embody an early tradition concerning the transfer of authority from Samuel to Saul, originally independent of the sophisticated theological reflection that has been added in the redactional process.

In vs. 5 the original account probably had Samuel concluding his deposition by the appeal to the newly acclaimed king, "And a witness is Yahweh's anointed *hayyôm hazzeh.*" [191] Although the longer form is used, it yields foremost place to the word receiving special stress, $w^{e'}\bar{e}d$. It is an identifying characterization that epitomizes a situation in which Samuel's successor's presence is guarantee of the truth of all that he is declaring concerning his lifelong behavior (cf. *'ad hayyôm hazzeh* in vs. 2). The redactor has enlarged this to include Yahweh as witness alongside the king, since for him Saul was a witness whose testimony ultimately turned out to be worthless.

In vs. 17 *hayyôm* is part of another identifying characterization typical of the deuteronomistic redaction. This introduces the sign episode, which is concluded by the statement of vs. 18 that Yahweh sent thunder and rain *bayyôm hahû'*—leading directly to what was for the redactor the climactic statement of the entire chapter, *viz.*, that "all the people greatly feared Yahweh and Samuel."

I Sam. 14:33

We have previously argued that I Sam. 14:32b-34 contains the *hieros logos* for an unknown shrine, and that in vs. 33 the MT's היום should be retained over against the word read in the LXX's *Vorlage*, חלם.[192] This report severely abbreviates the formula that the officiant must have used; in any case it is apparent that the command with *hayyôm* led to the central symbolic action of the day in question.

---

190. Samuel's declaration begins with parallel noun-clauses, the first of which has the predicate noun, the subject, and a prepositional phrase, *bākem*, the second of which repeats the predicate noun, inserts a new subject, substitutes the temporal phrase for the prepositional phrase, and continues on into a *kî*-clause containing an indirect quotation. It is clear that Yahweh's witnessing was an apologetic testifying against someone (cf. Deut. 4:26, 8:19), whereas Saul's witnessing was a mere attestation of fact. A redactor added the first noun-clause, along with a renewed statement in vs. 6, found in the LXX text, to the effect that Yahweh was witness (it does not appear why the MT should have dropped out the word עד, but the Hebrew text makes no sense without it).

191. The LXX has the peculiar double reading, σήμερον ἐν ταύτῃ τῇ ἡμέρᾳ.

192. See Chapter Two, n. 126.

I Sam. 14:28, 30, 38, 41 LXX, 45

Our previous analysis of I Sam. 13f. has identified one of two hero-saga/holy-war narratives as extending through 13:15b-18, 14:1, 3b-5, 15, 23b-30, 37-46.[193] It is noteworthy that this story contains the greatest share of time-designatives within these two chapters, including all the occurrences of *hayyôm* (*hazzeh*) except the single occurrence in 14:33. *Hayyôm* appears as part of identifying characterizations in a citation of Saul's curse in 14:28 and in Jonathan's complaint about it in vs. 30, as an appeal for decisive action in Saul's summons of vs. 38, and according to the LXX text, as an epitome in Saul's lament of vs. 41;[194] *hayyôm hazzeh* appears as an epitome at the end of the substantiating clause concluding the people's oath in vs. 45.

The reason for the heavy stress on the time element in this story is found in the conflict between Saul's oath and the oath of the people, the latter prevailing, in the end, over the former. To assure victory, Saul had emphatically put the entire day ("until the evening," vs. 24) under a taboo that ironically came to endanger the very person whose valor had opened the possibility of victory. Assuredly there is pathos in that the transgressor is Saul's son, but the real tragedy lies in that he is also the hero, the one who "with God has wrought this day" (עם אלהים עשה היום הזה).

The successive occurrences of *hayyôm* and *hayyôm hazzeh* signalize the dramatic turning-points of this moving narrative: in vss. 28 and 30 the day is characterized first negatively and then positively with regard to the taboo and its military effect; following *bayyôm hahû'* in vs. 37, *hayyôm* in vs. 38 belongs to a summons to the people to resolve the question of who has sinned; in vs. 41 (LXX), *hayyôm* is part of an identifying characterization in the unusual form of a question; in the climactic affirmation of vs. 45 the day is finally and definitively identified as the day when God has been at work in Jonathan. This last is a clear and emphatic epitome; in the preceding passages with *hayyôm* the identifying characterizations and an appeal have helped produce the polarity and the tension that are at last resolved here in this grand epitomizing affirmation.

I Sam. 15:28

Hayyôm functions in an especially dramatic declaration in I Sam. 15:28, which contains Samuel's words to Saul following the latter's failure to carry out the prescribed *ḥerem* against the Amalekites. Here the declaration with *hayyôm* accompanies and interprets an ominous occurrence, which, although presented in the narrative as happening accidentally, has

---

193. Above, pp. 84-88.
194. On the textual problem, see the commentaries; almost all critics are in agreement that the Hebrew text has been damaged.

all the revelatory force of a prophetic symbolic act.[195] As Samuel turns away from Saul, the latter snatches at the fringe of his robe so that it tears, whereupon Samuel announces, "Yahweh has torn the kingdom of Israel away from you[196] *hayyôm* and has given it to your neighbor who is better than you." Most commentators agree that the section containing this verse is not part of the original narration in this chapter; it seems more likely, though, that vss. 24-29 constitute the climax to a parallel account than that they derive from literary supplementation, in which event the position of this epitomizing declaration with *hayyôm* is especially impressive.[197]

I Sam. 17:10, 36 LXX, 46

Our analysis of I Sam. 17 in connection with the occurrence of *bayyôm hahû'* in 18:2 has identified a prophetic hero legend that developed as a late accretion to a primitive hero saga in this chapter, being preserved in what many critics take to be the superior text.[198] In three of the speeches belonging to this legend, one by the Philistine challenger and two by David, a temporal designative appears in much the same role, first as identifying characterization, then as epitome. *Hayyôm hazzeh* occurs in vs. 10, where the Philistine taunts the fearful Israelites, characterizing the situation from his point of view (אני חרפתי את מערכות ישראל היום הזה). This emphatic form occurs again twice in vs. 46, where David concludes his challenge to the Philistine in rhetoric that eloquently expresses the characteristic prophetic theology of history, incorporating a highly stylized holy-war ideology. David has stated in pithy parallelism the starkly contrasting circumstances delineating the present situation (the Philistine armed, himself coming in the name of Yahweh Sebaoth). The forward position of the first *hayyôm hazzeh* shows that special stress is being placed on the time when David's god is to act; it is right now, this very day.[199] But there seems to be no reason to question when Yahweh

---

195. Cf. the more deliberately designed sign given to Jeroboam, I Kings 11:29-31. The present passage lacks the formal criteria of the prophetic *Botenspruch;* nevertheless Samuel speaks as an authoritative interpreter of Yahweh's intent; cf. the recollection of this passage in I Sam. 28:18.

196. Cf. BH³mg.

197. Cf. H. Seebaas, "I Sam. 15 (etc.)," *ZAW*, 78 (1966), 48-79 (especially pp. 149-54), assigning vss. 1, 11, 16-19, 24-28 to an independent narrative; although it is far from clear that these verses continue from chap. 14 (see above on 14:28, etc.), such elements as Saul's twofold confession of sin (25, 30) are evidence of parallel accounts. It is better to take vs. 29 as the conclusion to 24ff. than to assign it to the main narrative because its statement regarding the *nēsaḥ yiśrā'ēl* not repenting conflicts with vs. 35. The most extensive treatment of this chapter is by Artur Weiser, "I Samuel 15," *ZAW*, 13 (1936), 1-28, reprinted in *Glaube und Geschichte im Alten Testament*, pp. 201-28; he defends the literary unity of the chapter, except for vss. 25-29.

198. See above, pp. 88-90.

199. LXX, σήμερον. The forward positioning of *hayyôm hazzeh* occurs elsewhere in the deuteronom(ist)ic writings (Deut. 2:25, 5:24, 26:16, 27:9, Josh. 3:7) and in

will act; what is in question is what Yahweh will do. Hence the essential function of *hayyôm hazzeh*, even though emphatic, is to epitomize the expected outcome.

The series of perfect consecutives that follow include the grandiose claim that David will give "the corpse of the Philistine camps *hayyôm hazzeh*" to the birds and beasts—another epitome containing an ultimate symbol of Yahweh's triumph. All this is climaxed by the double word of divine self-demonstration (*Erweiswort*)[200] in vss. 46f. and by the concluding *kî*-clause, "for the battle is Yahweh's. . . ." It is very clear that, in David's expectation, "this day" was to be a day of eminent divine revelation.

The LXX contains σήμερον, the usual equivalent of *hayyôm*, as an addition to the second half of vs. 36,[201] where David is boasting to Saul about what he intends to do to the Philistine. Inasmuch as the clause in the Greek points to the ultimate meaning of this day of conflict, i.e., "I will remove reproach from Israel," there is a strong possibility that this reading may be closer to the original than that of the MT. It too epitomizes the central issue of the pericope.

I Sam. 18:21

The MT of I Sam. 18:21b contains a sentence that has no counterpart in the early LXX manuscripts: ויאמר שאול אל דוד בשתים תתחתן בי היום. Nevertheless the Hebrew reading may be more than a textual gloss; it could be an editorial insertion aiming to tie together the Michal and the Merab episodes, or—more likely—it could represent a variant reading to vss. 22-23a. In any event, the function of *hayyôm* is to be identified as epitomizing the situation, rather than as designating the time of occurrence.

I Sam. 20:27

In I Sam. 20:27 two adverbs of time (*gam temôl gam hayyôm*) are put in contrast to each other. Each simply identifies a particular day within a sequence.[202]

I Sam. 21:6 [E-5]

We have previously identified I Sam. 21:2ff. as an anecdote secon-

---

II Sam. 18:20, always with stress on the identification of time when. In I Sam. 24:11 it is foremost after *hinnēh*, but with no clear intent to identify time.

200. Cf. W. Zimmerli, "Das Wort des göttlichen Selbsterweises (Erweiswort), eine prophetische Gattung," *Gottes Offenbarung* (TB, 19, Munich, 1963), pp. 120-32. I Kings 20:13 contains a primitive example of this genre with *hayyôm* (see below). For further comment on this passage, see S. J. DeVries, "David's Victory over the Philistine as Saga and as Legend," *JBL*, 92 (1973), 23-36.

201. οὐχὶ πορεύσομαι καὶ πατάξω αὐτὸν καὶ ἀφελῶ σήμερον ὄνειδος ἐξ Ισραηλ. . . .

202. On I Sam. 20:18-20, 27, see G. R. Driver in *ZAW*, 86 (1968), 175-77.

darily developed by the author of the accession history from the early tale now contained in 22:6ff.[203] Important details are significantly different in these two accounts. Among them is that 21:2ff. accentuates the seriousness of Saul's (and Doeg's) offense by designating the ordinary bread that David received, according to 22:6ff., as the holy bread of the Presence. Hence the anxious query of Ahimelech, whether David's attendants, for whom the holy bread was intended, were in a condition of sexual purity (21:5); this is followed by David's affirmation (vs. 6) that, since in the past, whenever he would go on a foray, the *kēlîm*[204] of his men would be holy even if the mission were secular, certainly *hayyôm* they[205] would be holy too. *Hayyôm* functions here as a temporal identifier, making explicit the comparison between the specific situation of the present and the general situation of the past.[206] But the ultimate purpose of David's statement is simply to characterize his men in this situation.

I Sam. 22:15

I Sam. 22:15 contains *hayyôm* in one of its infrequent appearances as the first word of a sentence. Here it introduces what is unmistakably a rhetorical question in the mouth of the priest Ahimelech as he defends himself against the accusation of Doeg: היום החלתי לשאל לו באלהים ..., "Today have I begun to inquire[207] for him of God...?" As has been pointed out in connection with our analysis of *bayyôm hahû'* in vs. 18 of this chapter, this *hayyôm* must be taken literally, and as such is determinative for the entire time sequence of the original anecdote of which it is a part.[208] The foremost position of *hayyôm* gives it a very special emphasis, the purpose of which is to make as strong a contrast as possible to all the past days when, according to David's general and frequent practice, Ahimelech has been called upon to invoke the divine oracle, evidently in preparation for a military expedition of one sort or another. Thus the function of *hayyôm* is emphatic identification of time when. This passage's similarity to 21:6 in the function and styling of *hayyôm* suggests that, although the Doeg-Ahimelech narrative originated independently, the writer of the accession history has done extensive recasting of some of his materials.

---

203. Above, pp. 90-92.
204. Taken by most commentators to be a euphemism for the genitals, in accordance with the reference to sexual abstinence in 5b, 6a.
205. See BH³ mg.
206. David's words are often erroneously taken to mean that he now claimed to be on a holy mission, but the text states merely that what was generally true in the past (his men sexually pure even on common missions) is true now in the present.
207. We have transcribed the *qere* form. For the lexicography of seeking an oracle for the holy war, see C. Westermann, "Die Begriffe für Fragen und Suchen im Alten Testament," *KuD*, 6 (1960), 10-12.
208. See above, pp. 90ff.

I Sam. 24:11 [E-10], 19f. [E-18f.], 26:8, 19, 21, 23f.

That the two stories of David sparing Saul, in I Sam. 24 and 26, respectively, are literary doublets has long been apparent to biblical scholars. Although the attempt to prove them to belong to parallel ongoing documents has not been successful, the recognition of a formal schema common to both has made it clear that they at least go back to the same source in oral tradition.[209] Klaus Koch's recent book, *Was ist Formgeschichte?*, discussing the stories as an illustration of the hero-saga form, provides the valuable service of printing the two accounts in synoptic columns.[210] With the texts lying alongside each other, one is enabled to gain not only a firm impression of the overall structure, but specifically also of the functioning of a rather striking number of occurrences of the words presently under study, *hayyôm* (24:11, 19; 26:8, 19, 23) and *hayyôm hazzeh* (24:11, 20; 26:21, 24). One quickly sees the necessity of treating the occurrences of both chapters in conjunction with one another.

In a section on the redaction history of these parallel accounts, Koch argues effectively that chap. 24 belongs to a document that continues from chap. 23 and breaks off at 25:1, while chap. 26 is a continuation of 25:2ff. He identifies the former as the accession history of David, the latter as an independent document from a somewhat later period.[211] While we may agree in general with this redactional analysis, it is uncertain that the literary document of chap. 26 is actually younger than the accession history. Although it does contain extensive expansions from the original saga, it reflects in some respects a form nearer to the original than does chap. 24.

Even though it is the speeches that have come to receive, in the process of tradition development, the greatest amount and variety of expansion, close examination reveals that they also bear certain essential elements of the original schema, in particular such as are present in both accounts. Among elements lying in parallel are certain occurrences of epitomizing declarations with *hayyôm*, a recognition that will help immeasurably in discriminating which occurrences of the temporal formula are actually original, and in determining how the others came into the text.

One is particularly struck by the close proximity to each other of *hayyôm* and *hayyôm hazzeh* in three specific contexts, in 24:11, in

---

209. Cf. Gressmann, *SAT*², II, 1, *in loco*. H. U. Nübel, "Davids Aufstieg in der frühen israelitischen Geschichtsschreibung" (unpublished dissertation, Bonn, 1959), makes an unpersuasive attempt to isolate in both chapters elements taken from an original account of David's rise to power (pp. 47ff., 53ff.). See also H. J. Stoebe, "Gedanken zur Heldensage in den Samuelbücheren," Rost Festschrift (1967), pp. 208ff.; F. Mildenberger, "Die vordeuteronomistische Saul-David Ueberlieferung" (unpublished dissertation, Tübingen, 1962).
210. ET, *The Growth of the Biblical Tradition*, pp. 132ff.
211. *Ibid.*, ET, pp. 144-48.

24:19f., and in 26:23f. It should furthermore be pointed out that the *hayyôm* of 26:8 has a close counterpart in the expression *hinnēh hayyôm* *ʾašer* . . . of 24:5.

Looking first at 24:11, "Behold, *hayyôm hazzeh* thine eyes have seen how Yahweh gave (נתן) thee *hayyôm* into my hand . . . ," we may readily conclude that the introductory clause is secondary. The reasons are the following: (1) the artificial connective (את אשר); (2) the presence of the saying, "Yahweh gave (נתן) you *hayyôm* into my hand," in 26:23,[212] where it retains an original connection to the following statement of self-justification, "but I was not willing to put forth my hand against Yahweh's anointed" (paralleled by וידי לא תהיה בך in 24:13, 14); (3) that the summons to witness belongs within the formal structure of the controversy which the narrative of chap. 24 has developed at this point in David's speech,[213] an element that is completely lacking in the parallel section of chap. 26; and (4) that the statement about Saul's having seen evidence that Yahweh has put him in David's power comes too soon, before David has shown Saul such evidence (the fringe of his robe, vs. 12).

Thus, while the *hayyôm hazzeh* of 24:11 is from one of the stages of literary supplementation, *hayyôm* in all probability belongs to the original saga.[214] This means that the declaration that Yahweh has delivered Saul into David's hand, with all its theological implications, is integral to the saga in its primitive form[215] —a fact that is confirmed by the presence of this statement in closely similar forms in the parallel sections, 24:5 and 26:8, as well as in 26:23, the equivalent to 24:11 (cf. 24:19).

We turn next to 24:19f. Saul's closing speech to David in these verses contains elements that in themselves clearly identify the narrative of chap. 24 as belonging to the accession history: his declaration that David is more righteous than he, his prediction that David will rule, and his appeal for the protection of his lineage—all of which serve to legitimize David's takeover from Saul.[216] Yet not all the material in this speech could have been part of the original accession-history document. The double *ʾet ʾašer* clause in vs. 19 need not be taken as a sign of conflation, only of stylistic awkwardness: the second clause has been added to make specific what the first clause too hastily summarizes. What 19a summarizes is the substance of David's

---

212. Regarding the text, see BH[3] mg.
213. Analyzed in Boecker, *Redeformen des Rechtslebens im Alten Testament*, pp. 48-50; cf. Koch, ET, pp. 140f.
214. Contrary to various suggestions for deleting it, as by means of the *passeqs* in the MT; cf. BH[3] mg.
215. *Contra* Koch, ET, p. 146, arguing that theological elements are relatively late.
216. Saul's admission that David was more righteous than he (a proper conclusion to the preceding controversy episode), understandable in terms of the *Tendenz* of the accession history, has as little likelihood to be literally historical as Saul's admission in 26:21 that he had sinned; therefore Saul's concluding response in 26:25—appropriate to David's appeal of 24—may reflect more closely the original ending of the hero saga.

speech in vss. 11-16. That it cannot be the proper continuation of that speech is apparent from its needless and tardy restatement of the basis for Saul's climactic declaration in vs. 18, this being the original conclusion to vss. 11ff. Further evidence that vs. 19 has been added by a literary supplementer is that it employs a different verb than vs. 11 in the expression, "Yahweh has delivered me (you) up into your (my) hand."[217] But vs. 20a is the continuation of vs. 19; it adds a rhythmical wisdom-saying. Thus 19-20a is identified as an intrusion, leaving vss. 17, 18, 20b-23 as the probable content of the accession history at this point in the text. The conclusion is that *hayyôm* in vs. 19 derives from a supplementer, while *hayyôm hazzeh* in vs. 20, which contains Saul's final blessing on David, belongs to the accession history.

Next, *hayyôm* in 26:8. It occurs in the declaration that Abishai makes to David immediately upon finding Saul in a vulnerable situation. Although the Abishai material is a peculiar development of this account, and the declaration with *hayyôm* has a different verb than has the parallel declaration in 24:5 (סגר pi. for נתן; cf. also 24:11, 26:22), this being the same as the verb used in the supplement at 24:19, the mere occurrence of such declarations at this stage in both accounts is evidence that they derive from the original saga. There can be little doubt but that the form of speech in 26:8, employing *hayyôm* in a directly epitomizing declaration, is closer to the original than the modifying formula of 24:5, which interjects a divine oracle that promises what is elsewhere in these narratives simply declared, and of which we find no hint in the preceding accounts.[218]

Hayyôm occurs again in 26:19, and *hayyôm hazzeh* in 26:21. Here we find material not paralleled in chap. 24. That both vs. 19 and vs. 20 are introduced by *we'attâ* makes it virtually certain that one or the other is secondary. The choice readily falls on vs. 19 because its view of Yahweh's hypothetical involvement is quite inconceivable in the mind and mouth of the person who could utter vss. 23f.; that is to say, the confident affirmation of vs. 23 and pious prayer of vs. 24 are incompatible with the dark insinuation of vs. 19. Besides, the plea of vs. 20 is the appropriate continuation of the appeasement formula in vs. 18 (cf. the parallel in 24:10). Thus the *hayyôm* of 26:19 belongs to supplementary material. So also the *hayyôm hazzeh* found in vs. 21; here supplementation recapitulates vs. 24—coming too early, before David has shown Saul the evidence of the fact

217. The change of the verb in 19b, from the נתן of vs. 11 to סגר pi., may have been influenced by 26:8, where סגר pi. also appears (see below). The pi. of this verb occurs with ביד also in I Sam. 17:46, and without it in II Sam. 18:28. The hif. with ביד has a slightly different meaning (cf. Josh. 20:5, I Sam. 23:11f., 20, 30:15, Ps. 31:9, Lam. 2:7).

218. The parallelism of 24:5 and 26:8 offers important corroboration of the semantic correspondence between *hayyôm* in present discourse and forms with *hayyôm hahû'* in past narration, as has been assumed throughout this work.

here being affirmed (the spear, vs. 22)—again placing an unlikely confession of sin in the mouth of the king (cf. 24:18).

Probably original to the saga were the words of 26:23, affirming (1) Yahweh's act in giving Saul *hayyôm* into David's hand and (2) David's correct behavior in not harming Yahweh's anointed. As we have suggested, this represents the primitive schema. Vs. 24 may be an early literary phrasing of David's final appeal based on these affirmations;[219] with *hayyôm hazzeh* as an identifying characterization, it pointedly summarizes the meaning of David's act as a basis for this final appeal, preparing for Saul's concluding blessing (25).

Recapitulating the results of this analysis, we list the occurrences in 24:11b (*hayyôm*), 26:8, and 26:23 as deriving from the original saga, those in 24:11a (*hayyôm hazzeh*), 24:20, and 26:24 as from early literary formulation, and those in 24:19, 26:19, and 26:21 as from literary supplementation or redaction. It turns out that all in the first group have *hayyôm* and all in the second group have *hayyôm hazzeh*, while the third group has either form.

This usage is less a reflection of literary derivation than of formal function. In the original passages, *hayyôm* occurs in a prime epitomization of the outcome of the contest between David and Saul, as understood theologically. The epitome form is unmistakable in Abishai's mouth (26:8; cf. 24:4), but in terms of the narrative as a whole this epitome is reduced to the status of an identifying characterization (24:11, 26:23). In the verses of chap. 24 that belong to the accession history, *hayyôm hazzeh* is related to the controversy structure, coming in emphatic position in vs. 11, where it characterizes the situation as seen from the point of view of a dispute between Saul and David, with Yahweh as adjudicator; this form is echoed in less emphatic position as the concluding element of this controversy structure (20).[220] The *hayyôm hazzeh* of 26:24 is somewhat emphatic because this verse intends to repeat and reinterpret the declaration of vs. 23, containing *hayyôm*. No obvious explanation for the forms in the supplementary passages offers itself—and it is not at all certain that a simple explanation should be expected, since the writers responsible for these passages were most likely quite unaware of any special nuances for the words they were employing. The statement with the temporal adverb either makes an identifying characterization of the situation (24:11, 19, 26:19, 21, 23) or a climactic wish or appeal (24:20, 26:24). The former sets the

---

219. The appeal to Yahweh's intervention has probably been developed out of a request directly to Saul for clemency. In the parallel version (24:16), the appeal to Yahweh for deliverance (נצל hif.) becomes an appeal to him for adjudication (שפט qal).

220. Assuming that the MT has not undergone corruption at this point (compare what appears to be a paraphrastic LXX rendering), the temporal expression following חתת has to be read as a substantive, elliptical for the verbal clause that follows it—which may have been added secondarily.

scene, the latter bring it to a resolution, bestowing upon David the goodness that he has shown Saul *hayyôm hazzeh*. David's climactic appeal in
26:24 has been altered by the accession historian into a blessing placed in
Saul's mouth (24:20). Both employ dependent clauses that preserve a
summary, or epitomization, of what David has done to motivate the appeal
or blessing.

I Sam. 25:10, 32f.

The Nabal narrative in I Sam. 25:2ff. is connected literarily with
chap. 26,[221] but it arose from an independent tradition. It features
hayyôm in Nabal's gruff reply to David's servants in vs. 10, while in
David's response to the plea of Abigail in vss. 32f., it has a double
occurrence of *hayyôm hazzeh*. The LXX has σήμερον for each of these,
repeating this word in the relative clause of vs. 34, where a temporal
designative is lacking in the MT.

We can clarify the functioning of these adverbs only by identifying
some of the stages of the tradition development of the entire narrative. It
seems probable that its initial purpose was to recount how David began to
consolidate his position of leadership among the scattered clans of the
Judean southland (particularly among the dominant Calebites) through a
judicious and opportune marriage to the rich widow, Abigail; as such, this
narrative was originally recounted among David's followers at Hebron, his
first capital and the original center of Calebite influence. But once David
prevailed over the Saulides and moved his capital to Jerusalem, the tale
took on a new form, that of an apologetic for David's reign, similar in its
essential *Tendenz* to that of the accession history. The narrative reflects
this new concern particularly in Abigail's and David's speeches to each
other (vss. 26,[222] 28b-31, 33), and perhaps in the relative clause in 34.
This material forecasts the story's outcome while interpreting the narrative
theologically, i.e., in terms of David's innocence from blood guiltiness and
private vengeance, and hence of his fitness for the kingship over against the
house of Saul.

Nabal's contemptuous words in vss. 10ff. express very fittingly the
realities of the setting into which the story is placed. Though he was a
"fool," Nabal was quite aware why David and his men had been protecting
his herdsmen from other marauders, why they were now so humble and
solicitous in begging provisions from him (5ff.). David needed him—needed
him more than he needed David. Nabal's folly lay in his mistaking this
dependence and humility as weakness, a weakness that seemed all the

---

221. See above (n. 214). Note especially the fondness for the formulae with *bārûk*
in 25:32f., 39, 26:25.
222. Vs. 26a begins with *we'attâ*, which is repeated in 26b. But the original plea of
Abigail begins with the *we'attâ* of vs. 27.

greater to him in contrast to the overpowering might of king Saul. Thus Nabal chides David, as though he were a nobody: "Who is David? Who is the son of Jesse?"[223] —adding a characterization with *hayyôm* that implies an identification of his solicitant with the rabble of runaway slaves: "Today there are many servants breaking away from their proper masters!" The "today" is used, of course, in the readily understood sense of "at the present time."

As Nabal's taunt precipitates the crisis that supplies this story's dramatic tension, David's response to Abigail resolves it. It can be no accident that it, too, has the temporal designative—this time in strengthened form. However, the text is overfull in vss. 32ff.; one or the other of the sentences with *bārûk/bᵉrûkâ* and *hayyôm hazzeh* has to be identified as secondary, and the choice readily falls on the second. The reasons are: (1) it reflects the already mentioned recasting of the story; (2) it repeats *bārûk* in grammatical inflections agreeable to an alternating subject, first the abstract *ṭaʿmēk*, then the addressee *'āt*; (3) but vs. 39 has David "blessing" Yahweh, supporting vs. 32 both in form and in content as the original of these two alternatives. The bearing of *hayyôm hazzeh* is less on the temporal aspect of the situation (the reader will note that the present action is taking place during the night)[224] than on the quality of the situation in terms of event. So David's expression of praise to Yahweh, requiring the syntactical relegation to a subordinate clause of the verb and temporal adverb that define this event, is in effect an eloquent epitome, as is also David's declaration secondarily attached to it in vs. 33.[225]

I Sam. 27:10

In I Sam. 27:10 Achish, king of Gath, asks David, "Where[226] have you raided *hayyôm*?" The distributive form of David's reply, together with the distributive bearing of the introduction to this account (vs. 8a), the frequentative force of the verbs in 9abα and 11a, and the summarizing statement of 11b,[227] leads the reader to expect that the verb introducing Achish's question is meant as a frequentative too, in spite of its pointing—in which case the function of *hayyôm* would simply be to identify one

---

223. Cf. Judg. 9:38 (Zebul concerning Abimelech), II Kings 18:20 (the Rabshakeh concerning Yahweh).

224. See vss. 22, 34, 36f. It is not apparent whether this night is considered as part of the preceding or of the following day.

225. Though the relative clause in vs. 34 has a certain epitomizing force, it is a secondary element in the text. The LXX probably added σήμερον through the influence of vss. 32f.

226. Correcting the impossible MT according to variant readings; cf. BH³ mg.

227. The words following the *'athnaḥ* are to be taken as a quotation of what David's prisoners might say, not as superfluous and inappropriate (the perfect does not accord with the ostensibly frequentative context) parallel to the following clause with וכה משפטו.

particular day taken as typical of the many and various days on which this question would have been asked.

But close attention needs to be given to the vacillation of the verbal forms within this pericope. The form of unique narrative event (imperfect consecutive) occurs only in vs. 8a, in vs. 9b, here in the introduction to the direct discourse in vs. 10, and in the climactic statement in vs. 12 concerning the effect of David's deception on Achish;[228] this is probable evidence that this story was first told as the account of a single occurrence, perhaps very soon after the event.[229] Upon this assumption, the function of *hayyôm* is different: since no other days are in view, the question in which it occurs inquires concerning David's activity immediately prior to the conclusion of one, and only one, particular raid. *Hayyôm* is still a time-identification, but the question of which it is a part points to an epitomizing answer.

I Sam. 28:18

The emphatic form *hayyôm hazzeh* occurs at the climactic point of Samuel's ghostly oracle to Saul, I Sam. 28:18. What might appear to be a striking epitomizing function would be taken as especially significant, were it not for the recognition that Samuel's original speech has been secondarily expanded by the addition of vss. 17-19aα.[230] A late writer (probably the deuteronomistic redactor) has touched up an old saga, drawing it more closely into the overall narrative of Saul's downfall and David's ascent by having Samuel's spirit declare the fulfillment of his ancient prophecy as recorded in I Sam. 15:28. We have seen that that verse contained a striking epitomizing statement with *hayyôm*, reinforcing and interpreting the sign

---

228. Although mistakes in the Massoretic pointing are always a possible hypothesis, there is little likelihood that the distinctive morphology of the "defective" verbs in vss. 8f. would have become garbled in the process of textual transmission.

229. Inasmuch as David's practice continued during the entire period of his sojourn in Philistia, the form of this report was modified later to reflect what had become a habitual practice. This accounts for the frequentative construction in vs. 9abα (cf. *GK*, § 112[d, ee]; actually, this is a conditional sentence, with $w^e hikk\bar{a}$, "and whenever he would smite," in the protasis and the adversative clause with $w^e l\bar{o}$' $y^e hayyeh$ and $w^e l\bar{a}qah$ in the apodosis). It also accounts for vss. 7 and 11. Vs. 8 may originally have contained only one gentilic; its text is too jumbled to allow solid conclusions. Although David's reply in vs. 10b may have been expanded, all the names could have been included in the original form of the narrative; that is to say, he could conceivably have been raiding (hypothetically!) in the territory of the three groups mentioned, bringing his foray to a conclusion on the day of his confrontation with Achish, to which *hayyôm* refers.

230. This is most apparent from the double prediction of doom on both Saul (with his sons) and Israel (the Israelite army). Cf. Gressmann, *SAT*[2], II, 1, *in loco*; Hertzberg, *ATD*, 10, *in loco*; Schunck, *Benjamin*, pp. 94-96, 108. One surmises whether the peculiar ול at the beginning of this addition may have arisen inadvertently as the supplementer began to write of Saul in the third person, failing to correct himself as he shifted to the second person.

of the torn robe.[231] It may be that the *hayyôm* in that prophecy has stimulated the appearance of *hayyôm hazzeh* here; but the more emphatic form here has the special purpose of accentuating the correspondence between that day and this one, between the *hayyôm* when the live Samuel placed Saul under judgment and this *hayyôm* when the dead Samuel sees that judgment fulfilled. It is especially important to observe that this expression has little bearing on the immediate temporal situation, since the event narrated actually took place at night (vss. 8, 20, 25).

I Sam. 30:13

I Sam. 30:13 has the adverb *hayyôm* in an expression, placed in the mouth of a captive Egyptian, that functions to determine duration.[232]

II Sam. 3:8, 38f.

Hayyôm occurs twice in Abner's contemptuous reply to Ishbosheth (Ishbaal) reported in II Sam. 3:8; it occurs again in 3:39, where David bitterly complains concerning the ruthlessness of the sons of Zeruiah. *Hayyôm hazzeh* occurs immediately before it, in David's lament over the dead Abner, vs. 39. We have previously made a rather extensive analysis of this chapter, resulting in the identification of two separate narratives.[233] As we have seen, one narrative originates from David's court in Hebron, reflecting in a remarkably vivid and realistic way the frustration that David felt when his statesmanlike efforts at making an alliance with the Saulides were spoiled by the vengefulness of certain of his followers—specifically, the rambunctious Joab and his brother Abishai. It so happens that vss. 38f. provide the dramatic climax to this narrative. The second narrative originates in the Jerusalem scene; in it the deed of the bloodthirsty sons of Zeruiah drops somewhat from the center of attention, while David's complete innocence is emphasized (cf. vs. 37) as Abner is turned from an honorable and peace-loving man into a self-seeking scoundrel, quite deserving of the fate that befell him. It is to this account that vs. 8 belongs.

We shall briefly discuss the double *hayyôm* in vs. 8, taking it up first even though it belongs to the later of the two accounts. Although we immediately recognize in vss. 7-13 a verisimilitude with respect to the form of the dispute that is here taking place between Abner and Ishbaal, we also

---

231. See above, pp. 198f. Although I Sam. 15:28 is probably secondary in its own context, it is unlikely that the writer who added it was responsible for the insertion here in chap. 28. We note some subtle changes (e.g., מִיָּד instead of מֵעָלֶיךָ, the specific identification of רֵעַ as David) and at least one drastic change (חֲרוֹן אַף, a favorite prophetic term, for הַחֲרֵם). One should observe that the forward position of the verbal object (*haddābār hazzeh*) following 'al kēn makes the reference to 15:28 emphatic.
232. Cf. BH[3] mg.
233. Above, pp. 92ff., 148.

observe that the content of Abner's reply has been determined by the final outcome. The early narrative depicted Abner as an honest ambassador, with no intent of betraying his lord. It may be historically accurate that Abner was, in fact, scheming all the while to do Ishbaal in, but it is too much to believe that he would have openly declared his intent to Ishbaal's face, as vss. 9f. have him doing.

Thus the content of Abner's insolent reply is the narrator's artful and tendentious creation. It appears that the double use of *hayyôm* is to be explained from the narrator's desire to provide an effective introduction to vss. 9f. We need to pay special attention to the verb *'e'ᵉśeh* in vs. 8, occurring again in vs. 9. It is quite certain that the first *hayyôm* is not to be read with the preceding noun-clause.[234] Thus it precedes the frequentative *'e'ᵉśeh ḥesed bᵉ* . . . , which is immediately complemented by the adversative clause containing a negative and the perfect, "but (while, although) I have not let you encounter the power of David." This defines what Abner's behavior has been up until now, and is at the present moment. But Abner goes on in vs. 8b to declare the wrong that now threatens to upset this state of affairs, using a second *hayyôm* to terminate what is in effect a counter-charge against his lord.[235] This second *hayyôm* is used to offset the first. But what accounts for the first *hayyôm* and its emphatic position? Clearly it is the desire to make a striking contrast between what Abner is doing now (i.e., being loyal to the Saulides) and what he intends to do henceforward. (This in actuality amounts to treason, but as the narrator tells it, Yahweh's transcendent purpose will be fulfilled in Abner's roguery.) Thus, while the second clause with *hayyôm* is a simple epitome, the first is an identifying characterization that has the more ultimate purpose of establishing an emphatic temporal contrast.

The occurrence of *hayyôm hazzeh* in vs. 38 and of *hayyôm* in vs. 39 requires a less elaborate explanation. As has been said, both expressions belong to the early narrative—the one that takes a favorable attitude toward Abner. Following originally upon vs. 32, vs. 38 provides the climactic

---

234. This conclusion is not affected by a decision concerning the actual meaning of the odd expression *rō'š keleb*, or whether אשר ליהודה is a gloss (see the commentaries). *Hayyôm* with pure noun-clauses always provides an identifying characterization essential to the meaning of the pericope, never occurring in such a negative statement (direct denial or rhetorical question) as this one, for the reason that such a statement removes the characterization from the area of interest in the development of the narrative (cf. Gen. 31:48, 40:7, 42:13, 32, Deut. 1:10, 29:14, 31:2, Josh. 14:10f., I Sam. 12:5, 17, II Sam. 3:38, 18:20, 19:23, 36, Jer. 44:2, Job 23:2, Neh. 9:36, Ruth 4:9f.). For עשה חסד with *hayyôm*, cf. Gen. 24:12.

235. Whichever may be the correct reading (cf. BH³ mg), it is quite apparent that Abner regards "a fault concerning a (the) woman" as trivial; yet we know from II Sam. 16:22 and I Kings 2:19ff. that for an interloper to take a woman from the king's harem was a most serious offense. According to II Sam. 21:8ff., this same Rizpah was a woman of rank and importance in the household of Saul. Our narrator may have been deliberately accentuating Abner's roguery by having him minimize his offense in this way.

statement of David's funeral oration—a rhetorical question, exalting Abner in the manner of David's panegyric for Saul in 1:19, 27, in which the emphatic form of the epitomizing time-designative seems especially appropriate. The similarity to the question repeated in II Kings 2:3, 5 ("Don't you know . . . today?") suggests that there must have been a special solemnity in this particular form of expression.

But the real climax of this narrative comes in the double noun-clause of vs. 39, where David bitterly declares its ultimate meaning and commits the matter to Yahweh for adjudication. *Weʾānōkî* occurs foremost in emphatic contrast to *hāʿanāšîm hāʾēlleh*; then comes *hayyôm* because the characterization is more directly concerned with David's weakness[236] than with the harshness of the sons of Zeruiah. Although this double noun-clause has the usual form of the identifying characterization, its final and emphatic position within the narrative makes clear that its essential purpose is to epitomize the narrative as a whole.

II Sam. 4:8

The emphatic form *hayyôm hazzeh* next appears at the end of a dramatic declaration made by the brother-chieftains, Baanah and Rechab, who murdered their lord Ishbaal. Coming by forced march through the night all the distance from Mahanaim to Hebron, they first show David the evidence of their bloody deed, "Behold, the head of Ishbosheth the son of Saul, who sought your life," then follow this with a verbal clause containing the seldom-used imperfect consecutive: "So Yahweh has given to my lord the king vengeance *hayyôm hazzeh* from Saul and his seed!"[237] The gruesome head demonstrates the deed, while the declaration interprets it; together they epitomize the situation as the Beerothite brothers understand it.[238] As we read, they are in for an unpleasant surprise.

The final statement of the narrative, to the effect that Ishbaal's head was given an honorable burial in Abner's grave, is incontestable proof that Ishbaal and Abner had been on good terms immediately prior to their tragic deaths. (Moreover, David shows a highly favorable attitude toward Saul's son in calling him *ʾîš ṣaddîq*, vs. 11.) This clearly argues that this account of

---

236. MT רך has been read by the LXX as דד; the latter paraphrases the unique phrase that follows (משוח מלך).
237. The impf. cs. is used after a pf. with negative in the early narrative of II Sam. 3:8 (second *hayyôm*). The locution נתן נקמות is found elsewhere only in Ps. 18:48.
238. The Amalekite's report to David in II Samuel 1 provides an interesting contrast. Although the former brings concrete evidence to show that Saul is indeed dead (the crown and armlet, vs. 10), he shows these only after he has given his report. Moreover, his claim to have killed Saul is downgraded, being offered only as an effort to strengthen his reliability as an eyewitness (although there are certain discrepancies between his account and that of I Sam. 31) in response to David's probing. At any rate, the Amalekite makes no attempt to sum up the political-theological meaning of Saul's defeat, as here.

Ishbaal's murder is the immediate continuation of the early, favorable account in chap. 3, whose chief concern we have seen to have been to complain about the way certain unmanageable and ambitious underlings are able to frustrate the efforts of good leaders toward peace. Now we see that the two harsh sons of Zeruiah had their complete counterparts in the two harsh sons of Rimmon. The big difference is, of course, that although David may have felt himself weakened through the ruthlessness of Joab and his brother, he was strong indeed as compared with Ishbaal. Thus, as this narrator sees it, David ultimately prevailed not so much through anything that made him strong as through the things that showed the Saulides to be weak, hence bereft of Yahweh's favor.

II Sam. 6:20

Much more is required, in analyzing the function of the two *hayyôm's* in II Sam. 6:20,[239] than a simple statement regarding the form and syntax of the verse itself. It is immediately apparent that Michal's greeting to David is a taunt which David directly turns against her (21f.). The first clause (מה נכבד היום מלך ישראל) is meant as bitter mockery, accentuating the dignity that befits such a one as "the king of Israel," while the second clause (. . . אשר נגלה היום לעיני אמחות עבדיו)[240] states the contemptible reality that Michal sees in David's "leaping and dancing" before Yahweh. Together, the two clauses ironically epitomize the event and characterize the day, the first doing it negatively and the second positively. As in 3:8, the two *hayyôm's*, standing in stark contrast to each other, emphasize a disparity between what should be and what is.

Not so easy to resolve are the literary-critical and traditional-critical problems. It is rather widely agreed that this chapter provides the conclusion to the *hieros logos* for the ark, but no consensus has emerged regarding the relationship of the Michal episode to the ark legend, or regarding the religious and political rites that were actually involved. Proponents of the sacral-kingship hypothesis have naturally made much of this entire chapter, going so far as to claim that the Michal episode reflects an original *hieros gamos*, concluding the coronation of David, which is supposed to have taken place concomitantly with the enthronement of Yahweh.[241]   That the

---

239. This verse has been omitted in the Chronicler's story of the ark's entrance.

240. It is possible to point both nifals as participles; however, there is no question but that the second, referring to an action previously observed, has to be read as a perfect. The consequent likelihood that the first is similarly to be read, as in parallel with it, is strengthened by the observation that ironic exclamations in Jer. 22:23 and Job 26:2f. occur with unmistakable perfects (cf. *GK*, § 148[a,b]).

241. See J. R. Porter, "The Interpretation of 2 Samuel vi and Psalm cxxxii," *JTS*, 5 (1954), 161-73, followed by R. A. Carlson, *David the Chosen King* (Uppsala, 1964), pp. 91-96. Cf. also A. Bentzen, "The Cultic Use of the Story of the Ark in Samuel," *JBL*, 67 (1948), 37-53, refining the theories of Mowinckel and Pedersen.

story of the ark's entrance into Jerusalem originally had a cultic setting seems altogether assured; however, the story reports not the enthronement of Yahweh but merely the installation of the ark in a new cultic site—hence the transfer of the Yahweh Sebaoth tradition from Shiloh, lately the most prominent center of sacral-union ideology,[242] to the city that David had now captured from the Jebusites and intended to use as the basis for his religious-political program of uniting under his rule the formerly separate kingdoms of Judah and Israel.[243] If the text fails to mention the enthronement of Yahweh, it certainly says nothing of the coronation of David—already called "king" in vss. 12, 16; this can be discovered in the text only if one is previously committed to the sacral-kingship theory. Finally, the discernment of a *hieros gamos* in the Michal incident rests on several very questionable assumptions deriving from prior commitment to a patternistic methodology, such as a forced interpretation of the reference to Michal looking out the window and the notion that the "servants' maids" whom David expected to "honor" him would have been suitable substitutes for his wife Michal.[244]

---

242. For the view that the ark had been the peculiar possession of the Shiloh shrine, see R. Smend, *Jahwekrieg und Stämmebund*, pp. 56-70 (ET, pp. 76-97).

243. Cf. M. Noth, *History of Israel*, pp. 185ff. One may perhaps appropriately speak of a "re-enthronement," in the sense that the worship of the eclectic deity of Shiloh, Yahweh Sebaoth, probably incorporated, already in the premonarchic period, certain elements of the divine-kingship motif (cf. I Sam. 4:4, II Sam. 6:2, which add to the divine title the laudatory description, *yōšēb hakkᵉrubîm ʿālâw*). But it is extremely doubtful that "all the house of Israel" (vs. 15)—meaning a significant representation of the total membership of the sacral union, which as a whole had been strongly opposed to monarchistic ideology—would have tolerated any ritual that was openly designed as a divine enthronement. David was, of course, shrewd enough to see the possibilities inherent in the monarchistic associations of the Yahweh-Sebaoth ideology, using it not only to guarantee his own authority, but also to oppose the rival ideology of the Jebusite El-Elyon cult; cf. O. Eissfeldt, "Jahwe Zebaoth," *Kleine Schriften*, III (Tübingen, 1966), 103-23; and "Silo und Jerusalem," *ibid.*, pp. 417-25; G. von Rad, "Zelt und Lade," *Gesammelte Studien*, pp. 109-29; H.-P. Müller, *Ursprünge und Strukturen Alttestamentlicher Eschatologie* (BZAW, 109, Berlin, 1969), pp. 46f. In the liturgy of the temple, Ps. 24:7-10 is a full-blown embodiment of the Yahweh-Sebaoth kingship motif, while Ps. 132 expresses more closely the notion that must have informed the minds of most of those who participated in the original event of II Sam. 6, i.e., that Yahweh had found in Zion a "resting place" (this and the fact that the ark was placed in a tent, not a temple, are clear indications that important concessions were being made to the desert-wandering traditions that had heretofore been predominant within the sacral union); cf. H.-J. Kraus's commentary on these psalms in *BK* and in *Gottesdienst in Israel*, 237ff.

244. See especially Porter, *op. cit.*, pp. 164-67. The expression found in vs. 16, שׁקף nif. followed by *bᵉʿad hahallôn*, occurs elsewhere at Judg. 5:28; the hif. followed by *bᵉʿad hahallôn* occurs in Gen. 26:8 and II Kings 9:30 (cf. 32). Inviting as it may be to see a parallel to the harlotrous "woman in the window," only the reference to Jezebel's action in II Kings 9:30 can be construed as implying sexual enticement, and this passage involves a different verbal form than is found in II Sam. 6:16. Though David's threat to have himself "honored" by the maids may have implied sexual relations, none of them could have taken the place of the queen in a cultic

Careful study of the biblical text tends to substantiate the view of Leonhard Rost's classic study, *Die Ueberlieferung von der Thronnachfolge Davids,*[245] to the effect that the ark story did not originally contain the Michal incident. First of all, we see that vs. 16 has nothing to do with its context except as a device for joining the reference to David's dancing (vs. 14) to Michal's scornful comment of vs. 20.[246] Both it and vss. 20ff. require that Michal would have been absent from a public celebration where even the common women were present (19).[247] To accentuate the violence of David's dancing, and thus to make explicit the cause why David uncovered himself, it adds the unparalleled term $m^e pazz\bar{e}z$ ("jumping wildly," judging from cognate usage) to the $m^e kark\bar{e}r$ ("whirling"?) of vs. 14. However, the syntax of this section makes it unlikely that Michal would have seen David dancing if she had been looking out of her palace window because the dancing took place near Obed-edom's house, not before the palace. Vs. 14, with its double participial clause and David as subject, is intended to finish off the statement beginning with $way^e h\hat{i}$ in vs. 13; that is to say, David was dancing before Yahweh as part of the sacrificial ritual that took place after the ark has been moved six paces toward Jerusalem. Vs. 15 has another participle, but with the double subject, "David and all the house of Israel," thus marking a new episode, being the preface to the series of narrative verbs (imperfect consecutives) found in vss. 17ff.[248] Finally we add that the syntax of vs. 16 clearly marks itself off from its context.[249] Thus the Michal episode is to be identified as a secondary intrusion into the text.

---

marriage, and none of them could have borne him a proper heir without going through the legal formalities of becoming his wife. Furthermore, David would scarcely have come to his house for such a sacral marriage, especially not after having already sent the worshipers away to their homes (vs. 19). Finally we may add that the whole case for a *hieros gamos* depends on the mistaken assumption that chap. 6 is a literary unity.

245. BWANT, III, 6, Stuttgart, 1926; reprinted in *Das Kleine Credo und andere Studien zum Alten Testament* (Heidelberg, 1965), pp. 119-253. Regarding the Michal incident, cf. especially pp. 105ff. (212ff.). Rost bases his judgment on the consideration that form-critically the Michal incident plays no role in the structure of the *hieros logos*. The effort of Nübel ("Davids Aufstieg," pp. 78-82) to refute Rost's argumentation can hardly be called successful.

246. Vs. 17 would require a new subject if vs. 16 were original because the connection with vs. 15 is severed.

247. Even the maids of David's servants had been present to see David's nakedness (vs. 20).

248. Omitting vss. 6-9, a secondary intrusion (see above, pp. 66f.), we may outline the syntactical structure of the ark story as follows: Episode I, a series of narrative verbs (1-3) followed by descriptive participles (4-5); Episode II, a series of narrative verbs (10-12); Episode III, a series of narrative verbs (13) followed by descriptive participles (14); Episode IV, descriptive participle (15) followed by a series of narrative verbs (16-19). The foremost position of the participial phrase in vs. 15 has been occasioned by the special emphasis that is placed on the participation of "all the house of Israel" alongside David. Vs. 20a is a redactional device for introducing Michal's taunt.

249. The verse begins with $w^e h\bar{a}y\hat{a}$ (corrected by Chronicles and LXX to $way^e h\hat{i}$)

This analysis scarcely justifies the conclusion that the Michal narrative is the free invention of a redactor.[250] The apocopated introduction to David's reply—inviting emendation as a supposed corruption—and the unmistakable parallelism suggest that it may contain a saying in couplet form preserved from oral tradition.[251] This has been expanded into an anecdote that preserves the memory of an intense and damaging domestic quarrel within the royal family.[252] The purpose of the anecdote is, of course, to explicate the political effects·that followed from this quarrel, i.e., that Michal never gave David an heir (vs. 23), and that accordingly the bloodline of Saul lost any further hold upon the kingship.

But it may have been reflecting something even more essential than the political rivalry between the Saulides and the Davidides, viz., a substantial difference in religious ideology. We may suppose that Michal was offended not solely by the vulgarity manifested by David's nakedness, but also by the religious associations of the violent dancing that had occasioned that nakedness. Although the verse that originally reports David's dancing (14) makes no suggestion that he actually did allow himself to be exposed, this is precisely what our narrator makes of it. In other words, he has Michal objecting to the nakedness (by metonymy, sexual display and fertility orgies) that was commonly a part of baalistic rites, and thereby depicts her as impugning the ark ritual as baalistically tainted. And so, in truth, it may have been;[253] the fact that this is accurately reported even

---

followed by a participial phrase; this probably constitutes a circumstantial clause that is best given a temporal meaning in translation: "And it happened that, as the ark of Yahweh was coming into the city of David, Michal . . . looked down (etc.)."
250. Rost's painstaking argument that this incident represents the beginning of the "Thronfolgequelle" requires the assumption that, since the Michal story presupposes the ark story, the writer would have had it before him. Although this is a possibility, it is less likely than the theory that a redactor introduced the Michal narrative into the ark story as a device for binding it to the succession history, along with the Nathan prophecy and the account of the Ammonite war.
251. The original couplet could very possibly have looked something like this:

אשחקה לפני יהוה   ונקלתי עוד מזאת
והייתי שפל בעיני   ועם האמות אכבדה

252. Certainly Gunkel (*SAT*, II, 1, *in loco*) is wrong in suggesting that the story has to be fictional because no one would have known what happened in a private scene between a husband and wife. The narrative places the argument in a public place, at the gate of the palace. There would have been many eyes to witness this violent altercation, and many tongues to wag about it. Although the narrator-redactor may have been intending to suggest that the ensuing barrenness was a divine punishment for Michal's attitude toward the ark, the story leads ostensibly to what we would call the mediating cause of this ultimate effect, i.e., a perpetually strained relationship between the two royal personages.
253. In early texts "dancing" (from the roots חיל and שׂחק/ צ) is associated with women's role in victory celebrations (Exod. 15:20, Judg. 11:34, I Sam. 18:6f.) or idolatry (Exod. 32:6, 19). The dancing of the young women of Shiloh, mentioned in Judg. 21:21, was unquestionably erotic, involving ritualistic sexual liaisons, as may be inferred from the apologia that was offered to their fathers and brothers according to vs. 22; yet, at the time involved, Shiloh was counted as belonging to

though the narrator was not sympathetic with Michal's interpretation lends still greater credence to this account. The likelihood is, therefore, that Michal was acting as a true Saulide and primitive Yahwist, opposing an eclecticism that her father would never have tolerated.[254] The "today" of which Michal spoke so derisively was indeed a day of momentous consequence.

II Sam. 11:12, 15:20

We come next to a number of occurrences of *hayyôm* (*hazzeh*) in the throne-succession narrative. Since the problem of literary analysis is of minimal complexity here, our remarks may be restricted mainly to matters of style. The often-admired skillfulness of the author emerges in his great sensitivity for various possibilities in the use of the time-designatives that we have been studying. As we shall see, toward the climax of his account he puts effective speeches with epitomizing *hayyôm* into the mouths of his important characters, while in the minor scenes he prepares similar speeches that epitomize the essential meaning of particular events, in some instances using these time-designatives to tie the events together in the ongoing stream of narrative.

Before we comment on the individual epitomizing passages, mention must be made of two occurrences of *hayyôm* that function merely to identify one particular day in contrast to other days. The first passage, II Sam. 11:12, has the function of establishing a very important sequence in the Uriah-Bathsheba episode; the *hayyôm* of Uriah's presence in Jerusalem is contrasted with the *māḥār* of his departure (so likewise the reiterating *bayyôm hahû'* and *mimmāḥᵒrāt*).[255]

The second passage, 15:20, looking backward, contrasts the *hayyôm* of Ittai's presence with the *tᵉmôl* of his nonpresence, in this instance for the purpose of emphasizing the remarkable loyalty of David's mercenary.

Israel (otherwise it could not have provided suitable wives even for the Benjaminites; that Shiloh had to be identified, vs. 19, is indication that it was relatively obscure, perhaps only peripherally related to the sacral union). We also have the testimony of I Sam. 2:22, which, while secondary in its context, may reflect an authentic tradition. To some degree, these ideas seem to have attached themselves to the figure of Yahweh Sebaoth and to the ark. Thus the dancing, as well as the distribution of symbolic "portions," mentioned in II Sam. 6, appears to have been consciously or unconsciously associated with baalistic rites.

254. Elsewhere than in this chapter, early passages mentioning Yahweh Sebaoth are chap. 7 (8, 26f.), I Sam. 1:3, 11, 4:4 (pertaining to Shiloh and the ark), 15:2 (where Samuel, speaking in the name of Yahweh Sebaoth, undoubtedly represents a more orthodox tradition), II Sam. 5:10 (from the court historian, writing after the Yahweh-Sebaoth tradition had been fully assimilated). I Sam. 17:45 is from a relatively late, prophetically influenced legend (see above, pp. 199f.). Thus there is nothing whatever to associate Saul with Yahweh Sebaoth (or with the ark, I Sam. 14:18 having been altered from the original), which may in part account for Samuel's antipathy.

255. See above, p. 107.

II Sam. 14:22

Sublime subtlety lies in the interchange marking the climax of the episode concerning the wise woman of Tekoa, II Sam. 14:1-24. The narrator has told us that David really wanted Absalom back following his escape to Geshur, even though, for the sake of form, he refused to take the initiative toward effectuating his return (13:39). Joab sets out to allow the king to accomplish his wish by having him seem to be gracious to others, *viz.*, the woman, and, through her, himself. The woman comes to tell the story Joab has put in her mouth; David very quickly perceives that "the hand of Joab is in all this." He gives him the order to bring Absalom home, whereupon Joab replies (vs. 22), "*Hayyôm* thy servant knows that I have found favor in your sight, my lord, the king, because the king has acted according to his servant's word." *Hayyôm* is emphatic at the beginning, as though to underscore the possibility (very likely historical) that heretofore Joab may have had some reason to doubt whether he was fully in David's good graces. Now that David so forthrightly performs the request of his servant, thereby allowing him to function as the vehicle for the accomplishment of his own desire, Joab is more than assured that *hayyôm* is indeed a day of favor for him.[256]

II Sam. 16:3

The Mephibosheth (Meribaal) figure is surely one of the most pathetic in the entire throne-succession narrative. As the surviving pretender from the house of Saul, he is ever the occasion of suspicion in the mind of David; as the son of David's dear friend Jonathan, he is the object of David's ostentatious kindness. As a cripple, he may have fallen prey to villainous slander at a moment of crisis for all who had had any association with David.

The servant Ziba reports to David that Meribaal is remaining behind in Jerusalem, rather than joining David in his flight before Absalom (II Sam. 16:1-3abα). Later on, when David will encounter Meribaal upon his return to Jerusalem, the latter will explain that he had been tricked (19:27f.), but here in chap. 16 Ziba explains Meribaal's motive in a quotation (or pseudo-quotation) that epitomizes what he wants David to accept as Meribaal's expectation (3bβ): "*Hayyôm* the house of Israel will restore to me my father's kingdom." The time-designative has been placed foremost for emphasis, probably with the intent of depicting Meribaal as contrasting this day to all other days, i.e., as already savoring its uniqueness. It is this almost ludicrous image, together with Ziba's precipitous

---

256. Hence the story is as much concerned with Joab as with the wise woman, *contra* J. Hoftijzer, "David and the Tekoite Woman," *VT,* 20 (1970), 419-44; cf. R. N. Whybray, *The Succession Narrative* (London, 1968), p. 59.

solicitude reported in 19:18, that casts serious doubt on his report. Who then is the real scoundrel? It is part of the writer's artistry that he is able to keep the reader guessing.[257]

II Sam. 16:12

The Shimei episode in II Sam. 16:5-14 is, in fact, only the introduction to an intriguing narrative motif running through the entire succession narrative. That David took the curse of a prominent Saulide as a serious threat to the survival and well-being of his dynasty—more serious than the touching scene of reconciliation reported in 19:17ff. would seem to suggest—becomes quite clear from David's dying instructions to Solomon, reported in I Kings 2:8f., that Shimei's curse must be avenged with blood (cf. vss. 36ff.). That David did not immediately allow the outrageous curse to be avenged may not have been occasioned solely by gentleness, weariness, or piety;[258] Shimei very probably had a strong bodyguard with him, to judge from 19:18, where a force of one thousand supporters is mentioned, and for David to have allowed a clash at this awkward time would have seriously drained the manpower he needed for the inevitable showdown with Absalom. So David theologizes a rationalization for his restraint: "Yahweh has bidden him" (vs. 11); besides, "it may be that Yahweh will regard my punishment[259] and Yahweh will repay me with good for his cursing[260] *hayyôm hazzeh*" (12). The time-designative modifies the preceding infinitival gerund, which in a sense epitomizes the present day (this day is a day of curse). However, the emphatic form has a special purpose, one that becomes very clear when the reader turns to 19:20 and I Kings 2:8. "This day" is to have its adequate counterpart in a coming day of recompense and revenge. Hence in II Sam. 16:12 *hayyôm hazzeh* is primarily an emphatic identifier of one day in distinction from another, i.e., the one that in the narrator's viewpoint is sure to come.

---

257. Why should Meribaal have expected Absalom to allow the restoration of the Saulide rule? Could Meribaal have been so ignorant, or so naive? Yet we wonder why even a David in flight should have been so ready to believe Ziba's report if it was really as ridiculous as it seemed. In chap. 19 David shows by the half-measures he takes with regard to Meribaal's property (vs. 29) that he cannot be sure who is telling the truth; to our minds Meribaal's obsequious response (vs. 30) seems to put him under even darker suspicion than before.

258. David's more than annoyed rebuff to Abishai (vs. 10; cf. 19:22) can be understood only in the light of II Sam. 3. The extreme vengefulness of Joab and Abishai against the Benjaminites had frustrated David's strategy once before, and could do so now again.

259. So the *kethibh*, softened by the versions to "my affliction" (cf. BH³ mg). In characteristic enigmatic style, the narrator has David do two opposite things at the same time: admit he is being punished, yet suggest that the cursing is so much more severe than the offense that recompense is to be confidently expected.

260. So the *qere*, which is supported here by the fact that the noun required by the *kethibh* does not occur with the time-designative. Cf. I Sam. 24:20.

II Sam. 18:20, 31

Hayyôm occurs in the Cushite's announcement to David in II Sam. 18:31, while *hayyôm hazzeh* occurs twice in Joab's statement to Ahimaaz earlier in the same chapter. The Cushite's simple statement epitomizes, but the longer form in vs. 20 serves for emphatic time-identification.

It is important to see that the writer has artfully structured the entire account of Absalom's death in such a way as to emphasize its ambivalent meaning for David. This is accomplished chiefly through a play on forms from the root בשר, "bring (good) tidings,"[261] and by the skillful use of time-designatives. We have previously come to the discovery that *bayyôm hahu'* has been employed both to begin and conclude this account. In 18:7 it was used in a climactic statement that epitomized the outcome of the fighting between the army of David and the army of Absalom; in political terms, the day had already been established as a day of victory for David and his men. But in personal terms, the day is to turn out as an evil day. David is about to experience the futility of attempting to have everything his own way. He cannot win in war and keep his rebel son alive. Thus the *bayyôm hahû'* in vs. 8, synchronizing the account of Absalom's death with the larger narrative of which it is a part, is especially fraught with significance. It prepares for the irony inherent in the events that follow, leading to the epitomizing conclusion of 19:3, "So the victory *bayyôm hahû'* was turned into mourning for all the people." Absalom's dying and David's grief intervene to give this day the opposite of its appropriate character.[262]

Joab knows how to deal with Absalom, but he is less certain about how to deal with the king. His calculations in dispatching the two messengers (18:19ff.) seem to fall short of their purpose, for he certainly does not succeed in preventing David's breakdown and—of more personal concern—David's reprisal against himself. Joab apparently feels squeamish about sending the son of Zadok for this purpose, perhaps because, as David implies in vss. 26f., priests are supposed to be messengers of *good* tidings. Or perhaps, judging from Ahimaaz' words in vs. 22, Joab is simply fearful to risk so high a person to David's wrath. However this may be, he first refuses to let Ahimaaz go, telling him, לא איש בשרה אתה היום הזה, "no messenger shall you be this day" (20aα); the reason is given at the end of the verse: "because the king's son is dead." That the writer simply wishes to differentiate this particular day from other days is clear from Joab's intervening concession, "but you may be messenger another day *(b^eyôm 'ahēr)*, though *hayyôm hazzeh* you may not be a messenger." In any event,

---

261. Although the denotative range of בשר pi. is wide enough to include in one instance (I Sam. 4:17) the bringing of evil tidings, its general application is to the bearing of good tidings. Besides, in II Sam. 18 this form is deliberately ironic in passages like II Sam. 4:10, I Kings 1:42. The hithpael occurs only here (vs. 31).
262. See above, pp. 108f.

Joab's words eloquently express his characterization of this day as a day fraught with irony and peril.

That Joab so soon changes his mind may be due to his recollection of the open and naive nature of the Cushite whom he has sent in the place of Ahimaaz: this man will perhaps be too blunt and tactless. Thus he allows Ahimaaz to run. When Ahimaaz arrives ahead of the Cushite, he is deliberately ambiguous about the outcome of the battle—using less incisive words (vs. 28) than he first intended (19)—and evasive concerning the fate of Absalom (29).[263] The Cushite remains as the one who must give David a direct, factual account (31f.). First he happily epitomizes what he imagines the day ought to mean to the king: "Yahweh has vindicated you (שפטך) *hayyôm* from the hand of all who rose against you"; then he informs him, with a satisfaction that more prudent men would try to hide, of Absalom's bitter fate.

II Sam. 19:6f. [E-5f.]

Hayyôm occurs no fewer than five times in Joab's speech to David found in II Sam. 19:6f., eloquently expressing his agitation in an outpouring of protest against what he considers to be extremely harmful conduct on David's part, *viz.*, his pitiable weeping over Absalom at a time when he should have been leading his troops in a victory celebration.

Again we are helped by the recognition that this episode actually begins in vs. 4 with the statement containing *bayyôm hahû'*; it ends with the ambiguously optimistic note in vs. 9bα, "So all the people came before the king." We must look carefully at the beginning. As the preceding episode has been dovetailed into the present one with the preparatory remark that Joab was told of the king's weeping (vs. 2), so the present episode is dovetailed back into the preceding one by an abbreviated repetition of the king's pathetic words (vs. 5; cf. vs. 1). But this repetition is prefaced by the introductory statement of vs. 4, "Now the people went like thieves *bayyôm hahû'* as they entered the city, as the shamefaced people steal who have fled from battle." As we have seen, the time-designative provides the sequential link to this new episode; yet the verse also epitomizes the new situation and explains the vehemence of Joab's plea.

The function of the several occurrences of *hayyôm* in Joab's speech becomes apparent from an outline of its syntax. Joab starts right out by bluntly epitomizing the effect of David's conduct, as seen in the light of vs. 4: הבשת היום את פני כל עבדיך, "You have shamed today the faces of all your servants." Immediately Joab alludes to the irony of the situation, at the same time interjecting a note of stern reproach, by qualifying the

---

263. See BH³ mg and the commentaries concerning the text.

object-noun with a participial phrase containing *hayyôm* as an element of identifying characterization: ... הַמְמַלְּטִים אֶת נַפְשְׁךָ הַיּוֹם, "those who have saved your life today, etc." He next states the impression of startling paradox that results from David's behavior (vs. 7a), following this up with two epitomizing clauses with *kî*. The first *kî*-clause explicates the second half of the paradox ("hating those who love you"): כִּי הִגַּדְתָּ הַיּוֹם כִּי אֵין לְךָ שָׂרִים וַעֲבָדִים, "for you have revealed today that nothing to you are commanders or underlings." The second *kî*-clause explicates the first part of the paradox ("loving those who hate you"), but now—touching on the delicate matter of the king's dear son—Joab is circumspect enough to restrict his epitomization to a statement of his own opinion: כִּי יָדַעְתִּי הַיּוֹם ... כִּי לֹא ... כִּי אָז יָשָׁר בְּעֵינֶיךָ, "for I know that if[264] ∴. then it would be right in your eyes"; this "if" clause contains the fifth *hayyôm*, using it to make explicit the synchronization between the contrasting conditions it contemplates: לֹא אַבְשָׁלוֹם חַי וְכֻלָּנוּ הַיּוֹם מֵתִים, "if Absalom were alive and we all today were dead. . . ."

It must have taken a considerable amount of courage to talk to the king this way. Joab had to do it because he rightly saw the immense danger in David's unwillingness to deal forthrightly with a paradoxical situation. Joab in fact saved David's throne; yet we are not surprised to learn, a few verses further on (vs. 14; cf. I Kings 2:28ff.), that Joab was ungraciously cashiered, for David was not such a man as could love one who was willing to force him to do what he should have done himself.[265]

II Sam. 19:21, 23 [E-20, 22]

Once again, in II Sam. 19, we encounter the profuse collocation of *hayyôm*'s that evidences heated controversy and intense emotion. This occurs in the scene of Shimei's return, vss. 17-24. First Shimei uses an epitomizing *hayyôm* (vs. 21); then when Abishai attempts to interfere with David's decision to excuse him, the king three times reproves Abishai with clauses including the word *hayyôm*, all of which characterize or epitomize key elements in the scene.

When Shimei hastens to be reconciled with David, the latter quickly sees the wisdom of not attempting to punish him for the violent curse he had so lately put upon him (16:5-14). There are two reasons: (1) David needs him if he is to secure the loyalty of "the house of Joseph" (see the sequel in vss. 42-44); (2) Shimei has with him a thousand Benjaminites. At any rate, Shimei makes it easy for David to accept reconciliation by being

---

264. Reading the *qere;* cf. BH[3] mg.
265. "To tell the truth is useful to those to whom it is spoken, but disadvantageous to those who tell it, because it makes them disliked," Pascal, *Pensées*, 100. Regarding the crucial nature of this episode, see J. Jackson, "David's Throne: Patterns in the Succession Story," *CanJT*, 11 (1965), 193f.

properly courteous (in contrast to Joab's blunt rudeness) and humble. First Shimei attempts to set aside the past, asking to be forgiven for the wrong he did "on the day when my lord the king departed from Jerusalem" (20).[266] Without waiting for David to respond purely from a spirit of graciousness, Shimei gives him the hard, political reason he needs: "and behold, I am come *hayyôm* as the first from all the house of Joseph to come down to meet my lord the king" (21).

Again Abishai steps in as the nemesis of the house of Saul, demanding the death sentence because of the curse.[267] The king snaps back with the same words that he used in 16:10, "What have I to do with you, you sons of Zeruiah?" His exasperation is perhaps especially evident from the fact that his reply includes Joab, even though Joab has presumably not spoken.[268] David implicates them both in a countering reproach, "You (pl.) have become for me *hayyôm* an adversary"—which, because of the verb in the imperfect and the negative form of the whole charge, would be better described as an identifying characterization than as an epitome.

David seems almost to rant as he rushes on with two rhetorical questions, the first requiring a negative, and the second a positive, answer. Both have *hayyôm*, but the second involves an identifying characterization, while only the first properly epitomizes the entire situation. "*Hayyôm* shall any man die in Israel?" requires a "no" because this is a very special kind of day. What kind of day? The day of David's restoration to the kingship: "For do I not know that *hayyôm* I am king over Israel?" David will not tolerate the sons of Zeruiah preventing him from showing that he is king; the way to do this is to effectuate the old tradition that no man should die on the day of royal accession (I Sam. 11:12f.).[269] So the curse can wait; David swears that Shimei shall not die, meaning that *he* will not execute him. What another may do is another matter.

II Sam. 19:36 [E-35]

In the Barzillai episode, II Sam. 19:32-41, *hayyôm* appears in an identifying characterization similar to that put into Caleb's mouth in Josh. 14:10. David, grateful for Barzillai's generous treatment, invites him to

---

266. For the reasons stated, David sets aside the sentence of death (vs. 24), but he never forgives Shimei. On this passage, together with I Kings 2:8f., 37, 42, cf. Rost, *Ueberlieferung von der Thronnachfolge Davids*, pp. 101f. (209).
267. Cf. 16:9. The narrator allows an important difference between Joab's and Abishai's characters to come to light. Joab is bloody, blunt, and rude—but manages to do things that are practical even though they may annoy the king. Abishai is bloody and hotheaded, but more restrained in his relationship with David, managing to propose things that are impractical or impolitic.
268. So also in 16:9f. Abishai is at David's side because he commands one of the three divisions of the army (cf. 18:2ff.), while Joab has been replaced by Amasa (19:14).
269. Cf. p. 148. David will win the Saulides by seeming as gracious as Saul.

accompany him to Jerusalem, but his old friend excuses himself on the grounds of age and feebleness. The noun-clause in vs. 36, "An eighty-year old am I *hayyôm*," does not suggest that this day was his birthday, only that his age was an important factor in defining what he was, and therefore what he ought to do.

I Kings 1:25, 30, 48

Two of the scenes in the story of Solomon's coronation have the word *hayyôm*, while one other has *hayyôm hazzeh*. True to his accustomed style, the throne-succession historian uses the simpler form for epitomizing and characterizing statements, the longer, emphatic style for comparative time-identification.

The first *hayyôm* appears in I Kings 1:25, where Nathan gives David his report concerning Adonijah, defining succinctly the present situation of peril. Bathsheba has already entered the bedchamber to remind him of his oath to make Solomon his successor (17), apprise him that "Adonijah is king" (18ff.), and challenge him to decide who shall sit on his throne (20). As though to corroborate her by coincidence, Nathan bursts in. He makes no mention of Solomon, but pointedly asks whether David has played his proper authoritarian role in what is happening. He makes no such conclusive statement as Bathsheba has made, but simply describes, in a series of verbal clauses commencing with "for he has gone down *hayyôm*. . . ," what Adonijah is up to, suggesting that there is still time to counteract it, if the king will only give his command (25).

David responds by making the decision he has been too weak and selfish to make until this very moment. But before giving orders for Solomon's coronation (vss. 32ff.) he calls Bathsheba back for a tender scene that surely has a programmatic purpose in the succession history. David swears to her an oath confirming the oath he had evidently made long ago:[270] "As I swore to you . . . so will I do *hayyôm hazzeh*" (30). The primary purpose of the time-designative can only be to produce a contrasting time-identification. David swears to Bathsheba that what has been so long deferred is going to take place now, this very day, without further delay.

In vss. 43ff. the installation of Solomon is reported to Adonijah and his party. The messenger, Jonathan ben Abiathar, tells first every detail of what has been done with Solomon (43-46). To prevent the conclusion that Solomon may have been made king without David's approval, he next tells of how David has allowed his servants to wish Solomon a greater rule than

---

270. Cf. vs. 17. It can scarcely be an accident that the throne-succession history nowhere bothers to record the initial making of this oath. The author evidently put greater stock in Yahweh's promise (2:24) than in what David may have promised to a woman.

his own (47), and finally reports the words with which David has praised Yahweh, "Blessed be Yahweh, the god of Israel, who has appointed *hayyôm*[271] one to sit on my throne" (48). This is more than pious prattle: it effectively epitomizes David's understanding of the theological meaning of all that has happened, at the same time intimating his relief that a higher power has intervened to shape the course of events, where he had himself been too weak.

I Kings 2:24

The throne-succession history cannot end without telling how Solomon got rid of his rival Adonijah and those who had supported him. That Adonijah should have presumed to use Solomon's own mother to convey to him a suspicious request was all the pretext Solomon needed for putting him to death. In I Kings 2:23 the new king uses the self-cursing formula to bespeak the death decree; he makes this more explicit in vs. 24 (*weʿattâ*), this time swearing by Yahweh's life, while omitting the self-cursing in favor of two relative clauses that recall Yahweh's promise[272] and at the same time reveal Solomon's actual reason for wanting to get rid of Adonijah; finally, an apodosis states the verdict on Adonijah, היום יומת אדניהו. This is more than an ordinary epitome, though epitomizing force is evident in it: the foremost position of *hayyôm*, following directly upon the oath, indicates urgency and impatience, showing that there is unusual emphasis on the time element. The day defines the event at least as much as the event defines the day.[273]

I Kings 2:31 LXX

A final *hayyôm* may have been intended by the throne-succession narrator in Solomon's instructions for Joab's execution (I Kings 2:31). This is what the LXX has apparently read after the verb והסירת, "so you shall remove. . . ." Although the LXX confuses the words that follow, the Hebrew writer's great concern about Joab's bloodguiltiness, sustained throughout the narrative, may have added *hayyôm* to a command for decisive action at this point in the original text.[274]

---

271. The LXX insertion, "from my seed," has little meaning here since there was never any question whether one of David's sons would succeed him.
272. Concerning the promise of a house, see II Sam. 7:11f. Cf. Rost, *Thronnachfolge*, pp. 104f. (212f.).
273. Noting that the succession narrative has heretofore used only *hayyôm hazzeh* for time-identification, we may find an explanation for this exception in that it echoes, in reverse form, the customary death decree/amnesty formula with *hayyôm* (cf. I Sam. 11:13, II Sam. 19:23).
274. This would accord with his normal pattern; cf. vss. 24, 26, 37, 42. Contrariwise, the LXX may simply have been normalizing in recognition of this pattern.

I Kings 5:21 [E-7]

Following the throne-succession narrative, *hayyôm* occurs first in the flattering words of Hiram found in I Kings 5:21, "Blessed be Yahweh *hayyôm*, who has given David a wise son to be over this great people!" When we express agreement with the present consensus in identifying 5:15ff. as the free composition of the Deuteronomist, we do not intend to question the historical possibility of such an embassage and treaty as is reported here,[275] nor do we deny that some ancient dignitaries may have made a custom of bespeaking praise for the gods of their treaty counterparts.[276] The Deuteronomist inserts similar flattering words (in a different form, without *hayyôm*) into the speech of the Queen of Sheba (10:9).[277]

We have no reason to believe that the *bārûk*-formula used by Hiram belongs peculiarly to the introduction of treaty documents; the Deuteronomist has simply adapted a stereotyped phrase, adding the time-designative *hayyôm*. In this, he may have been immediately influenced by I Kings 1:48, where David uses *bārûk YHWH* together with *hayyôm* in a following relative clause—or possibly even by a more remote coalescence of these elements in I Sam. 25:32f. In any event, we note that the Deuteronomist has unaccountably brought *hayyôm* forward, as though to make it pertain to the act of blessing Yahweh (expressed by the passive participle) rather than to Yahweh's act of appointing Solomon king, thus producing an identifying characterization.

I Kings 8:28

It is again the Deuteronomist who is responsible for the next occur-

---

275. On this much-discussed historical problem, see now F. C. Fensham, "The Treaty Between the Israelites and Tyrians," SVT, 17 (1969), 71-87; cf. J. Priest, "The Covenant of Brothers," *JBL*, 84 (1965), 400-406.

276. A close parallel may be found in Tushratta's letter to Amenophis III in commemoration of a wedding alliance (J. A. Knudtzon, *Die El-Amarna Tafeln*, Leipzig, 1915, No. 21); ù aḫi-ia i-na ûmi[mi] ša-a-ši li-iḫ-du [ilu]šamaš ù ištar aḫi-ia ka-ra-ba ra-ba-a ḫi-du-ú-ta ba-ni-i-tú li-id-din-ú-neš-šu (lines 17-22).

277. Twice in I Kings 8 the Deuteronomist has put the words *bārûk YHWH* followed by a relative clause—as here—into the mouth of Solomon (vss. 15, 56). Although *hayyôm* is lacking in the Hebrew text in both verses, the LXX of each verse has followed the pattern of 5:21 in reading it immediately before the relative clause. The consistency of the LXX pattern tends to support rather than undermine the authenticity of the Hebrew text in all three passages, for it is more reasonable to suppose that the LXX would have supplied σήμερον in chap. 8 under the influence of 5:21 than that the MT would have dropped an original *hayyôm* in 8:15, 56 (see n. 171). Although II Chron. 6:19 faithfully repeats *kayyôm hazzeh* in chap. 8 of I Kings (vs. 25; it fails to copy I Kings 8:51-61, where this phrase reappears in vs. 61), II Chron. 2:11 and 6:19 lack the *hayyôm* of the corresponding passages in I Kings (5:21, 8:28, respectively; but LXX reads σήμερον in II Chron. 6:19); hence the failure of II Chron. 6:4 to support the σήμερον of I Kings 8:15 LXX is no decisive factor, either way (*contra* Gerhard Wehmeier, *Der Segen in Alten Testament*, Basel, 1970, pp. 127f., who conjectures that *bārûk* approaches in meaning the pual ptcp. and that *hayyôm* is a later addition to the text).

rence of *hayyôm*, this time at the climax of the prayer he has composed for the dedication of the temple, I Kings 8:28. Though there is no consensus as to precisely how much of this prayer derives from secondary expansion, vs. 27 is clearly parenthetical because it disrupts the syntactical bond between the jussive of vs. 26 and the waw-consecutive perfect introducing vs. 28. Solomon appeals to the covenant with David (23-26) as a basis for obtaining Yahweh's attentive regard for his prayer *hayyôm* (28), the burden of which is that Yahweh should heed his prayer and those of all Israel, whenever they may offer them ("night and day") (29f.). Even though the Deuteronomist is loosely echoing the promulgation formula so familiar in Deuteronomy,[278] the contrast between the two parts of his petition and the deliberate juxtaposition of *hayyôm* with *laylâ weyôm* indicate the essential function of these time-designatives to be that of temporal identification. Solomon asks for Yahweh's attention "today" in order that he may henceforth be continually assured of Yahweh's attention.

I Kings 12:7

In I Kings 12:7 *hayyôm* occurs as an emphatic time-identification. Standing in emphatic contrast to the phrase *kol hayyāmîm* at the end of the verse, its reference is to this one particular day as over against all future days. In popular interpretations of the narrative of Rehoboam's controversy at Shechem, the *zeqēnîm* who are speaking in this verse are often taken as favoring a pro-Israel position, while the *yelādîm* whose counsel Rehoboam accepted are supposed to be advocating a pro-Judah position. But the forward position of *hayyôm* is plain indication that the clause it defines embodies an exception.[279] The *zeqēnîm* are no less ardent than their younger counterparts in their zeal for the Davidic monarchy; they are simply more clever. They understand that temporary humility and compromise will gain the permanent subjugation which cannot be obtained through harshness and arrogance. It is altogether likely that the anecdote reporting their advice was composed by one of their own number or by a person who sympathized with their point of view.[280]

---

278. *Hayyôm* follows the participle in a relative clause, providing an elemental epitome of the most centrally significant activity of this particular day, but it is the central appeal of the prayer that defines its contextual function. However, the divergences from Deuteronomic usage are striking. Not only does Deuteronomy lack the verb involved in the participial phrase, but, according to the probably original LXX text, the participle does not modify its proper noun-cognate (התפלה) but an entirely different word (הרנה). It seems that the repetitious Hebrew text has been interpolated according to the recognized Deuteronomic form.

279. The LXX reading, ἐν τῇ ἡμέρᾳ ταύτῃ, tends to strengthen the contrast even more. Chronicles, on the other hand, quite ignores the point by omitting *hayyôm*, while altering the references to Rehoboam's humiliating himself (II, 10:7).

280. Cf. M. Noth, *BK*, XI, 270ff. On the situation underlying this passage see G. Fohrer, "Der Vertrag zwischen König und Volk in Israel," *ZAW*, 81 (1959), 1ff.

I Kings 13:11

If the *hayyôm* found in I Kings 13:11 is original, it represents a usage that is entirely unique in Biblical Hebrew. Occurring in indirect discourse and with unmistakably past reference, it has no parallel by which to give it a confident rendering, "that day."[281] Perhaps the best explanation is that it has come into the text through visual error on the part of an early copyist, who read twice the last three letters of האלהים immediately preceding it.[282]

I Kings 18:15, 36

All the remaining occurrences of *hayyôm* from within the Former Prophets appear in narratives about the prophets. We find two of these in the chapter dealing with Elijah's crucial encounter with the Baal prophets on Carmel: I Kings 18:15 has Elijah saying to Obadiah, "By the life of Yahweh Sebaoth, before whom I stand, (I swear) that *hayyôm* I shall appear to him," i.e., Ahab; in 18:36 the prophet prays to Yahweh, "*Hayyôm* let it be known that thou art God in Israel and that I am thy servant, and by thy word[283] have done all these things." Careful literary and form-critical analysis reveals that both these occurrences of *hayyôm* occupy climactic positions within their respective pericopes.

Among a number of impressive treatments of the Elijah stories appearing in print in recent years, Odil Hannes Steck's monograph, *Ueberlieferung und Zeitgeschichte in den Elia-Erzählungen,*[284] comes probably the closest to the mark. Steck resists, on the one side, the effort to identify all the stories in I Kings 17ff. as elements in a cohesive, ongoing original narrative,[285] and, on the other side, the effort to explain these chapters as arising from a mass of originally independent fragments.[286] Furthermore,

---

281. Noth, *BK*, XI, *in loco*, translating "an jenem Tage," is mistaken in adducing *way^ehî hayyôm* in I Sam. 1:4 as a parallel since this idiom, attested also in other passages, uses *hayyôm* as a substantive. As will be seen, the *hayyôm* in Jer. 34:15 is no parallel because it refers to an actual, though generalized, present. A very few translations (e.g., the earliest LXX witnesses with ἐν τῇ ἡμέρᾳ, and Luther, "des Tages") have remained deliberately ambiguous, but the overwhelming number both of translations and of commentaries render it so as to make it refer to the past. Montgomery-Gehman in *ICC* try to justify this by an appeal to the Arabic equivalent. Contrariwise, Gressmann (*SAT*², II, 1, *in loco*) elides it without explanation.

282. An error which the Massoretes sought to warn against by inserting *paseq* between the two words.

283. Cf. BH³ mg. In both verses, the LXX has σήμερον for MT *hayyom*; there is no sufficient reason to give preference to its paraphrastic rendering in vs. 36.

284. Published as WMANT, 26, Neukirchen-Vluyn, 1968. See especially pp. 9ff. for reference to chap. 18.

285. This is essentially the view of O. Eissfeldt, *Der Gott Karmel* (Berlin, 1953), and D. R. Ap-Thomas, "Elijah on Mount Carmel," *PEQ*, 92 (1960), 146-55.

286. G. Fohrer, *Elia* (ATANT, 53, Zürich, 1957; 2nd ed. 1968), isolates six original independent Elijah legends, plus another six stories added as expansions and embellishments. 18:15 belongs within the secondary expansion that comprises vss. 2b-16, while 18:36 belongs to the original contest narrative, vss. 19, 20-40.

he correctly sees that the narratives in chap. 18 are closer in genre to the prophet legend [287] than to the *hieros logos*, [288] being designed primarily to proclaim the power of Yahweh's word in historical event.

It is certainly clear that a redactor has been at work combining materials in chap. 18. Exegetes have long observed that the narrative concerning the giving of rain, terminating the drought predicted in 17:1, has nothing to do with the narrative of the fire upon Elijah's altar. Thus 18:41ff. must be severed from its preceding context and attached directly to vss. 17f. [289] Vs. 40 is almost certainly redactional, [290] and without it to tie the fire-on-the-altar narrative to the Carmel scene, we are inclined to view vs. 20 as redactional along with vs. 19, [291] which means that the original narrative had nothing at all to do with Carmel.

As for the redactional processes involved in the introductory sections of the drought narrative, we are inclined to agree with Steck over against Fohrer in identifying the Cherith episode (17:2-6) and the Obadiah episode (18:2b-16a) as belonging to its original structure, leaving 17:8ff. and 17ff. as secondary attachments. [292] The Obadiah episode scarcely has meaning as an independent anecdote, but—as we shall see when we scrutinize the function of *hayyôm* in vs. 15—does fulfill a very important role in preparing for the narrative's concluding episode in vss. 41ff. The Cherith

---

287. Pp. 142-44; cf. G. von Rad, *Theologie des Alten Testaments*, II (1960), 36ff. Cf. Fohrer, *Elia*; K. Koch, *The Growth of the Biblical Tradition*, p. 186, in defense of the genre "prophet legend."

288. E. Würthwein, "Die Erzählung von Gottesurteil auf dem Karmel," *ZTK*, 59 (1962), 131-44, makes a detailed argument for identifying I Kings 18:20ff. as the sacred legend for a Yahweh shrine on Mt. Carmel; cf. A. Alt, "Das Gottesurteil auf dem Karmel," *Kleine Schriften*, II, 135ff. However, this hypothesis fails to take sufficient account of the element that is really dominant in this pericope, *viz.*, the divine fulfillment of the prophetic word.

289. Ahab's charge in vs. 17, followed by Elijah's countercharge in 18a, is understandable only in reference to Elijah's word of 17:1. The narrator here provides reason and motivation for that word; therefore we ought to resist the suggestion that 18:18b is a deuteronomistic addition (אֶת מִצְוֹת, lacking in LXX, is a late intrusion). The drought legend *does* concern itself explicitly with the issue of whether Yahweh or the baals (compare the plural in vs. 18 with the singular in 19, 21ff.) provide rain and fertility.

290. So Steck, over against Fohrer and others. The fire-on-the-altar narrative comes to a clear dramatic conclusion in the people's exclamation of vs. 39, "Yahweh, he is God, Yahweh, he is God!" The redactor, influenced ideologically by II Kings 10:18ff., has added vs. 40 in order to anchor this narrative in the Carmel scene, itself original to the drought narrative.

291. Vs. 19, referring to four hundred prophets of Asherah, alongside the prophets of Baal who figure directly in vss. 21ff., is the main link between the drought narrative and the introduction to the fire-on-the-altar narrative. Though some exegetes view vs. 20 as the original introduction, it is suspicious because Ahab does not appear elsewhere in the story.

292. 17:7 is a redactional transition to 8ff. The intrusion of 17:8ff., 17ff. required the editorial transition at the beginning of 18:1 (וַיְהִי יָמִים רַבִּים, influenced by 17:15, is a superfluous addition to the original dating provided by this verse). Within the Obadiah episode are found a number of secondary expansions (vss. 3b-4, 10-11, 13-14, all of which disrupt the simple structure of the original).

episode is the proper preparation for the Obadiah episode, accounting for Elijah's mysterious absence between the time when he delivered his word to Ahab (17:1) and the time when he came to fulfill it.

We would reconstruct the original drought narrative as follows: 17:1, the word that is to be fulfilled (i.e., not the drought as such but that rain would return only by a new word from Elijah); 17:2-6, a transitional subsection in which Elijah's mysterious absence from political pressure, but also from the normal sources of human subsistence, is accounted for; 18:1aβb, 2a, introduction to the confrontation episode, Elijah responding to Yahweh's command to "show himself" to Ahab in order that Yahweh may send rain; 2b-3a, 5f., a transitional delineation of the situation in which Obadiah becomes the intermediary between Elijah and Ahab; 7f., Elijah "meets" Obadiah, ordering him to tell Ahab of his presence; 9, 12, Obadiah's protest concerning the danger to his person if the seemingly ephemeral prophet should be gone when he returns with Ahab, directly motivating the following; 15-16a, Elijah's oath that *hayyôm* he will indeed "show" himself to Ahab; 16b-18, the confrontation between Elijah and Ahab, in which the prophet declares the real reason for the delay of his appearance, i.e., that Ahab has been "troubling" Israel through his baalim; 41-42a, Elijah's instruction, placing Ahab in readiness to witness the power of his prayer for rain;[293] 42b-44a, Elijah's prayer on Carmel[294] and its result; 44b-46, the coming of the rain and its aftermath.[295]

Here each element builds suspense in preparation for the next. *Hayyôm* has been placed foremost in the apodosis of Elijah's self-cursing of vs. 15 as an answer to Obadiah's protest that he may be gone when he returns. Emphatically, Elijah declares that *today* he will appear. But the stress on the time-identification is to be understood in terms of the overall structure of the narrative rather than by reference to the issue raised in the secondary expansion in vss. 10f.[296] That is to say, Elijah is not responding to the implication of 10f. that he had been flitting from place to place, as it were, playing hide-and-seek (in which case *hayyôm* would contrast with the times of such occasions); he is simply affirming that, while he has been mysteri-

---

293. Ahab's eating and drinking apparently have quasi-magical or at least typical significance. Ahab is to ascend to a prominent place over against the summit where the prophet will be (the root עלה is thematic in this closing episode, occurring no fewer than seven times in vss. 41-44).

294. *Rōʾš karmel* apparently means the highest elevation in the Carmel range, but according to vs. 43 Elijah does not position himself on its very highest promontory. Carmel, a place of strong fertility traditions, is a favorite haunt of the Yahweh prophets (II Kings 2:25, 4:25).

295. Leah Bronner, *The Stories of Elijah and Elisha as Polemics against Baal Worship* (Leiden, 1968), p. 75, draws our attention to the parallel in Ug. 67, V, 6-8: wat.qh.rptk.rhk.mdlk.mṭrtk. Cf. *ANET*², 139a. The concluding reference to Elijah running before Ahab (vs. 46) accords with this narrative as a whole in emphasizing the prophet's charismatic mysteriousness.

296. See the essentially valid arguments in Fohrer, *Elia*, p. 36. Cf. n. 292, above.

ously absent since the day when he made his declaration to Ahab, he has now come to make the predicted appearance. Thus we discover a powerful epitomizing force in vs. 15, even though it concerns what is about to happen rather than what has already happened. This particular day is clearly of interest not because of its place on the calendar, i.e., its relation to other days, but because of its unique quality and content. Coinciding with and fulfilling the day envisaged in 17:1, it is the day for the prophet (and Yahweh) to act.[297] Far from this Obadiah episode being an aimless secondary expansion, it rises here in vs. 15 to the very climax of the entire drought narrative, with all that follows as denouement and anticlimax.

In analyzing the structure of the fire-on-the-altar narrative (21-39), we must pay particular attention to the successive time-designatives, for this will tell us why the heavily weighted *hayyôm* of vs. 36 receives stress in foremost position. This day is to be a day in which Yahweh will make known that he is God in Israel—yet consider the obstacles! Baal has four hundred and fifty prophets, while Yahweh has but one. Baal's prophets shout and leap and cut themselves, while Yahweh's prophet does nothing but pray. Their altar is dry, his is drenched. They have all day—from morning until noon (26), during the noon hour (27f.), and through the entire afternoon, until the time of the evening oblation (29, 36)[298] — leaving Elijah with no more than a few brief moments to get his god to act. So, if the challenge proposed in vss. 23f. is to be resolved, it must be in answer to the simple prayer of this one true prophet; it must come with the altar wet or dry; it must be now, immediately, while it is still *hayyôm*. And so it is: without further time-designatives we are told that Yahweh's fire falls, eliciting from the people an irrepressible confession (waw-consecutive imperfects in direct sequence), as though Elijah's prayer automatically produces the desired result. His prayer forcefully states the central issue of the entire narrative, asking that this day may even yet be proven to be the day of Yahweh's supreme self-disclosure, the day when he decisively makes himself known as Israel's god.[299]

---

297. Cf. the combination of epitomizing with stress upon time-identification as fulfillment of a prediction found, e.g., in I Sam. 28:18, I Kings 1:30 (see our preceding discussion).

298. The consideration that some time must have been consumed in Elijah's preparations envisaged in vss. 30-35 does not disturb the pericope's time schema. We are to understand that these preparations were being carried out while Baal's prophets were still raving on (vs. 30 begins with the waw-consecutive imperfect, without a time-designative).

299. This is the first passage, following I Sam. 17:46f., in which *hayyôm* (*hazzeh*) is directly connected with the ideology of Yahweh's self-revelation in an historical event; cf. I Kings 20:13. W. Zimmerli has correctly sought the traditional origin of the Ezekielian formula, "and so you shall know that I am Yahweh," in such primitive prophetic materials; cf. his comments on our passage in *Gottes Offenbarung*, p. 81. The σήμερον found in the Lucianic LXX at vs. 24 is to be noted. On I Kings 18:21-39 as a whole, see S. J. DeVries and Edward C. Meyer, "Preparation for Biblical Preaching XII," *Journal of the Methodist Theological School in Ohio*, IX, 2 (Spring, 1971), 9ff.

I Kings 20:13

Walther Zimmerli's interpretive work in Ezekiel has been greatly strengthened through its acknowledgment of the peculiar significance of the so-called "Erweiswort," concluding in the stereotyped formula, "and so you shall know that I am Yahweh."[300] Far from being a late editorial expression, as some commentators have claimed,[301] this formula proves to have its roots in preclassical prophetic formulation—particularly in two verses of I Kings 20 (13, 28).[302] Our analysis is specifically interested in the first of these two verses because it contains the word *hayyôm*; but it may be helpful to recall that we have already seen echoes of the *Erweiswort* ideology in other prophetically influenced passages, specifically the David legend (cf. I Sam. 17:46f.) and the fire-on-the-altar legend (cf. I Kings 18:36f.).

In order to gain a clear conception of the function of *hayyôm* in I Kings 20:13, it is necessary to make a careful comparison between the pericope to which it belongs and the pericope that contains vs. 28. Immediately some significant differences spring to our attention. First of all, regarding the styling of the respective verses themselves: though both follow the same general schema (the prophet approaches the king, announces himself with the messenger formula, mentions the situation, declares Yahweh's intent to "give this great multitude into your hand,"[303] and concludes with the *Erweis*-formula), the man who brings the message is called *nābî' 'eḥād* in vs. 13, but *'îš hā'elōhîm* in vs. 28; 13 puts the accusation (invective) element in the form of a question, while 28 styles it as a *ya'an 'ašer*-clause; 13 presents the judgment declaration (threat) in participial formulation following *hinnēh*, while 28 presents it in the form of the apodosis in a conditional clause with the perfect waw-consecutive; 13 has the *Erweis*-formula in the singular, as compared with the plural in 28.[304] We note also that vs. 13 introduces a new episode with the deictic

---

300. This occurs fifty-four times in pure form and eighteen times in mixed form within the book of Ezekiel; cf. Zimmerli, *BK*, XIII, pp. 55*-61* and *passim*.

301. E.g., H. G. May in *IB* (cf. p. 51 and *passim*).

302. Cf. Zimmerli's seminal discussion of these verses in relation to the Ezekielian formula in *Gottes Offenbarung*, pp. 54-56 (from the essay "Erkenntnis Gottes nach dem Buch Ezechiel"), 122-25, 128-31 (from the essay, "Das Wort des göttlichen Selbsterweises (Erweiswort), eine prophetische Gattung").

303. Reference to *kol hehāmôn haggādôl hazzeh* occurs in the accusatory question in vs. 13 and in the judgment declaration in vs. 28 (LXX[B] does not read כל in vs. 13, where it is probably a gloss); in view of the patent holy-war associations, "tumult" would be a better translation than "multitude" because of the intended pun on the symbolic holy-war word, המם. The phrase "give into your hand" is characteristically associated with the time-designative in the hero saga (cf. I Sam. 24:11, 26:8) and the holy-war narrative (cf. Judg. 4:14).

304. The LXX has harmonized by reading the singular in vs. 28. The singular, which predominates in Ezekiel, has every claim to being the more original (cf. Zimmerli in the essays cited), but I Kings 20:28 indicates that at a date long before Ezekiel the form suitable to the private oracle had already been adapted to the function of providing a theological witness to all Israel.

particle, the subject, and a verb in the perfect, whereas the imperfect consecutive in vs. 28 merges the oracle of this verse with the contiguous narrative sequence. Both narratives follow the general pattern of the time-hallowed holy-war narrative, [305] but we observe an important difference in their use of discourse. In the Aphek story of vss. 26ff., the oracle stands apart as the single element of discourse, epitomizing the significance of all that precedes and follows it. [306] In the Samaria story of vss. 1ff., discourse is expanded in such a way as to enliven each successive episode, first detailing the demands and negotiations that have gone on between Benhadad and Ahab, leading to the central situation of crisis (1-12), next detailing the instructions that Ahab receives from the prophet concerning the way in which the battle is to be fought (13-15), [307] finally detailing the confused situation within the Syrian camp (16-18).

Several conclusions flow from these observations. Not only is it evident that the two narratives derive from distinct tradents, [308] but we are able to discern that the Aphek narrative reflects more faithfully than the Samaria narrative the original structure from which the Ezekielian *Erweis-*

---

305. (1) Israel's distress; (2) the assurance of victory; (3) the battle and pursuit. Missing from this schema is the charismatic designation of a leader (inappropriate because Israel has an institutional kingship) and the summoning of the tribes (now present in the form of a regular army). The prophetic oracle has come to take the place of the traditional *Uebereignungsformel* found in such a passage as Judg. 4:14a. Regarding the fictitious perpetuation of the holy war during the dynastic period, cf. von Rad, *Heilige Krieg*, pp. 33ff. (on our present passage, pp. 54f.).
306. The "invective" element in the *ya'an* *ᵃšer*-clause is actually a citation, challenging the power of Yahweh; hence the entire *Erweiswort* with its narrative sequel constitutes a disputation oracle (cf. H. W. Wolff, "Das Zitat im Propheten-spruch," *Gesammelte Studien zum Alten Testament*, pp. 36-129). It will be observed that vs. 23 is paraphrastic and interpretive of this citation, leading to the conclusion that all the material connecting the Samaria narrative to the Aphek narrative, i.e., vss. 22-26aα, is probably redactional. Commentators have failed to take sufficient account of the fact that vs. 28 uses עֲמָקִים, not the (ה)מִישׁוּר of vs. 23; there is accordingly no good reason to identify the Aphek of our text with the Mishor region mentioned in Josh. 13:9 and elsewhere.
307. The name "Ahab" has been added to the text of vss. 2 and 13 in probably a secondary stage of redaction (it is missing in vs. 13, LXX [BL]), leaving "the king of Israel" anonymous, as in the Aphek story. Vs. 14a is most likely a secondary expansion because "Ahab" appears here without an appositional qualifier (LXX reads the name after וַיֹּאמֶר in vs. 14b); also because the messenger formula is out of place in the reply to a query (cf. vs. b) and because this half-verse exaggerates the role of the *na'ᵃrê śārê hammᵉdînôt* (in the sequel this group leads the army but it is "Israel" that actually accomplishes the victory).
308. For the Aphek narrative we find parallel material in II Kings 13:14ff. It has been persuasively argued that the narratives in I Kings 20 originated in the Jehu rather than the Omride period; cf. A. Jepsen, "Israel und Damaskus," *AfO*, 14 (1942), 154-58; C. F. Whitley, "The Deuteronomic Presentation of the House of Omri," *VT*, 2 (1952), 137-52; J. Maxwell Miller, "The Elisha Cycle and the Accounts of the Omride Wars," *JBL*, 85 (1966), 441-54. It is the references to Ahab rather than the references to a prophet that are secondary (so earlier, *contra* Hölscher, A. Jepsen in *Nabi, Soziologische Studien zur alttestamentlichen Literatur und Religionsgeschichte*, Munich, 1934, pp. 90f.).

wort has developed.[309] Yet the similarities that remain are all the more important for the mutual interpretation of these stories. The *Erweiswort* in vs. 28 does not have *hayyôm* because the Aphek story fails to develop the time factor as an element of suspense, as in vss. 1ff. Nevertheless the time factor is present in a highly stylized and traditional form: the two armies first face each other for seven days,[310] then join in devastating combat "in one day" (*b^eyôm 'eḥād*). The last is equivalent in function to *bayyôm hahû'* within a concluding casualty report, epitomizing the outcome of the traditional holy-war narrative. This helps us see more clearly what already is evident: that the participial clause with *hayyôm* in vs. 13 is an epitomizing climax to the entire account. As in the fire-on-the-altar legend (I Kings 18:21ff.), everything hangs on whether salvation can be accomplished in a single day; Israel has only until *k^e'ēt māḥār*[311] to neutralize Ben-hadad's threat (vs. 6), but resolves the situation by going out that very day, *baṣṣāh^orāyim*, "at noon" (vs. 16).

II Kings 2:3, 5

In the legend of Elisha's rapture, the word *hayyôm* occurs twice in the identically phrased revelatory messages of two distinct bands of prophets (II Kings 2:3,5),[312] the second confirming the first. That these respective messages are purely preparatory to the central narrative is evident from the observation that, while Elijah three times urges Elisha to remain where he is (vss. 2, 4, 6), only after the first and second instance does Elisha receive the message and respond to it.

All is shaped to build up suspense.[313] The two prophets are walking along on the way from Gilgal,[314] when suddenly Elijah receives the

---

309. The only secondary factor in the styling of vs. 28 is the shift to the plural in the *Erweis*-formula (see above). Syntactically, its elements flow naturally from one another: I, invective (*ya'an ^ašer* with the perfect); II, threat (perfect consecutive); III, *Erweis*-formula (perfect consecutive). According to this conception, Yahweh's self-revelation flows from the entire situation, including the hostile word of the enemy, not merely from his own saving act. In vs. 13 the accusatory question is artificially constructed; it does not repeat anything that Ben-hadad has said (showing that the discourse of vss. 1ff. is an embellishment) but is able merely to allude to the situation created by the presence of *kol hehāmôn haggādôl hazzeh*. Because I is in the form of a question, II is thrown into participial construction, leaving only III with the perfect consecutive.
310. For the ideology of the holy war by numbered sequence, cf. Josh. 6, Judg. 20.
311. A favorite form in threats; cf. I Kings 19:2.
312. The MT has *hayyôm* foremost in the *kî*-clause of each verse. There is little reason to prefer the variant word-order of the LXX, particularly in vs. 3, where *hayyôm* is read between *YHWH* and the participle.
313. Compare the three oracles and three troops of fifty in II Kings 1. The number three is structurally symbolic in the prophet legends, e.g., I Kings 17:21, 18:34, II Kings 2:17, 13:18.
314. The commentaries wrestle needlessly with the topographical problem, at-

revelation that Yahweh wants him to go as far as Bethel. He urges Elisha to stay behind but the latter refuses; he is, of course, being tested as to whether he will prove worthy to be Elijah's successor. As they approach Bethel, the local "sons of the prophets" meet Elisha and give him the revelation that they have received, "Do you know that *hayyôm* Yahweh will remove your master from his place of authority over you (*mē'al rō'šêkā*)?" Elisha's reply is, "I too know it, be still!" He does not need their revelation, for he is a prophet himself—a prophet before them. This pattern is repeated in an encounter with the local "sons of the prophets" belonging to Jericho (vss. 4f.), and again Elisha passes both tests. This leads, then, to the central episode (vss. 6-12a), in which Elisha again refuses to remain behind, going over the Jordan to pass the climactic test, whether he will "see" Elijah as he is being taken from him.[315]

The evident purpose of this narrative is to legitimize Elisha as the new leader among the prophets,[316] as emphatically affirmed in vs. 15, "Elijah's spirit abides on Elisha." This declaration is clearly the central epitome of the narrative as a whole, yet the question of the Bethel and Jericho prophets has an epitomizing force too. Elisha cannot receive Elijah's mantle until Yahweh shall first have taken Elijah away; this is what accounts for the closing episode (vss. 16-18), in which the fact of Elijah's rapture is confirmed by prophetic investigation. So the narrative begins and ends with the motif of Elijah's departure. The solemn, twofold designation of *hayyôm* as the day for this fateful passing on provides an aura of awe for all that is to transpire.[317]

II Kings 4:23

Critics have noted that the Elisha stories tend to exaggerate the

---

tempting to identify a Gilgal north or west of Bethel, attempting to account for "going down" to Bethel, and the like. In all probability the erratic course of the two prophets, as dictated by divine revelation, deliberately emphasizes the mysteriousness of the entire experience.

315. Vss. 12b-15, like vss. 16ff., are anticlimactic, confirming Elijah's word of vs. 10. For the significance of Elisha's cry, "My father, my father, the chariots of Israel and its horsemen" (cf. II Kings 13:14), see von Rad, *Heilige Krieg*, p. 55; K. Galling, "Der Ehrenname Elias und die Entrückung Elias," *ZTK*, 53 (1956), 129-48.

316. The "double portion" to which Elisha refers in vs. 9 is a metonymy for "birthright," which in turn is metaphorical for "place of leadership" among the sons of the prophets. Elijah's word of vs. 10 is fulfilled when the test that he sets is realized (12). On the significance of the mantle, cf. J. Lindblom, *Prophecy in Ancient Israel* (1962), pp. 64f. On the intent and classification of this entire narrative see now A. Rofé, "The Classification of the Prophetical Stories," *JBL*, 89 (1970), pp. 436ff.; R. A. Carlson, "Elisée le successeur d'Elie," *VT*, 20 (1970), 401-405.

317. Cf. our previous remarks on David's panegyric in II Sam. 3:38. There David's question (with the verb in the imperfect and *hayyôm* in unemphatic position) assumed an affirmative answer; here the verb is in the stative perfect and a negative answer is assumed.

miraculous element much more than the Elijah stories.[318] When one compares the Elijah story of restoring a boy to life (I Kings 17:17-24) with the Elisha story on the same theme (II Kings 4:8-37), it is evident that if the former is to be identified (correctly) as a prophet legend, the latter must be called something else. Strikingly lacking in II Kings 4 is the effective power of the prophetic word. Though this can scarcely be called a tale of magic,[319] it is certainly a wonder tale. All emphasis is diverted away from Yahweh to the charismatic person whose body possesses healing powers.

II Kings 4:8ff. has a number of peculiarities. One is the narrator's fondness for *way^{e}hî hayyôm* as a transitional device (vss. 8, 11, 18), a locution found elsewhere only at I Sam. 1:4, 14:1, Job 1:6, 13, 2:1. Another is his identification of Carmel as the prophet's place of residence (cf. 3:25). We may say that his use of *hayyôm* is another peculiarity, in comparison with the way it is employed in the prophet stories previously studied. It occurs here in vs. 23, where the Shunamite's husband, apparently unaware that the lad is dead, observes her preparations for a hasty departure and asks, "Why are you journeying[320] to him *hayyôm*? It is neither new moon nor sabbath." Although *hayyôm* is in an unemphatic position, it is nothing but a time-identifier, as its proximity to the following identifying terms discloses. Emphasis is on this day in contrast to other days, when the woman's behavior might be appropriate, and hence understandable, from the husband's point of view.

II Kings 6:28, 31

The last two occurrences of *hayyôm* within the Former Prophets are found in a pathetic anecdote introducing the prophet legend[321] about the deliverance of Samaria, II Kings 6:24–7:20. In 6:28 a woman petitioning the king of Israel reports her prior agreement with another mother: "This woman said to me, 'Give your son and we shall eat him *hayyôm*, and my son we shall eat *māḥār*.' " A few verses further on (31), the king utters a curse, "May God do thus to me and even more if the head of Elisha the son of Shaphat is still on him *hayyôm*!" It is evident that the first *hayyôm* is intended as a simple time-identification, contrasting the day when the first child was to be eaten with the time when the second child was to be eaten. The question of function is less certain with respect to the occurrence in vs.

---

318. On the theological significance of this difference, see the remarks of G. von Rad in *Theologie*, II, 27-44; cf. Lindblom, *Prophecy*, pp. 50f.

319. Cf. Bronner, *Stories of Elijah and Elisha*, p. 134.

320. Reading the *qere*; cf. BH³ mg.

321. Gressmann's interpretation of this narrative (*SAT²*, II, 1, *in loco*) remains one of the most insightful, though he makes a characteristic error in defining it as a saga, in contrast to 6:8-23, which he calls a prophet legend, evidently because of its more highly developed supernaturalistic element.

31: in spite of the fact that we have not previously encountered *hayyôm* with the imperfect in curse formulas, we receive the initial impression that the king is epitomizing the present day with respect to the fate of Elisha. This impression needs to be tested by way of an analysis of the structure of the narrative as a whole.

At several crucial points textual corruptions have encumbered the interpretation of this narrative. Nevertheless, it is possible to identify supplementary elements of various kinds. First of all, we recognize an editorial introduction in 6:24aα and a pedantic gloss at the end, 7:17b-20. In addition, the anecdote of the cannibalistic mothers (6:26-30) seems to have originally been independent because it rises to a climax in the reference to the visible signs of the king's participation in their distress (the sackcloth, revealed when he tears his cloak). The episode of the four lepers (7:3ff.) separates the prophetic word (7:1f.) from the report of its fulfillment (vss. 16-17a), but might be taken as the original narration between them, were it not for the fact that it suffers from several internal disharmonies. Specifically, at vss. 5ff. a retrospective reference to the supernatural noise of chariots, etc., and a double report of the Syrians fleeing [322] intrude between two separate references to the lepers approaching the edge of the camp; also, at vss. 13f. it is proposed that five horses be sent to reconnoiter but—without explanation—only two mounted men are actually sent. [323] Another point of great difficulty is within 6:32ff., where a number of further inconsistencies are discernible. [324]

The theory that seems best suited to account for the present form of this narrative would identify 6:26-33aα and 7:3-5, 7aα₂-13, 16a as secondary attempts to interject greater tension into the original narrative. Each of these additions appears to go back to independent anecdotal material, of equal, or perhaps even greater historical authenticity than that of the legendary material in the remaining verses. In an effort to dramatize the king's impatience (6:33aβb) and to motivate Elisha's prediction that only one more day will pass before Yahweh will act to relieve the famine (7:1), a redactor has inserted the anecdote about the cannibalistic mothers, adding the rather aimless and ineffectual material in 6:31, 32b-33aα. The anecdote of the lepers was then worked into the fulfillment episode, making more dramatic and suspenseful the laconic report of the original. [325]

---

322. There is strong textual witness to support an emendation to במחנה in vs. 7 in preference to removing וינוסו from vs. 7, as proposed in BH³ mg. There are a number of conflicting elements at this point in the Hebrew text and in the versions.
323. The text is confused with interpolations and dittographies at this point; cf. BH³ mg and the commentaries. מחנה ארם in vs. 14 should not be emended since the meaning "Syrian army" is consistent with original usage in vs. 6 (cf. the meaning "Syrian camp" in vss. 4, 5 *bis*, 7, 8, 10, 12, 16).
324. המלך is clearly original in vs. 33. Its misreading (mishearing) as המלאך may have accounted for the redactor's references to a person sent to Elisha to precede the king; cf. BH³ mg.
325. The original is rhythmic and pithy in its description of Yahweh's (אדני in the

From this emerges an original prophet legend with the following structure: (1) the situation: dire need in Samaria and the king's desperation lead him to the point of surrendering; (2) Elisha pronounces a salvation oracle[326] predicting a dramatic overabundance *kā'ēt māḥār*; (2a) the insolent unbelief[327] of the king's officer is answered by Elisha[328] in a simple prediction (not itself a Yahweh-word, but the prophet's charismatic interpretation of the revelation just proclaimed) that he should see the abundance but not eat of it; (3) the coming of Yahweh in mysterious sounds terrifies the Syrians into flight; (4) two scouts, sent to reconnoiter, pursue the Syrians to the Jordan and return; (5) the people plunder the Syrian camp, fulfilling Elisha's prediction; (6) the officer is crushed in the gate. A unique feature of this legend is the motif of retribution on one who has dared to challenge the divine word sent through the prophet.[329]

Except perhaps in a negative way, this analysis proves to be rather disappointing with respect to the function of *hayyôm* in 6:31. The king's curse does not actually epitomize anything central in the narrative; it is a threat introduced secondarily to dramatize the tenseness of the situation, and as such has essentially the function of a time-identifier. We are nonetheless impressed by how strongly tradition has asserted himself in an epitomizing use of time-designatives at other places in this narrative, particularly in the *kā'ēt māḥār* of Elisha's prediction[330] and in the lepers' words of 7:9, "This day is a day of good news!"

This completes our study of occurrences of *hayyôm* and *hayyôm hazzeh* in the Former Prophets, where relative frequency has been paral-

---

text very probably derives from original יהוה since this is holy-war ideology) intervention: "(And) the Lord caused the Syrian army to hear chariot sound, sound of horse, sound of great force, etc." It is difficult to determine whether the time-designative *benešep* (vs. 7) is original, influencing the redactional reference in vs. 5, or whether both are redactional; the former is more probable because *ke'ēt māḥār* (vs. 1) implies divine action during the intervening night. Vss. 7aα -8aα attaches this to the continuation of the leper story. If the leper story had a report of the scouts going out, it has been supplanted by the original material in vss. 14f. Vs. 16a is probably the conclusion of the leper story; the original merely reported the hasty departure of the Syrian army and the consequent availability of grain the following day.

326. The form is that of a portrayal of salvation in rhythmic pattern (2:3, 3:2), with elements in chiastic arrangement, countering 6:25.

327. The Hebrew text is difficult. It is possible that an original הן ("if") underlies the present הנה (cf. RSV).

328. In vs. 2 את איש האלהים has been added from vss. 17f. Cf. BH[3] mg.

329. Close parallels are in Jer. 28:16f., Ezek. 11:13; cf. Jer. 20:6 and Amos 7:17, where the word of judgment is recorded, but not the effect. A similar ideology is reflected in II Kings 2:23f.

330. Where *hayyôm* would occur in the *Uebereignungsformel* of the simple holy-war narrative (cf. Judg. 4:14), *māḥār* appears if the divine irruption is to take place during the intervening night; cf. Judg. 20:28b, I Sam. 11:9. This account witnesses to an ideology related to that of Exod. 12, 14, Judg. 5, 7, II Kings 19:37, with Yahweh doing his awesome and mysterious work at night, frightening his enemies into panicky flight. Particularly noteworthy is that, though everything occurs at night, the lepers refer to this as a "day."

leled by difficulty of analysis. We shall move forward to complete our examination with respect to the prophetic literature and the *kethubhim* before attempting to make a final systematic evaluation.

(4) The Latter Prophets

As with *bayyôm hahû'* in past usage, there are far fewer occurrences of *hayyôm* (*hazzeh*) in the prophetic corpus than within the narrative literature.[331] This is to be expected from the nature of the materials: here there is comparatively little dialogical discourse, and also very few contexts in which the experiential situation is described. Perhaps, therefore, there is special significance in that the few prophetic occurrences strongly echo the functioning of these time-designatives as seen in the narrative literature. At the same time, we must ponder the relationship to the characteristically parenetical usage so profusely attested in Deuteronomy.

Isa. 38:19

The only occurrence of *hayyôm* in the book of Isaiah is in 38:19. Not only is the section, chaps. 36–39, a late insertion into the book (= II Kings 18:13–20:19); the psalm of Isa. 38:9-20, containing this occurrence, is itself an insertion into the material borrowed from Kings. This "Psalm of Hezekiah" is certainly postexilic, hence the occurrence of *hayyôm* in 38:19 witnesses only negatively to the usage of the prophet Isaiah. A definitive study by Joachim Begrich[332] gives a general identification of this "Psalm of Hezekiah" as a thanksgiving psalm (*Danklied*), but it may be well to draw distinctions somewhat more precise than this, designating it, in Westermann's categories, as the second type of individual lament (involving a pattern in which the afflicted person not only appeals hopefully to Yahweh but records the fact of Yahweh's answer, going on in the conclusion to propose an offering of thankful praise).[333] Structurally, Pss. 22, 69, etc. are close parallels. We discern the simple schema: (1) the suppliant's distress, vss. 10-16; (2) the suppliant's relief, vss. 17-18; (3) the suppliant's rejoicing, vss. 19-20.[334] In vs. 19 all emphasis is on the repeated

---

331. Besides the nine passages analyzed below, in which *hayyôm* (*hazzeh*) is attested in the MT (see also *be'eṣem hayyôm hazzeh* in Ezek. 24:2, treated above), LXX^A offers σήμερον as the last word in Ezek. 8:9. The attestation is very weak and reflects a usage not found elsewhere in Ezekiel; it is an addition influenced by the Deuteronomic combination *pōh we hayyôm*.

332. *Der Psalm des Hiskia, Ein Beitrag zum Verständnis von Jesaja 38, 10-20* (FRLANT, 25, Göttingen, 1926).

333. Cf. C. Westermann, *The Praise of God in the Psalms* (Richmond, 1965; trans. by K. R. Crim from *Das Loben Gottes in den Psalmen*, Göttingen, 1951); especially pp. 68-78. Restricted essentially to text-critical matters is P. A. H. de Boer's essay, "Notes on Text and Meaning of Isaiah xxxviii 9-20," *OTS*, 9 (1951), 171-86.

334. The LXX provides a loose paraphrase in vs. 19. That vs. 19 is to be joined to vs. 20, rather than to vs. 18, is clear from the dramatic beginning and from a shift

word, ‏חי‎, thrust forward for explicit contrast with the mention of death (vs. 18) as a state of praiselessness,[335] and in syntactical and semantic parallelism with ‏אב‎ at the beginning of the second distich. The comparative clause, ‏כמני היום‎, is itself in synthetic parallelism with ‏חי חי‎, explicitly identifying the "living one" who praises Yahweh (parallel to the father who tells his children of Yahweh's faithfulness) as the psalmist himself, here and now in the full experience of Yahweh's saving help. There can be little question but that vs. 19 epitomizes the psalm as a whole; this is the first instance that we have observed of an identifying characterization with *hayyôm* functioning through internal parallelism in support of such a central epitome.

Jer. 1:10, 18

Within genuinely prophetic materials, *hayyôm* and *hayyôm hazzeh* are found hardly at all, and it is the book of Jeremiah that contains virtually all the occurrences, two of them in the very first chapter, in apparently similar epitomizing declarations. 1:10 has the more emphatic form, 1:18 the simple *hayyôm*,[336] but both are syntactically equivalent within a commissioning word of Yahweh to Jeremiah (deictic particle, perfect verb with pronominal suffix, temporal adverb, prepositional/infinitival phrase). The very characteristic that has induced various commentators to assume an original connection between these verses, and hence between the pericopes to which they belong, *viz.*, their similarity in content and form,[337] ought to be taken instead as evidence for distinct—even if analogous—settings for each.[338] This should be especially apparent with respect to the declarations with *hayyôm* (*hazzeh*), for we should hardly expect to see this construction twice within the same original context. A careful study of the function of the two time-designatives within their respective pericopes confirms that this attitude of caution is well justified.

Although critics are in agreement that 1:4-10 constitutes Jeremiah's call-vision, equivalent to Isaiah's in Isa. 6 and Ezekiel's in chaps. 1—3 of his

---

from the 3:2 meter, uniformly applied to this point, to the short-verse meter (2:2) as a device for expressing excitement. Begrich's attempt to emend the text in order to produce a regular 3:2 meter in these verses does not commend itself.
335. The arrangement of stichoi is partially chiastic, with deliberate alliteration between *yôdêkā* and *yôdî*ᵃ‵. On the ideology of the living praising God, see Chr. Barth, *Die Errettung vom Tode in den individuellen Klage- und Dankliedern des Alten Testaments* (Zollikon, 1947); cf. also Westermann, *Praise of God*, pp. 154-60.
336. The LXX rendering (σήμερον in vs. 10, ἐν τῇ σήμερον ἡμέρᾳ in vs. 18) departs radically from the usual LXX system of equivalents. Since the MT forms are required by the meter in the respective verses, there is no reason to favor the LXX.
337. E.g., W. Rudolph, *HAT*, 12, *in loco;* A. Weiser, *ATD*, 20/21, *in loco;* J. Bright, *AB*, 21, *in loco.* The opposite tendency is represented by J. P. Hyatt in *IB*, assigning vss. 17ff. to a "Deuteronomic editor."
338. Cf. H. Graf Reventlow, *Liturgie und prophetisches Ich bei Jeremia* (Gütersloh, 1963), pp. 61f.

book, it is Henning Graf Reventlow who has provided the first complete analysis of the formal schema of this call-vision.[339]   Reventlow examines the call of Moses in Exod. 3 and 4, Gideon's call in Judg. 6, and the "call" of Yahweh's servant in Isa. 42, comparing these with the parallel materials concerning Isaiah, Jeremiah, and Ezekiel, in order to obtain the following paradigmatic outline: (1) Yahweh-epiphany; (2) complaint; (3) introduction to the salvation oracle; (4) salvation oracle proper; (5) commission; (6) objection to the commission; (7) renewal of the commission; (8) symbolic act or sign; (9) interpretation of the symbolic act or sign. In Reventlow's opinion, Jer. 1:4-10 not only hews very close to the most primitive call-vision form, but clearly involves a cultic ritual installing the prophet-to-be in a special office. While serious objections may be brought against some of Reventlow's conclusions,[340]   his outline is helpful. It is especially important to see that the symbolic act in which Yahweh touches Jeremiah's lips (vs. 9) is schematically equivalent not only to the identical act in Isa. 6:6f. and to the giving of the scroll in Ezek. 2:9–3:3, but also to the confirmatory sign in some nonprophetic pericopes (Gen. 15:5, Exod. 3:12, 4:2-9, Judg. 6:17ff.). Since symbolic acts regularly are followed by interpretive declarations, we are to view Jer. 1:10 as the climactic interpretive word within the entire pericope, confirming and elaborating the terms of the initial announcement in vs. 5.

The section vss. 17-19 is hardly a repetition of this call-vision, since Yahweh here simply strengthens Jeremiah rather than commissions him, and the scope of Jeremiah's prophetic activity is now restricted to the "whole land" of Judah: kings, officials, priesthood, citizenry.[341]   Moreover, the metrical structure of the two pericopes is markedly different.[342] The question is, then, how vss. 17-19 are related to the verses that immediately precede them. Critics have understood that the connection

---

339. *Ibid.*, pp. 24-77. Cf. also N. Habel, "The Form and Significance of the Call Narratives," *ZAW*, 77 (1965), 297ff. On the significance of the Moses-image in shaping this pericope, see W. L. Holladay, "The Background of Jeremiah's Self-Understanding: Moses, Samuel, and Psalm 22," *JBL*, 83 (1964), 153-64.

340. There is no need to repeat here the numerous criticisms that have appeared in reviews of Reventlow's book. One of the most telling objections is that the wide variety of individual development makes a cultic setting for the call-vision *prima facie* unlikely. The priestly account of Joshua's ordination in Num. 27:12ff., on which Reventlow relies so heavily for evidence (pp. 67ff.), is a late stylization.

341. The effort of various interpreters, beginning with some scribes of the LXX, to emend the plural of גוי in vss. 5, 10, has been posited on the mistaken assumption of an identical background for the two pericopes.

342. It is questionable whether הנה נתתי דברי בפיך is to be taken in parallelism with ראה הפקדתיך היום הזה; the first declaration interprets the symbolic act, similarly to Yahweh's declaration in Isa. 6:7 (an analogous element is lacking in Ezekiel), while the second declaration constitutes the definitive commissioning, parallel to Isa. 6:9ff. Jer. 1:10 accordingly has two short verses in couplet form (2:2, 2:2)—assuming the emendation proposed in BH[3.] mg (cf. the commentaries). The meter in vss. 18f. is most probably 2:2:2, 2:2:2, 2:2:2, 2:2:3 (with intrusive נאם יהוה).

between 11f. and 13ff. is the work of a redactor—albeit an early one—and that accordingly the interpretive announcement introduced by כי הנני in vs. 15 is not to be regarded with suspicion on the grounds that it lacks a counterpart in 11f. To some extent, the same consideration ought to hold true with regard to vss. 17ff. Despite the fact that we have here the form of a private rather than a public oracle, there is no compelling reason to suppose that the prophet may not have received both as part of the same revelatory experience. 17ff. is not introduced as an independent oracle, and there is no justification for identifying it as secondary. Moreover, the situation is identical in 15ff. and in 17ff. (Yahweh is bringing enemies from the north as punishment upon Judah); the only difference is that Yahweh turns in 17ff. specifically to the prophet to strengthen him for the personal burden of speaking this word of judgment against his own people.

It should be clear, therefore, that the *hayyôm hazzeh* of vs. 10 and the *hayyôm* of vs. 18 identify two quite different occasions. In all probability both oracles were received very early in Jeremiah's career; but the first comes at the very first experience of Yahweh's call to the prophetic ministry, the second comes when Jeremiah is given to understand that his general commission to be Yahweh's deputy over nations and kingdoms requires the more intimate and heart-searching duty of announcing Yahweh's judgment on his own people.[343] Each declaration is an epitome of the entire oracle to which it belongs; the more emphatic form in vs. 10 may have its explanation in that the call-vision is constitutive to the entirety of Jeremiah's ministry, and that accordingly "this day" is to be memorialized above all others.

Jer. 34:15

A seemingly anomalous occurrence of *hayyôm* is found at Jer. 34:15. Vss. 8ff. concern an incident of serious infidelity during the last days of Jerusalem's existence: the release of the Hebrew slaves in the face of the Babylonian siege and their reinslavement as the Babylonians depart temporarily to meet the approaching army of Hophra (588 B.C.). Following an introductory explanation in vss. 8-11, a judgment oracle is introduced in vs. 12 in condemnation of the people's behavior; it contains an indictment charging them with breach of covenant fidelity (13-16) and a threat announcing the evils that will come when Yahweh brings the Babylonians back to Jerusalem (17-24). Since the addressees are currently in a state of apostasy, it is difficult to understand how *hayyôm* can literally mean "today" in vs. 15. The translators have been tempted to render it in a noncommittal way, with an ambiguous "now," or to allow its reference to slip into the past with "recently" (RSV), "just now" (Moffatt), or the like.

---

343. The substance of this announcement is strongly echoed in 15:20, where Yahweh responds to one of Jeremiah's complaints.

It is essential to observe here that the *hayyôm* of vs. 15, equivalent to the date of the covenant that the Jerusalemites had made, is contrasted to "the day when I brought them (the fathers) from the land of Egypt" (vs. 13)—the date when Yahweh had made the original covenant concerning the release of Hebrew slaves.[344] The fathers would not listen, thereby breaking that covenant and bringing the present distress. But *hayyôm* those who were experiencing that distress have taken steps to reestablish the covenant and alleviate the distress: they have covenanted anew to keep the commandment.[345] Thus a new situation prevails: the inhabitants of Jerusalem stand before Yahweh, not on the basis of the former covenant and former transgression, but on the basis of the new covenant which they themselves have sworn. All the worse for them, then, that they proceed to sin so lightly, showing themselves to be even more contemptible than their fathers! Immediately following upon the making of this new covenant two contradictory actions have occurred: (1) the release of the slaves and (2) taking them back—both in a sequence so abrupt that it would seem to have happened in a single day.

The confidence with which many scholars have argued for a relatively late "Deuteronomic" edition of Jeremiah has been challenged in recent studies demonstrating the close affinities between the prophet and his disciples, on the one hand, and the Deuteronomic movement on the other.[346] Those who have ascribed Jer. 34:8ff. to Jeremiah through

---

344. This passage is more familiar with the law as found in Deut. 15:1, 12, than as found in the book of the covenant, Exod. 21:2. The phrase מארץ מצרים מבית עבדים, which occurs only here in Jeremiah, seems to be a direct borrowing of a Deuteronomic locution (it is found elsewhere at Exod. 13:3, 14, 20:2, Deut. 5:6, 6:12, 7:8, 8:14, 13:6, 11, Josh. 24:17, Judg. 6:8, Micah 6:4). Our passage assumes the historicity of the tradition that the Deuteronomic laws derive directly from Moses.
345. In view of various discrepancies between the narrative introduction and the judgment oracle, criticism has tended to identify as secondary either the one or the other. Considerations favoring the originality of the oracle are the following: (1) its reference to the people (various classes of which are specified in vs. 19, without mention of the king) as making a covenant with Yahweh, rather than the king making one with the people (vs. 8), seems antecedently more likely; (2) the oracle depicts the people as releasing the slaves who had fulfilled six years of service, in accordance with the Deuteronomic law—presumably retaining others whose term had not yet expired—while vs. 10 seems to state that all slaves were released, without exception; (3) whereas the oracle minimizes the time-lapse between the releasing of the slaves and their recovery, placing them both within the temporal rubric of *hayyôm*, the introduction aims for a more understandable sequence by inserting *'aḥⁿrê kēn* in vs. 11; (4) the play on the root שוב, a favorite motif of Jeremiah's (cf. W. R. Holladay, *The Root Šubh in the Old Testament*, Leiden, 1958), is less discriminating in the introduction than in the oracle; (5) the oracle, though elaborate in content, runs more true to the normal schema than one would expect in secondary materials; (6) the form of the introduction to the oracle (vs. 12) is closer to the original than that of the redactional introduction in vs. 8.
346. The pioneer work along the lines of the former theory is S. Mowinckel's *Zur Komposition des Buches Jeremias* (Kristiania, 1914). A rather extreme restatement of this position is in J. P. Hyatt's commentary in *IB;* more moderate is W. Rudolph in *HAT.* 34:8ff. has been dated very late (*ca.* 450) by C. Rietzschl, *Das Problem der*

Baruch will find some support in that the combination of the exodus with the covenant-law (vs. 13) is characteristic of some of Jeremiah's authentic oracles, but is found in Deuteronomy only in the late addition, 29:24.[347] It is more with the late than with the early materials in Deuteronomy that Jeremiah's use of *hayyôm* is to be associated. Nowhere in our entire study have we observed an instance in which the actual temporal content of *hayyôm* would positively be required to extend over more than a single twenty-four-hour period. It is analogous only to the usage within the Deuteronomic parenesis, and especially in chaps. 4, 26—30, where *hayyôm* is employed again and again to define every new situation of covenant confrontation, with little or no stress on the actual time element. Here in Jer. 34:15 it is clear that *hayyôm* is used situationally. The statement, "But you repented *hayyôm* and did what is right . . . and made a covenant. . . ," defines the basis on which the people's apostasy is to be judged. This identifying characterization is essential to the central purpose of the pericope as a whole.

Jer. 40:4

It is clear that *hayyôm* functions in an epitome in Jer. 40:4, where the captain of the guard orders the removal of Jeremiah's bonds, interpret-

---

Urrolle (Gütersloh, 1966), p. 122. Favoring Baruch as the author of this pericope are such commentaries as Weiser's (*ATD*, 20/21, 4th ed. 1960) and Bright's (*AB*, 1965), together with the Introductions by Eissfeldt and Fohrer. On the affinities between the deuteronomists and the prophetic schools, see S. Herrmann, *Die prophetischen Heilserwartungen im Alten Testament* (BWANT, 5, Stuttgart, 1965); cf. J. W. Miller, *Das Verhältnis Jeremias und Hesekiels sprachlich und theologisch untersucht* (1955).

347. There is a strong consensus among scholars that Jeremiah is the author of at least several of the passages where the exodus is remembered as the occasion for the giving of the covenant law. In Jer. 7:22 (cf. vs. 25) and 11:4, 7, it is the command to be Yahweh's people that is stressed; in 31:32 the stress is on the covenant itself, but not without attention to the role of the law, as the positive counterpart in vs. 33 makes clear. In all these verses, save for 11:7, where we find the hif. of עלה, it is the hif. of יצא that is used, as in 34:13. I Kings 8:9, containing a deuteronomistic reference to the stone tablets, is not a close parallel because it differentiates syntactically (and hence ideologically) between the event of Horeb and the departure from Egypt. However, the secondary material in Deut. 29:19ff. contains a reference (vs. 24) that is closely akin to these Jeremianic references. The *kayyôm hazzeh* of vs. 28 is evidence that this section is exilic; the covenant mentioned in vs. 24 is conceived in terms of the commandment against worshiping other gods. It is with this passage, rather than with Deuteronomy as a whole, that the Jeremianic idea is affiliated, as one will see when he discovers that elsewhere in Deuteronomy (1:27, 5:6, 15, 6:12, 7:8, 15, 18, 8:14, 9:7, 10:19, 11:3f., 10, 13:6, 11, 15:5, 16:3, 20:1, 24:22, 28:27, 60, 68, 29:1, 15, 34:11) the exodus is remembered as the saving act that provides the basis for the covenant commitment, rather than the occasion when the covenant law as such was promulgated. Martin Noth explains this Jeremianic combination as arising from within a ritual in which the *Heilsfeiten* were recited in close connection with the covenant (*UGP*, p. 50, n. 162, noted by S. Herrmann, *op. cit.*, p. 180, n. 31, and Weiser, *op. cit.*, p. 286, n. 4); Ps. 81 may have been a liturgy for precisely such a covenant ritual.

ing this action in the declaration, "And now, behold, I have released you *hayyôm* from the chains on your hands."[348] This is followed by an explanation of the various options available to the prophet.

No doubt these words were meant to justify Jeremiah's decision to remain in Palestine, demonstrating his loyalty to his own land and people when he was offered the opportunity of obtaining favored treatment among the Babylonians.[349] But perhaps the redactor/editor who was responsible for the introductory rubric at vs. 1 intended more. There is no actual prophetic oracle here; though the text has been disrupted in this section, it will not do to identify vss. 2f. as containing the torso of an original prophetic oracle,[350] because vs. 1a has been supplied redactionally, i.e., after our passage had already substantially attained its present form. The only suitable explanation is to interpret the speech of the captain of the guard as—from the redactor's point of view—a word from Yahweh. What the Babylonian officer declares has the effect of authoritative revelation. Jeremiah's release may therefore be seen as the fulfillment of Yahweh's original promise, "Be not afraid of them, for I am with you to deliver you, says Yahweh" (1:8), or more particularly of the words in 1:18f., containing a previous *hayyôm*: "And I, behold, I make you this day a fortified city.... They will fight against you, but they shall not prevail against you; for I am with you, says Yahweh, to deliver you."[351]

Jer. 42:19, 21

Modern scholarship seems to be in general agreement that Jer. 42: 19-22 has been transferred from its original place following 43:3. *Hayyôm* occurs in epitomizing declarations twice within this section, but both times there is good ground to doubt its authenticity. The clause כי העידתי בכם היום in 19b is suspicious because it interjects itself before the *kî*-clause of 20aα, because it is not attested in the LXX, and because it echoes Deut. 8:19. The clause ואגד לכם היום at the beginning of vs. 21 is also lacking in the LXX; it states superfluously what is already obvious.

---

348. See BH³ mg.
349. This report, probably composed by Baruch, is intended as a continuation of the narrative in chap. 39, where only vss. 3 and 14 are original (see the commentaries; the LXX omits vss. 4-13). According to 52:12 Nebuzaradan was not present when the city was breached (9 IV) but came on 10 V to burn and destroy; hence we are to understand the action of the Babylonian officers in releasing Jeremiah to the custody of Gedaliah as preliminary. Somehow the prophet got swept up into the group gathered at Ramah for deportation, and it was there that Nebuzaradan first found him.
350. Cf. Weiser, *ATD, in loco.* Unmistakably, the speech of the captain of the guard has been restyled from a Hebraic point of view. Baruch himself would have done this, hence there is no need to assign this section to a late Deuteronomic editor (so Hyatt, *IB, in loco*) or to characterize it as legendary (so Duhm, Cornill).
351. See above on 1:10, 18.

Jer. 44:2

The second Jeremianic occurrence of *hayyôm hazzeh* is in 44:2, where it occupies an emphatic place at the beginning of a clause providing an identifying characterization. The feminine plural participle read by the versions is probably correct. This is a usage that has not been found in later materials except in the deuteronomistic literature (though there it is regularly the simple *hayyôm* that is used). The Septuagintal text of Jer. 44:2 does not read the time-designative, nor does it read כיום הזה in vs. 23, where this clearly seems to have been added in the MT through the influence of כהיום הזה in vs. 22. The last, together with כיום הזה in vs. 6 and עד היום הזה in vs. 10, represents typical deuteronomistic language. One would imagine that a Hebrew scribe familiar with these verses, and especially vs. 6, found it irresistible to insert the parallel time-designative in vs. 2.

Hos. 4:5

Hayyôm occurs adverbially in Hos. 4:5, but evidently in the meaning "by day" (normally *yômām*), in contrast to "by night" in the second half of the verse.[352] The only close parallel to this usage is found in the use of the substantive *hayyôm* (par. *hallaylâ*) in Neh. 4:16.

Zech. 9:12

Finally, *hayyôm* occurs within the Deutero-Zecharian collection at Zech. 9:12. The phrasing is unusual: גם היום מגיד משנה אשיב לך. Many problems surround the effort to restore a readable text,[353] and no solution to the literary-critical problem thus far proposed can be declared to be completely satisfactory,[354] yet it is possible to point to certain important

---

352. Most modern commentators follow the LXX, Syr., Tg., over against Vg.; there is nothing in this *rîb*-oracle to provide this particular day with any special meaning. The meaning "by day" seems secure even if the reference to the prophet stumbling by night is to be identified as a gloss (so Wolff, *BK*, XIV/1, *in loco*).

353. See especially T. Jansma, "An Inquiry into the Hebrew Text and Ancient Versions of Zechariah ix-xiv," *OTS*, 7 (1950), *in loco*. The chief difficulties in vs. 12 are the lack of a subject with מגיד and the 3mp summons in the middle of an address to the 2fs. Summarizing the versional readings, the author of a recent major study (Magne Saebø, *Sacharja 9—14, Untersuchungen von Text und Form*, WMANT, 34, Neukirchen, 1969, p. 55) reaches the following conclusion: "So zeigt die Textüberlieferung im 12. Vers von einer gewissen Aporie, die vielleicht im Gestaltungsprozess des MT selbst ihren Grund hat. Die Versionen scheinen weder im ersten noch im zweiten Versteil eine andere, vom MT abweichende Vorlage, die zu rekonstruieren wäre, hinreichend oder eindeutig begründen zu können; vielmehr scheinen sie nur Vermutungen zu einer Verbesserung des Textes hergegeben zu haben."

354. E.g., K. Elliger, *ATD*, 24/25, *in loco*, identifies vss. 11f. as the introduction to one (9:11-16) of four oracles constituting the core of the collection and dating from the beginning of the Hellenistic period, yet this introduction seems too abrupt

affinities. Though the expression "blood of your covenant" remains un-clarified because of the lack of any close parallel, the notion of a special covenant is found in Jeremiah (31:31ff., 34:8ff.) and in a late passage in Ezekiel (16:60ff.). The expressions "from the pit," "prisoners of hope," and "restore to you double" remind the reader especially of Deutero- and Trito-Isaiah. One is especially struck by the fact that *hayyôm* is accom-panied by the participle; this occurs predominantly as a Deuteronomic/ deuteronomistic construction.[355]   In any event, a postexilic date seems assured. It is difficult to determine the function of the temporal adverb in this passage, not only because of the remaining uncertainties in matters of text and literary composition, but especially because our writer is obviously borrowing freely from a wide range of traditional forms and expressions. The most we may say is that *hayyôm* is probably intended as part of an identifying characterization, with some unclarified emphasis on the time element.

(5) The Writings

We draw toward a close of our survey. Among the *kethubhim* we encounter a moderate number of occurrences of *hayyôm* in the narrative materials, but find that in the poetic materials its occurrence is virtually nil. *Hayyôm hazzeh* is not found at all. The most interesting poetic passages are two verses from the Psalms, where a strikingly epitomizing or characterizing function is evident, in both instances with special stress on the time factor.

Ps. 2:7

Psalm 2 has often been described as a Royal Psalm, more specifically as an Enthronement Psalm.[356]   There seems to be no reason to disagree with the emerging consensus in this matter: the entire psalm is spoken by

---

as it stands, and one must suppose redactional interference or mechanical damage; Elliger's reliance on the theory of mechanical damage for restoring vs. 12 suffers under the burden of improbability. On the other hand, there is a measure of improbability also in Saebø's theory (*op. cit.*, 188-93) that Deutero-Zechariah is comprised of a mass of unrelated, worked-over fragments, one of which is 9:11f. (an expansion of 9:1ff.). The strength of both Elliger's and Saebø's work, over against such a treatment as that of B. Otzen, *Studien über Deuterosacharja* (Copenhagen, 1964), pp. 126-30, 241f., is that they deal seriously with form and tradition history and refrain from such positivistic historicizing as leads Otzen to his theory of preexilic authorship (on the basis of the similarity to Ps. 2:7, Otzen is ready to leap to the conclusion that the *hayyôm* of our text refers to the "Tag der Thronbe-steigung").

355. The previously analyzed syntactic data will be summarized below. The only occurrences of the participial construction outside Deut./Dtr are in Exod. 34:11 (J), I Sam. 9:20, II Sam. 19:6, I Kings 20:13, II Kings 2:3, 5, 4:23.

356. Cf. S. Mowinckel, *Psalmenstudien*, III (1922), 80-93; H. Gunkel, *Die Psalmen, GHKAT*, II, 2 (4th ed. 1929), *in loco*; I. Sonne, *HUCA*, 19 (1945/46), 43-55; A. Weiser, *ATD*, 14/15, *in loco*; H.-J. Kraus, *BK*[3], XV/1, *in loco*.

the Davidic king at his accession; he ridicules the pretensions of subject rulers as a futile attempt to shake off the authority of the supreme God, citing specifically the royal protocol of adoption conferring worldwide dominion upon him. The grandiose ideology is probably influenced as much by the imperialistic claims of Israel's neighboring kingdoms, on whose ritual this psalm as a whole is modeled,[357] as by the specific achievements of the David-Solomon era.[358] Nevertheless, special pains have been taken to enunciate a clear distinction between the Israelite theory of kingship and the divine-kingship conception of Egypt; the occurrence of *hayyôm* in vs. 7 is particularly important.

Vss. 7-9 contain the precise wording of the divine protocol.[359] Following introductory formulae, Yahweh declares to the king that he has become his son: בני אתה אני היום ילדתיך. These words constitute the second and third stichoi in a tristich, followed by another tristich in vs. 8 and a distich in vs. 9 inviting the new king to receive and employ the authority that is germane to his office as Yahweh's son. Throughout the protocol, emphasis is on the conveying of this authority. We see this in the chiastic structure of 8a, where ממני and ואתנה are brought immediately together; similarly in the chiastic arrangement of 7, where independent personal pronouns stand back to back, representing the two principal figures. First, אתה is stressed to secure the identification of the addressee as Yahweh's son; next, אני (without conjunction) is stressed to secure the identification of the speaker as the one to whom the new king owes a filial allegiance.

Two important consequences emerge from this analysis. First, the verbal form $y^e lidt\hat{\imath}k\bar{a}$ must be seen as an unemphatic conventionalism, borrowed metaphorically from contemporary divine-kingship ideology and used here only to fill out the parallelism with $b^e n\hat{\imath}$. The Hebrew poet has been careful to preface the verb with the temporal adverb, "today," making impossible any impression of a literal begetting. This "today" is obviously the day of the divine protocol rather than the day of the king's birth— hence his inaugural day, when the protocol comes into force. This brings us to a second consequence, *viz.*, that *hayyôm* functions not to identify this one particular day (repeated typologically upon each royal accession), but as part of an epitomizing declaration that characterizes its central significance. *Hayyôm* may stand in the chronicles of men as the day when such

357. See S. Herrmann, "Die Königsnovelle in Aegypten und Israel," *Wissenschaftliche Zeitschrift der Karl-Marx-Universität Leipzig, gesellschafts- und sprachwissenschaftliche Reihe*, 3 (1953/54), 33ff.

358. Cf. Kraus, *BK*, XV/1, pp. 14ff., following A. Alt, *Kleine Schriften*, II, 66ff.; III, 129ff.

359. The radical emendations to vs. 7a proposed by Duhm, Mowinckel, and other scholars of a former generation have generally been given up. G. von Rad has clarified the meaning of *hōq* (= *'ēdût, b^e rît*) in "Das judäische Königsritual," *Gesammelte Studien*, pp. 208ff.

and such a king began his reign, but in the book of God it is the day when Yahweh confers his power upon his anointed, his son.

Ps. 95:7

Equally striking is the employment of an emphatic *hayyôm* in another liturgical psalm, Ps. 95 (vs. 7), and here again the temporal adverb identifies no particular date on the calendar—that of one specific temple service in this instance—but functions in the characterization of a typical situation that is potentially repeatable again and again. Most recent scholars agree that the occasion for this psalm is the worshipers' entrance into the temple area. [360] First, they are summoned by the liturgist (a priest?) to sing praise to their great Lord (vss. 1-5), then, at the very gates of the sanctuary, as his humble and trusting covenant people, to fall down before him in worship (vss. 6-7a). Abruptly, a new voice is heard appealing for inner integrity and reminding the worshipers that a generation whom Yahweh loathed learned that, in putting him to the test by coming before him with deceitful hearts, they failed to enter into his "rest" (vss. 7b-11). [361] We may speculate whether the speaker is a cult prophet, as in Ps. 81:6ff., 50:7ff., and perhaps 24:3ff. In this psalm he functions like the pareneticist of Deuteronomy; his use of *hayyôm* has its closest parallels in the Deuteronomic parenesis. This word is foremost, preceding the entire conditional clause, אם בקלו תשמעו. Thus, vs. 7b in effect epitomizes an ideal but hypothetical condition—the one which the speaker ardently desires and which alone will give validity to the worshipers' song and prayer—that of dutiful obedience to Yahweh's will. [362] We see again that the epitome and the appeal are closely akin. But the admonition immediately passes into a warning as the day of obedience which the speaker requires is contrasted to the day of disobedience at Massah. [363] The poignancy of this warning conveys to the sensitive reader the impression that the pareneticist was realistically anticipating the hardening and not the obedience, as in the words of the prophets elsewhere and in the appeals of Deuteronomy.

Ps. 119:91

The only remaining occurrence of *hayyôm* within the Psalter comes in the late torah-teaching of Ps. 119, where vs. 91 uses this word as a simple

360. Cf. Kraus, *BK, in loco;* on the Psalm as a whole see G. Henton Davies in *ZAW,* 85 (1973), pp. 183ff.
361. Cf. G. von Rad, "Es ist noch eine Ruhe vorhanden dem Volke Gottes," *Gesammelte Studien,* pp. 101-108.
362. It seems likely that the recital of an apodictic summary may have followed the speaker's warning; see the commentaries.
363. It should be considered whether *massâ* is to be read as an abstract verbal noun, "testing," rather than as a place name. The name "Meribah" appears alone in the gloss to P at Num. 20:13, while the references to "Massah" are clearly secondary in the J account at Exod. 17:1-7; cf. Noth, *UGP,* pp. 143ff.

time-identification. The reference is to Yahweh's word establishing the earth, which consequently stands *hayyôm* (= "now," "until this day") in obedience to that word.

Prov. 7:14

In Prov. 7:14 the meaning and function of *hayyôm* is immediately apparent. A harlot is depicted as laying hold on a foolish youth and beginning her enticement with a protestation of ritual purity: "Peace offerings are with me; *hayyôm* I paid my vows." The temporal adverb, foremost for emphasis, identifies the time of the harlot's sacrificing (she refers, of course, to the daytime immediately preceding this darkness, vs. 9), but it functions even more as an identifying characterization of the harlot's present condition, i.e., one of religious "rightness"—in ironic contrast to her lascivious intent. Is baalistic ideology implied?

Prov. 22:19

Hayyôm occurs in the preface to an admonitory series in Prov. 22:19; it is an element in the purpose clause, "That your trust may be in Yahweh, I have made known *hayyôm* even unto you. . . ."[364] This is an epitome of all that is to come; this day is a day of making known, of inculcating trust.

Job 23:2

The only occurrence of *hayyôm* in the book of Job (23:2) is suspect on a variety of grounds. For one thing, the text is uncertain;[365] but another consideration is that nowhere else in the poetic discussion is there any direct allusion to time.[366] As the MT stands, *hayyôm* is emphatic at the beginning of a new complaint by Job, but the reason for this emphasis is not apparent from the context. The function is that of identifying characterization.

Ruth 2:19

Hayyôm occurs a number of times in Ruth, exhibiting several distinct varieties of function.[367] In 2:19 it appears twice, in Naomi's query and in Ruth's answer, as an element of identifying characterization.

---

364. Cf. BH³ mg.
365. The LXX reads ידעתי; for discussion of the philological problems involved, see Driver-Gray, *Job, ICC*, p. 159.
366. Cf. S. Terrien, *IB, in loco.*
367. Time-designatives are characteristically frequent in this folk tale because sequences are important; cf. 1:1, 4, 22, 2:7, 14, 17, 23, 3:2, 3, 4, 8, 13, 14, 4:5, 7 (also 4:9, 10, 14). In this respect, Ruth resembles Esther.

Ruth 3:18

Hayyôm identifies time when in 3:18, where Naomi refers to the present day as the time during which the question of Ruth's marriage will be settled.

Ruth 4:9f.

In Boaz' final declaration he uses the phrase, "you are witnesses *hayyôm*," both at the beginning and end (cf. vs. 11). The form as such may be that of an identifying characterization (noun-clause), but the function is definitely intended to be that of an epitome; that is, what the kinsmen witness to is the central matter of the speech and, indeed, the structural climax of the entire book: Boaz' purchase of Mahlon's land and the purchasing of Mahlon's wife.

Ruth 4:14

The sentimental climax of Ruth comes a few verses further, where the women bespeak a word of praise to Yahweh because "he did not deprive you of a *gō'ēl hayyôm*." To judge from vs. 17, the *gō'ēl* referred to is the newborn child, not Boaz. In any event, it is clear that the women's praise epitomizes the entire narrative from the point of view of Naomi's personal concern.[368]

Esth. 5:4

Although time-designatives are common in the book of Esther,[369] *hayyôm* occurs only once, in a dubious text, 5:4, where Esther uses it as a simple identification of time when.[370]

Neh. 1:6, 11

The Chronicler, emulating deuteronomistic language, has composed words of prayerful lament to be placed in the mouths of Nehemiah and Ezra; it is solely in their prayers that the word *hayyôm* appears. The Nehemiah prayer is in Neh. 1:5ff., where Nehemiah is reacting to sad news from Palestine. Following a traditionally styled appellation (5), a plea for Yahweh's attention is made in verbose and ill-fitting language (6), employing *hayyôm* in an identifying characterization immediately before another temporal phrase (*yômām wᵉlaylâ* = "by day and night," i.e., "continually")

---

368. On the legalities of Naomi's adoptive action, see G. Gerleman, *BK*, XVIII, *in loco*.

369. See above, pp. 114f.

370. While the Vulgate supports the MT, the word *hayyôm* is missing from a number of Hebrew mss. and is not read by the Syr. The LXX has a grossly conflate text, apparently reading *hayyôm* three times.

that essentially contradicts it. The latter phrase apparently refers back to the *yāmîm* of vs. 4, but the juxtaposition of the two expressions in vs. 6 can be explained only in terms of the complete artificiality of this prayer. It makes a confused repetition of stereotyped language, in particular that of Solomon's prayer in I Kings 8:28f., where the same two phrases of time occur in near sequence, but more meaningfully than here.

Following a confession of sin and a recollection of the divine promise of restoration, the prayer culminates in a new plea in vs. 11. This appeal is not merely for Yahweh's attention, as in vs. 6, but for success *hayyôm* in obtaining mercy "before this man." These words are in anticipation of chap. 2, which records Nehemiah's interview with Artaxerxes, but this attempt to make an artificial prayer contemporaneous fails to reckon with the fact that the praying is not located temporally within the same episode (it is dated in Nisan rather than in Chislev). Yet the intended function of the temporal adverb, that of creating an epitomizing appeal, is evident in spite of the writer's bungling.

Neh. 9:36

In Neh. 9:36 it is Ezra who is praying—again in words put into his mouth by the Chronicler. *Hayyôm* appears somewhat emphatically in a characterizing noun-clause at the end, "Behold, we are slaves *hayyôm*." While confession has occupied much of this prayer, this statement is more complaint than confession. It is repeated at the end of the verse without *hayyôm*.

I Chron. 29:5

Although the Chronicler seems often to confuse the use of *hayyôm* when he tries to use it in original composition, and neglects it when copying from his sources, [371] he does appear to have some sense of its traditional function in the words he has put into king David's mouth in I Chron. 29:1ff. Having stated all that he himself has done to prepare for building the temple, David turns to the people in vs. 5, asking, "And who is willing to consecrate himself *hayyôm* to Yahweh?" Here *hayyôm* with the participle is an identifying characterization of what the king challenges the people to become.

II Chron. 35:21

The Chronicler has embellished the Deuteronomist's note concerning Neco's encounter with Josiah (II Kings 23:29f.) with traditions that some

---

371. Chr regularly drops the time-designative in passages copied from Samuel-Kings. The LXX seeks to restore these in II Chron. 6:19 (= I Kings 8:28) and 10:7 (= I Kings 12:7).

scholars consider to be historically trustworthy.[372]   At II Chron. 35:21 he
puts a speech into the Egyptian king's mouth containing the word *hayyôm*.
Denying hostile intent against Josiah, Neco characterizes himself first
negatively and then positively: "Not against you have I come *hayyôm*, but
against the house with which I am at war." The participle that has
apparently been read by the LXX (ἥκω translates Heb. *'ᵃnî 'ōteh*) not only
makes sense out of a garbled Hebrew text, but conforms to the usual usage
within identifying characterizations.[373]

3. Interpretation: The day present as a moment of crucial decision

It is necessary now to draw together the results of the foregoing
analysis and interpret its significance in systematic form. A number of
questions are in our mind: Do the functions of the time-designative vary
among the respective documents and in successive periods? Do these
functions arise in oral or in literary transmission, and if in each of them,
with what differences of form? In what way do the functions respecting
present time compare with the functions of *bayyôm hahû'*, respecting the
past? What relationship is there between the respective situations to which
the time-designatives have reference and the acting subject? Does it make a
difference if the one who acts is God or man? What is the correlation
between functions on the one hand and syntactical constructions and
literary genres on the other? Only when these questions have been answered will we be in a position to appreciate fully the Hebrew apprehension
of present time.

So massive is the material, and so numerous are the relevant details,
that some tabulation is required if we are to get the overview we need. It
will be well, first, to offer a display of the various occurrences according to
the respective functions and to correlate this with an identification of
tradents and literary sources. We do this in Table 4.[374]   Here passages with

372. So most recent commentators, relying on the Gadd chronicle.
373. Cf. Syr. The LXX paraphrases in I Esdras 1:24f., omitting σήμερον.
374. Special abbreviations used in Table 4 are as follows:

acc hist	= accession history (David)
Baruch	= biographical account
D	= D school
Dtn	= original Deuteronomic corpus
Dtr	= deuteronomistic history
E	= the Elohist
J	= the Yahwist
JE	= the redactional combination of the last two
P	= the priestly document
plur	= the pluralistic sections in Deut.
R, r	= redactor, redactional
s	= a supplement
sing	= the singularistic sections in Deut.
succ narr	= the throne-succession narrative

all four forms, *b^e'eṣem hayyôm hazzeh*, *bayyôm hazzeh* (both only as they refer to the historical present), *hayyôm hazzeh*, and *hayyôm*, have been structured in columns in consecutive order and in relationship to the primary function which the time-designative has been found to have in each.

We include under I:Time Identification, all passages where the time-designative is being used as a date, i.e., where the described action is further being categorized by its precise place in the pattern of time. A few of the passages listed have the additional purpose of indicating synchronism, sequence, or duration, but since they also do identify the time of the given event's occurrence, it has been deemed wise to combine them here, rather than separate them as in the tabulations at the end of Chapter Two. It must be further mentioned that in certain of the time-identifying passages an epitomizing function is at least on the periphery of the writer's intent; we have discussed this problem in detail as we took up the passages in question, hence there is no need to seek any schematic representation of this partial ambiguity.

We list next the epitomizing passages, and alongside them the passages in which an appeal (or command) for decisive action occurs, where this decisive action—still future—qualifies the day in question in the same way in which the past action described in the epitome qualifies the day to which it pertains. We see the appeal form as the structural counterpart of the epitome. It comes into use because "today" is likely to be composed of parts past, present, and future. If something has already happened on this day, or is happening at the moment, to give it its memorable qualification, the epitomizing indicative statement suitably declares the meaning of what is happening or has happened. (The same is true respecting something that is about to happen but is seen as already complete, such as Elijah's appearance to Ahab promised in I Kings 18:15.)[375] If an event is only desired for the present day, having not yet occurred, the appeal or command functions to bring this about; here the modal verb (imperative, jussive, cohortative, perfect consecutive) contemplates the event that will give this day its essential meaning.

Column IV lists the passages in which *hayyôm*, etc., occur as an element in an identifying characterization. Here the statement is likely to be in the indicative, as in the epitomizing structure, but with certain syntactical differences that will receive comment later. The clearest indication that a given occurrence actually is an identifying characterization, rather than what we choose to call an epitome, is its place and function within the pericope. Actually, it is a kind of epitome in miniature, offering a succinct description of one of the important elements in a given situation (thus, e.g., the brothers' explanation in Gen. 42:13, ". . . The youngest is

---

375. Since the future is always contingent, the prophets rarely dare use *hayyôm* in epitomes of events that are about to happen. A striking exception is I Kings 20:13.

Table 4
Function, Tradent, and Literary Source for Discursive Passages
with *hayyôm* and Equivalents

I Time iden- tification	II Epitome	III Appeal or command	IV Identify- ing char- acteri- zation	Primary (and secon- dary) tradent	Literary source
			Genesis		
	4:14			Judah tribe	J
			21:26	Isaac tribe (Beersheba shrine)	E
22:14				Isaac tribe (unknown shrine)	E
		24:12		Jerusalem court	J
24:42				"	J
30:32				Jacob tribes	J
			31:43	"	E
	31:48			"	J
			40:7	northern court	E
			41:9	"	E
	41:41 LXX			Jerusalem court	J
			42:13	"	E
			42:32	northern court	E
	47:23			Jerusalem court	J
			Exodus		
			2:18	Midianites	J
			5:14	—	J
	13:4			central shrine	D
		14:13(1)		"	J
			14:13(2)	"	J
		16:25(1)		Jerusalem shrine	P
16:25(3)				"	P
		19:10		central shrine	J
	32:29(1)			Levitical circles	JE
	32:29(2)			"	JE
			34:11	central shrine	J
			Leviticus		
9:4				—	gloss
			10:19(1)	—	Pˢ
			10:19(2)	—	Pˢ
			Deuteronomy		
			1:10	—	D (plur)

continue

Table 4 (continued)

I Time iden- tification	II Epitome	III Appeal or command	IV Identify- ing char- acteri- zation	Primary (and secon- dary) tradent	Literary source
			1:39	—	D (plur)
			2:18	—	D (sing)
2:25				—	D (sing)
			4:4	—	D (plur)
4:26				—	D (plur)
		4:39		—	D (sing)
			5:3	—	D (plur)
5:24				—	Dtn (plur)
		7:9 LXX		—	Dtn (sing)
8:19				—	Dtn (plur)
			9:1	—	Dtn (sing)
		9:3		—	Dtn (sing)
		11:2		—	Dtn (plur)
	11:26			—	Dtn (plur)
			12:8	—	lawbook^r (plur)
			15:15	—	lawbook^r (sing)
			20:3	—	lawbook (plur)
	26:3			—	lawbook (sing)
26:16				—	Dtn (sing)
	26:17			—	Dtn (sing)
	26:18			—	Dtn (sing)
	27:9			—	Dtn (sing)
			29:9	—	D (plur)
			29:11	—	D (plur)
			29:12	—	D (plur)
			29:14(1)	—	D (plur)
			29:14(2)	—	D (plur)
			29:17	—	D (plur)
	30:15			—	D (plur)
30:18				—	D (plur)
30:19				—	D (plur)
			31:2	—	D
			31:21	—	gloss
			31:27	—	gloss (sing)
			+26 promul- gation clauses	—	—
	Joshua				
3:7				—	Dtr

continued

Table 4 (continued)

I Time iden- tification	II Epitome	III Appeal or command	IV Identify- ing char- acteri- zation	Primary (and secon- dary) tradent	Literary source
	5:9			Gilgal shrine	—
		7:25		"	—
			14:10	—	Dtr
			14:11	—	Dtr
			22:16(1)	Transjordan shrine	priestly documen
			22:16(2)	"	"
			22:18(1)	"	"
22:18(2)				"	"
		22:22		"	"
			22:29	"	"
	22:31			"	"
			23:14	—	Dtr
		24:15		Shechem shrine	Dtr
		Judges			
	9:18			—	R
	9:19			—	R
		10:15		—	Dtr
		11:27		—	R
			12:3	Gilead tribe	—
	21:3			Bethel shrine	—
	21:6			Mizpah shrine	—
		I Samuel			
	4:3			Jerusalem shrine	ark legend
4:16				"	"
9:9				Gilgal shrine	—
9:12(1)				"	—
			9:12(2)	"	—
9:19				"	—
9:20				"	—
10:2				"	—
10:19				—	Dtr
	11:13(1)			Gilgal shrine	—
	11:13(2)			"	—
	12:5			Gilgal/Mizpah shrine	Dtr
			12:17	—	Dtr
			14:28	Gilgal shrine	—
			14:30	"	—
		14:33		"	—

continue

Table 4 (continued)

I Time iden- tification	II Epitome	III Appeal or command	IV Identify- ing char- acteri- zation	Primary (and secon- dary) tradent	Literary source
		14:38		"	—
			14:41 LXX	"	—
	14:45			"	—
	15:28			prophet circle	R
			17:10	"	—
	17:36			"	—
	17:46(1)			"	—
	17:46(2)			"	—
	18:21			—	R
20:27				David's court, Jeru- salem	acc hist
			21:6	"	"
22:15				Saul's court (David's court, Jerusalem)	"
			24:11(1)	David's army (court, Jerusalem)	"
			24:11(2)	"	"
			24:19	"	R
		24:20		"	acc hist
			25:10	David's court, Hebron	"
	25:32			David's court, Jerusalem	"
	25:33			"	R
			26:8	David's army	—
			26:19	—	R
			26:21	—	R
			26:23	David's army	—
		26:24		"	—
27:10				David's court, Hebron (Jerusalem)	acc hist
28:18				prophet circle	Dtr
30:13				David's court, Hebron (Jerusalem)	acc hist
	II Samuel				
			3:8(1)	David's court, Jerusalem	acc hist
	3:8(2)			"	"
3:9 LXX				"	"
	3:38			David's court, Hebron	"
	3:39			"	"
	4:8			"	"

continued

Table 4 (continued)

I Time identification	II Epitome	III Appeal or command	IV Identifying characterization	Primary (and secondary) tradent	Literary source
	6:20 bis			David's court, Jerusalem	R
11:12				Solomon's court	succ nar
	14:22			"	"
15:20				"	"
	16:3			"	"
16:12				"	"
18:20 bis				"	"
	18:31			"	"
	19:6(1)			"	"
			19:6(2)	"	"
	19:7(1)			"	"
	19:7(2)			"	"
			19:7(3)	"	"
	19:21			"	"
			19:23(1)	"	"
	19:23(2)			"	"
			19:23(3)	"	"
			19:36	"	"
	I Kings				
			1:25	"	"
1:30				"	"
	1:48			"	"
2:24				"	"
2:26				"	"
		2:31 LXX		"	"
			5:21	—	Dtr
8:28				—	Dtr
12:7				Rehoboam's court	—
	18:15			prophet circle	—
		18:36		"	—
	20:13			"	—
	II Kings				
	2:3			prophet circle	—
	2:5			"	—
4:23				"	—
6:28				Samaria court	—
6:31				—	R

continued

Table 4 (continued)

I Time iden- tification	II Epitome	III Appeal or command	IV Identify- ing char- acteri- zation	Primary (and secon- dary) tradent	Literary source
		Isaiah			
			38:19	—	supplement
		Jeremiah			
	1:10				oracle collection
	1:18				"
			34:15		Baruch
	40:4				—
	42:19				gloss
	42:21				"
			44:2		"
		Ezekiel			
	24:2				
		Hosea			
4:5					
		Zechariah			
			9:12		supplement
		Psalms			
	2:7			Jerusalem court (shrine)	
		95:7		Jerusalem shrine	
119:91					
		Proverbs			
			7:14		
	22:19				
		Job			
			23:2		
		Ruth			
			2:19 *bis*		
3:18					
	4:9				
	4:10				
	4:14				

continued

Table 4 (continued)

I Time iden- tification	II Epitome	III Appeal or command	IV Identify- ing char- acteri- zation	Primary (and secon- dary) tradent	Literary source
	Esther				
5:4					
	Nehemiah				
			1:6		
		1:11			
			9:36		
	I Chronicles				
			29:5		
	II Chronicles				
			35:21		

hayyôm with our father"; or Moses' description of the Israelites in Deut. 1:10, "You are *hayyôm* as the stars of heaven for multitude"). We make no absolute distinction between these two kinds of passages. They are related in form and in function, but what we designate as an epitome is the central declaration toward which the entire pericope (or entire episode within the pericope) builds. The identifying characterization sets the scene, as it were, while the epitome brings the resolution of the scene. Moreover, what is an epitome in terms of a particular episode may be reduced to a characterization in terms of the entire pericope. The identifying characterization fulfills the essential role of defining the situation, while the epitome provides a climactic word of authoritative interpretation, clarifying the significance of the event that has occurred or is occurring within the situation.

Let us observe now the patterns of usage followed by the various tradents and literary documents.[376] It certainly is striking that in the Tetrateuch epitomes occur only in J, each time as a primitive element of received tradition. E does not preserve this usage; it has, however, most of the passages in which identifying characterizations occur, the two important early exceptions coming in two J passages (Exod. 14:13[2], 34:11) that are highly liturgical in nature and where the characterization is itself part of a central appeal.[377] Except for Gen. 24:12, appeals or commands

---

376. We see no necessity for further argumentation to support our identifications since we offer this only for its general profile.

377. This offers us ground for speculating whether E's experience of history was

with *hayyôm* are climactic elements in liturgical narrative—more clearly so in the two J passages (Exod. 14:13(1), 19:10) than in the P passage, Exod. 16:25(1). Gen. 24, having an appeal and a time-identification occurring in nonclimactic positions, may reflect J's own peculiar style more than the epitomizing passages do. The P passage in Exodus and all the occurrences in Leviticus have a curiously fuzzy focus on the referent of the word *hayyôm*; always it is no more than a vaguely defined day of cultic celebration.

We come next to Deuteronomy. Much has already been observed about Deuteronomy's use of *hayyôm* and its equivalents, but in the context of our total study more needs to be said. First we remark about the time-identification passages. None are found in the lawbook; only three (5:24, 8:19, 26:16) are from the original framework; the rest belong to elements added later. Thus time-identification does not appear to have been an early concern of the Deuteronomic school. It apparently arose with the need to compare the present day of parenetic appeal with either the past or the future. 26:16, the only singularistic passage on this list, may have been the earliest to develop this concern; it is unique in (emphatically) identifying the present day with a paradigmatic day in the past—the day on which Yahweh gave his law, now identified as the day when Yahweh calls on Israel to obey it. The rest of the passages compare the present day with a day in the future. The other two that, like 26:16, use an emphatic *hayyôm hazzeh* (2:25, 5:24) contemplate the Israelites as they confront Moses in the wilderness and look into the future. This leaves 4:26, 8:19, and 30:18f., which depict Moses standing in the present, solemnly warning his hearers of the consequences of a future apostasy that, from the writer's point of view, is certain to come because it has already come.

We are scarcely surprised to find the epitomizing declaration among the relatively earlier sections of Deuteronomy. Certainly the liturgical declaration of 26:3 represents comparatively early material within the lawbook, while the primitive covenant affirmations of 26:17, 18 may be equally ancient, though now taken up into the parenesis. An elemental epitome, summarizing the entire situation for which Deuteronomy was originally promulgated, is 27:9, "*Hayyôm* have you become the people of Yahweh your god." 11:26 and 30:15 have the respective purposes of pinning the introductory parenesis to the lawbook and of bringing the covenant-in-Moab addition (chaps. 29—31) to a climax. Thus Deuteronomy offers us a clear example of how the epitome with *hayyôm* is used: it functions as the fulcrum either of the entire composition or of one of its important elemental units. Certainly its use is no casual one. Similar is the position and function of the appeal passages with *hayyôm* (4:39, 7:9, 9:3, 11:2).

---

quite equivalent to J's. E's passages with *hayyôm* appear to use it artfully (see especially the Joseph passages!) as part of a deliberate structure in which the time element is seen as helping depict the situation.

What impresses us most in looking at Deuteronomy is its frequent employment of *hayyôm* as an identifying characterization. Besides the twenty-six promulgation clauses having it in this function, there are no fewer than seventeen other passages with it. These additional passages are almost all relatively late, the earliest among them being probably those that depict Israel as about to invade new territory (2:18, 4:4, 9:1, 20:3) or as receiving the law (5:3). Several of the passages have to do with the generation problem. 1:10, 39, 4:4, 5:3, 12:8, and 29:9-14 attempt to bring the generation being addressed back into the situation in which Moses first spoke, making his law applicable to the present hearers as well as to those who first received it. The glosses in 31:21, 27, on the other hand, are concerned with the apostasy of generations still to come.

We see here a similarity between those passages that feature *hayyôm*, etc., in a time-identifying capacity and those which have *hayyôm* in an identifying characterization: both classes seem to emerge out of a concern for the generation problem, and for this reason give the impression of being comparatively late. The early Deuteronomic tradition seems to have taken it for granted that the covenant community could place itself typologically back in the time of Moses. For the later tradition—reflecting the experience of Israel's gross apostasy and the calamities of Yahweh's judgment—this could no longer be so easily assumed.

We note also that the time-identifiers and the characterizers tend to have the pluralistic styling, as contrasted with the epitomes and the appeals, which tend to have the singular. One can readily see from the table how relative this is—yet it is clear that the preponderance of passages in columns II and III are singularistic, and at the same time relatively early, while the preponderance of passages in columns I and IV are pluralistic and relatively late.[378]

The situation involved in most of the passages with the identifying characterization is that of Israel's being urged to acknowledge Yahweh, keep his covenant, and obey his law. That is, the manward side of the divine-human relationship is being stressed. Yahweh has already done his part, having given his law, made his covenant, prepared Israel as his people and set before them tne alternative of life or death (the epitomizing sections). Now Israel is being described as at the crisis-point of decision (the characterizations) or is actually being urged to decide (the appeals). The stereotyped promulgation clauses only underscore this relationship: they state what Yahweh through his mediator-spokesman has already done "this day," defining the present situation; but the syntax is pointed to the

---

378. Thus there is no simple solution to the question of the singularistic-pluralistic pattern. It is certainly more complex than a documentary hypothesis would suggest. Evidently the earliest levels were singularistic, yet there are some late singularistic passages, requiring that additional criteria be employed alongside the criterion of number for questions of composition and dating.

appropriate response, *viz.*, Israel's affirmation or confession or compliance. Since the appeals for Israel to respond are relatively infrequent, and the characterizations showing her responsible to respond are relatively frequent, one again receives the impression that the actuality of her affirmative response is highly questionable in the pareneticist's mind. She is responsible this day to decide for Yahweh; whether she will respond this day is a question only the future can answer.[379]

We come now to a review of the materials in the Former Prophets. We are impressed that in Joshua and Judges the passages with *hayyôm*, etc., are either very early or relatively late. Having just surveyed the use of these terms in Deuteronomy, we are especially interested to observe the Deuteronomist's relatively frequent (six out of twenty-one occurrences, five out of twelve passages) use of them. Josh. 3:7 shows every sign of being from the same hand as Deut. 2:25, using an emphatic *hayyôm hazzeh* to mark off the time of Moses from the time of Joshua. The Deuteronomist uses the identifying-characterization form employed in Deut. 31:2 (Moses) to introduce the farewell speeches of Caleb (Josh. 14:10f.) and Joshua (23:14). Although he is himself responsible for the typological appeal-prayer (vs. 15) that provides the climax for his extensive commentary in Judg. 10:6ff., it is likely that he derived Joshua's climactic appeal of Josh. 24:15 as part of an ancient tradition concerning the Shechem covenant.

---

379. Hans H. Schmid, in "Das Zeitverständnis der Geschichte in Deuteronomium," *ZTK*, 64 (1967), 1-15, makes an attempt to define the "today" to which the Deuteronomic parenesis is addressed. The actual addressees were living in a time of fulfilled promise, yet this promise was again being called into question as the (actual) past became (fictionally) future. Schmid denies the presence of a futuristically oriented eschatology, speaking rather of a "präsentische Eschatologie," in which "die Gegenwart ist eigentlich besser, schöner konzipiert, als sie in Wirklichkeit ist. . . . Israel hat sie noch nicht ganz ergriffen. Israel ist noch nicht 'zur Ruhe gekommen' " (p. 11). The reason is that she is in peril of forgetting her history and therewith her god. By remembering her history, Israel may realize the fullness of the promise. "Die Qualitätsdifferenz zwischen faktischer und von der Verheissung intendierter Gegenwart ist der Raum, in welchem Israel sich befindet. Daran, wie sich Israel innerhalb dieser Qualitätsspannung verhält, entscheidet sich Segen oder Fluch, Leben oder Tod. Dieser Qualitätsdifferenz schafft dem Hörer Zeit, schafft ihm Zukunft" (p. 13). Thus a "qualitativen Eschatologie—keine temporale Grosse, sondern Lebensraum." There is nothing in Schmid's elucidation that would be contradicted by our present study, which rather underscores its conclusions.

In "Vergegenwärtigung und Ueberlieferung, Bemerkungen zu ihrem Verständnis im dtn.-dtr. Ueberlieferungbereich," *EvT*, 30 (1970), 169-200, Joh. Michael Schmidt makes another important contribution to the meaning of "today" in Deuteronomy while criticizing Noth's "metaphysical-realistic" concept of how the "Vergegenwärtigung" of the *Heilsfeiten* occurs, von Rad's notion that Deut. 5:3 represents a crisis of developing individualism in Israel, and Ebeling's view that existential appropriation of revelation can occur in isolation from the historical tradition of the people who produced Scripture. An essential distinction is that the *Heilsfeiten* are in the actual past, being at the most remembered—thus in a way "re-presented" (Noth's term)—within the covenant ritual. But the covenant renewal as such takes place in an ever renewed present; this is not "re-presenting" the past but simply an extension of the present into the future.

The only other examples of time-identification and identifying characterization in Joshua-Judges appear in the late priestly narrative, Josh. 22, which, incidentally, offers clear examples of all the other functions as well (it is the only passage where all functions are represented). The special stress placed on the time factor in this narrative helps us identify its intention, which is to secure the perpetual twelve-tribe unity of Israel by absolving the Transjordanians of the charge of apostasy.[380]

The materials in Joshua-Judges that are early-original or early-redactional use the time-designatives as part of an epitome or appeal, always in a position of crucial transition or climax. In the case of Judg. 21:3, 6, epitomizing *hayyôm* is repeated from two distinct sources to provide the fulcrum for a redactional expansion. It is striking that most of the early epitomes and appeals derive from sacral-union shrine traditions.

In I-II Samuel the Deuteronomist has only a meagre contribution to make. Interestingly, the two passages where his time-identifiers appear (I Sam. 10:19, 28:18) have the purpose of contrasting or of correlating different times, similarly to the late strata of Deuteronomy. Part of the early material borrowed for Samuel's speech in I Sam. 12 contains a witnessing epitome (vs. 5); it was likely the Deuteronomist himself who composed the identifying characterization in vs. 17.

Almost all the other time-identifiers play an important role in carefully constructed narratives. Thus I Sam. 4:16 provides a synchronism of central significance in the ark story. The narrative of Saul's designation, I Sam. 9:1–10:16, repeatedly uses the time-identifying *hayyôm*, along with a variety of time-designatives, to establish a simple time sequence integral to the narrative's structure (a day of anticipation, a day of decisive action). The writer of the Davidic accession history includes a number of time-identifiers from his source material, but makes little direct use of them in establishing the sequence of his own narrative. The throne-succession historian, on the other hand, has deliberately used time-identifying adverbs at several crucial points. A special favorite of his has been *hayyôm hazzeh* (II Sam. 16:12, 18:20 *bis;* cf. I Kings 1:30).

It comes as no surprise that I-II Samuel contains a large number of epitomizing statements with *hayyôm*, alongside its numerous epitomes with *bayyôm hahû'*. It reports epitomizing statements as they appeared in original sources (I Sam. 4:3, 12:5, 18:21, 26:8, II Sam. 3:8(2), 38, 4:8, 6:20 *bis*, 14:22, 16:3, 18:31, 19:21), allowing these to stand in order to provide important transitions within the narrative. In other passages it places epitomizing statements in the mouth of one of the chief characters at the climactic point of the entire narrative, i.e., where the central

---

380. The influence of Deuteronomy is apparent, yet linguistic affinities are with P. Is the situation analogous to that of Num. 32:5ff. (see our comments on Num. 32:10, above)?

significance of what has happened, or is about to happen, is spelled out (I Sam. 11:13 *bis*, 14:45, 15:28, 17:36, 46 *bis*, 25:32f., II Sam. 3:39, 19:6f., 23(2); cf. I Kings 1:48). Closely related to the former group are the impressive number of identifying characterizations (distinguishable from this group of epitomes in that they are not so clearly the climactic element of primitive narrative material); closely related to the latter group are the appeals (or commands), in which a central character calls for decisive action.

In I-II Kings the time-identifiers predominate. The most interesting development to be observed in this material is the contribution of prophet legend, with its significant use of climactic epitomes and appeal. We observe these again in Jeremiah and Ezekiel, then again in the Psalms, Proverbs, Ruth, Nehemiah, and Chronicles.

It will be helpful now to present a tabular list of primary tradents for each of these four functions. In Table 5 we give these in their approximate

Table 5
The Functions of Present Time-Designatives
According to Their Tradents

	Functions			
	I	II	III	IV
Pre-amphictyonic tribes	2	2	0	4
Amphictyonic shrines	4	4	6	7
Saul's court	1	0	0	0
David's army	0	0	1	5
David's court, Hebron	2	3	0	1
David's court, Jerusalem	3	5	1	2
Solomon's court	8	9	1	6
Rehoboam's court	1	0	0	0
Jerusalem shrine	2	5	1	0
Jerusalem court	1	3	0	0
Northern court	0	0	0	4
Samaria court	1	0	0	0
Levites	0	2	0	0
Prophet circles	3	14	1	5
Deuteronomic-deuteronomistic	10	7	5	49
Priestly circles	2	1	0	6
Psalmists	1	1	1	0
Wisdom circles	0	1	0	2
Late folk narrative	2	3	0	2
Chronicler	0	0	3	2
totals	43	60	20	95

chronological order. This tabulation has little significance in itself except to show that shrines and the cultus have had a very minor role in shaping the way Israel spoke about its historical experience, while the court historians, the Deuteronomic-deuteronomistic school, and the prophets have influenced it very much. The shrines evidently operated more as the preservers than as the shapers of Israel's tradition concerning its historical experience.

It will be useful to offer also a tabulation of the individual linguistic forms (*hayyôm* and its structural variants) within the respective patterns of syntax and in relationship to the respective formal genres. Table 6 presents these several elements in combination, listed according to the respective functions of the time-designatives.[381]

We need to take note of the way in which our time-designatives relate to the various literary genres within the several syntactical patterns, as indicated in Table 6. It is extremely difficult to summarize these data in any helpful way. The most that can be done is to make certain generalizations which the reader may check out for himself on the basis of this table. First of all, we may say that certain syntactical patterns are directly related to each of the functions. The time-identifying function appears equally often with the imperfect or perfect consecutive (15) and the perfect or imperfect consecutive (15), while other syntactical constructions are relatively infrequent: infinitive (1), participle (4), noun-clause (1), imperative (1), and cohortative (1); this is so because the central concern is to define a given time in relation to other times in the past or future. We find, next, that the epitomizing function predominates with the perfect construction (40), appearing with relative infrequency with the infinitive (1), participle (5), noun-clause (5), and imperfect or perfect consecutive (7). The appeal or command to decisive action, pertaining to the immediate future, prefers the imperative (6), the perfect consecutive used as an imperative (7), the jussive/cohortative (4), the imperfect (1), or—in dependent clauses—the perfect (3). The identifying characterization has a somewhat different

---

381. Special abbreviations and signs used in Table 6 are the following:

*	time-designative foremost
BH	*bayyôm hazzeh*
BHH	*beʿeṣem hayyôm hazzeh*
coh	cohortative
h	deictic particle foremost
H	*hayyôm*
HH	*hayyôm hazzeh*
impf	imperfect
impf cs	waw-consecutive imperfect
impv	imperative
inf	infinitive
n-cl	noun-clause
neg	negated
pf	perfect
pf cs	waw-consecutive perfect
ptcp	participle

Table 6
Analysis of Form, Syntax, and Genre of Present Time-Designatives
According to Respective Functions

			Genre	
	Form	Predicate	Individual	Contextual

I. Time-identification

Gen. 22:14	H	impf	archeological note	shrine legend
24:42	H	impf cs	historical recital	folk history
30:32	H	impf	contract discourse	ethnological saga
Exod. 16:25(3)	H*	impf (neg)	sabbath torah	cult narrative
Lev. 9:4	H*	(pf)	—	—
Deut. 2:25	HH*	impf+inf	call to battle	historical review
4:26	H	pf	witnessing oath	parenesis
5:24	HH*	pf	historical recital	redactional transition
8:19	H	pf	witnessing oath	parenesis
26:16	HH*	ptcp	redactional transition	"
30:18	H	pf	warning	"
30:19	H	pf	witnessing oath	"
Josh. 3:7	HH*	impf+inf	interpretive gloss	—
22:18(2)	H	impf	warning	controversy narrative
I Sam. 4:16	H	pf	battle report	hieros logos
9:9	H	impf	archeological note	—
9:12(1)	H	pf	instruction	legitimation narrative
9:19	H	ptcp	"	"
9:20	H	ptcp	"	"
10:2	H	inf	"	"
10:19	H*	pf	denunciation	redactional transition
20:27	H	pf (neg)	investigative question	accession history
22:15	H*	pf+inf	avowal of innocence	"
27:10	H	pf	battle inquiry	"
28:18	HH	pf	threat	judgment oracle
30:13	H	pf	battle report	accession history
II Sam. 3:9	(BH)	impf	oath	"
11:12	H	impv	royal instruction	succession narrative
15:20	H	impf	remonstration	"
16:12	HH	inf	reproach	"
18:20(1)	HH	n-cl (neg)	battle command	"
18:20(2)	HH*	impf (neg)	"	"
I Kings 1:30	HH	coh	oath (renewal)	"
2:24	H	impf	decree of death	"
2:26	BH	impf	decree of amnesty	"
8:28	H	ptcp	prayer	historical narrative
12:7	H*	impf	casuistic counsel	"
II Kings 4:23	H	ptcp	investigative question	wonder tale

continued

Table 6 (continued)

	Form	Predicate	Genre	
			Individual	Contextual
6:28	H	impf	complaint	anecdote
6:31	H	impf	curse (threat)	—
Hos. 4:5	H	pf	invective	judgment oracle
Ps. 119:91	H	pf	—	torah teaching
Ruth 3:18	H	pf	transitional admonition	folk-tale
Esth. 5:4	H	impf	invitation	folk-history
		II. Epitome		
Gen. 4:14	H	h+pf	complaint	ethnological saga
31:48	H	n-cl	appeal to witness	covenant narrative
41:41	(H)	h+pf	decree of appointment	novella
47:23	H	h+pf	contract	"
Exod. 13:4	H*	impf	liturgical parenesis	cult legislation
32:29(1)	H	(pf)	liturgical declaration	legitimation narrative
32:29(2)	H	inf	"	"
Deut. 11:26	H	h+ptcp	call to decision	parenesis
26:3	H	pf	recital	festive liturgy
26:17 *bis*	H	pf+inf	declaration	covenant liturgy
27:9	HH*	pf	"	parenesis
30:15	H	h+pf	call to decision	"
Josh. 5:9	H*	pf	cult etiology	shrine legend
22:31	H*	pf	declaration of absolution	controversy narrative
Judg. 9:18	H	pf	denunciation	—
9:19	HH	pf	casuistic formula	—
21:3	H	pf+inf	lament	quasi holy-war narrative
21:6	H	pf	complaint	"
I Sam. 4:3	H	pf	lament	hieros logos
11:13(1)	BH	impf (neg)	decree of amnesty	accession narrative
11:13(2)	H*	pf	victory acclamation	"
12:5	HH	n-cl	appeal to witness	farewell address
14:45	HH	pf	declaration of acquittal	hero saga/holy war narrative
15:28	H	pf	prophetic threat	judgment oracle
17:36	(H)	pf cs	victory boast	hero-legend
17:46(1)	HH*	impf	"	"
17:46(2)	HH	pf cs	"	"
18:21	H	impf	marriage formula	accession history
25:32	HH	pf	praise	hero saga
25:33	H	pf	"	"

continued

Table 6 (continued)

	Form	Predicate	Individual	Contextual
			Genre	
II Sam. 3:8(2)	H	impf cs	complaint	accession history
3:38	HH	pf	funeral oration	"
3:39	H*	n-cl	complaint	historical narrative
4:8	HH	impf cs	victory report	"
6:20 *bis*	H	pf	taunt	court anecdote
14:22	H*	pf	formula of ingratiation	succession narrative
16:3	H*	impf	victory boast	"
18:31	H	pf	victory report	"
19:6(1)	H	pf	complaint	"
19:7(1)	H	pf	"	"
19:7(2)	H	pf	"	"
19:21	H	h+pf	plea for reconciliation	"
19:23(2)	H*	impf	decree of amnesty	"
I Kings 1:48	H	pf	praise	"
18:15	H*	impf	predictive oath	prophet legend
20:13	H*	h+ptcp	threat	"
II Kings 2:3	H*	ptcp	revelatory question	"
2:5	H*	ptcp	"	"
Jer. 1:10	HH	h+pf	commissioning declaration	call vision
1:18	H	h+pf	"	private oracle
40:4	H	h+pf	decree of amnesty	prophet history
42:19	H	pf	—	—
42:21	H	impf cs	—	—
Ezek. 24:2	BHH	pf	oracular instruction	judgment oracle
Ps. 2:7	H	pf	accession protocol	enthronement hymn
Prov. 22:19	H	pf	summons to instruction	admonitory series
Ruth 4:9	H	n-cl	appeal to witness	contract
4:10	H	n-cl	"	"
4:14	H	pf (neg)	praise	birth narrative

III. Appeal/command for decisive action

Gen. 24:12	H	impv	prayer	folk history
Exod. 14:13(1)	H	impv/impf	call to witness	deliverance narrative
16:25(1)	H	impv	sabbath torah	cult narrative
19:10	H	pf cs	ritual command	theophany narrative
Deut. 4:39	H	pf cs	call to confession	parenesis
7:9	H	pf cs	"	"
9:3	H	pf cs	"	"
11:2	H	pf cs	"	"
Josh. 7:25	BH	jus	appeal for punishment	etiological legend
22:22	HH	jus	appeal for judgment	controversy narrative
24:15	H	impv	call to decision	covenant narrative

continued

Table 6 (continued)

	Form	Predicate	Individual	Contextual
			Genre	
			Individual	Contextual
Judg. 10:15	HH	impv	prayer	theological résumé
11:27	H	jus	appeal for adjudication	holy-war narrative
I Sam. 14:33	H	impv	liturgical command	altar legend
14:38	H	pf	summons to lot	hero saga/holy-war narrative
24:20	HH	(=pf)	blessing	accession history
26:24	HH	h+pf	appeal for protection	hero saga
I Kings 2:31	(H)	pf cs	royal instruction	succession narrative
18:36	H*	jus	prayer	prophet legend
Ps. 95:7	H*	impf	parenetic appeal	covenant liturgy
Neh. 1:11	H	pf cs	plea for success	prayer

IV. Identifying characterization

	Form	Predicate	Individual	Contextual
Gen. 21:26	H	—	self-exculpation	ethnological saga
31:43	H	impf	treaty discourse	"
40:7	H	n-cl	investigative question	novella
41:9	H	n-cl	confession	"
42:13	H	h+n-cl	self-characterization	"
42:32	H	n-cl	"	"
Exod. 2:18	H	pf+inf	investigative question	ethnological saga
5:14	H	pf (neg)	reproach	contest narrative
14:13(2)	H	pf	promise	deliverance narrative
34:11	H	ptcp	ritual command	theophany narrative
Lev. 10:19(1)	H*	h+pf	complaint	midrash
10:19(2)	H	pf cs	"	"
Deut. 1:10	H	h+n-cl	historical review	farewell address
1:39	H	impf (neg)	parenesis	"
2:18	H	ptcp	"	"
4:4	H	ptcp	historical review	"
5:3	H	n-cl	parenesis	introduction to apodictic code
9:1	H	ptcp	call to battle	parenesis
12:8	H	ptcp	parenesis	—
15:15	H	ptcp	"	—
20:3	H	ptcp	call to battle	instruction
29:9	H	ptcp	protocol	parenesis
29:11	H	inf	"	"
29:12	H	ptcp	"	"
29:14 *bis*	H	ptcp	"	"
29:17	H	ptcp	warning	"
31:2	H	n-cl	self-characterization	farewell address
31:21	H	ptcp	—	—

continued

Table 6 (continued)

	Form	Predicate	Genre Individual	Contextual
31:27	H	ptcp	—	—
26 promulgation clauses	H	ptcp	—	—
Josh. 14:10	H	h+n-cl	self-characterization	farewell address
14:11	H	n-cl	"	"
22:16(1)	H	inf	investigative question	controversy narrative
22:16(2)	H	inf	"	"
22:18	H	impf	warning	"
22:29	H	inf	renunciation	"
23:14	H	h+ptcp	self-characterization	farewell address
Judg. 12:3	HH	pf	complaint	—
I Sam. 9:12(2)	H	n-cl	instruction	legitimation narrative
12:17	H	n-cl	rhetorical question	farewell address
14:28	H	impf	curse	hero saga/holy-war narrative
14:30	H	inf+pf	wish	"
14:41	H	pf (neg)	complaint	"
17:10	HH	pf	challenge	hero-legend
21:6	H*	impf	affirmation	accession history
24:11(1)	HH*	h+pf	appeal to witness	"
24:11(2)	H	pf	victory report	"
24:19	H	pf	résumé	"
25:10	H*	pf	taunt	hero saga
26:8	H	pf	victory report	"
26:19	H	pf	complaint	
26:23	H	pf	appeal for adjudication	hero saga
II Sam. 3:8(1)	H*	impf	affirmation of loyalty	accession history
19:6(2)	H	ptcp	complaint	succession narrative
19:7(3)	H	n-cl	"	"
19:23(1)	H	impf	reproach	"
19:23(3)	H	n-cl	decree of amnesty	"
19:36	H	n-cl	self-characterization	"
I Kings 1:25	H	pf	report	"
5:21	H	ptcp	praise	historical narrative
Isa. 38:19	H	—	proposal of praise	individual lament
Jer. 34:15	H	impf cs	invective	judgment oracle
44:2	HH	(ptcp)	parenetic review	"
Zech. 9:12	H	ptcp	portrayal	salvation oracle
Prov. 7:14	H*	pf	declaration of ritual purity	admonition

continued

Table 6 (continued)

	Form	Predicate	Genre	
			Individual	Contextual
Job 23:2	H*	n-cl	complaint	wisdom drama
Ruth 2:19(1)	H	pf	investigative question	folk-tale
2:19(2)	H	pf	identifying declaration	"
Neh. 1:6	H	pf cs	plea for attention	prayer
9:36	H	h+n-cl	self-characterization	"
I Chron. 29:5	H	ptcp	summons to giving	royal address
II Chron. 35:21	H	(ptcp) neg	rejection of hostilities	historical report

pattern than that of the epitome, using with relative infrequency the perfect (20) and the imperfect (7) while extending the use of the noun-clause (16) and strongly preferring the participle (18, plus 26 promulgation clauses).

We find that a great variety of genres are used with the time-designatives we are studying. The time-identifiers seem to have no significant correlation to them. The epitome, however, is found most often in complaints, decrees, declarations, reports, and summonses. The appeal is found in instructions, prayers, summonses, and wishes. The identifying characterization prefers to appear in challenges, complaints, and parenesis. The most highly stereotyped formulations are the epitomizing appeal to witnesses with the participle, the self-characterizing noun-clause, and the participial promulgation clause of Deuteronomy.

Rather than attempt to refine our analysis of the use of individual genres, it may be more helpful to suggest something about *Sitz im Leben*, as seen in the light of our listing of tradents and contextual genres. Here again, generalizations must suffice. We present the following scheme of the locus for the respective life-situations, listed again according to the several functions of the respective time-designatives:

I. Time-identification: early cult, 3; late cult, 1; tribal narrative, 1; folk narrative, 3; court narrative, 17; literary redaction, 3; law-giving and parenesis, 6; prophetic proclamation, 3.

II. Epitome: early cult, 5; late cult, 2; tribal narrative, 1; folk narrative, 15; court narrative, 17; literary redaction and editing, 4; law-giving and parenesis, 3; cult legislation, 1; prophetic narration and proclamation, 8; Levitical legitimation, 2; wisdom, 1.

III. Appeal/command: early cult, 5; late cult, 2; tribal narrative, 1; folk history, 4; court narrative, 2; prophet narrative, 1; parenesis, 4; redactional, 1; late history, 1.

IV. Identifying characterization: early cult, 2; late cult, 5; tribal narrative, 3; folk narrative, 13; court narrative, 12; law-giving and parenesis,

20 (+26 in promulgation clauses); prophet proclamation, 3; wisdom, 2; late history, 4; redaction, 4; midrash, 2.

The main value of this tabulation will be to underscore what has long since become apparent in this study: that the significance of "today" was not celebrated in psalmody or in wisdom, nor even in cultic narrative, but in the narration of the people. And what had happened in a day passed by is given new life and urgency in the new "today" of covenant parenesis.

We would like to conclude this discussion by turning our attention specifically to the epitomes and appeals having *hayyôm* and its equivalents, in order to make a comparison with the epitomizing use of *bayyôm hahû'*. We are curious to know who has acted or is acting, and what has happened or is taking place, on the days designated by these respective time-referents. The question is: "What kind of event is celebrated by the epitomizing statement, past and present?" What is it, precisely, that happens or has happened on the memorable days of Israel's history?

Going back, then, to the tabulations at the end of Chapter Two, we recall that the epitomizing statement with *bayyôm hahû'*, when used in redactional or supplementary materials, referred to those days when Yahweh exalted Joshua in the crossing of the Jordan (Josh. 4:14), when Ai was defeated by Israel (8:25), when Benjamin was defeated by Israel (Judg. 20:46), and when Josiah kept the passover (II Chron. 35:16). When used at the end of episodes, as an original transition to a new episode, *bayyôm hahû'* referred to the day when the Levites showed zeal for Yahweh (Exod. 32:28), when Benjamin defeated Israel (Judg. 20:21), when Saul and his sons were slain (I Sam. 31:6), when David's servants defeated Israel (II Sam. 18:7), when Absalom's death turned victory into mourning (19:3), when Yahweh annulled his covenant (Zech. 11:11), and when the assembly held a feast in celebration of Solomon's accession (I Chron. 29:22). When used at the end of pericopes, as part of a concluding formula, *bayyôm hahû'* had reference to those days when Yahweh made a covenant with Abram (Gen. 15:18), Jacob departed from Esau (33:16), Yahweh saved Israel from the Egyptians (Exod. 14:30), Joshua subjugated the Gibeonites (Josh. 9:27), Joshua made a covenant with Israel (24:25), Israel subdued Moab (Judg. 3:30), Israel defeated Jabin (4:23), Jerubbaal earned his name (6:32), Israel defeated Benjamin (20:35), the Philistines returned the ark (I Sam. 6:16), Yahweh routed the Philistines at Mizpah (7:10), Yahweh delivered Israel at Michmash (14:23), David entered Saul's service (18:2), Doeg slaughtered the Nob priests (22:18), Israel cleared David of blame for Abner's death (II Sam. 3:37), Eleazer defeated the Philistines (23:10) and Israel celebrated Zerah's defeat (II Chron. 15:11).

We are impressed once again by how often the situations referred to have to do either with victory over enemies or with covenant making (and breaking). These memorable days are generally days when Yahweh has acted or when Israel has acted in consort with him and in response to him.

Yahweh acts on his own initiative in the following *bayyôm hahû'* passages:
Gen. 15:18, Exod. 14:30, Josh. 4:14, Judg. 4:23, I Sam. 7:10, 14:23,
Zech. 11:11. A revelational mediator or charismatic person acts on Yahweh's behalf in Josh. 24:25, Judg. 6:32, II Sam. 23:10. Man acts in cultic
confrontation with Yahweh in Exod. 32:28, I Sam. 6:16, II Sam. 6:9, II
Chron. 15:11, 29:22. This leaves a number of passages in which man
confronts man (Gen. 33:16, Josh. 8:25, 9:27, Judg. 3:30, 20:21, 35, 46, I
Sam. 18:2, 22:18, 31:6, II Sam. 3:37, 18:7, 19:3), but since the events
referred to occur under the aspect of pan-sacrality, it can be said that they
too have to do with God's will in history.

What now are the events referred to in epitomizing declarations
containing *hayyôm* and its equivalents? Though the list is long, it is useful
to review it here: [382]   Yahweh drives out Cain; a heap witnesses to a treaty;
Pharaoh sets Joseph over Egypt, Joseph purchases the Egyptians; Israel goes
forth from Egypt; the Levites ordain themselves and receive Yahweh's
blessing; Yahweh confronts Israel with a blessing and a curse; a worshiper
celebrates the possession of the land; Israel and Yahweh declare that they
belong to each other; Israel becomes Yahweh's people; Yahweh confronts
Israel with life and good, death and evil; Yahweh rolls away the reproach of
Egypt; Phinehas acknowledges that the Transjordanians have not committed treachery; the Shechemites revolt against the house of Jerubbaal; a
tribe is lost from Israel; Yahweh has put Israel to rout; no man is to die,
because Yahweh has delivered Israel; witnesses testify that Samuel has
committed no fraud; Jonathan has wrought with God; Yahweh tears the
kingdom from Saul; Yahweh and David are about to deliver Israel from the
Philistines; David is to become Saul's son-in-law; Yahweh has sent Abigail
to keep David from bloodguilt; Ishbaal charges Abner with fault; a great
man has fallen in Israel, so that David the anointed king has been made
weak; Yahweh has avenged David upon the house of Saul; David has
dishonored himself by exposing his nakedness; Joab acknowledges that
David has favored him; Meribaal expects Yahweh to restore the kingdom of
Saul; Yahweh has delivered David from his enemies; David despises his
servants by weeping over Absalom; Shimei has come to support David's
return to power; no man shall die, because David has regained his kingship;
Yahweh has placed one of David's offspring on his throne; Elijah will show
himself to Ahab; Yahweh will defeat the Syrians; Yahweh will take away
Elisha's master; Yahweh commissions Jeremiah; the Rabshakeh releases
Jeremiah; Jeremiah warns the Judahites of apostasy; the king of Babylon
lays siege to Jerusalem; Yahweh adopts the Davidic king; a wisdom teacher
makes known his precepts; the people bear witness to Boaz' action; Yahweh provides a kinsman for Naomi.

Here the immediately past, the present, and the immediate future

---

382. Scripture references are those of the listing in Tables 4 and 6.

merge into one another. Certain memorable events have happened, are happening, and are about to happen to give "this day" its central significance. Always it is something that has decisive effect for the time to come: after "today" things will never be the same. However, the array of contemplated situations has been much broadened from that of the past epitomes; the covenant and the holy war are still included, but now every aspect of public life is touched upon. The epitome with *hayyôm* has its *Sitz im Leben* in Hebrew life and society as a whole.

The situation that calls forth the appeal or command with *hayyôm* and its equivalents is often that of the covenant confrontation (Deut. 4:39, 7:9, 9:3, 11:2, Josh. 24:15; Ps. 95:7) or, more broadly, any controversy in which sharp issues are to be resolved (Josh. 7:25, 22:22, Judg. 11:27, I Sam. 14:38, 26:24, I Kings 18:36, II Chron. 35:21). It may also be the moment of cultic dedication (Exod. 16:25, 19:10, I Sam. 14:33, I Chron. 29:5) or of divine self-revelation (Gen. 24:12, Exod. 14:13, Judg. 10:15, Neh. 1:11). Here the holy war, the cultus, the covenant-renewal festival, the liturgy of Yahweh's saving acts appear as predominant life-situations. The array of situations is more restricted than that covered by the epitomes with *hayyôm* and its equivalents, being roughly commensurate with that covered by the epitomes with *bayyôm hahû'*.

It will become possible to make a delineation of the interrelationship between these three groups, appeals, epitomes past, and epitomes present, after we have made one more refinement in our analysis. We need to observe that present epitomes function in two distinct ways within the several pericopes; either they remain as a fossil of an earlier narrative stage, wherein they appeared at the interpretive climax, now providing a transition to the new pericope's ultimate climax, or they continue to occupy the climactic position within the pericope. This is parallel to the situation observed regarding the epitomes with *bayyôm hahû'*, where the occurrences likewise fell into two categories: transitional and concluding. For our present purposes we may also refer to the epitomes with *hayyôm*, etc., under these two categories, listing them as follows: transitional: Gen. 41:41, Exod. 13:4, Deut. 26:3, 17f., Judg. 21:3, 6, I Sam. 4:3, 12:5, 18:21, 26:8, II Sam. 3:8, 38, 4:8, 6:20, 14:22, 18:31, 19:21, II Kings 2:3, 5, Ezek. 24:2, Ps. 2:7, Ruth 4:9f.; concluding or climactic: Gen. 4:14, 31:48, 47:23, Exod. 32:29, Deut. 11:26, 27:9, 30:15, Josh. 5:9, 22:31, Judg. 9:18f., I Sam. 11:13, 14:45, 15:28, 17:36, 46, 25:32f., II Sam. 3:39, 19:6f., 23, I Kings 1:48, 18:15, 20:13, Jer. 1:10, 18, 40:4, 42:19, 21, Prov. 22:19, Ruth 4:14.

A quick glance at the several passages that happen to contain both kinds of epitome will show us the difference of their function within a given pericope. Deut. 26:17f., along with vs. 16, functions transitionally to 27:9, where the original Deuteronomic parenesis comes to the point of ultimate gravitational equilibrium. David's lament over Abner in II Sam.

3:38 is instrumental to his ultimate declaration in vs. 39: "I am this day weak." Shimei's offer to help David found in II Sam. 19:21 is instrumental to David's climactic declaration of vs. 23, decreeing amnesty for him. The witnessing declarations of Ruth 4:9f. are transitional to Naomi's final exclamation (vs. 14) regarding the giving of a kinsman. It is possible, by extending this kind of analysis to all the instances, to determine what the ultimate concern and intention of each passage is.

When we select those passages in which past epitomes, present epitomes, and appeals happen to appear together, we are able to see how each of these is likely to function within a given pericope. There are nine passages that have a combination of two or more of these: Exod. 14 has an appeal in vs. 13 and a past epitome in vs. 30 (both featuring the vocable ראה); Exod. 32 has a past epitome in transitional position at vs. 28 and two present epitomes in the climactic declaration of vs. 29; Josh. 24 has an appeal in vs. 15, a past epitome in the narrative conclusion at vs. 25; Judg. 20:21 features a past epitome in transitional position at 20:35 (20:46 is redactional) and a present transitional epitome at 21:6 (vs. 3 being a narrative variant); I Sam. 14:23 has a past epitome that concludes one of the original narratives in this chapter, while the second narrative has a central appeal at vs. 38 and its own concluding present epitome at vs. 45; II Sam. 3 has a transitional present epitome at vs. 8 and a concluding past epitome in vs. 37 as elements in one of its constituent narratives, a double present epitome as the concluding element of its second constituent narrative (vss. 38f.); II Sam. 18 has a transitional past epitome at vs. 7 and another transitional epitome—now a present one—at vs. 31 (cf. the supporting time-identification in vs. 20); this leads in chap. 19 to still another transitional past epitome at vs. 3 and a climactic present epitome in Joab's declaration of vss. 6f.; finally, Josh. 22 contains both an appeal (vs. 22) and a concluding present epitome (vs. 31).

The meaning of all this is that appeals may appear with past epitomes, or even with transitional present epitomes, but not with concluding present epitomes—except where the appeal is for a test of truth, as in I Sam. 14 and Josh. 22. In other words, it is at only one place within a given pericope that narrative description, on the one hand, and declarative discourse or hortatory appeal, on the other hand, may express a narrative's ultimate meaning and intention.

Who, finally, is the acting subject in the present epitome or appeal? The subject is likely to be much the same as with the past epitomes. Yahweh acts on his own initiative in twenty-two present epitomes and in eight appeals. A revelational mediator acts in Yahweh's behalf in six present epitomes and in no appeals. Man acts in confrontation with God in eight present epitomes and in eleven appeals. Man acts in confrontation with other men in thirty-four epitomes and in two appeals.

Our study of "in this day" is now complete, standing alongside our study of "in that day" with reference to the past. We now have insight into the formal and traditional background of these expressions sufficient to enable us to approach a study of their equivalent within the context of eschatological expectation. However unique the future day may prove to be, it cannot be described except in terms of the day that is now past and the day that is now present.

CHAPTER FOUR

The Day Future: *bayyôm hahû'*

1. The future extrapolated from the past and present

AS THE SACRED historiographers interpreted the interconnectedness and essential quality of particular days in the past, and the pareneticists identified the significance and challenge of particular days in their own present, so there were some to declare the meaning of particular days yet to come. They scarcely did this solely by unaided human calculation, and it made a difference whether the predicted day lay in the immediate or remote future. The future might be forecast on the basis of preparations already made, and on the analogy of the past, but something transcending the human factor was needed if the future day was to be identified—and awaited—with any degree of confidence.

We moderns readily think of ourselves as moving forward into the future. The model that many of us have is that of a railroad timetable or the program for a space flight. Time is simply another quantum which man can control and predict. In the area of historical event, however, the once-popular image of undisturbed meliorism has been forced to undergo radical qualification because of the demonic element that has sporadically manifested itself in human behavior. Scientists may confidently predict the future landing spot of a space rocket, but historians and statesmen scarcely dare forecast exactly what nations or persons will do, and when. The wisest thing they can do is play the odds, try to manipulate the determinative factors, and hope for the best.

The ancient Hebrews and their contemporaries had little confidence in forecasting the future because they knew human frailty and aberration, as well as man's susceptibility before the uncontrollable powers of nature. Nevertheless, it must be significant that, among ancient peoples, those who were the most acutely aware of historical time, past and present—namely, the Hebrews of the Bible—were also the people who actually had the most to say about the future. They did not, like the Babylonians, depend on diviners and hepatoscopists. The Babylonians believed that the future could be predicted because it was predetermined; all that was needed was the services of one who knew the signs and omens, i.e., an interpreter who could identify future days by their foredetermined tokens. Even the gods, the embodiment of erratic, irrational force, were subject to the predetermined times. Not so for the Hebrews. For them the future depended solely on two factors: God's will and man's response to it. Somehow, even nature and historical event were unable to interfere with the interaction of these two factors because both were manifestations of the divine will and were therefore under God's control.[1]

---

1. Cf. in this connection the moving words with which Alfred Jepsen concludes his work, *Die Quellen des Königsbuches* (Halle, 1953), pp. 110-14.

The Hebrews were so intensely interested in the future because they knew they had a share in shaping it; also because they believed their God was waiting on their action. Actually, it was not until the prophets had made them aware of God's will and purpose in the ominous historical movements threatening their late nationhood that they began to think very much about what the future would bring, and then it was in terms of what God was about to do in response to man's doing, and what man would consequently do in response to God's doing—never in terms of bare "historical" occurrence. Always the future day that awaited them was predicted in terms that were calculated to influence their present behavior. If it was to be a day of woe, it was designed to move them to repentance and conversion; if it was to be a day of bliss, it was designed to move them out of despair. Thus Israel's concern with the future was, if anything, eminently practical and personalistic. It involved the personhood of God and the personhood of man in free interaction, both of which were guaranteed because the future was not predetermined but open to the loving, trusting partnership of God as history's purposeful shaper and man as history's responsible actor.[2]

We can say, then, that Israel's concern for the future was related to its momentary existential responsibility in a way analogous to its concern for the past. Israel's historiography was not simply antiquarian. The past was important because it informed the present.[3] "That day" was the illuminating image of "this day," helping the nation see how it should act now. So too the "that day" of the future, which we so often find deriving its model from an ideal in the past that no longer is, but which one hopes may be recovered through responsible action in the here and now. Thus, in an ultimate meaning, both historiography and eschatology are forms of parenesis, holding the covenant people to an ever present choice between "life and good, death and evil" (Deut. 30:15).

2. Māḥār: a deferred hayyôm

Ere we begin our study of futuristic *bayyôm hahû'*, we take note that the time word *māḥār* (in a variety of combinations: *māḥār, lᵉmāḥār, kā'ēt māḥār, māḥār kā'ēt hazzō't*) functions in a number of passages like a

---

2. These observations have been strongly influenced by the penetrating insights of Hartmut Gese in his essay, "Geschichtliches Denken im alten Orient und im Alten Testament," *ZTK*, 55 (1958), 127-45.

3. The point that Israel's memory of her past is a vehicle for enabling her to confront the crisis of the present is effectively made by Brevard S. Childs in his monograph, *Memory and Tradition in Israel* (SBT, 37, Naperville, 1962), especially in chap. VI, "Memory and Cult," and chap. VII, "Memory and History." Although Childs's study is restricted to passages in which the root זכר appears, its conclusions concerning Israel's interest in her past have received a broader corroboration in our foregoing study and have been generally supported by serious students of Israel's historiographic literature.

deferred *hayyôm*. This appears generally where a sequence of more than one day is involved. Although a number of occurrences are concerned with mere time-identification (Exod. 8:6, 19, 9:5, II Sam. 11:12, I Kings 19:2, 20:6, II Kings 6:28, 7:18, Prov. 3:28, Esth. 5:8, 9:13) or are part of an identifying characterization (Exod. 9:18, 10:14, 17:9, Josh. 11:6, I Sam. 19:11, Esth. 5:12), slightly more than half the occurrences are found in appeals/commands or in epitomes similar to those with *hayyôm*, always, as one would expect, in direct discourse as part of a momentous announcement. The appeals/commands with a form of *māḥār* are Exod. 8:25, 19:10, Num. 11:18, 14:25, 16:7, 16, Josh. 7:13, Judg. 19:9, and II Kings 10:6, plus the highly stylized call to battle found in II Chron. 20:16f., "*Māḥār* go down against them. . . . *Māḥār* go out before them while Yahweh is with you." The epitomes, always with the time word foremost, are the following:

> Joshua said to the people, "Sanctify yourselves, for *māḥār* Yahweh will perform wonders in your midst," Josh. 3:5.

> And Yahweh said, "Go up, for *māḥār* I will deliver him into your hand," Judg. 20:28.

> "*Kā'ēt māḥār* I shall send you to someone from the land of Benjamin, and you shall anoint him as leader over my people Israel and he shall deliver my people from the Philistines . . . ," I Sam. 9:16.

> "Thus shall you say to the men of Jabesh-gilead, '*Māḥār* you will have victory, at the heat of the sun'." . . . And the men of Jabesh said, "*Māḥār* we shall come out to you and you shall do to us whatever seems good in your eyes," I Sam. 11:9f.

> ". . . And *māḥār* you and your sons will be with me; moreover, the army of Israel Yahweh will deliver into the hand of the Philistines," I Sam. 28:19.

> And Elisha said, "Hear the word of Yahweh: Thus says Yahweh, '*Kā'ēt māḥār* a bushel of fine flour for a shekel and two bushels of barley for a shekel in the gate of Samaria!' " II Kings 7:1.[4]

> ". . . Let us eat and drink, for *māḥār* we die!" Isa. 22:13.

To this list of epitomes with adverbial *māḥār* we may add such a substantival occurrence as the ritual announcement found in Exod. 32:5, "*Māḥār* is a feast to Yahweh!" (cf. also Exod. 16:25, I Sam. 20:5, 18). Like *hayyôm*, *māḥār* is the name of a day, in this case the day next following today.[5] Like *hayyôm*, *māḥār* is a substantive that functions adverbially. As

---

4. We observe how a redactor's weak repetition in vs. 18 carelessly displaces the time-designative.

5. In point of fact, *bōqer*, which also means "morning," is the prime Hebrew word for "tomorrow." *Māḥār* has come to receive that meaning in the majority of its occurrences, but this must be seen as a specification of its broader and probably more original meaning, "later," "in the future." This original meaning remains in the foreground in Gen. 30:33, where Jacob declares to Laban that his integrity will answer for him *beyôm māḥār*, "in a future day"—certainly not on the day immediately following. The same general meaning comes out in four cult-legislative passages (Exod. 13:14, Deut. 6:20, Josh. 4:6, 21) in which there is the same reference to future children asking their parents for an etiological explanation of an

substantive or as adverb, it designates a today that is stretched out past the coming night into the day that is to follow. The person who announces it can envisage it as though it were today. It lies just over the horizon of time. But when that horizon gets extended, deferred beyond immediate expectation, it becomes *hayyôm hahû'*—"that day," a day out there, beyond man's immediate reach and in the hand of God.

3. Bayyôm hahû' pointing to the coming day

a. Referring to the gnomic-cultic present/future

While *māḥār* is essentially a projection of *hayyôm* into the proximate future, *bayyôm hahû'* refers adverbially to a time that may be as distant from today futuristically as when it lies in the past. It should be obvious at this point in our investigation that futuristic *bayyôm hahû'* can scarcely be understood except on analogy with *bayyôm hahû'* past.

We cannot proceed, however, without first carefully setting aside a small group of passages with *bayyôm hahû'* that are only apparently futuristic. The usage involved here is a gnomic-cultic future, parallel to the gnomic-cultic present observed in Chapter Three. The passages belong to three genres. Representing cult legislation are Exod. 13:8,[6] Lev. 22:30,[7] 27:23,[8] Num. 6:11,[9] and Ezek. 45:22;[10] representing casuistic law is

---

established rite. It also appears, in contrast to *hayyôm*, in Josh. 22:18, 24, 27f., and is probable in Isa. 56:12 and Prov. 27:1. Further treatment of *māḥār* is found in S. J. De Vries, "The Time Word *māḥār* as a Key to Tradition Development," forthcoming in *ZAW*, 87 (1975).

6. See our analysis of *hayyôm hazzeh* in vs. 3, above, pp. 160f. Many levels of composition are reflected in Exod. 13:3-10. Vs. 3 may be an old apodictic law; vs. 4 integrates this redactionally into the narrative context; vss. 5-7 are torah; vss. 8-10 incorporate legislation about instructing the new generation. Editorially, *bayyôm hahû'* refers to the futuristic day of vs. 5, but in terms of the cult legislation it is understood as having continuous effect.

7. K. Elliger, *HAT*, 4, *in loco*, assigns this law for the *zebaḥ tôdâ* to the fourth level of Holiness Code legislation. *Bayyôm hahû'* is foremost in contrast to *'ad bōqer*, "until morning." RSV, "on the same day," brings out the emphatic time element: the eating of the sacrifice must take place on the same day as the killing of it (cf. apodictic law concerning this in Exod. 23:18, 34:25, also the ritual in Exod. 29:34; the law has been modified in Lev. 7:15-18, 19:5-8). The day designated is clearly any and every cultic day when the specified conditions obtain. Cf. the negative prohibition with *beyôm 'eḥād* in vs. 28, with which vss. 29f. have nothing to do.

8. Elliger (*ibid.*, *in loco*) assigns this passage to the *Grundschicht* of this separate law for redeeming vows and tithes. *Bayyôm hahû'* is equivalent to *šenat hayyôbēl*, "the year of the Jubilee" (cf. vs. 24), i.e., the first day of it.

9. This is a late ritual for reconsecrating a Nazirite's head, inserted in vss. 9-12 into priestly legislation for separating the Nazirites. *Bayyôm hahû'* acts as a synchronism, equivalent to *bayyôm haššemînî* ("on the eighth day") in vs. 10.

10. H. Gese, *Der Verfassungsentwurf des Ezechiel* (Tübingen, 1957), pp. 80f., and W. Zimmerli, *BK*, XIII, *in loco*, agree that vs. 21b is an editorial gloss binding 21a and 22ff. Thus *bayyôm hahû'* refers to the fourteenth day of the first month.

Deut. 21:23;[11] representing the wisdom saying is Ps. 146:4.[12] In each passage the time-designative refers to a day that is future only from the vantage point of the lawgiver or wisdom speaker who is prescribing for—or describing—action that regularly occurs in specific situations. That it is also sequential to the action on which it is contingent is less decisive than that it is consistently, predictably future as an enduring and habitual action, belonging to typical human behavior or to the cultus. This does not, therefore, represent a genuine historical future—the future of once-for-all, linear eschatology. It reflects that which is general and cyclical, rather than that which is uniquely significant for its own time and place.

b. Referring to the historical-eschatological future

At the beginning of Chapter Two reference was made to the monograph by P. A. Munch, *The Expression Bajjôm Hahu', Is it an Eschatological Terminus Technicus?*,[13] in which it was argued that in every instance the futuristic time-designative in question means no more than "then," providing a temporal or quasi-temporal link between two specific events. Our criticism of Munch was that he paid only peremptory attention to past references with *bayyôm hahû'*; this criticism should now be enlarged to the point of blaming him for quite ignoring all analogous time-designatives and the Hebraic language of time generally. Be that as it may, it is necessary to state also the positive side of what Munch has accomplished. Certainly Munch's treatment is a responsible and helpful study; it no doubt represents the best scientific evaluation attainable under the canons of its period. We shall have occasion, in what follows, to refer to particulars. Munch was still operating under the limitations of "pure" literary criticism—the kind that was innocent of insights into questions of form- and tradition-history.

Prior to Munch, Hugo Gressmann had been the scholar whose views were the most dominant on the question of the origin of Hebrew eschatology. In his book *Der Messias*, Gressmann had listed *bayyôm hahû'* as a uniquely important technical expression, possessing in itself a specific eschatological meaning.[14] Munch was ready to demonstrate, to the contrary, that *bayyôm hahû'* never possesses an eschatological meaning. Al-

---

11. RSV, "the same day," makes the obvious synchronism between the time of a man's hanging and the time of his burial. See the Gospel accounts of Jesus' crucifixion and burial.
12. Cf. I Mac. 2:63f.
13. P. 57; publication data in Chapter One, n. 37.
14. FRLANT, 43, Göttingen, 1929, pp. 82-84. He cautions, however, against making a linguistic identification with "the day of Yahweh": *"Jener Tag* und *der Tag Jahves* sind sachlich zweifellos identisch; aber ביום ההוא lässt sich nicht als Abkürzung von ביום יהוה verstehen, einem Ausdruck, der uns überhaupt nirgends begegnet und der darum auch nicht direkt mit jener Redewendung zusammenhängen kann" (83).

though Munch has himself received criticism from various quarters,[15] it is this dictum of his that has subsequently shown up in the standard summaries, such as Koehler's *Lexicon* and Jenni-Westermann's new *Theologisch Handwörterbuch zum Alten Testament*. It is now our task to test it against our own comprehensive analysis of the evidence.

(1) Outside the prophetic corpus

Exod. 8:18 [E-22]

There is every reason to believe that Exod. 8:18-19a is a late insertion.[16] An interpolator has used *bayyôm hahû'* to create a synchronism between the coming of the flies and the separation of Goshen, inexplicably equating this time-designative with the more proximate (also unoriginal) *lᵉmāḥār* of vs. 19b.

Deut. 31:17f.

The pericope, Deut. 31:16-22, in which futuristic *bayyôm hahû'* thrice occurs alongside a past *bayyôm hahû'* in vs. 22 and *hayyôm* in vs. 21, has been previously discussed.[17] This passage was identified as a very late insertion; it is an editorial introduction to chap. 32. But vss. 17f., where the three futuristic occurrences of *bayyôm hahû'* are found, are themselves probably a later expansion of vss. 16, 19ff.[18] In vs. 16 Yahweh predicts that Israel will break his covenant, which is specifically the motive for giving chap. 32's song as a witness (vs. 19; cf. 20); vss. 17f. break this sequence by having Yahweh threaten personally to bring the evil that is objectively envisioned in vs. 21, having the people react with a confession of guilt and having Yahweh threaten once more to hide his face. Each of these three elaborations contains *bayyôm hahû'* in unemphatic position; the third occurrence, with the pronoun subject, infinitive, and imperfect, is climactic and conclusive. The occurrences in vs. 17 may be said to provide synchronizing transitions, while the occurrence in vs. 18 is definitely meant to be epitomizing.[19]

---

15. E.g., M. Saebø, *Sacharja 9–14* (cf. Chapter Two, n. 274), pp. 261-76.
16. The theme of setting apart the land of Goshen finds no echo in the statement of the execution of the threat (vs. 20); only the plague on the Egyptians is referred to. Perhaps this is an expansion modeled after 9:4, 26.
17. Pp. 69, 173.
18. As we shall see, in the other passages where past and future *bayyôm hahû'* appear together, the two belong to separate literary strands (I Sam. 3:1ff., I Kings 22:1ff.). This adds the weight of improbability against the original homogeneity of Deut. 31:16-22.
19. "That day" is future from the point of view of Yahweh's speech to Moses; cf. the *hayyôm* of vs. 21 (cf. vs. 27). From the interpolator's point of view it is present or already past, since Moses' "today" is long gone.

I Sam. 3:12

As *bayyôm hahû'* belongs to secondary literary expansions in Exod. 8:18 and Deut. 31:17f., so it does apparently also in I Sam. 3:12, which is especially interesting because it appears to be the very earliest passage where the futuristic use is found. Having previously discussed the function of past *bayyôm hahû'* in I Sam. 3:2, 4:12, and of *hayyôm* in 4:3,[20] we are particularly concerned to know what interconnectedness there may be between them and the time-designative in 3:12, especially since we have here *bayyôm hahû'* future, in contrast to *bayyôm hahû'* past in vs. 1.

We are dealing with a passage that has repeatedly come under discussion.[21] While it cannot be said that any completely satisfying solution to the problem of its origin has yet been offered, Martin Noth has pointed the way, combining tradition and literary criticism in his important study, "Samuel and Silo" (1963). Noth identifies three independent strands of tradition in I Sam. 1–3: the first is the Samuel birth narrative (1:1–2:11, 18-21); the second is the narrative of the wickedness of Eli's sons, leading to the prophecy of the punishment of Eli's house (2:12-17, 22-25, 27-36); the third is the narrative of the revelation to the lad Samuel (all of chap. 3 except vs. 21).[22] Our own analysis of these chapters reveals that chap. 3 presupposes two independent oral narratives, *viz.*, those of Samuel's birth, comprising 1:1-28, 2:11, 19-21, and of the wickedness of Eli's sons, comprising 2:12-17, 22a, 23-25. The narrator of chap. 3 added 2:18, 26 to the first story when he joined it and the second to his own.[23] To the second story a Zadokite polemicist (from the time after David) added 2:22b, 27-36—which, however, was itself further expanded in the time of Josiah.[24]

---

20. Above, pp. 63f., 104f., 194.

21. See the commentaries for the extensive bibliography on these chapters. The older literary analysis represented by W. Caspari, *Die Samuelbücher* (1926), O. Eissfeldt, *Die Komposition der Samuelisbücher* (1931), and I. Hylander, *Der literarische Samuel-Saul Komplex* (1932), has been superseded. A broader methodology is represented in the work of R. P. Knierim, "The Messianic Concept in the First Book of Samuel," *Jesus the Historian*, pp. 20-51, and J. T. Willis, "An Anti-Elide Narrative Tradition from a Prophetic Circle at the Ramah Sanctuary," *JBL*, 90 (1971), 288-308. Among other recent studies we may mention J. Lindblom, "The Political Background of the Shiloh Oracle," SVT, 1 (1953), 78-87; J. Dus, "Die Geburtslegende Samuels I. Sam. 1," *RSO*, 43 (1968), 163-94; and the articles named in the following notes.

22. *VT*, 13 (1963), 390-400. Noth argues that the birth narrative is not a misplaced etiology of Saul (against Hylander, pp. 12f.); its bad pun is understandable as a secondary attempt to explain Samuel's name. It is essentially historical, deriving from the Shiloh shrine in premonarchic times. The second narrative dates from the early post-Solomonic period. The composer-redactor who drew on these two to write chap. 3 intended to legitimize Samuel as a prophet. 3:21 was added after the destruction of the Shiloh shrine (!) to legitimize it by further reference to Samuel's authority.

23. As modern critics agree, 2:1-10 was added in the late monarchic period.

24. A thorough analysis appears in Gunneweg, *Leviten und Priester*, pp. 109-14.

But chap. 3 has also been expanded beyond what was included in the writing of the original redactor-historian. As we have seen, vss. 1, 19-20 (21) are a framework for vss. 2-18; they were added to legitimize Samuel as a prophet—a tradition found elsewhere only in 9:9.[25] Besides this, the Zadokite polemicist added vss. 12-13aα in order to identify the event of chap. 4 as the specific fulfillment of the prophecy in 2:22b, 27-36.[26] The artificiality of this synchronism is evident in that the syntax of 3:11 (deictic particle, pronoun, participle of imminent action) envisages the very near future, while the activity covered by the foremost *bayyôm hahû'* in vs. 12 is spread out in time to at least the polemicist's own date (כל אשר דברתי . . . החל וכלה).

The commonly accepted theory that I Sam. 1–3 is a separate redactional unit, having nothing originally to do with chaps. 4ff., needs serious reconsideration.[27] Not only should we resist the temptation to identify 4:1a as a gloss; we need to observe that, together with 3:11, it specifically ties together the narratives of chap. 3 and chap. 4. "The word of Samuel" referred to in 4:1 is not the prophetic word of 3:19, 21, but the threat of 3:11: Yahweh is "about to do a thing (*dābār*) in Israel" at which every ear shall tingle; before this *dābār* shall be fulfilled in the events of chap. 4, all Israel shall come to know of it.[28] It is called *d^ebar š^emû'ēl*, "the word of Samuel," because the lad Samuel was the vehicle of its revelation (a most noteworthy phenomenon!).

Thus chap. 3, together with chaps. 1 and 2, is only the prelude to chap. 4, which is not the actual beginning of a separate ark legend.[29] One

---

Whether or not Gunneweg is correct in stating that Abiathar and the priests of Nob are secondarily identified with the Elides (I Sam. 22:11), it is altogether probable that our polemicist made this equation. A Zadokite, he was intent on attacking his contemporaries within the family of Abiathar by blaming them for the sins of Eli and his sons. It is important to observe that his polemic was against the Elides as priests, not against Shiloh as a shrine. Since the latter had ceased to function as a worship center, there would be no point in attacking its legitimacy, but there was a need to combat the claims of a rival priesthood. Cf. M. Tsevat's discussion in *HUCA*, 32 (1961), 191-209, and in *JBR*, 32 (1964), 355-58.

25. Cf. I Sam. 15, 28. Since 9:9 has been shown to be probably genuine (see above), these additions may have been made by Benjaminites (Saulides?) to underscore the legitimacy of Saul's designation (cf. 10:6ff., identifying Saul's affinity with the prophets). Cf. M. Newman, "The Prophetic Call of Samuel," Muilenburg Festschrift (1962), pp. 86-97.

26. So already K. Budde, *KHCAT*, 8, *in loco;* H. Gressmann, *SAT*[2], II, 1, *in loco*.

27. See now Willis, "An Anti-Elide Narrative Tradition," whose arguments, in spite of the title, are based less on tradition analysis than on a consideration of redactional procedures.

28. It is easier to explain the Hebrew text, ויהי דבר שמואל לכל ישראל, as original than to explain why the LXX translators would have suppressed it in favor of their own reading, καὶ ἐγενήθη ἐν ταῖς ἡμέραις ἐκείναις. The two evidently represent independent recensions. As it stands, the Hebrew text of 4:1a is intended as the transitional introduction to 2ff.

29. Rost's dictum that I Sam. 4–6, II Sam. 6 constitute a distinct composition has been called into question by such scholars as Vriezen and Dhorme. Our argument

needs to observe that chap. 5 begins with a transitional formula: "When the Philistines captured the ark of God they carried it from Ebenezer to Ashdod, etc.," as though the narrator already had (at least) chap. 4 before him. In spite of the dominance of the ark theme throughout chaps. 5 and 6, in chap. 4 this is secondary and instrumental to the question of the fate of the Elide priesthood, coming to a rising climax in the episodes of Eli's death (vss. 12-18) and the symbolic naming of Phinehas' child (vss. 19-22).[30] In chap. 4 we find, simply, the redactor-historian's conclusion to a complex prediction-fulfillment narrative comprising the core of chaps. 1–4. This is perhaps the earliest example of Israelite historical narrative, being more than mere saga. It was probably oral in form until the insertion of 3:1, 19f. in the early Saulide period. We can only speculate as to who our redactor-historian may have been; evidently it was someone who thought highly of Shiloh and considered its downfall a catastrophe.

I Sam. 8:18

The conclusion of Samuel's remonstration regarding Israel's request for a king (I Sam. 8:11ff.) contains two occurrences of futuristic *bayyôm hahû'*, first, as a synchronism, in a prediction of the people's response ("you will cry out"), then, as an epitome, in a prediction of Yahweh's refusal to heed this response ("will not answer"). This represents a sudden shift in subject following a long tabulation of how the prospective king was to behave. There is every reason to suspect its originality.

A number of scholars have attempted to dissect this pericope, among them Horst Seebaas in his essay, "Traditionsgeschichte von I Sam. 8, 10[17ff.] und 12," published in 1965.[31] Seebaas has identified a very old, authentic tradition in I Sam. 7:2, 5f., 8f., 15-17, 8:1f., 4-7, 10 (= 10:18aα, 19a), 19:22aα, 9, 22b, 10:17, 19b-24, 12:1-6a, 7a, 6bα, 10:25b-27. To this, in his opinion, two traditions hostile to the kingship were added in 8:11-18 and 12:16-25 (the latter is copied from 7:5-12). To a great extent this analysis has benefitted from Artur Weiser's stimulating study, *Samuel, seine geschichtliche Aufgabe und religiöse Bedeutung* (1962).[32] Weiser had argued with considerable cogency that chap. 8 goes back to a reliable old tradition deriving from the circle of Samuel's followers, also that the "royal

---

does not preclude the possibility—rather, likelihood—that this material came to be used as a *hieros logos* for the Jerusalem shrine; it only challenges the view that this would have been a special, independent composition.

30. Vs. 21b is an explanatory (but superfluous) gloss. After naming the child (21a), the mother declares in an epitomizing statement with the perfect the main upshot of the entire narrative as seen from the fate of the Shiloh shrine, גלה כבוד מישראל, "Gone into captivity is glory from Israel," substantiating this in a following *kî*-clause concerning the capture of the ark.

31. *ZAW*, 77 (1965), 286-96. Cf. also F. Langlamet, *RB*, 77 (1970), 161ff.; J. T. Willis, *op. cit.*

32. Pp. 25-45.

law" of vss. 11ff. does not reflect conditions under the later monarchy but those of the contemporaneous Canaanite city-states.[33]

We need to observe the affinities between 8:18 and Deut. 31:17f., analyzed above, where a similar series of divine and human consequences (expressed with the perfect consecutive and imperfect, as here) are determined for some vague future day of apostasy. The same excessive fondness for the expression *bayyôm hahû'* was evident there, being used three times within two verses. There can be little doubt but that it is the Deuteronomist who has reworked our chapter. The internal structure[34] and affinities with Deut. 31:17f. (also 4:26ff., 8:19ff.) make it likely that this redactor is responsible for vss. 7b-10, 18. "That day"—the day of the people's outcry and Yahweh's nonanswer—is no particular day of accession, not even every day of accession, but the final day of Israel's judgment, when the results of kingly rule shall have become fully manifest.[35] Thus the double *bayyôm hahû'* creates a synchronism that is entirely artificial.

I Kings 13:3

The occurrence of *bayyôm hahû'* in I Kings 13:3 has generally been interpreted as a past reference, with the "man of God" as subject rather than Josiah. This demands that the verb at the beginning of the verse (ונתן) be read as a simple perfect with conjunctive waw.[36] But this seems highly unlikely in light of the fact that two imperfect consecutives have been used for narrating past events in the immediately preceding context. Actually, it

---

33. Against the view of Noth and others. Cf. I. Mendelsohn in *BASOR*, 143 (1956), 17-22.
34. Thrice in this pericope Yahweh commands Samuel to "hearken to the voice of the people" (vss. 7, 9, 22). The third time this is entirely positive, with no restriction or expression of censure. It is probably original; so also 7a. The Deuteronomist added the *kî*-clause in 7b to introduce his long insertion about Israel's history of apostasy. This includes a new injunction to hearken to the people (9a), followed by a command to warn them solemnly (העד תעיד בהם) about the "ways" of the king in an emphatic *kî*-clause. Vs. 10, introduced by ויאמר, is the Deuteronomist's transition to Samuel's original address beginning in vs. 11, likewise introduced by ויאמר. Weiser's judgment that Samuel was not actually giving Israel a "king like all the nations" is hardly supported by our analysis. In fact, Samuel does give them a king—not the one deplored in vs. 18 but the one described in vss. 11-17. This is the only logical way to resolve the contradiction between vss. 7b, 18 on the one hand and vss. 7a, 9, 22 on the other hand. Samuel is displeased, praying to Yahweh to back him up; but Yahweh indicates that he should accede. Nevertheless, Samuel first informs Israel of what having a king will entail, hoping they will be dissuaded. When they refuse, he again asks Yahweh and receives the answer as at first. But Samuel does not give in even then, sending them away. This story was certainly not originally antimonarchic in principle, representing as it did both Yahweh and the people as in favor of a king (these are the two essential factors in the legitimation of a king; cf. 10:24). Thus the tradition records that only the institution of the *šōpᵉṭîm* stood against it.
35. Observing the incongruity of time, the LXX offers a plural in vs. 8b.
36. So LXX[AN], Syr., Vg., modern translations such as RSV, NEB, and most commentators. This is also the understanding of the late addition in vs. 5.

seems reasonably certain that not only the identifying words, יאשיהו שמו,
but the entirety of vss. 1b, 2aβbα has been inserted into the text by the
deuteronomistic redactor. The last four words of vs. 2, not represented in
the text of LXX^A, may be a still later addition. The original narrative did
not report the actual words spoken by the "man of God" from Judah,
recording only that he "cried" against the altar in Bethel on the authority
of Yahweh. Vs. 3, on its part, is hardly a continuation of the original
narration in vs. 1a. The reasons are the following: (1)ונתן, which would
have to be taken as a simple perfect with waw if the connection were
original, breaks the syntactical sequence from the imperfect consecutive in vs.
2aα; (2) there is incongruity in that the sign is quoted in full while the
prophet's threat remains unreported; (3) in spite of vs. 5, the narrative
sequel makes nothing of the sign, mentioning only the prophetic word (cf.
the climactic declaration in vs. 32). Hence vs. 3 is best taken as the
Deuteronomist's continuation from vs. 2aβbα.

But did this redactor perhaps intend vs. 1's "man of God" as the
subject of ונתן? This is clearly the interpretation taken by vs. 5, which will
have to be identified as a postdeuteronomistic addition if we judge otherwise. If the "man of God" were the intended subject, *bayyôm hahû'* would
have to be past, and this would involve the Deuteronomist in the above-
observed syntactical inconcinnity, since we have ascribed ויאמר to him.
There might be a way out of this difficulty if we were to omit the
last-mentioned verb, following LXX^B. A formidable objection, however, is
that *bayyôm hahû'* is without explanation on the assumption that the
Deuteronomist is using it with reference to the past. If vs. 3 were an
addition to vs. 2, we could understand it as an introductory synchronizer,
but as part of the same stratum it is functionless. No one would need to be
told that the prophesying and the giving of the sign occurred on the same
day—this would be abundantly evident from the narrative development—
nor is there evidence that the time formula is used for dating.

The only likely solution, then, is to take ונתן as a futuristic perfect
consecutive, with Josiah as the subject. The Deuteronomist has filled out
the text by putting words into the mouth of the "man of God" that predict
the birth and drastic action of this king. He goes on to state that Josiah will
justify his action by appealing to a sign that was once spoken by Yahweh.[37] Even though the sign (the altar splitting and pouring out its fat)
may seem only remotely associated with Josiah's projected deed (sacrificing
the priests on it), the Deuteronomist apparently intended the former as a
symbolic explanation and justification of the latter. Thus vs. 3, with
futuristic *bayyôm hahû'*, mysteriously epitomizes the "reform" of Josiah.

---

37. Where the quotation came from is unclear, but it evidently arose between the
time of the legend and the Dtr interpretation. Our analysis is partly indebted to M.
Noth, *BK*, IX, *in loco*. For נתן מופת in the meaning, "announce or designate a sign,"
see Exod. 7:9, Deut. 13:2, II Chron. 32:24.

I Kings 22:25, II Chron. 18:24

Coming to the final occurrence of futuristic *bayyôm hahû'* outside the prophetic corpus (I Kings 22:25 = II Chron. 18:24), we discover that it appears in the same pericope as a past *bayyôm hahû'* (II Kings 22:35 = II Chron. 18:34).[38] Inasmuch as, in the only other passages where *bayyôm hahû'* future and *bayyôm hahû'* past are found together (Deut. 31:16-22, I Sam. 3:1ff.), these belong each to separate literary sources, it would be remarkable—and surely significant—if both were original here. Our analysis reveals, however, that they belong each to different sources, and that is significant too.

Until recently, little question was raised about the unity of I Kings 22:1-38, once the deuteronomistic insertions and later glosses (1-2a, 28b, 35bβ, 38) were removed. Ernst Würthwein, following Schwally and Volz,[39] has now taken a number of internal inconsistencies within the predeuteronomistic narrative as evidence for a complex process of development, involving a basic tale about the attack of the two kings against Ramoth-gilead plus a prophet story with three distinct levels of accretion.[40] The story of the kings, originally independent of the prophet story, comprises only vss. 2b-4 and 29-37; it is no genuine historical account but a "marchenhaft" tale aimed as polemic against the pride and stupidity of those who rely on deceit. Within the Micaiah account, only vss. 5-9, 13-17 (18?), 26-28 are original; this is an old narrative about how a prophet's words were put to the test by locking him in prison. This received a revision with the addition of vss. 10-12, 24f., explicating the manner and ideology of the *Heilspropheten.* Somewhat later a third layer was added; it consists of vss. 19-22, with a redactional adaptation in vs. 23, and its purpose is to interject the point of view of the *Unheilspropheten*, who laid no claim to the Spirit but professed to enjoy access to the secret council of Yahweh.[41]

Würthwein's analysis places the past *bayyôm hahû'* of vs. 35 into a source separate from that of the futuristic *bayyôm hahû'* of vs. 25, but one is hard put to discern any significant function for the latter on the basis of his theory that it concludes a revision. Micaiah seems here to have the last word—but to what purpose? It is supposed to be Zedekiah's viewpoint that has shaped this stage of supplementation.

Although Würthwein is surely justified in emphasizing the unhomogeneity of this passage, his reconstruction fails to solve a number of problems. First, he leaves the kings' disguising of themselves in vss. 30f.

---

38. See above, pp. 112f.
39. F. Schwally, "Zur Quellenkritik der historischen Bücher," *ZAW*, 12 (1892), 159-61; P. Volz, *Der Geist Gottes* (1910), p. 20. See also J. Gray, comm., *in loco*, who hints at internal growth without specifying the process.
40. "Zur Komposition von I Reg. 22$^{1-38}$," Rost Festschrift (1967), pp. 245-54.
41. Cf. later attempts to solve the problem of the *Unheilspropheten* in Jer. 23:9-32, 27-28, Ezek. 12:21—13:23, Lam. 2:14, 4:13.

unmotivated and ascribes the tragic outcome to accident, rather than to a divine purpose. More serious is the objection that his theory assumes a highly complex process of supplementation—unlikely, to say the least. Even more telling is the objection that, while making much of internal inconsistencies,[42] he glosses over some that are the most glaring. Specifically, he fails to make anything of the fact that vs. 12 is just a rephrasing of the prophets' advice in vs. 6; he does not observe that the king summons a *sārîs* in vs. 9, instructing him to fetch Micaiah, whereas it is an unidentified person known as *hammal'āk*, "the messenger," who performs this duty in vs. 13; he overlooks the inexplicable inconsistency between Micaiah's oath in vs. 14 to repeat "whatever Yahweh will say to me"[43] and his lie about what Yahweh actually said, recorded in vs. 15.

We see in the predeuteronomistic material two originally separate tales about a certain Micaiah, put together by a redactor because of their similarity in theme.[44] The earlier of these tales probably belonged to a prophet-legend cycle, dating perhaps from the ninth century B.C. It is, in fact, a prediction-fulfillment narrative, proclaiming the power of Yahweh to realize in historical event the word of his true prophet. It has three scenes: the occasion (1b-4a, 4bβ-9), the confrontation (15-18, 26-28a), and the fulfillment (29-35bα, 36-37). An unnamed king of Israel, having summoned Jehoshaphat, informs his "servants" of a serious political-military problem, then invites Jehoshaphat to join him in a common effort to solve it.[45] Since an attack on the city involved must be carried out under the

---

42. In addition to the ones noted below, we must observe the following: Jehoshaphat's speech is twice introduced, with inconsistent replies (4b, 5); vss. 10f. shift the scene from some unspecified place (the palace?) to the *gōren*, making a superfluous reference to the prophets' action (cf. vs. 6); there is constant fluctuation in the prophets' address to the king(s) (6, 11f., 15); unaccountably the subject changes in vs. 19 (RSV supplies the name); after one vision oracle with *rā'îtî* (17), Micaiah gives a second (19ff.); Micaiah is twice rebuked/punished (24, 26f.) and twice delivers climactic oracles (25, 28).

43. Micaiah does not use the familiar herald formula with the perfect of אמר. His formula is plainly futuristic, containing a locution that is common to all the other futuristic passages (אשר with the imperfect of אמר, plus a divine subject including the name אלהים with a first-personal pronominal suffix), Exod. 8:23, Deut. 5:27, Jer. 42:20. (The imperfect of אמר in present reference occurs in Isa. 1:11, 18, 33:10, 40:1, 25, 41:21 *bis*, 66:9, Ps. 12:6.) Hence Micaiah has not yet received Yahweh's message; it comes in the form of the vision's interpretation, vs. 23.

44. The redactor's work is seen particularly in vs. 4bα, normalizing our text to II Kings 3:7; in the pluralization of the king of vs. 10; in the superfluous oracle of vs. 12b and the "messenger's" advice to Micaiah in vs. 13, seeking to explain the inconsistency involved in combining vs. 14 with vs. 15; perhaps also in the pluralization of the verbs in the king's question of vs. 15 (this may be a later textual change; cf. the VSS, Chronicles). The redactor may have added ויאמר in vs. 19. He filled out Yahweh's question in vs. 20aβ to harmonize the two narratives.

45. As suggested in the previous note, II Kings 3:7 has influenced our text. But the framework of II Kings 3 is late and artificial; it introduces Jehosphaphat only to serve as the pious counterpart to an Israelite king so wicked that Elisha will not prophesy for him (vs. 14). This is blatant pro-Judahite polemic. Nevertheless, it has colored the earlier text of I Kings 22, as in the gloss of vs. 4bα. Since, according

theory of the holy war, Jehoshaphat demands first a favoring oracle; not satisfied with the unanimous encouragement of the four hundred prophets, he gets the king of Israel to summon Micaiah, who always prophesies evil. When this man arrives he first answers the king's question as the others did, but when rebuked, reports a gloomy vision he has seen; it implies that though Israel will return home $b^e\check{s}\bar{a}l\hat{o}m$, "in peace,"[46] their master/ shepherd will not do so (vs. 17). The king of Israel confirms that this applies to him, but seeks to avoid its fulfillment by giving instructions for the imprisonment of the prophet under conditions of privation "until I come in peace" (vs. 27). This leads, then, to the climactic declaration of the entire narrative (vs. 28a), in which the ultimate issue is stated, whether the prophet's word or the king's action is to be the stronger: "If you return in peace, Yahweh has not spoken by me." But the king cannot frustrate the prediction since it is in fact Yahweh's true word. The king's elaborate effort to disguise himself is thwarted by a seeming accident that is verily Yahweh's own deed; propped up to seem alive, he bleeds to death. At the end, the army flees safely home, but the king is brought home only to be buried.

The second tale is a controversy narrative, probably dating from the eighth century at the earliest—to judge from its affinities with Isa. 6. Its schema is simpler than that of the prediction-fulfillment narrative. Vss. 10-12a describe the occasion, then comes a confrontation scene in which Micaiah reports a vision that he has seen (14, 19-23) and engages in a climactic diatribe with Zedekiah (24f.).

The introductory participial clauses in vs. 10 make it quite clear that this is actually the beginning of a new story. The scene is set at the *gōren* opposite the gate of Samaria; the (two) king(s) is (are) sitting, arrayed; the prophets are prophesying. Zedekiah ben Chenaanah performs and then interprets a symbolic action; promising victory over the Syrians (not expressly at Ramoth-gilead since 12b is a redactional harmonization), his word is confirmed by the others who are there, except for Micaiah, who swears that he will speak an independent message from Yahweh. It is in the form of a vision oracle. Opposed to the throne(s) of the (two) king(s) at the gate of Samaria is the throne of Yahweh; opposed to the entourage of favoring prophets is the entire host of heaven (כל צבא השמים) standing on Yahweh's right and on his left. The issue is plainly, Which of these two courts has the greater authority? Obviously Yahweh's. And how does one account for the false favoring oracle? What Micaiah has seen gives the answer: Yahweh has sent out a lying spirit (רוח שקר) to deceive the

---

to the original text, it is the king of Israel who declares that he and Jehoshaphat are allies, the supposition that the latter was a vassal to Ahab (accepted as actual fact in almost all the histories) stands in jeopardy. Cf. J. D. Shenkel, *Chronology and Recensional Development in the Greek Text of Kings* (1968), pp. 106f.

46. On the phrase, "return in peace," see now W. Eisenbeis, *Die Wurzel šlm im Alten Testament* (BZAW, 113, Berlin, 1969), especially pp. 116-20, "Excursus on Micaiah ben Imlah, I Reg. 22:13-28."

prophets and entice Ahab.[47]   All this is plainly interpreted in vs. 23, concluding with the negative judgment, "Yahweh has spoken evil about you." This understandably provokes Zedekiah into a rebuke and challenge. He questions how Micaiah can claim to have the same "spirit of Yahweh" that he has. Micaiah's concluding word gives his rival the only answer that can be given (vs. 25): "Behold, you will see (participle) *bayyôm hahû'*, when (אשר) you shall go into an innermost chamber (חדר בחדר) to hide yourself."[48]

The *'ašer*-clause is not to be taken as defining this future day, which is already made definite by the demonstrative adjective. It is not a question of whether Zedekiah will hide himself; this is certain, an unavoidable consequence of the coming of "that day." To what then does "that day" refer? There can be no other answer than: the day of the prophecy's fulfillment. If Yahweh has spoken evil concerning Ahab it will surely come to pass. He has "a day" for it. No man knows when it will be. The event or events that will fill it are still hidden. But Yahweh has "that day" prepared. Zedekiah shall surely see it, and when he does, he will try to hide.

Several things are remarkable about this occurrence of futuristic *bayyôm hahû'*: it is the only narrative occurrence that is closely associated with the prophets; it is, thus far, the only occurrence that belongs to original material; it is the only one that does not provide some kind of synchronism. In terms of formal function, it produces an identifying characterization. There can be no doubt, however, that Micaiah's characterization of Zedekiah is intended as an epitome of the entire controversy between these two kinds of prophets.

As we proceed to an examination of futuristic *bayyôm hahû'* within the prophetic corpus, we shall find several passages in which this time-designative seems to be used as absolutely as here. We need to keep this passage constantly in mind because the usage it reveals has every claim to having been the model on which the classical prophetic pattern was based.

(2) Within the prophetic corpus

Remaining to claim our attention are one hundred and one passages in the Hebrew text containing a futuristic *bayyôm hahû'*, plus one other probable reading from the Septuagint. It will not be necessary, however, to treat each of these with equal attention. We need to be detained only momentarily by a few that are glosses and to review in brief order a large number—the majority—that function in a stereotyped way to provide an

---

47. Cf. Jer. 20:7, Ezek. 14:9. "Ahab" is probably original in this narrative; it is more likely that the designation has been changed in vs. 10, where normalization has been redactionally introduced, than here, where there is no suggestion of a double title.
48. Cf. Isa. 26:20.

editorial transition to a new pericope. Our major analytical energies will be expended on a small minority that function as transitional or concluding formulae, for here we shall discover the closest affinities to the phenomena that have heretofore come under scrutiny and have proven to be so significant. Rather than list the futuristic passages *seriatim*, it will prove advantageous to treat them according to this order of importance.

(a) Glosses

To begin, we set aside those passages where *bayyôm hahû'*, alone or with additional words, reveals itself to be one sort or another of scribal gloss. These have little significance for our study because the connection they make existed only in the mind of the scribes who inserted them.

The first gloss is in Isa. 4:1, where the LXX has not read *bayyôm hahû'*, which disturbs the meter in the portrayal of judgment, 3:25–4:1. More complex is the problem of Jer. 39:16, where *bayyôm hahû'* appears at the end of the verse, preceding a verb and another *bayyôm hahû'* in vs. 17; the latter is genuine and will be discussed below, but the former is almost certainly a gloss, for the following reasons: (1) the LXX omits the entirety of vs. 16b, (2) the double *bayyôm hahû'* is meaningless, (3) a strained translation is required to make any sense, and (4) Yahweh is the subject in vss. 16a and 17a, making a change of subject in 16b unlikely.[49]

Next come a pair of doublets, Jer. 48:41 = 49:22 and Jer. 49:26 = 50:30. There can be little doubt but that 48:41b is a gloss from 49:22 since it disturbs the meter and is lacking in the LXX;[50] thus 49:22 is the original passage containing the eagle metaphor, though here the expression *bayyôm hahû'* disturbs the meter and must be identified as a gloss. This expression has probably been added as a gloss in both 49:26 and 50:30, to judge from the LXX, which makes only slight alterations in the Hebrew text of 50:30

---

49. There has been a great variety of opinion about this passage. Munch held *bayyôm hahû'* to be original in both verses. P. Hyatt, *IB, in loco,* calls the whole section fictional and assigns it to the D school. A. Weiser, *ATD,* 21, *in loco,* assigning it to Baruch, binds 16b to 17 by translating: "Und wenn sie an jenem Tage vor deinen Augen eintreffen, 17 dann werde ich dich an jenem Tage retten. . . ." Rudolph, *HAT,* 12, *in loco,* follows Cornill in identifying 16b as a dittograph from 17. He recognizes this as a genuine Baruch fragment, originally belonging after 38:13, *contra* Mowinckel, who assigns it to his "C" source, and Duhm, Cornill, and others, who say it is a late insertion. A more thorough discussion is to be found in Gunther Wanke's monograph, *Untersuchungen zur sogenannten Baruchschrift* (BZAW, 122, Berlin, 1971), pp. 110-12, where it is argued that (1) 39:15-18 fits nowhere in the context; (2) it is compiled of allusions to a variety of other passages; and (3) it shows acquaintance with chaps. 38 and 45 in their present form. The conclusion is that the section is un-Jeremianic. Cf. also O. Eissfeldt, "Baruchs Anteil an Jeremia 38,28b—40,6," *OA,* 4 (1965), 31-34; F. Planas, "Jeremías y Abdemelec," *CB,* 120/21 (1954), 302f.

50. Against the view of J. Bright in *AB,* 21, *in loco,* to the effect that the LXX has simply omitted it here in conformity with its general habit of omitting repeated phrases.

(LXX, 27:30), identical to that of 49:26 (LXX, 30:15), but in both passages omits *bayyôm hahû'*.

Bayyôm hahû' has been added as a gloss also in Ezek. 24:26, immediately before an original *bayyôm hahû'* in vs. 27. The central problem of Ezekiel's location hangs on the analysis of these two verses. They give the impression that the prophet heard the report of Jerusalem's fall on the very day when it fell, the *b⁰yôm qaḥtî*, etc., of vs. 25 and the *bayyôm hahû*'s of 26f. producing an emphatic synchronism. This of course conflicts with the chronology assumed in 33:21f. The best solution is to identify the time-designative in vs. 26 as a gloss, as we have done; together with the difficult את הפליט of vs. 27, it represents a late attempt to interpret 33:21f. and harmonize it with this passage. We shall comment further on this passage when we discuss vs. 27.

Finally, we list as a gloss the expression *bayyôm hahû'* at the end of the first distich in Zeph. 1:9, where it disturbs the meter and produces an awkward syntactical construction.

(b) Incorporating supplements

This brings us to the very sizable number of passages in which *bayyôm hahû'* serves as an editorial or redactional transition to a body of added material, short or long. In most cases it appears to be an original part of the expansion, though at times the added material may have had an independent existence and was attached to its context by the use of *bayyôm hahû'* and perhaps other connectives.

Very often, but not necessarily always, the time-designative stands foremost at the beginning of the expansion, and when it does, it may be preceded by the perfect-consecutive form, *w⁰hāyâ*, "and it shall come to pass." It produces an artificial synchronism between the event of the original material and the event of the expansion, like *bā 'ēt hahî', b⁰yāmîm hāhēm*, and similar connectives. In this respect it is identical in function to *bayyôm hahû'* introducing supplementary material in past pericopes. The only major difference is that it is used with relatively far greater frequency in futuristic than in past pericopes, sixty-nine times out of one hundred two (almost seventy percent), as compared with fifteen out of eighty-eight (slightly more than one sixth). This does not include five out of nine of the futuristic occurrences outside the prophetic corpus (Exod. 8:18, Deut. 31:17(1), I Sam. 3:12, 8:18(1), and I Kings 13:3). We see here reflected the special susceptibility of futuristic material to the need and opportunity for revision. The relative frequency of this editorial connective has, of course, not escaped the notice of the commentators; as a matter of fact, many of them (notably Duhm) have taken it as the self-evident mark of secondary material.

It will not suffice, however, simply to mark off this sizable group of

passages as secondary. We need seriously to inquire whether the supplementers in question have had some kind of special temporal ideology. Is
bayyôm hahû' a mechanical connective, joining two bodies of unrelated
material, or does the redactor-editor have a particular purpose? We would
guess the latter, since otherwise it could have been omitted entirely, as in
the case with the vast majority of the artificial connections that have been
made within the prophetic corpus. But does it merely mean "then," as
Munch has so confidently affirmed? We may get a clue to the answer as we
pay special attention to the kinds of prophetic material that have been
joined together by the use of *bayyôm hahû'*.

Arranging the occurrences in a logical or systematic order, we observe
certain significant affinities among the passages in question.

I. Judgment against Israel, expanding judgment against Israel:

Isa. 2:20. A foremost *bayyôm hahû'* introduces an epexegetical
expansion (20f.) to the fragment that precedes it (19); to the motif of
fleeing into the holes and caves on Yahweh's day of terror (here as
judgment for Israel), the expansion adds the deuteronomistic theme
of casting away idols (cf. vs. 18).[51]

Isa. 3:18. A foremost *bayyôm hahû'* incorporates a secondary word
of censure against female love of adornment (vss. 18-23) into a
probably Isaianic invective-threat against the pride of the women of
Jerusalem, vss. 16ff.; *wᵉhāyâ* is used as a terminal connective to vs.
24. This expansion could be very late.

Isa. 5:30. The time-designative is set back in order to give emphasis to
וינהם, producing a pun on the root נהם in vs. 29; the expansion
enlarges the scene of Assyria's coming attack on Judah into a scene of
cosmic judgment.[52]

Isa. 7:18, 20, 23. Foremost *wᵉhāyâ bayyôm hahû'* in vss. 18, 23 and
simple *bayyôm hahû'* in vs. 20 introduce three scenes of military
disaster, expanding the Isaianic image of "such days as have not come
since the day that Ephraim departed from Judah" (vs. 17); although

---

51. Cf. H. Wildberger, *BK*, X/2, *in loco*. Regarding the time-designatives Wildberger
depends heavily on Munch and A. Lefèvre, "L'expression 'en ce jour-là' dans le
Livre d'Isaie," Robert Festschrift (1956), pp. 174-86. Regarding the origin of the
day of Yahweh, he follows von Rad. Isa. 2:20 has probably been borrowed from
31:7, where *bayyôm hahû'* has a more-than-editorial function (see below).
52. Lefèvre, p. 175, identifies the supplementer as one of Isaiah's immediate
disciples. His methodology is not exact enough, however, to justify his conclusion
that the disciple is using *bayyôm hahû'*, like his master, "pour marquer le point
culminant de la catastrophe." Duhm is wrong in interpreting vs. 30 as a salvation
saying; it is judgment on judgment. Procksch is scarcely justified in removing only
bayyôm hahû', since the ill-fitting pun marks the whole verse as secondary (so most
critics).

the last is apparently from a disciple, the first two were probably spoken by Isaiah himself and added editorially.[53]

Hos. 1:5. To Hosea's original threat, blaming the house of Jehu for "the blood of Jezreel" (vs. 4), an initial *wᵉhāyâ bayyôm hahû'* attaches a later, geographical explanation of the Jezreel symbolism, itself a judgment threat against Israel.[54]

Amos 8:9, 13. To the vision of the summer fruit, with its accompanying oracle of judgment (vss. 1-3), a disciple-redactor has added a series of oracles (4-6, 7f., 9f., 13f.; 11f. is probably deuteronomistic), all predicting judgment on Israel and epexegetical of the original oracle. In vs. 9 an initial *wᵉhāyâ bayyôm hahû'* depicts the judgment as "a bitter day" (*yôm mar*); in vs. 13 foremost *bayyôm hahû'* introduces the ironic image of the youth who swear by the "life" of false gods, yet faint for thirst.[55]

Mic. 2:4. To a complete Mican oracle, including a denunciation and a threat introduced by *lākēn* and the herald formula (vss. 1-3), a redactor-disciple added a taunt song with an epexegetical interpretation introduced by another *lākēn* (4f.). The addition begins with *bayyôm hahû'*; it seeks to explicate the *'ēt rā'â* of vs. 3 by identifying the land-grabbing of 1f. as the cause for the loss of land predicted in 4f.[56]

Zeph. 1:10, 12. To an original day-of-Yahweh oracle in vss. 7-9, employing the imagery of a sacrificial feast, a disciple-redactor has attached a number of epexegetical interpretations; not only are these identified as occurring on the same day, but they are joined as a series

---

53. So Wildberger. Cf. W. McKane, "The Interpretation of Isaiah VII 14-25," *VT*, 17 (1967), 208-19. Lefèvre, p. 177, argues that all is from Isaiah. Vss. 21f. are a salvation saying added by the later glossator of vs. 15 (see below).

54. As H. W. Wolff observes (*BK*, XIV/1, p. 8), the original Hoseanic connective is *kî* (vss. 4, 6, 9). W. Rudolph, *KAT*, XIII/1, pp. 5f., admits that vs. 5 was added when chaps. 1-3 were put together, but ascribes it to Hosea himself. A. Weiser, *ATD*, 24/1⁴, *in loco*, accepts Hosean authorship. Munch identifies it as a later insertion, with most of the older critics; so also M. Buss, *The Prophetic Word of Hosea, A Morphological Study* (BZAW, 111, Berlin, 1969), p. 7, omitting *wᵉhāyâ bayyôm hahû'* as a gloss without explaining why it should have been inserted.

55. Many commentators agree that these supplements are originally from Amos himself. Vs. 9a is in anacrusis and redactional; the antecedent of "it" (f.) in 10c is probably ארץ in vs. 9, since *yôm* is masculine in gender. In vss. 13f. parallelism is difficult to identify except in the words of those who do the swearing. Since the rest is apparently prose, there can be no valid reason for eliminating *bayyôm hahû'* as a gloss.

56. Although Micah himself may have at some time spoken vss. 4f., there is little likelihood that Weiser (comm., *in loco*) and J. T. Willis, "The Structure, Setting, and Interrelationships of the Pericopes in the Book of Micah" (dissertation, Vanderbilt, 1967), pp. 255-58, are right in seeing this all as an original unity. While vss. 1-3 are poetry, the introduction to the taunt song is in prose.

of characterizations of the dread day predicted in the original oracle (punishment for certain groups, the sounds of battle). The redactor makes the connection explicit with *w*^e*hāyâ bayyôm hahû'* (plus the oracle formula) at the beginning of vs. 10 and—according to the probably original reading of the LXX—of vs. 12.[57]

We are able to conclude that when a day of judgment on Israel was expanded by mention of new acts of judgment "on that day," it was almost without exception the immediate followers of one of the preexilic prophets (one of the *Unheilspropheten*) who were at work. The new word may have come from the prophet or from a disciple, but was attached as though both were one and the same, even as the predicted day of judgment was described as one and the same.

II. Judgment against the nations, expanding judgment against the nations:

Isa. 17:9. Using initial *bayyôm hahû'*, an interpolator of uncertain date has expanded (vss. 9-11) Isaianic judgments against Syria and (northern) Israel (vss. 1-3, 4-6)—the latter being viewed as an enemy— in terms of an additional prediction of desolation, including in his expansion an independent judgment oracle that may be itself Isaianic.[58]

Isa. 19:16, 19. To a probably non-Isaianic oracle against Egypt (vss. 1-15), at least two late interpolators have attached words of judgment and of salvation, making constant use of (usually) foremost *bayyôm hahû'*. The words of judgment, such as they are, probably reflect the conditions of the Achemenid period: Yahweh will make the Egyptians fear Judah (16f.) and an altar to him will be established in their land (19a).[59]

---

57. MT: *w*^e*hāyâ bā'ēt hahî'*. This may have resulted by contamination from 3:19, 20, where a different redactor/editor has been at work. We have seen that *bayyôm hahû'* is a gloss in vs. 9. In vs. 10 *bayyôm hahû'* with a following noun-clause is like an identifying characterization, except that the oracle separates these elements syntactically.

58. The pronominal suffix to the subject apparently refers to the Syria of vss. 1ff. There is no need to emend the text as in the LXX (cf. BH³ mg); so most commentators. The critics have been divided concerning the unity of vss. 1-11, some defending it (Duhm, Kissane), others denying it (Munch, Procksch, Scott, Lefèvre). To us it seems that 1-3, 4-6 are Isaianic, being joined by the catchword *k*^e*bôd*, and that 7-8 is a late, universalistic (so *contra* Kissane) prose comment, put here because of the idolatry theme mentioned in vs. 10. Vs. 9, with *kî* in vs. 10, is the redactional introduction to an indictment (10a) and threat (10b-11).

59. Vs. 19b is a gloss. On the salvation words of vss. 18, 21, 23, 24f., see below. They date from the Ptolemaic period, when Judah was administratively part of Egypt. The critical positions regarding this chapter range from a defense of Isaianic unity (Kissane) to analysis into late fragments (e.g., Procksch, assigning 16f. to the time of Cambyses, 18-22 to the late Persian era, 23-25 to the third century B.C.).

Isa. 23:15. Isaiah himself is the probable author of an oracle against Tyre in vss. 1-14, but there seems to be little question but that $w^e h \bar{a} y \hat{a}$ *bayyôm hahû'* in vs. 15 introduces a very late (after 333) supplement taunting her as a forgotten harlot (vss. 15f.).[60]

Jer. 25:33. Into the middle of a Jeremianic poem of judgment against all the nations, including the announcement (vs. 32) and portrayal (vss. 34-38) of coming desolation, a late prose interpolator has inserted an image of battle devastation, thrusting the thematic word ($hal^e l \hat{e}$ *YHWH*, "Yahweh's casualties") forward before the time-designative, following the stereotyped $w^e h \bar{a} y \hat{a}$.[61]

Ezek. 30:9. Ezekiel's judgment oracle against Egypt (vss. 6-9) was expanded in the Persian period to include anguish among the Kushites as the latter hear of Yahweh's day against Egypt.[62]

Here we discover that, though all the original oracles of judgment against the nations are probably from the prophets after whom the respective books have been named, their expansions with *bayyôm hahû'* are too late to come from their immediate schools. This simply reflects the fact that Israel/Judah continued in periods remote from the days of the great prophets to hate those who were once their enemies, continued to predict a day of divine judgment for them.

III. Judgment against Israel, expanding judgment against the nations:

Isa. 17:4. It is because vss. 1-3 have identified Syria and northern Israel that a second Isaianic judgment word, attached to it by foremost $w^e h \bar{a} y \hat{a}$ *bayyôm hahû'* (vss. 4-6), speaks of famine in Israel as judgment on an enemy.[63]

---

60. Vss. 17f. are still later. Regarding the much-confused text of vs. 14 the commentators are much at variance. It should be carefully observed, however, that vs. 14 is like a refrain to vs. 1. Cf. Jer. 25:11ff., 29:10.

61. The locution $hal^e l \hat{e}$ *YHWH* occurs elsewhere only in a late exilic passage, Isa. 66:16. The LXX has ἐν ἡμέρᾳ κυρίου, which represents a combination ($b^e yôm$ *YHWH*) found nowhere in the Hebrew Bible. The section, Jer. 25:15-37, is the introduction to the collection of foreign-nation oracles in the LXX text, displaced in the MT to chaps. 46–51. Most critics sever vs. 33 from its context (so Rudolph, Bright, Hyatt). Against Weiser (*ATD*, 20/21, *in loco*), who argues for the unity of this pericope, it may be observed that: (1) vs. 33 is prose while vss. 32, 34ff. are poetic; (2) *bayyôm hahû'* has no function in its context except as an artificial synchronism, being precluded by "the days of your slaughter, etc.," in vs. 34; (3) vs. 33 predicts lamenting while vss. 34ff. call for wailing, etc.; (4) the judgment of vs. 33 is emphatically universal, but that of 34ff. is only against the "shepherds."

62. The redactor intends $b^e yôm$ *miṣrayim*, "on the day of Egypt," to be understood as explicative of *yôm YHWH*, "the day of Yahweh," in vs. 3. On the text, cf. BH[3] mg. Initial *bayyôm hahû'* introduces this expansion.

63. See above on vs. 9.

Ideologically, this is scarcely a separate category. Israel, Yahweh's own nation, becomes his enemy when it acts contrary to his will. During the Syro-Ephraimite attack upon Judah (II Kings 16:5ff.; cf. Isa. 7:1ff.), the Judahite prophet lumps his fellow Yahwists with the heathen.

IV. Salvation, expanding salvation:

Isa. 11:10f. The Isaianic hymn of messianic restoration in 11:1-9, portraying a scene of idyllic peace, has received two expansions beginning with *w^ehāyâ bayyôm hahû'*; the first of these (vs. 10) predicts the universal glory of "the root of Jesse," while the second (vss. 11-16) predicts the return of the diaspora and Yahweh's universal rule. The noun-clause in vs. 10, followed by a verbal clause, has the form of an identifying characterization. Both additions are from the late postexilic period.[64]

Isa. 12:1, 4. To the Isaian collection, chaps. 1–11 (ending in a salvation saying), a late postexilic editor has attached two hymns of declarative praise; the first of these gives personal testimony (vss. 1f.), while the second calls on Zion to praise Yahweh for his great deeds (4-6). All of 1aα and 3-4aαא, including the twice repeated "and you shall say *bayyôm hahû'*," is redactional.[65]

Isa. 25:9. To the great eschatological poem of Isa. 24:21-23, 25:6-8, a stirring hymn of gratitude has been attached as epexegetical interpretation (vss. 9-10a). The awkwardness with which the connection has been made (the Hebrew text has *w^e'āmar bayyôm hahû'*, "and one shall say on that day") is probable testimony to a relatively late date for this editorial work.[66]

Hos. 2:18, 20, 23 [E-16, 18, 21]. To Hosea's plaintive poem of restoring love (vss. 4-17), a redactor-disciple has attached a series of epexegetical additions concerning the ideal husband/baal relationship

---

64. So most commentators. Vs. 10 borrows from 11:1, 5:26, 11:12, 2:3; vss. 11-16 borrow from 10:14-27 (cf. O. Kaiser, *ATD*, 17, *in loco*). Even Kissane, defending vs. 10 as Isaianic, admits that vss. 11f. are later than Isaiah's lifetime. Although the critics are divided as to whether vss. 1-9 are original, the recent tendency is toward accepting them as from Isaiah himself.

65. Probably 1f. was added first, then 3ff., because of the change from the singular "you" to the plural "you." (On the significance of this variation see Wildberger, *BK*, X, 6, 480.) The LXX, followed by Kissane, normalizes by making both singular. The hymns are similar to such late psalms as Pss. 118, 138, and 145 (cf. Gray, *ICC, in loco*).

66. LXX and 1QIs^a normalize to 12:1, 4 by reading the verb as second-personal. Because the hymn is in strict meter (3:3, 3:3, 3:2), the redactional introduction has to be seen in anacrusis and as probably secondary. Cf. M.-L. Henry, *Glaubenskrise und Glaubensbewährung in den Dichtungen der Jesajaapokalypse* (BWANT, 86, Stuttgart, 1967), pp. 184f., opting for the likelihood that the hymn was expressly composed as a reflex to vss. 6-8, and that the connective is merely "schematisch."

(18f.), the ideal covenant/marriage (20-22), and ideal responsiveness (23-25). To introduce the first and third he employed a foremost $w^e h\bar{a}y\hat{a}$ *bayyôm hahû'* (as in 1-5), but his intent to emphasize the covenant theme led him to defer the time-designative in the second.[67]

Joel 4:18 [E-3:18]. It is a question whether Joel himself could have composed the poem of refuge in Zion on the day of Yahweh found in vss. 14-17, but surely it was a late editor who used $w^e h\bar{a}y\hat{a}$ *bayyôm hahû'* to attach to it the concluding poem of vengeance and paradisaical bliss in vss. 18-21.[68]

Mic. 4:6. An exilic poem of restoration for Zion (vss. 1-4) attached to Micah's prophecies received an early expansion promising return for the downcast exiles (vss. 6-8), introduced by initial *bayyôm hahû'* and the oracle formula.[69]

Mic. 5:9 [E-10]. An original Mican judgment oracle against the nations (vss. 9aβ-13), threatening destruction on all that has made the enemy strong, has been editorially connected by $w^e h\bar{a}y\hat{a}$ *bayyôm hahû'* and the oracle formula to a probably exilic poem of salvation for Israel, vss. 6-8. The ideology of both is strikingly similar: salvation for Israel is seen in terms of its power—or Yahweh's power—to defeat its enemies.[70]

Zeph. 3:11. A disciple of Zephaniah, living in the exile, composed a salvation oracle (vss. 9a, 11aaɔ-13) proclaiming an end to haughtiness and deceitfulness; into this a postexilic interpolator inserted a lame

---

67. The likelihood is that the same redactor is responsible for all four occurrences of *bayyôm hahû'* in Hosea. He is the disciple who was responsible for putting together chaps. 1–3 (cf. Wolff, *BK*, XIV/1, pp. 57ff.). As for the prophet, in the view of the disciple "that day" could be both a day of judgment and one of salvation. On the text of vs. 23 (cf. BH³ mg) see A. Guillaume in *JTS*, 15 (1964), 57f. Without explanation, Buss (*Prophetic Word of Hosea, in loco*) takes $w^e h\bar{a}y\hat{a}$ *bayyôm hahû'* in vs. 18 as secondary, along with 17a, 19-20, 23-25.

68. Wolff, *BK*, XIV/2, *in loco*, points out that Joel's own eschatological transition is either *kî hinnēh bayyāmîm hāhēmmâ*, "for behold in those days" (4:1), or $w^e h\bar{a}y\hat{a}$ *'ah^{a}rê kēn*, "and it shall happen afterward" (3:1).

69. Most commentators agree that vss. 6ff. do not belong to the preceding. Because 1ff. comes to a clear conclusion in vs. 4, vs. 5 is a separate late insertion. The redactional introduction to 6ff. is in anacrusis; there is no need to rearrange the poem, with Smith, *ICC, in loco*. As elsewhere in Micah, Willis, "Structure . . . of the Pericopes," pp. 216-18, sees here the purposeful arrangement of overall redaction.

70. The introductory rubric fits the 3:2 meter but falls outside the pattern of couplet parallelism. Noting the kinship to Isa. 2:6-8, most commentators are ready to see this addition as preexilic in origin—probably from Micah himself—even though it was added to the text in the exilic period. So O. Eissfeldt, *Einleitung* (2nd ed., 1956), pp. 499, 502f; cf. also Willis, *op. cit.*, pp. 114-16, 229f. Vs. 14 disturbs both the thought and meter of this expansion, hence is revealed as a still later addition.

expansion about the coming of the remnant to worship Yahweh (vss. 9b-11aα‬ℵ). The latter evidently ended his expansion with *bayyôm hahû'* because of the emphatic time-designative (*kî 'āz*, "for then") in vss. 9 and 11.[71]

Zeph. 3:16. Two victory hymns (14f., 16-18), dating perhaps from the time of Zephaniah himself, have been artificially joined together by the phrase, *bayyôm hahû' yē'āmēr lîrûšālayim*, "in that day it shall be said to (about) Jerusalem"; both call on Jerusalem to rejoice in the victory that Yahweh has wrought.[72]

Zech. 2:15 [E-11]. An original summons to rejoice over Yahweh's return to Zion (vss. 14, 16) has received in vs. 15 a late prose expansion in the spirit of Zech. 8:20-23, proclaiming the coming of many nations as a condition of this return; *bayyôm hahû'* is placed laconically at the end of its clause, conceding the emphatic place to the thematic words, the verb and subject.[73]

Zech. 3:10. To a secondary salvation oracle, acclaiming Joshua as high priest (vss. 8f.), a redactor's initial *bayyôm hahû'* plus the oracle formula attaches the last in a series of additions to this chapter, an idyllic image of blissful harmony (vs. 10). Here our time-designative seems equivalent to *bᵉyôm 'eḥād* at the end of vs. 9, bringing the oracle of 8ff. to an epitomizing conclusion.[74]

Wherever salvation oracles have been secondarily enlarged by new salvation oracles or hymns, using *bayyôm hahû'*, the likelihood of literary affinity is remote. Only in Hosea does a prophet's own disciple seem to have been at work. Otherwise, expansions to the original writings of the preexilic prophets were made by editors living many years later. However, when we come to the postexilic materials (Joel, Zechariah), the refocusing

---

71. Cf. K. Elliger, *ATD*, 25, *in loco*. The two time-designatives would scarcely come from the same writer. 9ff. is itself an expansion of an original prophecy of Zephaniah (3:1-8).

72. The phrase is probably from the editor who arranged the book into three sections. The LXX reads *bā'ēt hahî'*, probably through contamination from the late insertions, vss. 19, 20. We see in Zephaniah the tendency to supplant *bayyôm hahû'* with *bā'ēt hahî'*; perhaps in later times the latter expression became more popular for introducing eschatological additions because the vision of one particular historical day of fulfillment became sublimated to the idea of an era of divine action.

73. Vs. 14 appears to be epexegetical to 2:5-9 (so Elliger; also K. Galling, *Studien zur Geschichte Israels im persischen Zeitalter*, Tübingen, 1964, pp. 116, 123); vs. 16 belongs with it in spite of the change to the third person, thus vs. 14 is a citation while vs. 16 is comment on the citation. A date during the building of the temple, proposed by Galling, is probably correct. Cf. also W. Eichrodt, "Vom Symbol zum Typos. Ein Beitrag zur Sacharja-Exegese," *TZ*, 13 (1957), 509-22; Albert Petitjean, *Les oracles du Proto-Zacharie, un programme de restauration pour la communauté juive après l'exil* (EtB, Paris-Louvain, 1969), pp. 136-43.

74. Cf. Petitjean, pp. 186-206.

of salvation imagery seems to have occurred in close affinity to the context of its original promulgation.

V. Salvation, expanding judgment against the nations:

Isa. 10:20. An editor has used foremost *wᵉhāyâ bayyôm hahû'* to expand Isaiah's invective (vss. 12-15) and threat (vss. 16-19) against Assyria into a promise of return for the remnant of Israel (vss. 20-23); besides following the catchword principle, attaching an expansion with *šᵉ'ār yiśrā'ēl*, "the remnant of Israel," to a pericope with *šᵉ'ār 'ēṣ*, "the remnant of trees," he was likely attracted by the epitomizing *bᵉyôm 'ehāḏ*, "on one/a certain day," in vs. 17.[75]

Isa. 17:7. To a collection of judgment oracles (vss. 1ff., 9ff.) a late prose addition (vss. 7f.) promises a universal turning to Yahweh; the connective is an initial *bayyôm hahû'*.

Isa. 19:18, 21, 23, 24. A second addition to an oracle against Egypt (vss. 1-15), pro-Egyptian in attitude and probably dating from the Ptolemaic period, uses *bayyôm hahû'* (foremost except in vs. 21) to introduce predictions that five Egyptian cities will be proselytized to Yahweh, Yahweh will be the Egyptians' covenant God, there will be common communication and worship from Egypt to "Assyria," and Israel, Egypt, and "Assyria" will share alike in being a blessing to all the earth. Surely this must be the most astoundingly universalistic image of peace in all the Old Testament!

Isa. 24:21. An eschatological poem of the day of Yahweh in vss. 1-20 receives an expansion in the form of a poem of apocalyptic bliss (24:21-23, 25:6-8) predicting Yahweh's universal rule, removing even death, for the sake of his people. Judging from the fact that *wᵉhāyâ bayyôm hahû'* is the introductory formula, as only in 27:12f. elsewhere in the "Little Apocalypse" section, another editor is probably at work here than in 25:9, 26:1, 27:2.[76]

Isa. 26:1. A threat against Moab (25:10b-12), including a prediction that Yahweh will destroy its fortifications, has been expanded, with

---

75. Cf. Zech. 3:9; there is no reason to prefer the Septuagintal text, which reads *bayyôm hahû'* at the beginning of vs. 18. Our editor intended vss. 20-23 as a salvation saying, though it is ambivalent in itself, decreeing judgment as well as salvation; it may be Isaianic, while the editor's work is late. On vs. 20 Lefèvre writes (p. 178): "Il donne une explication du reste. . . , il annonce le succès de l'oeuvre de Yahweh décute par le vs. 16-19; c'est le rôle classique de notre formule."

76. See Henry, *Glaubenskrise*, pp. 148-79; cf. O. Plöger, *Theokratie und Eschatologie* (WMANT, 2, Neukirchen, 1959), pp. 69-79; G. W. Anderson, "Isaiah XXIV-XXVII Reconsidered," *VT*, 9 (1963), 118-26. The earliest LXX witnesses do not read the time-designative in vs. 21, having rather a different text; cf. Gray, *ICC*, p. 424.

bayyôm hahû' as a transition, into a hymnic celebration of refuge in Zion, made certain by Yahweh's humbling of "the lofty city," i.e., Moab (26:1-6).

Isa. 27:2. An eschatological poem of the day of Yahweh (26:20–27:1) has had attached to it in an unusually artificial manner (*bayyôm hahû'* is in anacrusis, hence is no part of the noun-clause) a song of divine protection for the "pleasant vineyard," Israel (27:2-5).[77]

Ezek. 29:21. An Ezekielian judgment oracle against Egypt, announcing that Egypt will be given to Nebuchadrezzar in compensation for his fruitless toil before the walls of Tyre (vss. 17-20), has been expanded, with foremost *bayyôm hahû'* as connective, into a salvation oracle combining prominent Ezekielian themes.[78]

Since judgment on Israel's enemies means salvation for Israel, it is no surprise to find this kind of expansion. As with salvation oracles that have been expanded with salvation sayings, the new material proves to be late editorial in those cases where the original oracles were relatively early (Isa. 10, 17, 19), while it may have come from within the same school where the original oracles were relatively late (Isa. 24–27, Ezek. 29).

VI. Expansions to early apocalyptic:

Ezek. 38:10, 18, 39:11. To Ezekiel's original prophecies there has been added an apocalyptic oracle against the archetypal enemy, Gog (38:1-9, 39:1-5, 17-20).[79] This has been expanded in as many as eight places, and not surprisingly four of the eight expansions have *bayyôm hahû'*, three of them with *weḥāyâ* at the beginning. In 38:10 this introduces a postexilic addition in which Yahweh taunts Gog for his subjective motivation in devising the still-future attack on Yah-

---

77. This is probably very late material; cf. Henry, *Glaubenskrise*, pp. 195-98; see also L. Alonso-Schökel, "La cancion de la viña," *EE*, 34 (1960), 767-74. BSHmg recommends that we read *we'āmar* before the time-designative, as in 25:9; but the phrase may have become such a stereotype that in this case a verb was simply omitted (so Dillmann; cf. Gray, *ICC*, p. 454). To place *bayyôm hahû'* at the end of vs. 1 (BH²) would involve an unprecedented doubling of this expression at the beginning and end of a poetic unit.

78. The expansion may be from Ezekiel's school since it repeats the prophet's words in altered form. Inasmuch as it is unique, it may have been added to 17ff. (the latest dated oracle) before it was transferred here by the editor who put Ezekiel's book into substantially its present form. There is a difference among the commentators as to whether vs. 21 is messianic.

79. The most helpful analysis is that of Zimmerli in *BK*, XIII/2, *in loco*. The occurrences of *bayyôm hahû'* in 38:14 and 19 will be discussed below. The acute sensitivity of one of the late interpolators is seen in 38:17, where three separate past time-designatives are put into equivalence (*beyāmîm qadmônîm*, "in former days"; *bayyāmîm hahēm*, "in those days"; *šānîm*, "years").

weh's people (vss. 10-13), who are yet in exile from the point of view of Ezekiel's own prophecies but are here seen as resettled in the land. In 38:18 it introduces a late baroque elaboration of Gog's judgment scene, in which Yahweh summons every sort of terror against him (vss. 18-23). And in 29:11 it introduces a late reflection on how the land will be purified following the great slaughter (vss. 11-16).

Zech. 12:3, 6, 8 *bis*, 9, 11, 13:1, 2, 4. Of the ten occurrences of *bayyôm hahû'* in Zech. 12:1–13:6, nine introduce new predictions. The core was evidently the postexilic *Jahwerede* in 12:2a, appointing Jerusalem to be "a cup of reeling to all the peoples round about." Three groups of expansions became attached to this (12:3-8, 12:9–13:1, 13:2-6); each began with $w^e h\bar{a}y\hat{a}$ *bayyôm hahû'* and a new speech by Yahweh, the first of which (12:2-4a) predicted disaster on those who will attack Jerusalem, the second (12:9f.), defeat for the nations and repentance in Jerusalem, and the third (13:2f.), the end of idol-worship and false prophecy. To each of these expansions new material came to be added, sometimes in the form of a speech by Yahweh but generally in the speech of the prophet; not always, but usually, these new expansions begin with a foremost *bayyôm hahû'* (12:6, 8a, 11, 13:1), in two cases with preceding $w^e h\bar{a}y\hat{a}$ (12:8b, 13:4).[80] Here is evidence of the ever expanding power of the apocalyptic vision. There was no limit to what Yahweh could do on his supreme and final day.

Zech. 14:4, 6, 8, 9, 13, 20. Of the seven occurrences of *bayyôm hahû'* in Zech. 14, all but one (vs. 21) introduce new predictions. If Magne Saebø's analysis is correct,[81] an original prediction in vss. 1-3, to the effect that on the day of Yahweh Jerusalem will be rescued from defeat, has been expanded by successive stages. First were two accretions introduced by $w^e h\bar{a}y\hat{a}$ *bayyôm hahû'*, both elaborating the holy-war imagery: vss. 6, 7b (cooperating natural elements; cf. Josh. 10:12ff.), and vss. 13f. (great panic; cf. Judg. 7:21f., etc.). Later came several additions enlarging the scope of the theophany and

---

80. 12:8b begins a new expansion with the verb, subject, temporal expression, and comparative phrase (cf. 9:16); there is no valid reason to remove *bayyôm hahû'* (so BH[3] mg, most commentators). For the tradition history of Zech. 12:1-8, see H.-M. Lutz, *Jahwe, Jerusalem und die Völker* (WMANT, 27, Neukirchen, 1968), pp. 11-19. The best formal analysis is that of Saebø (*Sacharja 9–14*, pp. 264-76), who has greatly advanced our understanding of this perplexing chapter by his identification of 12:3, 12:9, and 13:2 as the beginnings of separate blocks of tradition.

81. *Op. cit.*, pp. 282-309. Saebø goes against the consensus (Plöger, Lutz, Lamarche, *et al.*), which tends to see only two rival traditions at work in this chapter. The commentators generally deal arbitrarily with the various occurrences of *bayyôm hahû'*; e.g., Elliger, *ATD*, 25, *in loco*, removes it from vs. 4 as a gloss, with only meager textual support. One LXX manuscript reads *bayyôm hahû'* in vs. 3.

reflecting the influence of Ezekiel's temple vision: vss. 4f. (Yahweh on the Mount of Olives) and vss. 8, 10aα, 11 (living waters from Jerusalem, the land laid out in an ideal pattern); vs. 4 has *bayyôm hahû'* following the verb, while vs. 8 begins with *wᵉhāyâ bayyôm hahû'* (cf. 7a, *wᵉhāyâ yôm 'eḥād*). A third stage is represented mainly by fragments reflecting a priestly interest and point of view: vs. 9 (universal rule, monotheism), vs. 19aβb (exaltation of Jerusalem), vs. 7a (one single day), vss. 12 and 15 (plague as a holy-war weapon), vss. 16-19 (plague on the nations who do not worship Yahweh), and vss. 20f. (absolute holiness in Jerusalem); here only one of the new fragments, vss. 20f., is introduced by the time-designative, and it is probably the latest addition. In this passage so many diverse interests have been at work that a diffused and even conflicting pattern results. The last great day of Yahweh has been crammed with everybody's dream and stretched into an era of endless bliss.

The apocalyptic vision with *bayyôm hahû'* may be seen as an extension of the late prophetic tendency to interpret the day of judgment on the nations as a day of joy and salvation for Israel. Here is the old holy-war motif with a vengeance. Everything tends to be absolutized. There is no more judgment on Israel, only blessing. But of course this is an image that remains only as a transcendentalized ideal; no such day could ever appear literally on the scene of actual history.

VII. Salvation, expanding judgment on Israel:

Isa. 4:2. The Isaianic oracles of judgment in chap. 3 have been counteracted by what appears to be a late image of bliss in 4:2-6; commencing with *bayyôm hahû'*, this predicts glory for Yahweh's *ṣemaḥ*, cleansing, and the cloud of Yahweh's presence within Jerusalem.[82]

Isa. 7:21. To the scenes of judgment on Israel in Isa. 7, images of salvation have been added in vss. 15 and 21f., in the latter section with foremost *wᵉhāyâ bayyôm hahû'* in imitation of the other later additions to the prophet's oracle (18, 20, 23). The interpolator's ambition was modest: he wished only to announce survival for some in the midst of disaster.

Isa. 27:12f. To an exilic lament over the fallen city (vss. 7-11), a

---

82. Cf. J. G. Baldwin, "Ṣemaḥ as a Technical Term in the Prophets," *VT*, 14 (1964), 93-97. Though some critics argue for Isaianic authorship at least in vs. 2 (Eissfeldt, *Einleitung*, 3rd ed. 1964, p. 426; Lefèvre, "L'expression 'en ce jour-là'," p. 177), those who follow Duhm in identifying it as late have everything on their side (so Wildberger, *BK*, X/2, *in loco*, suggesting that 3-5a expanded vs. 2, 5b-6 expanded 3-5a).

supplementer has added two salvation sayings concerning the return of the diaspora, vss. 12 and 13, introducing each with the customary *wᵉhāyâ bayyôm hahû'*.[83]

Isa. 28:5. An early follower expanded Isaiah's oracle of judgment (vss. 1-4) against "the drunkards of Ephraim" (seen as Israel, or as an enemy?) into a prediction of Yahweh's perfect rule (vss. 5f), introducing this with *bayyôm hahû'*.[84]

Jer. 30:8. An editor living probably late in the exile made a very pertinent, but especially drastic emendation to Jeremiah's moving portrayal of judgment against Israel in vss. 4-7. Jeremiah had graphically described every face turned pale and every man grasping his loins as if in labor, exclaiming, "Woe, for great is that day (*hayyôm hahû'*), there is none like it! And a time of distress (*'ēt ṣārâ*) shall it be for Jacob: and from it shall anyone be saved?"[85] This is a dramatic epitome, coming at a crashing climax, crystallizing all his dread concerning his people's future. But in a time of hope someone dared to predict the opposite; using foremost *wᵉhāyâ bayyôm hahû'*, our editor made a collage of earlier salvation themes to predict restoration and renewed service to Yahweh and his king (vss. 8f.). The day that had begun in disaster—now stretched out over many years—would continue in bliss.[86]

Amos 9:11. The last genuine oracle of Amos (9:9f.) decreed the death of "all the sinners of my people." Probably in the exile, a redactor-supplementer corrected this bitter image to the extent of

---

83. Cf. Henry, *Glaubenskrise*, pp. 192-94. *Contra* Munch, these verses are not poetic in form. Duhm's argument that they constitute the proper conclusion of the Isaiah apocalypse is countered by the consideration that they do not concern its major theme. They are editorially akin to 11:10ff., 19:16ff. (cf. Scott, *IB, in loco*).
84. *Wᵉhāyâ* would be out of place because the main verb is from היה. Though some defend the unity of vss. 1-6 (Kissane, Lefèvre), the longer meter and the catchword *'ᵉteret* show that vss. 5f. are secondary (so Duhm, Gray, Munch, Scott, *et al.*).
85. On irony in vss. 5-7 see W. Holladay in *JBL*, 81 (1962), 53f. Some critics, among them Holladay, connect these verses to 10f., but they probably constituted a separate oracle.
86. The epitome with *hayyôm hahû'* in the original verses makes it impossible for *bayyôm hahû'*, etc., to be its genuine continuation (*contra* Weiser, *ATD*, 21, *in loco*). Vss. 8f. borrow from Isa. 10:27, Jer. 2:20, 5:19, Hos. 3:5, Ezek. 34:23 (cf. Rudolph, *HAT*, 12, *in loco*). It is significant that this kind of expansion occurs in the so-called "Book of Consolation," chaps. 30, 31, regarding which S. Herrmann writes (*Heilserwartung*, p. 218): "In den Kern der . . . Heilssprüche in Jer. 30/31 schieben sich andere ein, die zu einem Teil ihren sekundären Charakter sogleich verraten. . . . 30,8-9 [ist] ein Wort gegen falsche Gottesverehrung und eine Davidverheissung; Gott und David soll paritätisch gedient werden—eine in dieser Form sehr knappe, wenig differenzierte Ausdrucksweise, die aber deutlich ein Reflektieren über das Verhältnis von Gott und König verrät, wie es in der deuteronomistischen Literatur seine Parallelen hat." Although a major concern of this expansion was indeed to express the ideal God-king relationship, its major concern was unmistakably to counteract the prophet's grim portrayal of Israel/Judah's fate.

predicting the restoration of the Davidic house and victory over Israel's enemies (vss. 11f.), attaching this to the judgment oracle with initial *bayyôm hahû'* (cf. the paradisaical portrayal in vss. 13-15, introduced by *wᵉhinnēh yāmîm bā'îm*, "and behold days are coming," with the oracle formula).[87]

Although some of Isaiah's original oracles of judgment were apparently corrected within the century after he lived (Isa. 4, 7, 28), the oracles from the Little Apocalypse, Jeremiah, and Amos were corrected during or after the exile. The hope of seeing Israel's fortunes reversed "on that day" lived on from age to age.

(c) Transitional formulae

We are ready now to examine a small group of futuristic passages in which *bayyôm hahû'* provides a transition within a given block of material deriving from one particular source. Analogous use in past reference was seen to have been restricted to synchronisms and sequences (see Table 1). In future reference it is impossible to know whether a synchronism or a sequence is intended; perhaps the Hebrew eschatologists did not distinguish logically between them.

Isa. 3:7

The Isaianic judgment poem of 3:1-9 has three clearly distinct elements: (1) threat, vss. 1-5; (2) an illustrative scene, vss. 6f.; (3) statement of the results of sin (= invective), vss. 8f. Both the second and the third elements are introduced by *kî*, which may mean "for" in vs. 6 as well as in vs. 9.[88] In any event, vs. 6 is a kind of protasis to vs. 7, asserting the condition under which the speaker of vs. 7 is moved to say what he says. Therefore, the "that day" of vs. 7 is qualified by the conditions of vs. 6, according to which anyone possessing a mantle in the midst of chaos will be chosen as a leader. Equally, however, "that day" is qualified by the vehement refusal of such a person to be a leader. The syntax is different here from the customary form by which secondary materials have been introduced; i.e., the time-designative is allowed to follow the unemphatic verb in normal order, introducing here a quotation, as in Isa. 12:1, 4, 20:6, 25:9. This is characteristic of transitional and concluding formulae, which almost never have *bayyôm hahû'* in foremost position.

---

87. Though some still defend the originality of these supplements (so Ward), the imagery and ideology are unmistakably exilic.
88. Cf. Wildberger, *BK*, X, 120, identifying this passage as Isaianic and from a time in Ahaz' reign when anarchy was impending. We have here a typical example of the ironic "kleine Szenen" (Procksch) that characterize Isaiah's early prophecies; cf. 4:1.

Isa. 22:20, 25

Isa. 22:15-25 is of peculiar interest not only because it represents one of the very few examples from within the prophetic corpus of the private oracle, but also because it illustrates beautifully the process of expansive redaction within a given prophetic tradition. Although the unity of this oracle is still defended (Lefèvre), everything favors the argument of Duhm, Munch, Gray, and others, that vss. 19-23 and vss. 24f. constitute two successive supplements. Vss. 15-18 was an oracle delivered by Isaiah to Shebna; it contains the prophetic commission (15), an accusatory question = invective (16), and a threat (17f.).[89] The very severe threat (exile,death) is mitigated as Yahweh's speech continues in the first expansion (the punishment being reduced to deposition from office); this expansion is concerned, however, not with Shebna but with Shebna's successor, correlating the former's downfall by use of $w^e h\bar{a}y\hat{a}$ *bayyôm hahû'* with the empowering of the latter. But apparently things did not go as well with Eliakim as had been expected; a second supplementer was obliged to change the favoring peg image of vs. 23 into a negative metaphor, correlating the hanging of a weight of trivialities with the giving way of this peg and the "cutting off" of that burden. In this second expansion, which is in effect a new judgment oracle, an artificial synchronism is created by foremost *bayyôm hahû'*, followed by the oracle formula.

Isa. 29:18

The next occurrence of *bayyôm hahû'* in a transitional position is within a salvation pericope belonging to the Second Isaiah tradition (so Duhm, Gray, Scott, Munch, and others, *contra* Kissane, Lefèvre). In Isa. 29:17-24, a rhetorical question introduces the salvation theme by reference to nature (17); the poet shifts from this, using *bayyôm hahû'* after the verb, to a spectacle of the marvelous transformation of four representative classes of the oppressed (18f.). A parenthesis (20f.) introduced by *kî* depicts the judgment of oppressors (= invective). This leads to the concluding strophe (22-24), introduced by *lākēn* and an expanded herald formula, in which salvation is put within a specific covenant context. Because of the time-designative at the beginning of the pericope, *'ôd m^e'aṭ miz'ār*, "only a little longer," the action introduced by *bayyôm hahû'* lies plainly in the very near future.

Isa. 30:23

Another salvation saying containing transitional *bayyôm hahû'* is Isa. 30:23-26. Here the time-designative is entirely unemphatic, following, as it

---

89. Cf. C. Westermann, *Grundformen der prophetische Rede* (BEvT, 31, Munich, 2nd ed. 1964), pp. 101ff.

does, the verb and subject and preceding the object, which, because of its unusual separation from the verb, receives special stress. Formally *bayyôm hahû'* is only a synchronizer, yet it is given special poignancy because it is plainly equivalent to *yôm hereg rab*, "the day of great slaughter" (vs. 25). The highly complex intermingling of judgment and salvation metaphors may seem to argue in favor of those who prefer a late, rather than early, date for this pericope.[90]

Jer. 39:17

In Jer. 39:16 *bayyôm hahû'* belongs to a gloss, but in vs. 17 it is an original transition within a redactional expansion.[91] This is a private salvation oracle for Ebed-melech: Yahweh tells him that the evil word against the city will be fulfilled (16); the perfect-consecutive verb, followed by *bayyôm hahû'* and the oracle formula, instructs him that he will nonetheless be delivered.

Ezek. 24:27

An almost identical situation pertains in Ezek. 24:25ff., where *bayyôm hahû'* is first part of a gloss (vs. 26), then provides a transition to a new element; also, the entire pericope is redactionally secondary.[92] Here, however, the transition has *bayyôm hahû'* foremost in its clause in order to make an emphatic synchronism between vss. 25 and 27. The day of Jerusalem's fall (not the day of the fugitive's arrival) will be the day when the prophet's mouth is opened. There can be no doubt but that, from the redactor's point of view, this coincidence of occurrences is the most symbolic in the entire book.

Ezek. 38:14, 19

We have seen that *wᵉhāyâ bayyôm hahû'* introduces expansions in Ezek. 38:10, 18, 39:11.[93] At 38:14-16 an interpolator uses the form of divine address to recapitulate vss. 1-9. Yahweh speaks this time directly to Gog, predicting the latter's coming and his own purpose—which is that the nations may know him and that his holiness may be vindicated (16). The two time-designatives, *bayyôm hahû'* in vs. 14 (equivalent to *bᵉšebet ʿammî yiśrāʾēl lābeṭaḥ*, "when my people Israel dwell safely") and *bᵉ'aḥᵃrît hayyāmîm* ("in the latter days," a reduction of *bᵉ'aḥᵃrît haššānîm*, "in the

---

90. The commentators disagree widely, but even Munch opts for Isaianic authorship. It is clear that vss. 18-33 are redactionally secondary to vss. 1-17, whose severe judgment they seek to counteract.
91. See above, p. 296.
92. See above, p. 297.
93. Pp. 306f.

latter years," vs. 8) in vs. 16, are intended as equivalents, contrasting Gog's intent and action with Yahweh's intent and action ("I will bring you against my land").[94]

A similar expansion in `38:18-23, introduced by *wᵉhāyâ bayyôm hahû'*, has Yahweh declare in the form of an oath (*'im lō'*) that *bayyôm hahû'* there shall be a great shaking in the cosmos. The time is the same as that of vs. 17: the time of Yahweh's wrath, the time of all the other catastrophes of this awful day.

Zech. 6:10

Since Wellhausen, the first four words of Zech. 6:10b, *ûbā'tâ 'attâ bayyôm hahû'*, "and go you on that day," have generally been regarded as a gloss, but it is more probable that the word following this, a second *ûbā'tâ*, is secondary, having come into the text through dittography.[95] It is impossible to explain why the time-designative would have intruded as a gloss, hence we are obliged to interpret it as an original synchronizer. The synchronism it makes between the command to take what the returned exiles have brought (made more specific in vs. 11) and the command to go to Josiah's house is, in fact, an emphatic one, with special stress on the acting subject. The prophet is to go: he is to go on the very day he takes. *Bayyôm hahû'* expresses an accentuated urgency and heightened enthusiasm in the action that is about to take place. Evidently the time could not be fixed as *hayyôm* or *māḥār*, but it must have been in the very immediate future.[96]

Conclusion

Although transitional occurrences of futuristic *bayyôm hahû'* appear in secondary pericopes (Isa. 22:20, 25, 29:18, 30:23, Jer. 39:17, Ezek.

---

94. In point of fact, all of 14b-16a, introduced by the interrogative negative (*hᵃlô'*) before *bayyôm hahû'* (cf. Obad. 8), is nothing but a series of temporal and circumstantial clauses leading up to the main clause (16b) introduced by *bᵉ'aḥᵃrît hayyāmîm*. *Bayyôm hahû'* of course makes a synchronism with the event of the original oracle, vss. 38:1ff. The fact that it can be equivalent to *bᵉ'aḥᵃrît hayyāmîm* shows how loosely apocalyptic had come to employ the concept of time and historical event.

95. This word does not appear in the LXX, hence is regarded by F. Horst in *HAT*, 14, *in loco*, and by Petitjean in *Les oracles du Proto-Zacharie*, pp. 271-79, as a gloss. Regarding the final form of the very confused text in vss. 9-15, cf. Petitjean, pp. 302f. On its purpose and composition, see K. Galling, *Studien zur Geschichte Israels im persischen Zeitalter* (Tübingen, 1964), pp. 121-23.

96. If Galling (*loc. cit.*) is right in identifying 1:7 as the original introduction to 6:9-15, we have a precise date for the revelation to the prophet. His response must have followed immediately afterward. The date (24 XI, 2 Darius) is not inconsistent with that of Hag. 2:10, 20 (24 IX, 2 Darius), which introduces an oracle (vss. 21-23) in which Zerubbabel's investiture is predicted for *hayyôm hahû'* in the very near future. It is conceivable that Zechariah may have intended an innuendo on his colleague's striking oracle (see below on this passage).

24:27, 38:14, 19) far more often than in original pericopes (Isa. 3:7, Zech. 6:10), this fact seems to have no special significance. We are struck by two characteristics of this group of passages: (1) the time-designative produces a synchronism, often emphatic, and (2) the syntax generally thrusts the time-designative backward from the initial position typical of passages where it is used as an editorial or redactional connective.

(d) Concluding formulae

And now we arrive at our very last group of raw data: the passages that have a futuristic *bayyôm hahû'* in the conclusion. As with *bayyôm hahû'* past, a strong preference for the epitomizing function asserts itself.

Isa. 2:11, 17

It has already been seen that the second chapter of Isaiah is a compilation of diverse fragments, including vss. 20f., a deuteronomistically tinged day-of-Yahweh saying introduced by an editorial *bayyôm hahû'*.[97] One of the elements that has a strong claim to Isaianic authorship is the day-of-Yahweh poem in vss. 12-17, terminating with virtually the identical concluding words of vss. 10-11, including *bayyôm hahû'* at the very end. Both in vs. 11 and in vs. 17, *bayyôm hahû'* falls within the metrical pattern, hence there can be no thought of its being secondary.[98]

The function of this final *bayyôm hahû'* is seen most clearly in vss. 12-17. Powerful in its unified impact, this dramatic poem of universal judgment first posits the central reality: that Yahweh Sebaoth has a "day" (literally, "there is a day to Y. S."). In the tristichs and distichs of vss. 12b-16 it goes on to specify against whom (עַל) this day's terrors are directed, maintaining close parallelism throughout. The conclusion (vs. 17) comes abruptly: two parallel perfect consecutives predict the humbling of human pride, then a third predicts the contrasting goal of divine exaltation, filling out the parallelism with *bayyôm hahû'*.

The central image of this poem is the theophanous power of Yahweh as seen both in nature and in the affairs of men. Beginning with the declaration that Yahweh's day is "against all that is proud and lofty, against all that is lifted up and high," it specifies first the awesome giants of nature

---

97. P. 298.
98. Wildberger, *BK*, X, *in loco*, identifies vss. 10f. as a fossil of vss. 12-17. The critics have been deeply impressed by *bayyôm hahû'* in these verses. Duhm, viewing 11-17 as a unity, spoke of vss. 11 and 17 as "Kehrverse." Procksch agreed with Duhm on the authenticity of this pericope. Lefèvre ("L'expression 'en ce jour-là'," p. 175), who has made a special study of our expression in Isaiah, offers the somewhat flamboyant interpretation: "Les bayyom hahu' marquent comme des points d'orgue le moment pathétique." But it is tradition rather than pathos that has inspired the appearance of this expression at the crucial point in these two pericopes.

("cedars of Lebanon . . . oaks of Bashan . . . high mountains . . . lofty hills"; cf. Ps. 29), then, by similitude, the most imposing works of man ("tower . . . wall . . . ships . . . craft") as the objects to be humbled. The series of perfect-consecutive clauses at the end state the purpose and result, and the final clause, with *bayyôm hahû'* as the chiastic counterpart to *yôm laYHWH ṣᵉbā'ôt* at the beginning, is in effect an epitome of the entire poem. Here is abundant evidence that the future day of Yahweh's decisive action is equivalent to "the day of Yahweh."

In vs. 11 the concluding lines of this great poem have been attached, with somewhat altered wording, to a dramatic call to flee before the terror of Yahweh's theophany. Although the day of Yahweh is not directly mentioned, the similarity to vss. 12ff. makes the epitomizing function of *bayyôm hahû'* apparent here also.

Isa. 10:27

Isa. 10:24-27 is an independent poetic salvation oracle that again appears to have an epitomizing conclusion with *bayyôm hahû'*. Although the precise date is uncertain, its reference to the menace of Assyria makes Isaianic authorship likely. Introduced redactionally by *lākēn*, the oracle depicts Yahweh as comforting his oppressed people with the assurance that *'ôd mᵉ'aṭ miz'ār*, "in a very little while" (cf. 29:19), he would turn his anger from them toward the Assyrians. Because it shifts to a third-person reference to Yahweh, vs. 26 has aroused suspicion, but it may nevertheless belong here because of the reference to Egypt in vs. 24, drawing this in as a kind of parenthesis. In vs. 27 the time-designative stands foremost with *wᵉhāyâ*. This introduces a rhythmical line (emended from the corrupt MT)[99] that may be a citation; cf. 9:4, 14:24, both referring to Assyria, the former also to Midian. In any event, this verse epitomizes by stating the purpose and effect of Yahweh's action.

Isa. 20:6

Isa. 20:1-6 appears to be another early Isaianic passage clearly reflecting an epitomizing usage with *bayyôm hahû'*. It is a symbolic-act oracle containing an account of Isaiah's nakedness (vss. 1f.) with an interpretation making an explicit comparison between Isaiah on the one hand and the Egyptians and Kushites on the other hand (vss. 3f.). The interpretation goes on in vs. 5 to predict the dismay of a group identified only by their having made Kush their hope and Egypt their boast. Suddenly, at vs. 6, a certain *yōšēb hā'î hazzeh*, "inhabitant of this coastland" (Phoenicia?), is introduced as spokesman for this group. He points dramatically (הנה) to what

---

99. Cf. BHSmg and the commentaries. The time-designative stands in anacrusis.

had happened to those in whom they had hoped, then asks plaintively, "And how shall we escape?" The punitive expedition of the Assyrians of 711 B.C. was to occasion despair among those who were tempted to side with Kush and Egypt. This included Judah, who witnessed Isaiah's act and for whom this oracle was primarily intended. *Bayyôm hahû'* is hardly meant as a synchronism since the sequence of events would be self-evident without it. [100] It is to be seen rather as introducing the interpretive declaration of the bystander, representative of all who were involved in intrigue against Assyria. "That day"—the day of the Assyrians' coming—is epitomized, then, as a day of despairing lament.

Isa. 27:1

Among a number of occurrences of *bayyôm hahû'* in the Little Apocalypse, the one at the beginning of Isa. 27:1 is the only one belonging to a conclusion. Following a summons to the people to hide themselves *kim'aṭ rega'*, "for a short moment" (cf. I Kings 22:25), a theophany poem announces Yahweh's imminent coming to punish the earth, giving this as the reason for the summons (26:20f.). Continuing in long-verse meter, 27:1 adds an explanation to the effect that *bayyôm hahû'* Yahweh will punish the mythological Leviathan and will slay the mythological *tannîn*, "serpent." 26:21 uses the futuristic participle to announce Yahweh's deed, then a perfect consecutive and an imperfect to describe the consequences ("earth will disclose . . . no more cover"). 27:1 starts afresh syntactically: following *bayyôm hahû'*, an imperfect and a perfect consecutive describe Yahweh's action. Although there is no proof that this verse could not be secondary, the likelihood is that it is the interpretive (and epitomizing) conclusion not only to 6:20f. but to an original day-of-Yahweh poem comprising 24:1-6, 17-20, 26:20—27:1. [101] If so, the day of which 27:1 speaks is not only the day of mythological combat but "that day" on which Yahweh will shake the earth and scatter all his mortal enemies.

Isa. 31:7

It would be difficult to prove that the occurrence of *bayyôm hahû'* in Isa. 31:7 (foremost following *kî*) represents anything but a synchronism, even though it introduces a conclusion to the short exhortation inserted

---

100. There remains some doubt whether *bayyôm hahû'* is original to the text, in spite of Munch's confident affirmation, since it is missing in some early Septuagintal witnesses. Without explanation, Duhm omits it from his translation. The commentators seem generally agreed that the context derives from the Isaianic school.

101. Cf. Henry, *Glaubenskrise*, pp. 116-47, against the general view that 27:1 is a gloss (so Munch). Here again, "that day" is seen as being very near. The mythological imagery is intended as a metaphorical transposition and theological interpretation of 6:20f., and perhaps of the entire poem.

into the text at vss. 6-7, rudely disturbing the structure of the Isaianic salvation oracle, vss. 4f., 8f.[102] This prose gloss appears to be an expansion from Isa. 2:20,[103] hence is probably very late.

Isa. 52:6

Only once does *bayyôm hahû'* occur in the poems of Second Isaiah, and then in a secondary insertion.[104] There seems no valid reason to dissent from the view that Isa. 52:4-6 is a marginal gloss playing on the word "nothing" in vs. 3.[105] The difficulty we encounter in following the thought of this insertion and in determining the function of *bayyôm hahû'* in its apparent conclusion, vs. 6, is attributable to the corrupt text. Following the herald formula (cf. the double oracle formula in vs. 5), Yahweh states the fact of his people's sojourn and oppression (vs. 4); *wᵉ'attâ* then introduces the equivalent of a complaint or indictment (vs. 5), to the effect that Yahweh's name is being continually despised. This leads to the promise of vs. 6, introduced by *lākēn*,[106] that Yahweh's people shall "know his name" *bayyôm hahû'*. Although this is in parallelism with the concluding words of attestation, "for I am he who speaks, look at me!" the promise would seem remarkably lame in any context but that of the Second Isaiah school, for whom such ambivalent sayings were charged with meaning. So also the phrase *bayyôm hahû'*, which appears here absolutely, without any referent or antecedent. "That day" is, to us, only vaguely the eschatological day of Yahweh's power; but to the writer of these lines it had to be one specific and realistic day which he awaited with confident expectation. The very unconcreteness of vs. 6 seems to suggest that it was meant as a heavily loaded, theologizing epitome.

Jer. 4:9

The function of *wᵉhāyâ bayyôm hahû'* at the beginning of Jer. 4:9 cannot be discerned until we have taken account of several problems surrounding the interpretation of vss. 1-10. Vss. 11f., beginning with *bā'ēt hahî'*,[107] and vss. 13ff. are obviously separate blocks of material; the question is whether our time-designative also introduces a secondary inser-

---

102. On 31:4-9, cf. B. S. Childs, *Isaiah and the Assyrian Crisis*, pp. 57-59; Lefèvre, *op. cit.*, p. 177.
103. See above, p. 298.
104. Second Isaiah himself was proclaiming Yahweh's new work of a new today, not the hope of a tomorrow.
105. Cf. C. Westermann, *ATD*, 19, *in loco*.
106. Munch writes off *bayyôm hahû'* as a marginal gloss, but the LXX and some other versions retain the temporal expression while omitting the second *lākēn* of the MT; cf. BHSmg.
107. Elsewhere in Jeremiah, at 8:1 and 31:1, this time-designative followed by the oracle formula introduces late supplements.

tion, or provides a transition to an original conclusion, and we must seriously consider the possibility that it may be the latter. The occurrence of the longer formula, *weḥāyâ bayyôm hahû'*, as the introduction to a concluding epitome in Isa. 10:27 shows that this expression is not to be taken as immediate evidence of secondary interpolation. On the other hand, *ne'um YHWH* appears with epitomizing *bayyôm hahû'* in Amos 2:16, 8:3, Obad. 8, and in initial position in Hag. 2:23, Zech. 12:4 (see below). According to the MT, the first word of Jer. 4:10 must be read as the first-personal imperfect of אמר with conjunctive waw, but there is some versional support for reading a third-personal verb with waw-consecutive, making the action futuristic rather than past and requiring as subject (at least) the prophets of vs. 9.

In recent discussion two contrasting positions have been taken. H. Graf Reventlow has strongly defended the unity of this pericope, using this in support of his thesis that Jeremiah spoke for the people suffering under Yahweh's wrath;[108] although he is able to appeal to the MT and most textual witnesses for support, a major difficulty in Reventlow's thesis is that the prophet neither speaks of himself nor is mentioned in the third person in the opening part of this pericope, requiring vs. 10 to be taken as a kind of personal annotation, reflecting Jeremiah's personal reaction to the oracle he had received. The majority of scholars have preferred to emend vs. 10 and identify vss. 9f. as an intrusion;[109] they are to be criticized for allowing a preconceived notion of the prophet's ministry to play the dominant role. A third alternative seems attractive to us. In spite of the weak attestation, we too take vs. 10 as the protest of the *Heilspropheten*, predicted in an epexegetical interpretation to the original doom oracle of vss. 5-8. The perfect consecutive of אמר in vs. 10 follows naturally after the perfect consecutive of שמם in vs. 9. Yahweh states the psychic reaction of Jerusalem's leaders, including the prophets, and then predicts the protest they will make to him. All this is, in effect, an expanded epitome of vss. 5-8; the day of alarm and terror, of lamenting and wailing, is the day when the proud leaders will be dismayed, complaining that the sword has reached the very life of the people in spite of their own confident promise that all would be well.

Amos 2:16

There is a general inclination among critics to regard *bayyôm hahû'* in Amos 2:16—its very earliest occurrence within the prophetic corpus—as

---

108. *Liturgie und prophetisches Ich bei Jeremia*, pp. 119f., 124, where supporting literature is cited.
109. E.g., Rudolph, *HAT*, 12, *in loco*, following H. Bardtke, "Jeremia der Fremdvölkerprophet," *ZAW*, 53 (1935), 217.

original.[110]   Following Wolff and most critics, we identify vss. 13-16 as a separate pericope, spoken by the prophet himself and exhibiting an intricate pattern of chiasis, with *bayyôm hahû'* falling within the regular meter.[111]   The sparse, vivid imagery progresses from a statement of Yahweh's act (pressing down) to a description of its effect, seen first in categories of quality ("the swift," "the strong"), then in specific representatives of these categories ("he who handles the bow," "he who rides the horse"). Vs. 16 returns to the description of one who represents the superlative quality of all the others ("the one who is bravest among the warriors"), predicting that even such a one shall both flee and be naked "on that day." If anything is an epitome, this is it, for it clearly restates in more poignant form what has already been declared. *Bayyôm hahû'* at the end does not synchronize; it is not a time-identifier. Used absolutely, it stands here filled with content by the epitomizing statement that precedes it.

Amos 8:3

Bayyôm hahû' appears absolutely in one other of Amos' original prophecies. This is at 8:3, where it is part of a dramatically epitomizing conclusion. The summer-fruit pericope of 8:1-3 shares the structure of the plumbline pericope in 7:7-9 to the extent that it contains (1) a report of the symbolic object, (2) Yahweh's query and the prophet's identification of that object, and (3) an applicatory oracle. In both passages Yahweh's oracle contains two parts, an interpretation and an announcement. 7:8f. presents these in close parallelism in the form of two 3:3:3 tristichs. 8:2b-3, on the other hand, offers the interpretation in the form of a 4:3 distich, balancing this in the announcement with two 3:2 distichs (the oracle formula is probably secondary and is, in any event, in anacrusis). We are to understand a very close parallelism between vs. 3a and vs. 3b; the first announces that "the mistresses[112] of the palace shall wail on that day," while the second dramatizes the cause of that wailing with a striking noun-clause and imperative: "Many the corpses in every place; cast (them) out in silence!" Although "that day" has not been identified timewise, it is plainly identical to "the end," which is seen as already come. In any event, it is with the

---

110. So also Munch, admitting that it is an original climax, though for him it means no more than "then."
111. Cf. Wolff, *BK*, XIV/2, *in loco*. We see הנה (13) and נאם יהוה (16) in anacrusis. וגבור לא ימלט נפשו (14) and וקל ברגליו לא ימלט (15) are expansions (otherwise Wolff), leaving an original oracle with 3:3:3, 3:3; 2:4, 3:4.
112. The MT's *šîrôt*, "songs," is impossible with an active verb, hence we follow the popular suggestion that *šārôt*, "mistresses," is the original. On the numerous problems connected with this passage see BH³ mg and the commentaries. Munch takes *bayyôm hahû'* as the introduction to a secondary addition. Wolff, *BK*, XIV/2, accepts it as original on p. 366, but identifies it as secondary on p. 373. On the formula *ne'um YHWH* see Wolff, pp. 174, 366ff.

dreadful quality of that day, rather than its specific place in time, that the oracle is concerned.

Obad. 8

Alongside Ezek. 38:14, the eighth verse of Obadiah is the only passage where *bayyôm hahû'* is preceded by the interrogative particle and the negative, *hᵃlô'*,[113] turning the threat of vss. 8f. into a rhetorical question. This phrase, with the oracle formula, is in anacrusis before a couplet composed of a tristich and a distich, all in a regular three-foot meter. We see this as epexegetical and epitomizing. An original poem by Obadiah is found in vss. 1b-9, being followed by a separate invective-threat oracle in vss. 10-14 and further expansions in vss. 15ff. This original poem commences with an audition-report, intimating Yahweh's intent to attack Edom (1b); this issues into a threat in vss. 2-4, concluded by the oracle formula. A new strophe in vss. 5-7 begins in the form of wisdom sayings and ends as a mock lament, with special emphasis on the fact that "there is no understanding (*tᵉbûnâ*) to it"—i.e., Edom's destruction proceeds contrary to the prudential preparations that have been made to prevent it. Vss. 8f., in which Yahweh renews his threat, but with emphasis on his intent to destroy *hᵃkāmîm*, "wise men," and *tᵉbûnâ*, "understanding," from Edom, are not to be taken as redactional word play but as a final strophe summarizing or epitomizing the whole oracle. The rhetorical question introduced by the interrogative negative and *bayyôm hahû'* is intended as a climactic revelation of the crucial transcendental factor that is at work in frustrating the vaunted wisdom and strength of Edom.[114]

Hag. 2:23

The final verse of Haggai appears to be an epitome introduced by *bayyôm hahû'* and the oracle formula. The special solemnity of this conclusion to the prophet's private oracle to Zerubbabel, appointing him to messianic office, is underscored by two further occurrences of the oracle formula, at the end as at the beginning with the full, sonorous divine name, Yahweh Sebaoth. 21b-22 has Yahweh's announcement for the near future, employing the usual syntax with the independent pronoun followed by a participle. As in vss. 6f., Yahweh declares that he is going to shake (רעש)

---

113. See also *hᵃlô' bᵉyôm qahtî* . . . in Ezek. 24:25.
114. Cf. J. D. W. Watts, *Obadiah: A Critical Exegetical Commentary* (Grand Rapids, 1969). There is nothing to support Munch's suggestion that *bayyôm hahû'* is a gloss. The fact that Jer. 49:7-11 has no parallel to Obad. 8a, whereas Obad. 8b-9 is reflected in Jer. 49:7, can hardly be taken as proof for Obad. 8a's late origin since the Jeremiah passage gives every indication of being later than the Obadiah passage. A date soon after 586, increasingly preferred in recent scholarship (e.g., Eissfeldt, *Einleitung*, 2nd ed., p. 492) over against the Wellhausen school, which dated it in the fifth century, is probably correct.

hif.) all the cosmos, now not in order to bring in the world's treasures for his temple but in order to subdue all kingdoms to his rule. Ancient holy-war imagery fills the regular parallelistic lines. In vs. 23 Yahweh abruptly turns to Zerubbabel, to whom the preceding announcement has been given, declaring to him the meaning of his cosmic war in terms of the latter's messianic rule. Yahweh will do two things: take him (identified by name, lineage, and honorific office, "my servant") and appoint him to be a *ḥôtām*, "signet." A final *kî*-clause gives divine election (בך בחרתי) as the ground for this action. This declaration epitomizes the entire oracle, revealing Yahweh's overriding purpose in the events of this tumultuous time.[115]

Zech. 9:16

In identifying the function of *bayyôm hahû'* in Zech. 9:16, it is important to use the insights of form and tradition criticism, in addition to literary analysis. Many critics have followed Wellhausen in simply deleting these words *metri causis*, then filling out the second stich of vs. 16a for balance.[116] The recent painstaking study by Magne Saebø has led to the conclusion that vss. 14f. form the core of this pericope (a late theophany poem), which was later provided with a framework consisting of vs. 13 and vs. 16a, which turn the theophany poem into a holy-war hymn.[117] There is every indication that Saebø's analysis is correct. This means that 16a is a conclusion at the stage of secondary expansion; turning back to the objects of concern in the introduction (Judah, Ephraim, and Zion as weapons against Javan), it declares the final effect of Yahweh's theophany, *viz.*, that Yahweh will save them/give them victory (perfect consecutive of ישע hif.) "on that day" as the flock of his people (*kᵉṣō'n 'ammô*). This is unmistakably intended as an epitomizing of the whole.

Zech. 12:4

Our previous treatment of Zech. 12:1–13:6 has argued that foremost *bayyôm hahû'* is regularly used to introduce new additions, in an initial stage with foregoing *wᵉhāyâ* and in subsequent stages without it.[118] For

---

115. The originality of *bayyôm hahu'* has hardly been disputed (cf. Munch) and is made especially probable by our observation of its epitomizing function in this concluding position.

116. Cf. BH³ mg; Elliger, *ATD*, 25, *in loco*. Munch retains it as part of a secondary expansion. The date is definitely in the Greek period. For a detailed study of the text, see T. Jansma, "Inquiry into the Hebrew Text and the Ancient Versions of Zechariah ix-xiv," *OTS*, 7 (1960), *in loco;* also B. Otzen, *Studien über Deuterosacharja*, Copenhagen, 1964, pp. 245f.; Saebø, *Sacharja 9–14*, p. 62.

117. *Op. cit.*, pp. 193-200. Vss. 16b-17 are a later expansion of vss. 13-16 (pp. 206f.).

118. P. 307.

the reason that vs. 4a, commencing with *bayyôm hahû'* and the oracle formula (a combination not found elsewhere in this section), is ideologically akin to vs. 3b, which in turn depends syntactically on vs. 3a, we must exempt the occurrence in 4a from this general observation. It is the conclusion to vss. 3-4a, and appears to epitomize by employing stereotyped holy-war imagery to suggest the inevitable outcome of the nations' attack upon Jerusalem.

Zech. 14:21

Zech. 14:20f. must certainly be one of the very last additions to the prophetic corpus, having come into the text at such an advanced stage of development that it lacks any trace of the holy-war ideology with which this late chapter begins.[119]   Priestly interests appear to have been at work in defining the ideal conditions of absolute sacrality. Initial *bayyôm hahû'* is followed by a series of verbal clauses, the first three of which have a form of היה, establishing a state of being rather than defining action. The first verb is in the imperfect, while all the rest through vs. 21a, in syndetic relationship with it, have perfect consecutives. Vs. 21b, however, is tacked on as a syntactical afterthought, with the negative particle and another imperfect of היה defining the negative quality of holiness by denying the presence of anything to defile it. It is the *kᵉnaʿᵃnî*, "trader," who will have no place in Yahweh's temple (cf. Mk. 11:15ff. and parallels), and if such a one is missing, all will be perfectly holy. Thus again, even in this very late passage of the Old Testament, *bayyôm hahû'* in concluding position signalizes an epitomizing intent.

Conclusion

With but one exception (Isa. 31:7, concluding a late prose gloss), conclusions with *bayyôm hahû'* are epitomes. The similarity to past references in parallel position is striking. Especially significant is that the majority of occurrences appear in original oracles of the preexilic and exilic prophets (in probable chronological order, Amos 2:16, 8:3, Isa. 2:17, 10:27, 20:6, Jer. 4:9, Obad. 8, Isa. 2:11, 27:1, 52:6) and in an original oracle of the return (Hag. 2:23). In some of these epitomizing passages "that day" is mentioned absolutely, as though known and familiar (Isa. 2:11, 52:6, Amos 2:16). In most early passages "that day" is a day of judgment on Israel or one of the nations (Isa. 2:11, 17, 20:6, Jer. 4:9, Amos 2:16, 8:3, Obad. 8), while in most late passages it brings salvation for Israel by way of judgment on her enemies (Isa. 10:27, 27:1, 52:6, Hag. 2:23, Zech. 9:16, 12:4, 14:21). In Isa. 20:6, Jer. 4:9, and Obad. 8 it brings an historical event, an invasion. One very early original prophecy specifi-

---

119. Cf. pp. 307f.

cally equates "that day" with the day of Yahweh (Isa. 2:17); the same is done redactionally, completely transcending its original imagery, in the very late passage, Zech. 14:21. Isa. 27:1, Hag. 2:23, Zech. 9:16, 12:4 strongly imply the same equation as in Isa. 2:17, while Amos 8:3 identifies "that day" as "the end," a term that in Ezek. 7:1ff. is synonymous with the "day" of Yahweh. In the passages from Second Zechariah "that day" is so highly abstracted as to seem quite remote, but among all the others it seems very near, three passages, Isa. 10:27, 27:1, and Hag. 2:23, specifically emphasizing its imminence.

4. Interpretation: The day future as a new opportunity for decisive action

What we have painstakingly taken apart we must now pull together. What impresses us most is the vast preponderance of synchronisms; about four out of five occurrences of futuristic *bayyôm hahû'* belong to this category, far more than with past *bayyôm hahû'*. All the glosses, all but one of the incorporating formulae, all the transitional formulae, and one of the concluding formulae provide a synchronism. It is all the more striking, therefore, that all save one of the concluding formulae are in epitomes or what amounts to an epitome, i.e., an identifying characterization (II Kings 22), underscoring the affinity with past *bayyôm hahû'*, which likewise occurs most frequently as a concluding formula in epitomes.

We are especially interested to inquire whether there is any significant difference between the preprophetic and the prophetic passages. An obvious difference is that the preprophetic passages use five of their nine occurrences as transitional or concluding formulae, in comparison with twenty-five out of one hundred two occurrences in the prophetic passages; yet this difference loses much of its impact when we observe that only one of the preprophetic passages (II Kings 22) is original, while twelve of the prophetic transitions and conclusions are original. The data may be summed up as follows:

	preprophetic	prophetic
glosses	0	8
incorporating formulae	4 (0 original)	69 (0 original)
transitional formulae	1 (0 original)	10 (3 original)
concluding formulae	4 (1 original)	15 (9 original)
total	9 (1 original)	102 (12 original)

Although four of nine preprophetic occurrences are epitomes or identifying characterizations, the three epitomes are from the deuteronomistic school, and the identifying characterization is itself prophetic.

Before going on to a more detailed analysis of forms and tradents, a word is in order concerning the specific intent of these various kinds of literary materials in their use of the formula, *bayyôm hahû'*. Where this is inserted as a gloss the intent is, of course, to specify the time when the action in question occurs; the gloss in effect creates a time-identification. Wherever *bayyôm hahû'* is used to incorporate supplementary material, two actions, that of the original pericope and that of the secondary material, are equated in time; hence the synchronizing function. But we need to realize that the redactor was doing more. He was in effect extending the day of the original pericope to include his new action, stretching it and coloring it to include new conditions. Hence synchronizing *bayyôm hahû'* can never mean merely "then," as Munch has claimed. The same is true when this formula is used in a transitional position. And in conclusions its force is almost always to epitomize. That is, the entire day—and the narrative that fills that day—is characterized by the epitomizing statement.

In Table 7 we offer a complete breakdown of this material, showing the form, syntax, genre, and tradent of the various passages, when grouped according to function.[120] We comment first about the form, observing that this is more a matter of individual style than of technical meaning. While synchronisms have the time-designative foremost in more than two thirds of the total, calling special attention to the time element, only six of the eighteen epitomes and characterizations—exactly one third—have it at the beginning. It will be useful to tabulate the data as follows:

	BH*	WBH*	+ of	total
1. Synchronisms				
preprophetic	1	0	0	5
Isaiah	16	11	3	36
Jeremiah	2	1	3	8
Ezekiel	5	2	1	9
Hosea	1	2	2	4
Joel	0	1	0	1
Amos	2	1	1	3
Micah	2	1	2	3
Zephaniah	1	2	1	5
Zechariah	7	7	1	18
totals	37	28	14	92

---

120. Abbreviations used in this Table are the following: BH—*bayyôm hahû'*; WBH—*wᵉhāyâ bayyôm hahû'*; *—foremost; + of—followed by the oracular formula, *nᵉ'um YHWH* or its variant. Additional abbreviations are as in n. 381 of Chapter Three. A dash under the tradent listing indicates uncertainty or remoteness. "School" means the immediate circle of disciples.

2. Epitomes and characterizations

preprophetic	0	0	0	4
Isaiah	1	2	0	7
Jeremiah	0	1	1	1
Amos	0	0	2	2
Obadiah	0	0	1	1
Haggai	1	0	1	1
Zechariah	1	0	1	3
totals	3	3	6	19

In all but two of the synchronisms, the oracle formula follows a foremost time-designative, but in only half of the epitomes/characterizations (3 of 6) is this true, despite the fact that the latter use it in one third of the passages (6 of 19) as compared with fewer than one sixth of the passages (14 of 92) involving synchronisms. The largest proportions with the oracle formula are found in Jeremiah (3 synchronisms and 1 epitome out of 9), Hosea (2 synchronisms out of 4), Amos (1 synchronism and 2 epitomes out of 5), Obadiah (1 epitome out of 1), Micah (2 synchronisms out of 3), and Haggai (1 epitome out of 1). Whereas the time-designative occurs foremost in only one of the preprophetic passages (a synchronism), it appears foremost with relative frequency in the synchronisms of Isaiah, Ezekiel, Hosea, Joel, Amos, and Zechariah. The preprophetic passages make no use of the oracle formula.

The syntax is what we should expect of futuristic materials. With the exception of Deut. 31:18, an epitome in which the infinitive strengthens the imperfect, I Kings 22:25 par., where *hinnēh* plus the participle marks an identifying characterization, and two synchronisms at Isa. 27:2 and Zeph. 1:10, with a noun-clause(s) followed by the imperative, the verb is throughout either imperfect or perfect consecutive. As one would expect, the perfect consecutive almost always follows a time-designative that is not foremost in the sentence. Contrariwise, foremost *bayyôm hahû'* takes the imperfect in every passage save Isa. 27:2, and foremost *wᵉhāyâ bayyôm hahû'* takes the imperfect in all but six passages having the perfect consecutive (Isa. 22:20, 23:15, 24:21, Hos. 1:5, Amos 8:9, Mic. 5:9) and in Zeph. 1:10, having the noun-clause and imperative. It is interesting that of the passages with the time-designative foremost, the verb is from היה, "to be," in Isa. 4:2, 7:23, 17:9, 19:16, 18f., 23f., 28:5, Ezek. 39:11, Ezek. 13:1, 14:6, 9, 13, 20. Almost all of these are very late. היה also occurs when the time-designative is not foremost, once with the imperfect (Zech. 14:21) and five times with the perfect consecutive (Jer. 25:33, 39:16, 48:41, 49:22, Zech. 12:8, all late; the last three follow with a comparative clause). This last is syntactically anomalous because היה expresses a state of being while the perfect consecutive is the verbal aspect of ongoing action.

Table 7
Analysis of Form, Syntax, Genre, and Tradent of Sentences with
Futuristic *bayyôm hahû'*, Listed According to Function

	Form	Predi-cate	Genre, individual (and contextual)	Tradent
			I. Synchronism	
Exod. 8:18	BH	pf cs	salvation oracle	J school
Deut. 31:17(1)	BH	pf cs	threat	D school
31:17(2)	BH	pf cs	"	"
I Sam. 3:12	BH*	impf	"	Zadokites
8:18(1)	BH	pf cs	judgment saying	Dtr
Isa. 2:20	BH*	impf	judgment portrayal	D school
3:7	BH	impf	illustrative scene (judgment oracle)	—
3:18	BH*	impf	judgment portrayal	—
4:1	BH	pf cs	gloss	scribal
4:2	BH*	impf	salvation portrayal	—
5:30	BH	pf cs	judgment portrayal	Isa. school
7:18	WBH*	impf	"	"
7:20	BH*	impf	"	"
7:21	WBH*	impf	salvation portrayal	—
7:23	WBH*	impf	judgment portrayal	Isa. school
10:20	WBH*	neg+ impf	salvation saying	—
11:11	WBH*	impf	editorial transition to salvation portrayal	—
12:1	BH	pf cs	editorial transition to declarative praise	—
12:4	BH	pf cs	"	—
17:4	WBH*	impf	threat	Isa. school
17:7	BH*	impf	salvation saying	—
17:9	BH*	impf	editorial transition to judgment oracle	—
19:16	BH*	impf	judgment saying	—
19:18	BH*	impf	salvation saying	—
19:19	BH*	impf	judgment saying	—
19:21	BH	impf	salvation saying	—
19:23	BH*	impf	"	—
19:24	BH*	impf	"	—
22:20	WBH*	pf cs	appointive oracle	Isa. school
22:25	BH*	impf	private judgment oracle	"
23:15	WBH*	pf cs	editorial transition to taunt oracle	scribal
24:21	WBH*	pf cs	salvation portrayal	—

continued

Table 7 (continued)

	Form	Predi-cate	Genre, individual (and contextual)	Tradent
25:9	BH	pf cs	editorial transition to declarative praise	—
26:1	BH*	impf	editorial transition to salvation hymn	—
27:2	BH*	n-cl+ impv	editorial transition to salvation oracle	—
27:12	WBH*	impf	salvation saying	—
27:13	WBH*	impf	"	—
28:5	BH*	impf	"	Isa. school
29:18	BH	pf cs	salvation portrayal	Second-Isa. school
30:23	BH	impf	"	—
31:7	BH*	impf	exhortation	—
Jer. 25:33	BH	pf cs	judgment portrayal	—
30:8	WBH* +of	impf	salvation saying	—
39:16	BH	pf cs	gloss	scribal
39:17	BH	pf cs	private salvation oracle	Jer. school
48:41	BH	pf cs	gloss	scribal
49:22	BH	pf cs	"	"
49:26	BH +of	impf	"	"
50:30	BH + of	impf	"	"
Ezek. 24:26	BH*	impf	"	"
24:27	BH*	impf	appointive oracle	Ezek. school
29:21	BH*	impf	salvation oracle	"
30:9	BH*	impf	threat	—
38:10	WBH*	impf	taunt	—
38:14	BH	neg+ pf cs	"	—
38:18	WBH* + of	impf	threat	—
38:19	BH	neg+ impf	"	—
39:11	WBH*	impf	"	—
Hos. 1:5	WBH*	pf cs	"	Hos. school
2:18	WBH* + of	impf	salvation oracle	"
2:20	BH	pf cs	"	"
2:23	WBH* + of	impf	"	"
Joel 4:18	WBH*	impf	salvation portrayal	—

continued

Table 7 (continued)

	Form	Predi-cate	Genre, individual (and contextual)	Tradent
Amos 8:9	WBH* + of	pf cs	threat	Amos school
8:13	BH*	impf	judgment portrayal	"
9:11	BH*	impf	salvation oracle	—
Mic. 2:4	BH*	impf	editorial transition to taunt (threat)	Mic. school
4:6	BH* + of	impf	salvation oracle	"
5:9	WBH* + of	pf cs	"	—
Zeph. 1:9	BH	pf cs	gloss	scribal
1:10	WBH* + of	n-cl + impv	editorial transition to threat	Zeph. school
1:12 LXX	WBH*	impf	"	"
3:11	BH	neg + impf	salvation oracle	—
3:16	BH*	impf	editorial transition to victory hymn	—
Zech. 2:15	BH	pf cs	salvation oracle	—
3:10	BH* + of	impf	"	—
6:10	BH	pf cs	instruction for private oracle	Zechariah
12:3	WBH*	impf	threat	—
12:6	BH*	impf	"	—
12:8(1)	BH*	impf	salvation oracle	—
12:8(2)	BH	pf cs	"	—
12:9	WBH*	impf	threat	—
12:11	BH*	impf	salvation portrayal	—
13:1	BH*	impf	salvation saying	—
13:2	WBH*	impf	salvation oracle	—
13:4	WBH*	impf	salvation portrayal	—
14:4	BH	pf cs	"	—
14:6	WBH*	neg + impf	"	—
14:8	WBH*	impf	"	—
14:9	BH*	impf	salvation saying	priests
14:13	WBH*	impf	judgment portrayal	—
14:20	BH*	impf	salvation portrayal	priests

continued

Table 7 (continued)

	Form	Predi-cate	Genre, individual (and contextual)	Tradent
			II. Epitome	
Deut. 31:18	BH	inf + impf	threat	D school
I Sam. 8:18(2)	BH	neg + impf	judgment saying	Dtr
I Kings 13:3	BH	pf cs	threat	Dtr
Isa. 2:11	BH	pf cs	theophany poem	Isa. school
2:17	BH	pf cs	"	"
10:27	WBH*	impf	salvation oracle	Isaiah
20:6	BH	impf	threat (symbolic act oracle)	Isa. school
27:1	BH*	impf	threat (theophany poem)	—
52:6	BH	impf	announcement (judgment/ salvation oracle)	Second-Isa. school
Jer. 4:9	WBH* + of	impf	epexegesis to judgment oracle	Jeremiah
Amos 2:16	BH + of	impf	threat	Amos
8:3	BH + of	pf cs	threat (vision oracle)	"
Obad. 8	BH + of	neg + pf cs	threat	Obadiah
Hag. 2:23	BH* + of	impf	private salvation oracle	Haggai
Zech. 9:16	BH	pf cs	holy-war poem	—
12:4	BH* + of	impf	threat	—
14:21	BH	neg + impf	salvation portrayal	priests
			III. Identifying Characterization	
I Kings 22:25	BH	h+ptcp	announcement (controversy narrative)	prophetic circles
II Chron. 18:24			"	"
Isa. 11:10	WBH*	impf	salvation saying	—

Somehow, a day that should be filled with action becomes frozen into a permanent condition or state of being—one of the hallmarks of developing apocalypticism.

When we ask the question whether *bayyôm hahû'* belongs more to judgment or to salvation pericopes, the answer is that the occurrences are fairly equally divided. Only in epitomes does the judgment scene strongly predominate over the scene of salvation. We may list the statistics for the various genres as follows:

1. Synchronisms: threat, 14; judgment saying, 3; judgment oracle, 2; judgment portrayal, 9; illustrative scene of judgment, 1; taunt, 4; exhortation, 1; salvation oracle, 17; salvation saying, 12; salvation portrayal, 13; salvation hymn, 2; declarative praise, 3; appointive oracle, 2; instruction for salvation oracle, 1.
2. Epitomes: threat, 8; judgment oracle, 1; judgment saying, 1; theophany poem, 2; announcement, 1; salvation oracle, 2; holy-war poem, 1; salvation portrayal, 1.
3. Identifying characterizations: announcement, 1; salvation saying, 1.

As the future day may be either a day of judgment or a day of salvation, so it may be a day for God to act or for man to act; in the vast preponderance of passages, it is Yahweh who acts directly, with man responding to his action. Following the pattern used with respect to past and present time-designatives, we list the passages as follows (glosses are excluded):

I. God's action
    A. Yahweh as the acting subject
        1) in the first person: Exod. 8:18, Deut. 31:17f., Isa. 11:11, 22:20, 27:2, Jer. 30:8, 39:17, Ezek. 29:21, 30:9, 38:18f., 39:11, Hos. 1:5, 2:20, 23, Amos 8:9, 9:11, Obad. 8, Mic. 4:6, 5:9, Zeph. 1:12, Hag. 2:23, Zech. 12:3f., 6, 9, 13:2, 14:9, 13.
        2) in the third person: I Sam. 8:18(2), Isa. 2:11, 17, 3:18, 7:18, 20, 10:27, 27:1, 12, 28:5, Joel 4:18, Zeph. 1:10, Zech. 9:16, 12:8, 14:4.
    B. Yahweh acting through a mediator: Isa. 4:2, 11:10, Zech. 6:10.
II. Man's action or condition
    A. In relation to God: I Sam. 8:18(1), I Kings 13:3, 22:25, Isa. 2:20, 5:30, 10:20, 12:1, 4, 17:4, 7, 19:16, 18f., 21, 20:6, 25:9, 26:1, 27:13, 29:18, 31:7, 52:6, Jer. 4:9, 25:33, Ezek. 24:27, 38:10, 14, Hos. 2:18, Amos 2:16, 8:3, 13, Mic. 2:4, Zeph. 3:11, 16, Zech. 2:15, 12:11, 13:1, 4, 14:20f.
    B. In relation to man and the world: Isa. 3:7, 7:21, 17:9, 19:23f., 22:25, 23:15, 30:23, Zech. 3:10.
III. The world: Isa. 7:23, Zech. 14:6, 8.

The epitomes we have observed fall into this pattern as follows: I, A, 1: Deut. 31:18, Obad. 8, Hag. 2:23, Zech. 12:4; I, A, 2: I Sam. 8:18(2), Isa. 2:11, 17, 10:27, Isa. 27:1, Zech. 9:16; I, B: I Kings 13:3; II, A: Isa.

20:6, 52:6, Jer. 4:9, Amos 2:16, 8:3, Zech. 14:21. One identifying characterization (Isa. 11:10) belongs to class I, B, and the other (I Kings 22:25
par.) belongs to class II, A. Thus epitomes and identifying characterizations
solely involve God's action or man's action in direct response to him.

This brings us to inquire, finally, about the tradents. Putting the
occurrences in roughly chronological order, we produce the following list:

> Synchronisms: J school, 1; Zadokites, 1; Amos school, 2; Hosea
> school, 4; Isaiah school, 8; Micah school, 2; deuteronomistic school,
> 3; Zephaniah school, 8; Jeremiah school, 1; Ezekiel school, 1; Second
> Isaiah school, 1; Zechariah, 1; priests, 2; scribes, 9. Undetermined are
> 51 others.

> Epitomes and identifying characterizations: early prophets, 1; Amos,
> 2; Isaiah, 1; Isaiah school, 3; deuteronomistic school, 2; Jeremiah, 1;
> Obadiah, 1; Second Isaiah school, 1; Haggai, 1; priests, 1. Undeter-
> mined are 4 others.

In view of the secondary nature of most of the material, it can hardly
be surprising that only one of the numerous synchronisms may with
confidence be ascribed to a particular writer, *viz.*, Zech. 6:10—and that
because it occurs in a narrative report. It seems all the greater gain,
therefore, that we have some assurance in identifying two epitomes from
Amos himself and one each from Isaiah, Jeremiah, Obadiah, and Haggai.
Together with I Kings 22:25 par., which is closely defined as to its narrative
situation, these original, unanonymous epitomes seem to be of unique value
in revealing the affinity of early and classical prophetism for the traditional
Hebraic concept of historical time.

The only other remarkable thing about the tradents involved in
futuristic *bayyôm hahû'* is that the redactors of Isaiah, on the one hand,
and the apocalypticists of the Second Zechariah tradition, on the other
hand, display a particular fondness for it. Strikingly, these two groups were
the most active in altering the original scene of "that day." If we knew
more about their respective dates and historical backgrounds, we would be
in a position to judge the theological relevance of their activity.

What then is "that day" future? It is God's or man's new opportunity
for decisive action. Although it may not be immediately present, like
hayyôm or *māhār*, it is imminently certain—except in apocalyptic, which
extends it to ages remote from the here and now. Like "that day" past, it
marks a new turning point in man's journey through history in conversation
with God.

CHAPTER FIVE

The Texture and Quality of Time in Old Testament Tradition

LIKE AN EXPLORER who has traversed a vast and little-charted territory, we look back to where we have gone, sensing now more fully the significance of distant contours. None who had passed by before us had paused to look so closely as we at what was there to be seen, leaving every report inescapably fragmentary, lacking both in detail and in proportion. We have, on our part, made a serious effort at surveying every salient feature, attempting to show the important interrelationships as we proceeded on our way. Since it is a final synthesis that is now required, it would be confusing as well as superfluous to repeat the summaries that appear at various stages within the framework of this book. We shall do no more than draw up the most obvious and far-reaching results emerging from our total study, pointing out some of the specific ways in which it may serve to influence ongoing exegetical, historical, and theological discussion.

1. The vindication of a comprehensive methodology

It is certainly important to declare emphatically that this study of the Hebraic tradition about time demonstrates that the only effective methodology is a comprehensive one. It is this realization above anything else that justifies the length of this book. As scholars have worked at the time problem from the viewpoint of philology, results have been partial and unsatisfying because the philologist has so often confined his analysis to the identification of cognates and the enumeration of statistics, without careful attention to the textual setting of specific occurrences. As theologians and religion-phenomenologists have attempted to assay the distinctiveness of the biblical view of time over against the views of Israel's ancient contemporaries, the results have seemed overdrawn and unconvincing because, once again, exegetical analysis has often been slighted, or ignored altogether, in haste to identify some basic principle of understanding. The linguistic phenomena fascinating the philologist may not be studied in isolation: words gain their full meaning only when put to use within a specific communicative context. The concepts that the theologian, phenomenologist, and philosopher find so interesting remain as disembodied spirits until they are identified concretely within specific passages, and are related to the experiential concerns of the people.

We may anticipate that some will complain about the difficulty of classifying the methodology of this book. It is neither—in an exclusive sense—a philological study or a theological-phenomological analysis or a critical-exegetical examination. One should observe the title of this chapter.

Because the book has aimed to employ its study of the Hebraic vocabulary of time as a tool for further understanding, we avoid the word "language." Because the book identifies the primary concern of the Hebrews to be that of describing and witnessing to an experience of time, we also avoid referring simply to a "concept" or a "theology," which would have been adequate had the Hebrews indulged in abstract speculations about time. A more meaningful way of identifying the point of our primary concern is to speak of an "Old Testament tradition," since this term alone is able to suggest the historical depth and cultural breadth of our perspective. If the inclusion of this term in the chapter title suggests that we see our work primarily as a study in tradition history, such we have earnestly endeavored to make it. But we take now the expression, "tradition history," to include every facet of modern criticism, including literary analysis, form criticism, and the tracing of usage from primitive stages of oral transmission to the most sophisticated levels of redactional combination. All this has been pinned down as accurately as possible in a specific, systematic, and detailed exegesis of the numerous individual passages where the most relevant phenomena occur.

We offer our study as a demonstration of the validity of a comprehensive approach, urging it on every serious exegete, critic, and theologian. Its results will justify its methods. We believe that the stage has been reached where the philologist must give up his effort to determine word-meanings without a comprehensive study of the function of words within specific formal schemata, within the ongoing stream of tradition history, and within particular literary contexts. The time has come likewise for the theologian and the phenomenologist to base their generalizations on a more specific and comprehensive exegetical analysis.

2. Lexical data and contextual function

As one assesses the contribution of this book to an extension of lexicographical knowledge, a great deal may depend on whether one is concerned only with denotative, "etymological" meaning, or also with the semantic aspect, as seen contextually and historically. Little may have been added to the dictionary meaning of time-words, but our study has proven to have important implications for the Hebrew language of time in the broader sense.

We have argued that the meaning "later," "in the future," is no extended or metaphorical signification for the word $m\bar{a}h\bar{a}r$, but is itself primary, coming by extension to do service as a name for the day next following today. Two time-words that derive from or incorporate a demonstrative particle, $'\bar{a}z$ and $'att\hat{a}$, are primarily logical and situational (this is especially true for the form $w^{e}'att\hat{a}$ and has important implications for the

etymology of the word '*ēt*), leaving *yôm* as the elemental Hebrew word for
time. This reflects the psychological and ideological impact of the day upon
the primitive Hebrew (and early Semite) mentality. Only the day (and
alternating night) had independent significance; all other divisions of time,
whether extensions of the day (week, month, year, etc.) or fragments of it
("watches" of the day and night) were artificialities and semi-abstractions.

There is little wonder, then, that so much emphasis seems to be
placed on the quality of particular days. Although *yôm* in all its combinations retains its reference to this elemental unit of time (*bayyôm hahû'*
never means merely "then"), it is what fills a day with meaning and gives it
its uniqueness, rather than its chronological dimensions, that makes it
important. It is for this reason that very occasionally (I Sam. 25:10, Jer.
34:15), *hayyôm* comes to refer to the present time as a period or situation;
the day on which the speaker speaks is typical and representative of other
days characterized by a special situation.

These are items that may be suitable for dictionary entry. What the
dictionaries and lexicons will have difficulty recording is the wide-ranging
functional variation observed with respect to various Hebrew time-words. It
is precisely here that philology reaches beyond itself into form and tradition analysis, as well as into phenomenology and theology.

3. Time-designatives determinative for literary criticism

The recognition of the central significance of *yôm* in determining the
Hebraic apprehension of time has forced us into a long process of analyzing
exegetically and critically the numerous passages where the most formal—
but also most revealing—combinations of this word occur. One of the most
immediate benefits of our procedure will, we hope, be the enrichment of
exegetical and critical discussion. Not only has our study drawn from
current insights in an effort to see a time-word in its exegetical context; our
study has in numerous passages itself led to drastic revisions of current
opinions. The commentaries and exegetical monographs will henceforth
need to pay more serious attention to the presence of a time-word,
recognizing that it may in fact be providing the indispensable clue to
unraveling a whole complex problem.

In certain instances our study has led to suggestions respecting the
criticism of one particular biblical book. A negative example is our demonstration that the centrally important time-designatives in Deuteronomy
lend little support to a theory of separate redactions characterized respectively by the singular and plural second-personal pronoun. This conclusion
tends to support Lohfink's approach, in opposition to the dominant position in current Deuteronomy criticism.

A more positive example would be the refinements we have suggested respecting the editorial introductions for literary supplements to the original prophetic writings, using a futuristic *bayyôm hahû'*. Or we could refer to the new insights that have emerged with respect to the techniques and ideology of the throne-succession historian, with all that this implies for the understanding of history in this foundational work of Hebrew historiography.

Very often the implications of our study have seemed to have been restricted to the interpretation of specific passages, whether short or long. Everywhere the role of time-designatives affects interpretation to some degree, but there are a great number of passages where the time-word proves to have a determinative effect, requiring radical changes in the accepted criticism. It is hoped that one of the important uses of this book will be with respect to the passages that have come into this kind of new light, and in particular those that have received a special, and in some cases extensive, literary and form-critical analysis, of which we may mention the following as being the most important: Deut. 31:16-22; I Samuel 13—14; I Sam. 17:1—18:6; I Sam. 24:1ff. and I Sam. 26:1ff.; II Sam. 3:1ff.; II Sam. 6:20-23; I Kings 13:1-6; I Kings 22:1-38; II Kings 6:24—7:20; II Chron. 35:1-17.

4. The formal function of time-designatives

Our analysis has produced a number of significant results in the area of form criticism, demonstrating how one or another of the time-designatives under study may function in a formal way within a given pericope. This is true to some extent of such time-designatives as *'āz*, *wᵉ'attâ*, *bā'ēt hahî'*, *hăškēm babbōqer*, *mimmāḥᵒrāt*, and the like, but it is especially true of combinations with *yôm*. We have, for instance, identified ways in which *bayyôm hazzeh* and *bᵉ'eṣem hayyôm hazzeh* occur as dating formulae, but far more impressive have been our discoveries with respect to the roles played by *hayyôm* and *bayyôm hahû'* in their various guises as epitomizers, characterizers, or time-identifiers. We have seen how an appeal or epitome with *hayyôm* may relate to an epitomizing past *bayyôm hahû'* in determining the structure of a particular narrative. We have studied the significance of *hayyôm* in the promulgation formula and the *Bundesformular* of Deuteronomy. We have attempted to draw up the evidence for genre and *Sitz im Leben*, showing that the time-designatives with *yôm* are historically, rather than cultically, oriented.

One of the greatest gains of this study has been an insight into the several functions of the time-designatives and the interrelationships between these functions. It has proven possible in almost every case to determine whether (1) a particular time ("day") is being defined according to a quality or event, or (2) an event is being defined with respect to its position within chronological time. Where an event's position within the structure of time becomes important, a time-identifier is used; this becomes a specific dating formula when calendrical concerns are introduced. Where the given day's significance is being determined, on the other hand, an identifying characterization may come into play for defining the situation, while an appeal or epitome may be used to provide a climactic word of interpretation. In synchronisms and sequences the role of the time-designative is apt to be more ambiguous: with the emphasis on the interconnectedness of two or more events, matters of chronological order or coincidence seem equally as important as qualitative definition.

The impossibility of making a clear choice with respect to the function of the time-designative in a very few of the passages studied in this book may now be interpreted positively. We recognize in the light of our total discussion that this ambiguity may have been deliberate. We have reference particularly to six passages that seemed to combine an epitomizing with a time-identifying use. Deut. 26:16, I Sam. 28:18, and I Kings 1:30 epitomize while identifying the day in question as a day to which another day has pointed. I Kings 18:15 and 36 epitomize or characterize by making an appeal, while emphatically contrasting the day in question to all other days. Deut. 27:9 is the most impressive of all. Not only does it provide the supremely climactic epitome within the entire Deuteronomic parenesis, defining the day of speaking as the day on which Israel became[1] Yahweh's people; the foremost *hayyôm hazzeh* emphasizes also the element of time, contrasting "this day" to all other days. We are thus to understand that "this day" was unique for its quantitative (i.e., chronological) relationship as well as for its qualitative character.

As the various functions of the time-designatives are related to levels of composition, some striking patterns emerge. One sees that synchronisms tend to reflect (and introduce) secondary material. Most sequences and time-identifications are original, though they do comparatively little to determine the internal structure of a given pericope. Identifying characterizations are original within sophisticated compositions, appearing with notable frequency in Deuteronomy. Almost all the epitomes and all of the appeals are original; they tend to appear in fairly early and fairly primitive narratives, determining schematic structure. This is true whether the reference is to the past, present, or future, whether the day in question is comparatively remote (*bayyôm hahû'*) or imminently present (*hayyôm, māḥār*).

The regular place of appeals and present epitomes is at the climactic point in the narrative; the place of past and future epitomes is at the end. One way or the other, the narrator/pareneticist/prophet provides a central

---

1. On the significance of the nifal perfect of היה see G. S. Ogden, "Time and the Verb היה in Old Testament Prose," *VT*, 21 (1971), 466f.

interpretation of the event's significance. This has much to do with the situation and the content of appeals and epitomes. With some exceptions, the person who acts (and often speaks) is Yahweh, a spokesman for Yahweh, or the people in response to Yahweh. In past epitomes the situation is almost always the holy war or a covenant—in other words, a situation of portentous conflict or confrontation. In present epitomes and appeals the situation becomes somewhat broader, but almost always involves some kind of confrontation. In future epitomes the scenes of judgment predominate, salvation coming in only as an aspect of Yahweh's judgment of Israel's enemies. From all this we may conclude that historical event is understood as revelatory, but definitely requires an interpretive word in order to break through into human apprehension. The epitomist is thus the authoritative interpreter of a past, present, or future confrontation filled with significance as a revelation of transcendent meaning.

Although appeals and epitomes with a time-designative claim our attention as potent bearers of revelatory meaning, we must not overlook the ideological significance of synchronisms. As we have noted, these almost always introduce new literary material. When '*āz* or *bā'ēt hahî'* are used, the intent is little more than to equate in time a second event with a first. But when *bayyôm hahû'* is used, and especially in futuristic reference, the intent seems to be to extend the qualification of the day in question. The editor/redactor is acting as a new epitomist, extending the original description to include additional qualifying events. The possibilities for expanding the qualification of the past are limited because the past is fixed in the people's memory, but the future is open to all sorts of new possibilities. Yet the degree of willingness to speculate with respect to the future is noticeably related to the supplementer's affinity with the original speaker; for only those expansions that add judgment to judgment have proven to come from within a prophet's intimate circle of disciples. It was ongoing historical experience that brought a new perspective, stimulating later generations to interpret judgment as a means of salvation. History interpreted by the word is susceptible to a new word of interpretation. Commensurate with God's power to create new things is his power to reveal himself in this new and more final word.

5. "Yahweh's day," past, present, and future

Another insight of central importance emerging from our study is that the revelatory interpretation concerning the past and the revelatory interpretation concerning the future have a parenetic concern. In other words, their intent is to motivate the present. Israel is anxious to understand its past and to anticipate its future in order to make a right choice in its present moment of responsible decision. "That day," past and future, has no other function than to illuminate "today."

Historiography provides the model for parenesis, employing the image of revelatory event in the past to illuminate the revelatory significance of the present. Eschatology is, then, an analogical projection of the past and present into the future, positing Yahweh's coming action on his action already experienced.

Since tradition clearly provides the pattern for eschatology, there is no sense in trying to assess the meaning of "the day of Yahweh" or of any other futuristic image except on the model of "that day" past and "this day" present. The future "day of Yahweh" is like any prior day in which God has confronted man. It is simply the coming day, so often introduced by the formula ($w^e h\bar{a}y\hat{a}$) $bayy\hat{o}m\ hah\hat{u}$', when Yahweh will act decisively once again. At least one prophetic passage, Isa. 2:11-17, makes this explicit, beginning with the announcement, "For Yahweh Sebaoth has a day . . . ," and concluding with the interpretive epitome, "So Yahweh alone will be exalted on that day."

In the early passages, at any rate, "the day of Yahweh" is not to be understood as the termination of history. It is analogous to $bayy\hat{o}m\ hah\hat{u}$' used absolutely in a futuristic sense, as in I Kings 22:25, Isa. 52:6, and Amos 8:3. The interpretive framework is not chronological, placing this day within or at the end of a sequence of days, but qualifying, characterizing it as a day of Yahweh's decisive action in which all the complexities and ambiguities of the present situation are brought to a complete—and in this sense final—resolution. But, as Yahweh has often acted decisively in the past, so there may need to be recurring days of Yahweh in the future. In fact, "today"—this very day—may be a "day of Yahweh."

As we have seen in Chapter One, there are an intriguing variety of ways in which the future day of Yahweh's acting, specifically the "day of Yahweh," may come to manifestation. In some passages it is described adjectivally, in others it is characterized by an action or event. One way or another, it finds its essential identity in that it is Yahweh's special day. Any day is potentially Yahweh's day since he made the day and the night (Gen. 1), but only those days become actively his day on which he manifests himself decisively and revealingly, in judgment or in salvation.

It is a relatively late book, Malachi, that seems to bring this to greater clarity than any other. A situation of unfaith with respect to Yahweh's ability to act gives rise to Malachi's trenchant pronouncements. In 3:1 he repeats Yahweh's word pointing to the sending of his "messenger" as a sign that he himself will come suddenly (פתאם) to his temple. This is defined as $y\hat{o}m\ b\hat{o}'\hat{o}$ ("the day of his coming"), equivalent to the act of his appearing, $h\bar{e}r\bar{a}'\hat{o}t\hat{o}$ (cf. vs. 19). Vs. 3 specifies what Yahweh will do when he comes; because he will come to effectuate his word, vss. 17 and 21 specifically describe this day as $y\hat{o}m\ {}^{a}\check{s}er\ {}^{'}n\hat{i}\ {}^{'}\bar{o}\acute{s}eh$, "the day when I act." So ultimately it is not the interpreter's (prophet's) speech about this day that determines its quality but the actuality of Yahweh's action (cf. Jer. 28:9,

Ezek. 33:33). Although the event cannot be apprehended without the word, the word without the event is vain and lifeless.[2]

6. The coming day—imminent or remote (prophecy and apocalyptic)

The impressive prominence of interpretive statements containing present time-designatives leads us to affirm that the normal relation between word and event is one of close temporal proximity. We have seen that epitomes and similar constructions with *hayyôm* refer to events already experienced, events currently being experienced, and events yet to be experienced on a particular day. What happens when the event is deferred beyond the day of interpretation? In many instances it is scheduled for *māḥār*, "tomorrow," and with equal certainty as if it had been this very day, because today has already seen the preparation for it. In prophetic speech, however, the fulfillment may be less immediate. *Bayyôm hahû'* is the locution that is demanded as a time-designative. Nevertheless, a number of passages (cf. Isa. 10:27, 27:1, 29:19, Hag. 2:23, Zech. 6:10) emphatically identify "that day" as very near, just over the horizon of the morrow. This may be taken as typical of the prophetic outlook. In agreement with the majority of modern interpreters, we affirm that Israel's prophets were predicting the future only as a proximate projection of the present. They were immediately deducing the future out of the present, less by way of political astuteness than out of faith in the being and nature of Israel's covenant God.

We do not as a rule find "that day" lying far in the future. This does occur in I Sam. 3:12 and 8:18, where secondary writers actually speak of their own time while taking the stance of being in the narrative past. This phenomenon is strikingly similar to the method of Deuteronomy, presenting Moses, the authoritative figure of remote antiquity, as promulgating the law while calling the Israel of late-monarchical times to crucial, fateful decision (cf. also the deuteronomistic "then/now pattern" seen in Num. 32:10, Josh. 14:9, 12).

Something different from this remarkable typological fiction is the method of apocalyptic. Apocalyptic follows in the train of the late expansions to the prophetic oracles that use (*wᵉhāyâ*) *bayyôm hahû'*, in which the day of Yahweh's action often becomes so full and complex that it loses any proximate resemblance to an original situation of crisis. The future has become increasingly abstracted from the present. It is no longer an extension of the present but an epoch of its own, detached from the present and irrelevant to it. Chronological interests intervene to define a duration of

---

2. Cf. the observations with which Bertil Albrektson concludes his penetrating study, *History and the Gods* (pp. 119-22).

time lying ahead ere Yahweh will come to act. Zech. 14:21 reflects this mentality by epitomizing the future day as a state of being rather than as the bearer of a decisive event (other *bayyôm hahû'* passages with forms of היה reflect the influence of this mentality). Inevitably, the reference to a single day becomes unsuitable. Isa. 61:3 makes *šānâ*, "year," parallel to *yôm*, "day." A number of eschatological passages speak vaguely of *yāmîm bā'îm*, "coming days," or of *'aḥᵃrît hayyāmîm*, "in days afterward." Or they exchange *bayyôm hahû'* for *bā'ēt hahî'*. Within the canonical literature, Daniel takes the ultimate step in equating the *'ēt* of God's coming with the absolute end (*qēṣ*). Only by ending history can God act in it.[3]

7. The quantitative and the qualitative approach to time

We come now to express an opinion with regard to the debate over the uniqueness of Israel's view of time. The distinctiveness of the Hebraic concept has been too apparent for the theologians and phenomenologists to ignore, yet most attempts to define it have gone astray or fallen short. Clearly it is wrong to suggest that the biblical writers were not concerned at all with chronology. Distinctions between an "outer" history and an "inner" history, between linear history and cyclical history, between "man's time" and "God's time," or between "secular time" and "sacred time" fall wide of the mark with respect to the data we have been studying. The only ready-to-hand polarity that seems really applicable is a contrast between what we would call two different approaches to the identical temporal phenomena: the quantitative approach and the qualitative approach. The first sees time as a succession of essentially commensurate entities—a given number of days or months or years. These temporal entities are susceptible to being spanned by the same measuring-staff, hence can be tabulated mathematically. This is time as a *quantum*, comparable to space (and, as Einstein showed, simply another dimension of it). The other approach sees time as a succession of essentially unique, incommensurate experiences. The day is an apprehensional unity, primitively conceived according to the event that gives it its character. Because such an event is revelatory of something more ultimate than the finite concerns of creaturely man, it points beyond itself to an eschatological fulfillment in an ultimately decisive day of divine action.

Both of these approaches appear within the Old Testament. In estimating their relationship to each other, it is important to bear in mind the

---

3. Taking its clue perhaps from Ps. 90:4, fully developed apocalyptic solves the problem of the indefinite extension of God's *yôm* by declaring that "one thousand years are as one day in the testimony of the heavens" (Jub. 4:30; cf. Ep. Barn. 15, 2 En. 33, II Pet. 3:8). In other words, God's time is not measured like man's time. But this procedure emphatically divorces God from human history.

various ways in which Israel's ancient neighbors thought and spoke about time. The Egyptians resisted a qualifying approach to time, just as they resisted any real conception of history.[4] For them time was an endless, meaningless continuum, caught in a perpetual seasonal pattern of alternation. Individual human life had no goal or purpose, except perhaps to extend itself beyond death, and thus everything unique within human experience was finally reduced to a common denominator. Being able to maintain themselves through a long succession of dynasties without having to face the threat of serious foreign irruption, the Egyptians were unprepared to accept history in a cataclysmic sense and accommodate themselves to it ideologically. At the end their civilization was catastrophically submerged in historical forces beyond their comprehension.[5]

The Hittites and the peoples of Mesopotamia were much more aware of the significance of historical event. We have evidence that the Babylonians and Assyrians were as ready to characterize temporal event as to measure it chronologically. It is true that their annals count the years of a king's reign, but we note also that there was a system of naming the years by eponyms, as though each one were unique. Many annals read like epitomes, identifying each year not only by a regnal number but also by its most significant occurrence.[6] Early Mesopotamian writings are much more prepared to emphasize the distinctiveness of successive temporal entities than to explain their interconnectedness, speaking of times of good, times of evil, times of deliverance, times of judgment, etc.[7] But while each successive "time" was conceived of as something special in itself, the succession of such times had little meaning. There was nothing to provide the perspective of purpose. The various times were seen not as a series of opportunities for realizing the goal of human existence—as the Hebrews came to understand it—but as an endless array of hazards to be endured. Accordingly, the whole trend of Mesopotamian religion was historically pessimistic, moving away from the concept of personal responsibility. As the unique became the irrational and the arbitrary, history became demonic while institutional religion tended to become purely manipulative.

In ancient Israel, however, one God was Lord of history. History

---

4. Cf. E. Otto, "Altägyptische Zeitvorstellungen und Zeitbegriffe," *Die Welt als Geschichte*, 14 (1954), 135-48.
5. On the Egyptian philosophy of history, cf. H. Frankfort, *Ancient Egyptian Religion* (New York, 1948), p. 88. A characterizing usage similar to that of Old Testament epitomes with *hayyôm* may be found in the "Dialogue of a man weary of life" (*ANET*, pp. 405-407), which, significantly, comes from a time of upheaval within the Egyptian social order. Disruption made the Egyptians conscious of history but led them to despair.
6. E.g., *ANET*, pp. 301ff.: "First year of Belibni: Sennacherib destroyed the towns Hirimma and Hararatum. Third year of Belibni: Sennacherib marched down to the country of Akkad, etc."
7. Cf. H. Gese, "Geschichtliches Denken im alten Orient und im Alten Testament," *ZTK*, 55 (1958), 127ff.

therefore was filled with positive potentiality. It had a goal and a meaning. Temporal event was seen as an ever renewed opportunity and challenge for bringing this goal to realization. In the Old Testament the quantitative approach to time provided the framework of continuity, allowing for the interconnectedness of specific events. But it was the qualitative approach that gave historical event its revelatory significance, keeping Hebrew man continually alert to the possibility of the creatively new in his relationship to God and his fellow men.

It is very true that the quantitative approach at times predominates within Israel's ancient records, but one is instructed by observing precisely where this appears. It is in three places: (1) the royal annals belonging to the divided kingdom, (2) the priestly writer's reconstruction of the nation's primal history, and (3) apocalyptic.

It is sufficient to say, with respect to annalistic chronology, that its rationale was determined by the political structures that Israel shared with other nations of the ancient Near East. It served to provide an ideological continuity within the context of historical change. To the extent that Israel was a nation like any other nation, it required all the institutional guarantors of orderly succession. Chronology is a tool of institutional order, a foil against chaos. But we take note that the Deuteronomist incorporates his extracts from the royal annals in order to show the ultimate breakdown of this order in the face of the irrational forces of historical destiny.

Apocalyptic, on its part, developed the notion that the years and days of history are numbered. It cannot be gainsaid that the practical result was to make contemporary history meaningless, something to be endured until the predestined number of days and years have transpired. Some spiritual benefit may be acknowledged in the strength the faithful were able to receive from the assurance that the time of the end was very near. But "hope deferred maketh the heart sick," leading often to aimless rationalization. Man grew weary of waiting for God, but when he presumed to count for God he fell into inevitable error.

The third genre giving prominence to the quantitative approach to history is the priestly scheme of patriarchal chronology. P went beyond the Deuteronomist's pattern of generations, the purpose of which had been to demonstrate the relentless cycle of repeated failure in Israel's past history. P evidently thought it important to improve on J and E by adding numbers to the patriarchal histories and genealogies, giving a rigid quantitative structure to the ideal, typological era during which Israel's forefathers wandered with no visible token of Yahweh's presence, moving on toward the promise. If the priestly narrative was in fact composed during the exile, as Karl Elliger has argued,[8] this interjection of chronology may have had an

---

8. "Sinn und Ursprung der priesterlichen Geschichtserzählung," *Kleine Schriften*, pp. 174-98.

intent similar to that of emerging apocalyptic, *viz.*, to comfort the faithful with the assurance that Yahweh has control of history because he has it all measured up and counted out. This tendency seems to come to full fruition in the ideology of Jubilees, a late book combining priestly with apocalyptic interest, providing precise dates for every significant event in the Genesis history while giving patriarchal sanction to the salient features of the cultic institution—all for the purpose of setting a typological pattern for the life of Israel in its actual history, i.e., its history since the time of Moses and the law.

8. Cultic/gnomic versus historical event

It seems very apparent that the priests were more prepared to think of time in quantitative than in qualitative terms. It is they who theologized about history as a chronological quantum, but most of their concerns were quite practical. They had to administer a calendar (to judge from Jubilees, I Enoch, Qumran, a subject of intense dispute within the priestly ranks) and regulate the cultic apparatus. It is they, therefore, who are found speaking of durations, of specific periods of time. When they define a particular day or time, it is with respect to its cultic character. Certainly the priests were very much aware of the distinctiveness of certain days, and especially of the great days of festival, for their greatest concern was to guard the sacred days, marking them off from all the other days on the calendar. But while they were ready to recognize—rather, eager to emphasize—the specialness of the holy days and seasons, they displayed little interest in unique historical event.

It was mainly the bearers of Israel's charismatic tradition—continuing from the time when the nation came into being, then passed on toward extinction, only to come to life again as Yahweh's new creation—who recorded the significance of unique historical event. To them time was not a phenomenon that levels every human experience but something that lends it purpose and distinctiveness. Every day has its own special character. Every day is potentially revelatory. Every day presents a new choice, a new opportunity, a new responsibility. In each day man is at work, but God is at work too. This is the approach to time that dominates the pages of the Old Testament.

One of the results of the present study has been the definition of a cultic/gnomic and an historical way of speaking about past, present, and future time. The special significance of this discovery is to be seen in the context of the preceding discussion. We recognize that within the priestly scheme of things there is a before and an after, but for the guardians of ritual this sequence is more cyclical than linear. Cultic "events" as well as gnomic "events" are put into a before-and-after order only that they may be repeated in undisturbed sequence when their proper time comes around again.

It is instructive to observe an irrepressible ritualizing of historical event, seen especially in liturgical recitals like that of Exod. 13:3f.: "Remember this day, in which you came out from Egypt. . . . This day you are to go forth, in the month of Abib." This liturgical command displays a radical "re-presenting" of *Heilsgeschichte*, a festal repetition of the original event from generation to generation. But the ritual fails to lead to any practical response, ending with no other command than to "keep this ordinance at its appointed time from year to year" (vs. 13). The tendency manifest here is for *heilsgeschichtliche* memorialization to become a touching but powerless, self-perpetuating ritual.

We need to keep this in mind when we hear it said that Israel's great festivals are historicizations of agricultural, and hence mythological, feasts. It is quite true that Israel substituted *Heilsgeschichte* for myth, but these festivals represent a compromise as much as a triumph. They manifest the tendency of cultic institutionalization to reduce the historically unique to something manageable, regularized, repeatable. It is striking that very little of the qualitative description of time belongs to the ritual for these festivals. The very essence of sacramentalization seems to be the reduction of the *timely* to the *timeless.*[9]

It was perhaps only at an annual covenant-renewal festival, if there was one (strangely, there is no direct reference to such a festival, which must be inferred from such passages as Ps. 95), that it was possible for the sacred past to move the faithful to responsible action in the present. This seems to be the whole impact of Deuteronomy, combining memorialization with urgent parenesis. For Deuteronomy the present generation is addressed as the generation that heard Yahweh speak from Horeb, being called not only to a new remembrance but to a new obedience.

It must be emphasized that the Deuteronomic event of parenetical confrontation itself appears to occur according to a pattern of liturgical order, bringing the moment of qualitative uniqueness into convergence with the sacramental orbit. The *hayyôm* of Moses becomes a *hayyôm* of revelatory meaning renewed for every generation. Regularization irresistibly arises when the epiphany of God, appearing from time to time in events of his sovereign choosing scattered among all the days of man's existence,

---

9. Cf. H.-P. Müller, *Ursprünge und Strukturen alttestamentlicher Eschatologie* (BZAW, 109, Berlin, 1969), pp. 48f.: "Wollte man also die Ungegenständlichkeit des Eingreifens Gottes gegen die von seinem Gegenstandsbezug her drohende Vergegenständlichung in Schutz nehmen, so droht nun gerade von diesem Versuch her eine Vergegenständlichung. Denn letztlich behauptet der mythisch fundierte Kult doch nur die Ueberlegenheit eines Endlichen über anderes Endliche. Eine bestimmte Zeit—die in der Urzeit fundierte begrenzte Festzeit—und ein bestimmter Raum—das Heiligtum als Stätte seiner sakramentalen Präsenz—erlangen letztgültigen Wert und letztgültigen Würde."

becomes memorialized in ritual repetition. Yet all the difference in the world remains between a liturgy that is repeated in order to commemorate a past day of divine appearing, for the purpose of eliciting in the present a response of renewed devotion, and a ritual that simply seeks to bring the worshiper into contact with numinous power through cultic manipulation.[10]

As wisdom tends to reduce everything to a set of rules, thus imposing order on nature's and on history's bewildering array of seemingly meaningless and unrelated occurrences, so the cult tends to reduce every moment of revelational uniqueness to ritualistic regularity and cyclical repetition. This fact is the best explanation for the prophets' antipathy to the shrines. The prophets saw that not only pagan worship, but Yahweh's own official apparatus, was susceptible to corruption and capable of stifling the imperative for responsible decision. "Rivers of oil" all too readily took the place of responses based on personal integrity, such as justice, covenant faithfulness, and creaturely humility (Mic. 6:6-8). Although Amos may have been prepared to abandon the cult completely, seeing it as the ineluctable enemy of personalistic religion, most of the other Old Testament prophets hoped for the cult's restoration and renewal. Even Malachi, deploring the deadening effect of perfunctory ritual and predicting a sudden new irruption of God into history, saw its purpose as cleansing and not destroying (Mal. 3:1ff.). Whether or not the pattern of the ninety-fifth Psalm was regularly repeated, it is its wedding of parenesis to liturgy that represents the ideal. To an Israel gathered to praise Yahweh for his wonders in history and in nature comes the new, urgent appeal, "Hayyôm, if you will hear his voice, harden not your heart!"

What distinguished biblical religion, even in its primitive forms, from all its ancient rivals, was its emerging awareness of the personalistic basis for the encounter between God and man, and for this, time had more revelational significance than place.[11] For the man of myth, the supernatural was

---

10. This is a matter that has important bearing on the question of Christ's presence in the Eucharist. When the supremely revelational event of Christ's death and resurrection becomes subordinated to a mystical re-creation of his physical body, the historically unique has clearly given way to metaphysical conceptions transcending all considerations of time. Following the analogy of Israelite religion, the degree of ethical response in the life of the masses elicited by the celebration of the cult ought to be the test of how far a particular eucharistic conception has departed from the biblical norm.

11. Whereas numerous historiographic passages end with interpretive verses containing "in that day," it is remarkable that none concludes with "in that place." Only subordinate elements such as cult legend and etiology are concerned with establishing the identity of place. This does not mean that place was insignificant to the Hebrews. Far from it: they took for granted that revelatory event must occur in a specific place as well as in a specific time. But the place where an event occurs is always one of the givens, already known and specified. What is not known until the narrative is concluded is the essential quality of the day. It is this that the action of God and of man at this particular place reveals.

In this light, the traditional fervor of Christian pilgrims for the "holy places"

everywhere in principle but realistically present in the apparatus of the shrines. Thus place was all important. Holy time was strictly subordinated to holy place, being instrumental in bringing the worshiper into the presence of numinous power. When the Israelite seminomads settled down in the land of Canaan, they assimilated the shrines, along with many cultic accoutrements, some of the ritual, and much of the priestly personnel, of their pagan predecessors. This was a process that was intensified, receiving the support of the political institution, when David brought the ark into Jerusalem. (Solomon made this permanent by building the temple.) Formerly Yahweh had been anywhere and everywhere;[12] he had given his revelations to the patriarchs at remote spots in the desert, far from established shrines, while the special "place" of cultic encounter remained a movable tent. But now Yahweh had found a "resting place" in the formerly pagan shrine of Jerusalem (Ps. 132). It was a fateful moment: Israel's unparalleled insight that God was available to man everywhere and always was being threatened by overpowering forces. From this moment, biblical religion was a compromise.[13]

These are the considerations that aid us in deciding whether the quantitative or the qualitative approach to time is more central to biblical religion, and whether those who try to adapt biblical principles to modern life need to emphasize the parenetic or the sacramental element in worship. These two can never be completely separated, for the extremest kind of parenetic worship requires at least some simple form for its performance. But, if it is to remain true to what is genuinely unique in biblical faith, modern religion must hold parenesis in the center, keeping sacramental memorialization strictly instrumental.

In the Hebrew Scriptures the quantitative measurement of time and the qualitative identification of time are joined in dynamic tension, helping man see his place in nature and in history. He belongs to the world of universality but, in personalistic relation to his covenant God, he belongs more importantly to the world of unique events, the succession of opportu-

---

of Palestine falls under serious question as a paganizing distortion of biblical religion.

12. Instructive is the contrast between the respective climaxes of the E and J stories in Gen. 28. E, derived ultimately from a *hieros logos* for a Canaanite shrine at Bethel, has Jacob exclaim, "How awesome is this place! This is assuredly a house of God, this is the gate of heaven." (17) In contrast, the more primitively Yahwistic J source has Jacob say, "Truly, Yahweh is in this place, and I knew it not." (16) Even though the site had nothing to commend itself as a potential place of revelation, Yahweh had chosen to reveal himself there. But he did it for the well-being of Jacob and to fulfill his promise, not to make the place as such holy. E represents the cultic, J the personalistic, historically oriented conception.

13. It is in the light of this observation that we must see the special significance of the fact that epitomes and similar forms with *hayyôm* and *bayyôm hahû'* are frequent in literature deriving from the premonarchic period but begin to disappear in David's reign, being found thereafter largely in the speech of the prophets.

nities ("days") that make him aware of an ever imminent responsibility to respond to the new crisis of God's address. It is this dialogue and interaction between a transcendent but infinitely concerned Deity and a finite but eminently responsible humanity that creates the Bible's most special contribution to mankind's continuing effort to apprehend the meaning of historical existence.

Παρακαλεῖτε ἑαυτοὺς καθ' ἑκάστην ἡμέραν, ἄχρις οὗ τὸ σήμερον καλεῖται.
Heb. 3:13

Glossary

–A–

accession history (narrative), Davidic. A document probably composed during David's residence in Jerusalem, legitimizing that king's accession instead of the house of Saul; it is dispersed through I Samuel 17–II Samuel 5.

Achemenid (also spelled Achaemenid) period. The time of Persian rule in Palestine and the Near East, from 539 to 333(2) B.C.

amphictyony (adj. -ic). From the Greek. The hypothetical twelve-tribe organization of ethnic groups in ancient Israel, joining them for worship and the holy war; a more neutral term is "sacral union."

anacrusis. A position outside the pattern of poetic meter.

apocalyptic (adj. -al). A literary and spiritual movement prominent in early Judaism and Christianity whose theological program was oriented toward the radical irruption of divine power in ending history, consigning the just and the unjust to their respective places of eternal destiny. Typically employing extensive allegory and bizarre imagery, it lent itself to cosmological and eschatological speculation.

apodictic. Esp. law. Referring to unqualified, authoritative prohibition or demand.

apodosis. The "then" or result clause of a conditional sentence.

ark narrative. I Samuel 4–6, II Samuel 6; also referred to as the *hieros logos* for the ark.

***ᵃšer*-clause.** A relative clause in Heb., introduced by the particle *ᵃšer*, "that," "which," "who," etc.

'athnaḥ. A Massoretic sign indicating the major disjunctive accent within a sentence.

attributive adjective. One that directly modifies a noun and is in grammatical agreement with it.

Auditionsbericht. German: audition report, a literary form in which a prophet repeats words purportedly heard in the heavenly council.

–B–

baalism (adj. -istic). A general term for fertility-religion beliefs and practices in Palestine and the ancient Near East; after the Phoenician-Canaanite god Ba'al.

Botenspruch. German for "herald formula," *q.v.*

Bundesformular. German: covenant formula, a special four-part schema used in covenant liturgies.

–C–

casuistic law. Israelite and ancient Near Eastern secular legislation structured conditionally and defining specific penalties for special cases (in contrast to apodictic law).

charismatic. Motivated by a principle of transcendental, interiorly received authority, in opposition to institutional and official.

351

chiastic. Crosswise, i.e., with parallel elements in reverse positions relative to one another.

Chronicler. The responsible author of I-II Chronicles and the author-compiler of Ezra-Nehemiah, usually dated from 400 to 300 B.C.

cohortative. A Heb. verbal inflection (tense), restricted to the first person, expressing strong desire or determination.

construct. A (usually shorter) form of the Heb. noun tying it genitivally to a noun or pronoun following it.

Covenant Code. A probably pre-exilic collection of intermixed apodictic and casuistic law presently preserved in Exodus 21—23.

covenant-renewal festival. A hypothetical assemblage of the Israelites at some central shrine, probably at the autumn harvest feast, centering in the reading of apodictic law and the renewal of covenant dedication.

cult, cultus (adj. -ic). Official, institutional religion, especially as expressed in public worship.

cultic present. See gnomic/cultic present.

—D—

decalogue. Any series of ten apodictic commandments, but especially the "ten words" (Decalogue) of Exod. 20:1-17, Deut. 5:6-21.

deictic particle. Heb. *hēn* or *hinnēh* (sometimes with pronominal suffixes), with the primitive force of "there!," dramatically pointing to, and calling attention to, a person, object, or action indicated by the word or phrase that follows. English "lo!," "behold!"

demonstrative adjective. One of the Heb. adjectives indicating proximity ("this," "these") or remoteness ("that," "those"), inflected in agreement with the noun that it modifies.

determinative. The Heb. definite article *ha* in its various modifications.

Deutero-Isaiah. More usually, Second Isaiah; Isaiah 40—55, generally dated toward the end of the exilic period, *ca.* 540 B.C.

Deuteronomic. Pertaining to the book of Deuteronomy, more especially in its primitive form.

Deuteronomist (= deuteronomistic history). The writer or school, influenced by Deuteronomy, responsible for the major redactional labors (collecting, arranging, interpreting) in the block of literary materials, (Deuteronomy) Joshua to II Kings. The date is probably early exilic.

Deutero-Zechariah. See Second Zechariah.

distich. A metrical line of two stichoi; alternative term: bicolon.

dittography. A scribal error, the writing of the same words twice (or more).

dodecalogue. A series of twelve apodictic commandments, as in Deut. 27:15-26.

doublet. Parallel version of identical literary material.

D school. A combinational term, covering Deuteronomy, the deuteronomistic history, and deuteronomistic redaction in the Tetrateuch.

dynastic period. Israel's history from David to the exile.

—E—

E. The Elohistic writer, document, or strand in the Tetrateuch (Pentateuch), probably dating *ca.* 850 B.C.; so called because of the characteristic appearance of the divine name Elohim.

editor (adj. -ial). A literary worker responsible for the formal structuring of pregiven materials; usually, but not necessarily, distinguished from the redactor.

Elide priesthood. Successors of Eli and erstwhile custodians of the Shiloh shrine, perhaps surviving in the person of Abiathar.

El Elyon. "God Most High," the deity of Salem (Jerusalem?); cf. Gen. 14:18-20.

El Olam. "The Everlasting God," the deity of Beersheba, identified with Yahweh in Gen. 21:33.

epexegetical. Interpretive of a passage to which material so designated is attached.

epitome, epitomization (vb. epitomize). The product and process of succinct, formal summarization; particularly through authoritative interpretion in narrative conclusion.

Erweiswort (Zimmerli). German: word of proof or demonstration, particularly in the Ezekielian formula, "so you shall know that I am Yahweh."

eschatology (adj. -ical). Discourse or doctrine about the future (not necessarily final) actions of God in human history.

etiology (also spelled aetiology; adj. -ical). Having to do with origins or first causes; discourse or forms specially designed with this concern.

exegesis (adj. -etical). Interpretation; especially the sympathetic, yet scientifically critical, analysis and elucidation of the Hebrew-Christian Scriptures.

existential. Experiential; having to do with man's spiritual-psychological response to historical (esp. catastrophic) event.

—F—

first-fruits. Heb.: *rēʾšît perî* (Deut. 26:10), the offering dedicated at the feast of weeks, seven weeks after passover.

form·criticism (adj. -critical). The exegetical discipline having to do with genre, structure (schema), and life-situation, esp. of elemental units within oral and literary compositions.

Former Prophets. The first half of the second part of the Jewish Canon, called *nebiʾim*–"Prophets": all the books from Joshua through Kings in the Hebrew order.

framework, literary. The surrounding structure, oral or written, but usually redactional, secondary to an original unity.

—G—

Gattung. German for *genre, q.v.*

genre. From the French (= *Gattung,* literary type); a distinct form or pattern, whether in speech or action, whose structure is communicative alongside the content of the pericope containing it.

gentilic. Designating peoples or nations.

gloss. An explanatory or corrective intrusion, usually remote from the setting and intent of the original.

glossator. The writer (scribe) responsible for a gloss.

gnomic. Having to do with popular wisdom, esp. in the form of proverbs or aphorisms.

gnomic/cultic present. An ahistorical present (verb form) found in gnomic and cultic materials; pertaining to action that is customarily or perpetually repeated.

Grundschicht. German: basic literary strand.

—H—

hapax legomenon. Greek: "once read"; i.e., a unique reading in the original text.

Heilsfeit (pl. *-en*). German: God's saving act.

Heilsgeschichte (adj. *heilsgeschichtliche*). German: salvation history, as recited in Scripture.

Heilsprophet (pl. *-en*). German: A prophet, usually but not necessarily attached to the court or temple, who characteristically predicts the wellbeing of his people.

Hellenistic. Post-classical (following *ca.* 400 B.C.) Greek. With reference to the Near East, under Greek influence following the conquest of Alexander the Great.

herald formula. Heb. *kōh 'āmar yāhwēh*—"thus says Yahweh," appearing regularly at the beginning of oracles or at the beginning of the threat/announcement within an oracle.

ḥerem. Heb.: devotion to destruction, a special feature of the holy war (cf. Joshua 6–7, I Samuel 15).

hieros gamos. Greek: sacred marriage; specifically, ritual intercourse between a king, representing the deity, and his consort.

hieros logos. Greek: sacred word or story; a technical term for the founding legend pertaining to a cultic object, practice, or site.

hifil (traditional spelling: hiphil). In Heb., the causative stem or conjugation.

historiography (adj. *-ical*). Literature having to do with real history, esp. when concerned with factors and motivations effectuating historical change.

hithpael. In Heb., the reflexive stem or conjugation.

Holiness Code. The collection of law contained in Leviticus 17–26 (probably exilic in date), so called because of its characteristic appeal to holiness.

holy war. The originally defensive war fought by volunteer Israelites and led by a charismatic person in the name of Yahweh, who was acknowledged as the actual leader.

—I—

imperative. The Heb. verbal aspect (tense) commanding a specific action.

imperfect. The Heb. verbal aspect (tense) expressing action that is possible, incipient, progressive, and/or unfinished.

imperfect consecutive. A special form of the Heb. imperfect (more complete terminology: waw-consecutive imperfect) containing a preformative waw and used almost exclusively for narration in the past.

indictment. A special form of the invective (*q.v.*) in which the misdeeds of the addressee(s) are expressly stated.

infinitive absolute. The unmodified Heb. infinitive, often used gerundively.

infinitive construct. A Heb. infinitival form adapted to modifying nominal and pronominal elements.

inseparable preposition. Heb. *bᵉ*—"in," *kᵉ*—"like," *lᵉ*—"to," and *mē*—"from," regularly attaching themselves to following nouns or pronouns.

invective. The first part of a prophetic oracle of judgment, in which a charge or accusation is brought against the addressee(s).

—J—

J. The Yahwistic (Jahwistic) writer, document, or strand in the Tetrateuch (Pentateuch), probably dating *ca.* 950 B.C.; so called because of the regular appearance of the divine name Yahweh.

Jahwerede. German: Yahweh-speech, a structure in which Yahweh speaks without prophetic mediation.

jussive. A Heb. verbal aspect (tense), occurring only in the second and third persons, in which desire or determination is expressed.

—K—

kerygmatic. Containing or pertaining to a transcendental message of hope and salvation; proclamatory of the divine benevolence.

kethibh. Aramaic: that which is actually written in the biblical text; i.e., the fully vocalized form implied by the preserved writing, antedating the (re)vocalization of the Massoretes.

Kethubhim. Heb. for Writings, *q.v.*

kî-clause. A motivational clause introduced by *kî*—"for," "because."

—L—

Lachish letters. Communications inscribed on potsherds and addressed to the Judahite garrison at Lachish (Tell ed-Duweir) during the Babylonian attack of 592 B.C.

Latter Prophets. The second half of the second part of the Jewish Canon: Isaiah, Jeremiah, Ezekiel, and the Twelve (Minor Prophets).

lectio deficilior. Latin: the more difficult reading, assumed to be original because defective, unless proven otherwise.

legend. An imaginative narrative dealing with cultic sites or religious personages and practices, usually with ostensible etiological intention, and only tangentially related to historical reality.

legitimation. Pertaining to and designed for the public acceptance of a new person or practice.

Levitenspruch. German: a legitimizing pronouncement pertaining to the Levites, a quasi-cultic order from early Israel.

life situation. Technical term for the specific place or setting in life to which a given genre pertains. German *Sitz im Leben.*

literary criticism (adj. -critical). Scientific analysis of strands and documents within extant literature; concerned mainly with literary vs. oral processes of composition.

literary type. See *genre.*

Little Apocalypse. The probably postexilic materials in Isaiah 24—27.

long-verse meter. 4:3 rhythm.

—M—

mashal. Heb.: likeness, allegory, proverb.

Massoretes (adj. -etic); also spelled Masoretes. Early medieval compilers of the Massora ("tradition"), a system of technical annotations on the form and grammar of the biblical text, and inventors of a system of vocalization, accentuation, and cantillation added to the received consonantal text of the OT.

mazzoth. Heb. *maṣṣôt*—"unleavened bread."

metri causis. Latin: due to the meter; i.e., where a regular metrical pattern indicates late additions to the text.

midrash (adj. -ic). As used here: biblical explanation (exegesis) of pre-existent biblical material.

morphology (adj. -ical). Pertaining to the formal or structural elements within words.

Muruba'at letters. First and second century A.D. writings recently found at Wadi Muruba'at near the Dead Sea.

mysterium tremendum. Latin: fearful mystery; *apud* R. Otto, the feeling of tremulous awe in the presence of the supernatural.

myth (adj. -ological). As used here: a cult-oriented, etiological tale, involving the world of deity in interaction with man and concerned with matters of essential reality (cosmology, cultural institutions).

—N—

Nazirite. Belonging to an order of sacral persons specially dedicated (*nāzîr*) to Yahweh.

Nehemiah memoirs. Autobiographical records left by Nehemiah and used by the Chronicler to compose his history.

nifal (traditional spelling: niphal). The simple Heb. stem or conjugation, passive, middle, or reflexive.

noun-clause. A Heb. structure with nonverbal predicate.

—O—

oracle (adj. -ular). A divine communication, announcing salvation or doom.

oracle formula. "Says Yahweh" (*neʾum yāhwēh*), usually at the end of early prophetic oracles.

original. Pertaining to material belonging to the earliest crystallization of literary elements, as distinct from secondary.

—P—

P. The priestly writer, strand, or document within the Tetrateuch (Pentateuch), usually dated in or after the exile.

pan-Israelite. Involving all twelve tribes joined in sacral union.

pan-sacrality. The concept involving divine interaction in every human and natural event.

parallelism, poetic. The principle and structure of balancing, metrical syntactical elements, constitutive of biblical poetry.

parenesis (also spelled paraenesis; adj. -etical). Urging, exhortation; particularly when voiced by an official spokesman for Yahweh, the covenant God of Israel.

pareneticist. One voicing parenesis.

paseq. Aramaic/Hebrew: a Massoretic sign, *viz.*, a vertical dash separating words.

patternistic. Conceived in the notion that cognate cultures copy patterns (esp. cultic, ritualistic) from one another.

Pentateuch (adj. -al). The five books of Moses, the Jewish Torah.

perfect. The Heb. aspect or tense that indicates the bare fact or occurrence of an event or action.

perfect consecutive. A special form of the Heb. perfect (more complete terminology: waw-consecutive perfect) containing a preformative waw and used as a substitute for the imperfect to indicate the indicative or modal present and future.

pericope. A unitary, cohesive segment of literature, whether in original or in expanded (secondary) form.

piel. The intensive (sometimes causative) Heb. stem or conjugation.

predynastic period. The period prior to David.

programmatic. Designed and intended by the responsible writer to indicate the moral, message, or distinctive point of view of a given literary document.

proleptic. Representing the future as present.

promulgation clause. In Deuteronomy, the locution, "as I have commanded you this day," with its variants.

pronominal suffix. An objective pronoun affixed to Heb. verbs, adjectives, nouns, and prepositions.

protasis. The "when" or "if" elements in a conditional sentence.

Ptolemaic. Pertaining to the Ptolemies, Greek rulers in Egypt after Alexander the Great; more particularly, their rule in Palestine from 301 to 198 B.C.

—Q—

qere. Aramaic: that which is to be read in the biblical text in the place of what is indicated by the *kethibh (q.v.).*

Qumran. Khirbet Qumran near the Dead Sea and associated caves, yielding materials, particularly scrolls, from the first century B.C. to the first century A.D.

—R—

recension. Group or family of documents, representing the peculiarities of a given translation tradition.

redaction (adj. -al). The compositional process, oral or literary, that transforms elemental units by combination, restructuring, and/or amplification. In contrast to editing, redaction involves considerable substantive addition to earlier forms of the text.

redaction criticism (adj. -critical). Analysis of redactional processes and reconstruction of the development of the biblical text through such processes.

redactor. The person responsible for redaction.

Religionsgeschichte (adj. *religionsgeschichtliche*). German for religion-phenomenology (-ical), *q.v.*

religion-phenomenology (adj. -ical). The discipline that has to do with the "clinical" aspects of religion; it is descriptive rather than evaluative.

rîb-**oracle.** From Heb. *rîb*—"controversy," "lawsuit." An oracle structured as a lawsuit in which Yahweh appears as plaintiff, prosecutor, witness, and/or judge against the persons or peoples accused.

rubric. A rigidly stereotyped formula, usually at the end or the beginning of the pericope to which it pertains.

—S—

sacral kingship. The theory or practice according to which the ruler is conceived of as being or representing the deity.

sacral union. The amphictyony (*q.v.*).

saga. A primitive, imaginative narrative involving sociological rather than cultic-religious concerns; closely rooted in historical event, it aims to represent the relation of political or sociological entities in simple dialogue and interaction between protagonists of these entities.

schema (pl. -ata). An essential structure shared by a significant number of passages representing a given genre.

secondary. Contrasted to original; anything added, whether by the first composer or another.

Second Zechariah. Zechariah 9–14, dating from *ca.* 450 B.C. downward.

Septuagint (adj. -al). The Greek translation of the Heb. Bible, begun in Egypt *ca.* 250 B.C.

Sitz im Leben. German for life situation, *q.v.*

source-analysis. The literary identification of strands or documents; a virtual synonym of "literary criticism."

stich (pl. -oi). An elemental combination of words in Heb. poetry, metrically balanced against similar combinations to form a distich or tristich; alternate terminology: colon.

strophe. A unity within Heb. poetry lying outside the pattern of poetic parallelism.

substantive. A noun or an adjective serving as a noun.

supplement(ation), literary. Reinterpretation of earlier material through addition.

synoptic. Pertaining to doublets or parallels, as most familiarly with the Gospels Matthew, Mark, and Luke.

Syriac. The early Christian translation of the OT into Syriac.

—T—

Targum. Periphrastic Aramaic rendering of the OT, mainly from the early Christian era.

Tendenz. German: tendency, especially as manifested in the program or intention of a particular document.

terminus technicus. Latin: technical term.

Tetrateuch. An artificial term (cf. Pentateuch) for the first four of the "five books of Moses"; i.e., Genesis through Numbers, containing the narrative sources J, E, and P.

text(ual) criticism (adj. -critical). The scientific comparison of the MT, as exhibited in its various manuscript witnesses, with the ancient versions, with a view to determining the probable original reading in the light of the history and tendency of the MT and these versions.

theologoumenon (pl. -a). A significant theological concept.

theophany (adj. -ic, -ous). God's awesome self-revelation and the narration concerning it.

theophoric. Bearing as an integral element a divine name; used especially of human names.

time-designative. An element or construction designating time.

threat. The second element in a prophetic oracle of judgment, often introduced by the herald formula (*q.v.*).

three-foot meter. 3:3 rhythm.

throne-succession narrative (history). A document probably composed during the reign of Solomon to legitimize that king's accession instead of his older brothers; with II Samuel 6 and 7 as problematical prologue material, it extends through II Sam. 9:1–20:22, I Kings 1–2.

torah. Priestly instruction in correct ritual; not the Torah (Mosaic law) of later Judaism.

tradent. Institution, school, or circle in which a given tradition was preserved and passed forward.

tradition history. The analysis of concepts, motifs, and themes preserved in tradition, together with the history of the process of their preservation and development; redaction criticism (*q.v.*), concerned with secondary literary developments, deals with an element in tradition history.

Transjordanians. Peoples of the tribes east of the Jordan: Reuben, Gad, and half-Manasseh.

tristich. A poetic line of three stichoi.

Trito-Isaiah. Also called "Third Isaiah"; Isaiah 56–66, dating from *ca.* 540 B.C. downwards.

typology (adj. -ical). A conceptual process in which an early figure or event comes to serve as a model for one later; e.g., the exodus for the return from Babylon.

—U—

Ueberarbeiter (Lohfink). Redactor.

Uebereignungsformel (Richter). The "arousing" formula of Judg. 4:14 and elsewhere.

Unheilsprophet (pl. *-en*). A prophet who characteristically pronounces judgment or doom upon his people.

United Monarchy. The Heb. kingship from Saul through Solomon.

—V—

vaticinium ex eventu. Latin: a purported prediction that actually originates after its fulfillment.

version (adj. -al). As here used: one of the ancient translations important for the textual criticism of the OT, chiefly the Septuagint, Targum, and Vulgate.

Vorlage. German: the Heb. text underlying a given version or manuscript.

Vulgate. The Latin version prepared by St. Jerome in the fourth century A.D.

—W—

waw-consecutive imperfect. See imperfect consecutive.

waw-consecutive perfect. See perfect consecutive.

wisdom (literature). Writings regulating social and political behavior (e.g., Proverbs, Sirach) or reflecting on cosmological and theological problems (e.g., Job, Ecclesiastes).

Writings. The third part of the Jewish Canon, containing Psalms, Job, Proverbs, the five Megilloth (Song of Solomon, Ruth, Lamentations, Ecclesiastes, Esther), Daniel, Ezra-Nehemiah, and Chronicles.

—Y—

Yahweh Sebaoth. "Yahweh of hosts," the deity of Shiloh; later a prestige name for Israel's God.

—Z—

Zadokite priesthood. The dominant priesthood of the Jerusalem cult from Solomon to the exile; probably reinstated after the exile under the name "Aaron."

INDEXES

1. Subjects

2. Modern authors

Aharoni, Y. 150n, 171n
Albrektson, B. 31n, 35n, 342n
Alfrink, B. J. 147n
Alonso-Schökel, L. 306n
Alt, A. 83n, 148n, 165n, 228n, 247n
Amsler, A. 69n
Anderson, G. W. 305n
Ap-Thomas, D. R. 227n

Baldwin, J. G. 308n
Baltzer, K. 175n
Bardtke, H. 318n
Barr, J. 31n, 32n, 34, 35n, 38, 39n, 40n
Barth, C. 239n
Barth, J. 40n
Barth, K. 33
Begrich, J. 238
Bentzen, A. 212n
Bergson, H. 32
Bertheau, E. 80n
Beyerlin, W. 162n, 163n
Bin-Nun, S. R. 110n
Birch, B. C. 104n
Blenkinsopp, J. 76n, 85n
Boecker, H. J. 78n, 83n, 91n, 105n, 192n, 195n, 203n
Boer, P. A. H. de 65n, 188n, 238n
Boman, T. 31n, 34, 38n
Brandon, S. G. F. 33n, 35n, 36n
Brekelmans, C. H. W. 147n
Bright, J. 113n, 115n, 239n, 243n, 296n, 301n
Brockelmann, C. 39n
Bronner, L. 229n, 235n
Buber, M. 195n
Budde, K. 288n
Buhl, M. L. 103n
Bultmann, R. 33n
Buss, M. 299n, 303n

Caird, G. B. 89n
Carlson, R. A. 212n, 234n
Caspari, W. 287n
Çazelles, H. 167n, 169n
Cerny, L. 36n
Childs, B. S. 72n, 76n, 101n, 121, 145n, 147n, 188n, 282n, 317n
Clements, R. 73n
Cornill, C. H. 296n
Cross, F. M., Jr. 37n
Cullmann, O. 34

Davies, G. H. 248n
De Vries, S. J. 90n, 120n, 186n, 200n, 230n, 284n
Dhorme, E. 288n
Dillmann, A. 306n
Driver, G. R. 40n, 200n
Driver, S. R. 84n, 96n, 107n, 249n
Duhm, B. 121, 247n, 296n, 297, 298n, 308n, 309n, 311, 314n, 316n
Dus, J. 287n

Ebeling, E. 263n
Eichrodt, W. 34, 304n
Eisenbeis, W. 294n
Eissfeldt, O. 77n, 80n, 89n, 213n, 227n, 243n, 287n, 296n, 303n, 308n, 320n
Eliade, M. 33
Elliger, K. 47n, 95n, 96n, 124, 145n, 146n, 164n, 245n, 284n, 304n, 307n, 321n, 345

Fensham, F. C. 37n, 225n
Fichtner, J. 79n
Fischer, A. 43n
Fohrer, G. 124n, 160n, 226n, 227n, 228, 229n, 243n
Frankfort, H. 32n, 344n
Fuss, W. 109n

Gale, R. M. 32
Galling, K. 72, 88n, 89n, 110n, 115n, 144n, 234n, 304n, 313n
Gehman, H. S. 227n
Gerleman, G. 250n
Gese, H. 35n, 144n, 282n, 284n, 344n
Gray, G. B. 118n, 249n, 302n, 305n, 306n, 309n, 311
Gray, J. 80, 81, 110n, 113n, 194n, 292n
Gressmann, H. 36, 37n, 70n, 89n, 91, 100n, 107n, 108n, 160n, 202n, 208n, 227n, 235n, 285, 288n
Grünbaum, A. 33
Guillaume, A. 303n
Guitton, J. 33
Gunkel, H. 99, 157n, 215n, 246n
Gunneweg, A. H. J. 64n, 102, 163n, 183n, 287n

Haag, H. 79n, 191n
Habel, N. 240n
Harrelson, W. 161n
Hauer, C. 84n
Hegel, F. 32
Heidegger, M. 32, 33
Heintz, J. G. 37n
Hempel, J. 35n, 43n
Henry, M.-L. 302n, 305n, 306n, 309n, 316n
Herrmann, S. 36n, 243n, 247n, 309n
Hertzberg, H. W. 76n, 77n, 85n, 95n, 103n, 104n, 108n, 208n
Hoftijzer, J. 40n, 217n
Holladay, W. L. 240n, 242n, 309n
Holm-Nielsen, S. 103n
Hölscher, G. 35n, 37n, 232n
Horst, F. 185n, 313n
Humbert, P. 43n
Humboldt, W. von 32n
Hyatt, J. P. 114n, 239n, 242n, 244n, 296n, 301n
Hylander, I. 287n

Jackson, J. 221n
Jacob, E. 34
Jansma, T. 245n, 321n
Jaubert, A. 141n
Jean, C. F. 40n
Jenni, E. 38, 40n, 42n, 286
Jepsen, A. 34n, 232n, 282n

Kaiser, O. 302n
Kant, I. 32
Katz, E. 38n
Keller, C. A. 78n
Kilian, R. 155n
Kissane, E. J. 300n, 302n, 309n, 311
Knierim, R. 88n, 287n
Knight, G. A. F. 34
Knudtzon, J. A. 225n
Koch, K. 100n, 133, 145n, 164n, 202, 203n, 228n
Kraus, H.-J. 76n, 143n, 144n, 213n, 246n, 247n, 248n

Langlamet, F. 83n, 289n
Largement, R. 37n
Leeuw, G. W. van der 33n
Lefèvre, A. 298n, 299n, 300n, 305n, 308n, 309n, 311, 314n

3. Scripture references

Versification and order of books are as in the Hebrew Bible.

GENESIS

1	141n
1:5ff.	42n
4:1-16	154f.
4:14	140n, 154f., 254, 268, 275
5	141n
6:4	52n
7:10	141n
7:11, 14	140n, 141
7:12, 24, 8:3, 5, 13f.	141n
8:22	42
11	141n
12:41, 51	140n, 142
15:3	240
15:7-11, 17f., 19-21	73f.
15:18	64n, 73f., 128, 130, 273f.
16:5	192n
17:23, 26	140n, 141f.
17:24f.	142
18:11	44n
19:2	142
21:26	140n, 155, 254, 270
21:33	217n
22:13ff.	155n
22:14	140n, 155, 254, 267
24	160
24:1	44n
24:11-49	155f.
24:12	140n, 155f., 210n, 254, 260f., 269, 275
24:12-14, 34-41	156
24:42-49	156
24:42	140n, 155f., 254, 261, 267
24:54	42
25:24	44
25:31, 33	52n
26	74n
26:8	213n
26:17, 19-23, 25	99
26:26-31	98f.
26:32	64n, 97-99, 116, 128, 130
27:41	50
28:16f.	349n
29	160
30:14	44
30:25-33	156
30:32	140n, 156, 254, 267
30:33	156, 283n
30:35	101, 117, 128, 130, 156
31	74n
31:43-57	157
31:43	140n, 156f., 254, 270
31:46	157
31:48	140n, 156f., 210n, 254, 268, 275
31:49-52	157
33:12-15	74f.
33:16	74f., 128, 130, 273f.
33:17	74f.
35:4	83
39:11	52n
40	158
40:7, 41:9, 42:13, 32	140n, 158, 210, 253f., 270
40:12f., 18-20	158
41:9, 26-38	158
41:41	140n, 158, 254, 268, 275
41:50	47n
42:13, 32	158
47:9	46
47:13-26	159
47:23	140n, 159, 254, 275
48:1f., 8ff., 15f.	99
48:20	97, 99, 116, 128, 130
49:1	50
50:3f.	44
50:20	52n

EXODUS

2:11	52n
2:15-22	160
2:18	140n, 160, 254, 270
2:23	52n
3-4	105, 123, 240
3:12	188n, 240
4:2-9	240
5:6	59f., 127
5:14	140n, 160, 254, 270
6:2-9	123
7:9	291n
8:6, 19	283
8:18f.	286f., 297
8:18	326, 330
8:20	286n
8:23	293n